PALACE

Lee Jackson is a well-known Victor~~......~~ ~~......~~ ~~......~~ ~~......~~ on
Victorian London (victorianlondon.org). He is the author of *Dirty Old London:
The Victorian Fight Against Filth* and *Walking Dickens' London*.

Further praise for *Palaces of Pleasure*:

'It turns out that the Victorians were very much amused. Lee Jackson's entertaining chronicle of 19th-century entertainment depicts a riot of laughter and
hi-jinks.' *Oldie*

'Jackson creates an unfamiliar picture: gone are the stern, upright, moral men
and women of popular imagination. Instead, the Victorians are revealed with
all their foibles and desires.' Joanne Cormac, *BBC History Magazine*

'A lively and engaging study of the unstoppable development of nineteenth-
century commercial entertainment.' Jane Darcy, *TLS*

'The industrialisation of the modern world is all too often described entirely in
terms of coal, iron and desperate factory lives. In *Palaces of Pleasure*, by contrast,
Lee Jackson has produced a detailed look at the industrialisation of pleasure:
how the Victorians turned enjoyment into Big Business.' Judith Flanders,
author of *The Victorian City*

'This fascinating book is a guide to the pleasure domes of 19th-century
England, most of which would have been closed if campaigners for moral
improvement had got their way.' Clive Aslet, *Country Life*

'From flying bulls to music hall: a gleeful account of how the Victorians created
mass entertainment.' *Sunday Times Ireland*

'Wonderfully comprehensive and engagingly readable.' Andrew Lycett, *Spectator*

'A fascinating book exploring the history of light entertainment in this country.'
David Leafe, *Irish Daily Mail*

'This frequently amusing and always fascinating book is wonderfully entertaining. It is as authoritative as it is accessible form the first page to the last. *Palaces of Pleasure* is a delight.' Catherine Curzon, *All About History*

'This entertaining book provides a valuable insight into just what our Victorian ancestors got up to in their leisure time when they had more free time and money in their pockets … Hold on to your hats, it's an exhilarating ride that smashes the stereotypes!' Karen Clare, *Family Tree Magazine*

'Jackson writes well, has researched widely, has an eye for telling detail … and has something new to add on each of his topics.' Hugh Cunningham, *Cultural and Social History*

'In this wide-ranging survey of Victorian fun, Jackson … takes the reader on a journey through gin palaces, music halls, seaside resorts and football stadia to counter the narrative that the Victorians were all about moral asceticism and po-faced imperialism.' Charlie Connelly, *The New European*

'[A] readable and immensely informative discussion of Victorian popular attractions and venues … Open[s] the door on a variety of delights.' Jacqueline Banerjee, *Cercles*

'There is a sense, throughout Jackson's book, of the sheer bustling energy of our nineteenth-century forebears when it came to finding ways to spend their leisure time.' Mark Jones, *Albion*

'It is a pleasure to stagger (in print, of course) from pub to gin-shop to music hall with Lee Jackson as your companion. This is outstanding scholarship that changes our notions of nineteenth-century entertainment. It is original, thorough, accessible and fully explains the commercial underpinnings of change in this sector across the century.' Sarah Wise, author of *The Blackest Streets*

'Inspired and fascinating. Jackson leads the reader on an incredible journey and breaks new ground in our understanding of the pioneering entrepreneurs who created mass entertainment for the Victorians.' Alex Werner, Lead Curator, Museum of London

Palaces of Pleasure

of

From Music Halls to the Seaside to Football,
How the Victorians Invented
Mass Entertainment

LEE JACKSON

YALE UNIVERSITY PRESS
NEW HAVEN AND LONDON

Copyright © 2019 Lee Jackson

First published in paperback in 2021

For information about this and other Yale University Press publications, please contact:
U.S. Office: sales.press@yale.edu   yalebooks.com
Europe Office: sales@yaleup.co.uk   yalebooks.co.uk

Set in Minion Pro by IDSUK (DataConnection) Ltd
Printed in Great Britain by Clays Ltd, Elcograf S.p.A

Library of Congress Control Number: 2018962166

ISBN 978-0-300-22463-4 (hbk)
ISBN 978-0-300-25478-5 (pbk)

A catalogue record for this book is available from the British Library.

10 9 8 7 6 5 4 3 2 1

Contents

CONTENTS

Illustrations

10. George Cruikshank, *Dancing-Rooms*, coloured etching from Cruikshank, *The Drunkard's Children* (1848), plate 3. Wellcome Collection.

11. A cartoon of a 'Cinderella ball' at Holborn Town Hall by Tom Browne, from Machray and Browne, *The Night Side of London* (1902). Author's collection.

12. Phoebus Levin, *The Dancing Platform at Cremorne Gardens* (1864), oil on canvas. Courtesy of the Museum of London.

13. A coloured photograph of the entrance to the Egyptian Court, Crystal Palace, Sydenham (1854–66). By permission of Historic England Archive.

14. A coloured lithograph from a photograph by P.H. Delamotte of the Pompeian Court, Crystal Palace, Sydenham; frontispiece to M. Digby Wyatt, *Views of the Crystal Palace and Park* (1854). © The British Library Board.

15. A drawing of the official opening of the 1862 International Exhibition by Edward Sherratt Cole. © Victoria and Albert Museum, London.

16. George du Maurier, *Development of Species under Civilisation*, printed in *Punch* (16 July 1887). Author's collection.

17. A plan of Imre Kiralfy's *Venice in London* (1889). Courtesy of Getty Research Institute, Los Angeles (90-B26537).

18. The catalogue cover for the India and Ceylon Exhibition (1896). Courtesy of Getty Research Institute, Los Angeles (90-B26509).

19. An advertisement for the 'Hong Kong Opium Smoking Parlour', Earl's Court (1899). Courtesy of the Museum of London.

20. A postcard of the 'Witching Waves', White City (1909). Author's collection.

21. A photochrom postcard of Clacton Pier (c.1900), Detroit Publishing Co. Courtesy of the Library of Congress.

22. E.T. Reed, *A Quiet Drive by the Sea*, from *Punch* (19 April 1890). Author's collection.

23. A photograph of Blackpool Winter Gardens (early twentieth century). © Look and Learn / Peter Jackson Collection.

24. A photochrom print of Blackpool Tower and beach, Detroit Publishing Co. (c.1900). Courtesy of the Library of Congress.

25. A photograph by Paul Martin of couples on the sand, Yarmouth (1892). © Victoria and Albert Museum, London.

26. An engraving depicting the FA Cup Final at the Crystal Palace on 15 April by Ralph Cleaver, printed in the *Illustrated London News* (22 April 1899). © Look and Learn.

Acknowledgements

MY THANKS TO HEATHER MCCALLUM and her colleagues at Yale University Press, who have made publishing this book a genuine pleasure. Many of my primary sources have been culled from the ever-increasing number of online databases available to researchers. I must thank, therefore, my part-time employer, the London School of Economics, for making its online and print resources available to all staff, including those, like myself, working in support roles. I am also particularly grateful for the encouragement and support of the following people: Alex Werner; Sarah Wise; Bob Nicholson; Rohan McWilliam; Alistair Owens; Simon Cope (for his generous visit to the Bodleian); Margaret Brown (for her thought-provoking replies to my random queries on Twitter); David Turner and Tim Dunn (for their online expertise on railways and rollercoasters); Christopher Burton (for translating accounts of the Portland Rooms in German); Terry Morris (for a football tip); Fabian Macpherson (for pointing out Cambridge alumni); and Jude Dicken (for her guidance about the Isle of Man). I would also like to thank Stef Dickers at the Bishopsgate Institute, and Dave Walker at Kensington and Chelsea Local Studies and Archives, for their cordial assistance; and, likewise, the many other library and archive professionals who have assisted me at the Blackpool History Centre; Guildhall Library; Ceredigion Archives, Aberystwyth; Lambeth Archives; Conwy Archives, Llandudno; Haringey Archives; the London Metropolitan Archives; LSE Women's Library; Manchester Archives; the Manx Museum; the Museum of London; the National Archives; Tower Hamlets Local History Library and Archives; and the V&A Theatre & Performance Archives.

Finally, thanks again to Mum and Dad for everything, and Joanne and Clara, for being lovely and generally putting up with me.

A Note on Money

FOR THE SAKE OF CONVENIENCE, I have sometimes used or quoted the traditional abbreviations *l* (pounds), *s* (shillings) and *d* (pence) in the text of this book. For example, 11s 8¼d means eleven shillings and eight and a quarter pence. Readers unfamiliar with pre-decimal currency should note that twenty shilling coins constituted a pound, and there were twelve pence in a shilling. A pound coin or 'sovereign', therefore, was worth 240 pence. The smallest coin was a farthing, worth a quarter of a penny. Readers will also find occasional mentions of sums in guineas. The guinea coin itself, worth twenty-one shillings, was defunct by the start of the Victorian era, but was still often used as a notional unit in pricing certain articles. This peculiar amount, fixed in 1717 when Britain adopted a de facto gold standard, was retained because it had aristocratic connotations. To pay in guineas was to be rich enough to add a shilling tip, as it were, to every pound.

As for incomes, Victorian male manual labourers rarely earned more than fifty pounds a year (and often considerably less). Skilled male workers in factories and workshops might earn seventy or eighty pounds a year. Male clerks, beginning their career, might earn similar sums; but depending on their employer, they could aspire to more senior positions with better remuneration. For example, well-paid post office clerks in the mid-century began on £90 p.a., potentially rising to £260 p.a. with annual increments. Senior administrators at the Post Office were paid £350–£500 p.a. Women, meanwhile, at the start of the nineteenth century, were generally employed in very poorly paid roles, including the manufacture of clothing, laundry work and domestic service. The low pay of female servants, typically £10–£25 p.a., was at least mitigated by free food and accommodation. Better-paid careers in department stores, schools and offices opened up for women towards the end of the century. Female telegraphists, for example, could earn from £40 to £100 p.a., depending on their skills and experience.

Introduction

EXPENSIVE AND DANGEROUS AMUSEMENTS

QUEEN VICTORIA PROBABLY NEVER SAID, 'We are not amused.' The words first appeared in print in an 1885 novel by the writer James Payn, the tart response of an unspecified 'royal' to a dubious anecdote. They were later attributed to Victoria, with a conveniently long-dead courtier cited as the source. Princess Alice, Victoria's granddaughter, having playfully quizzed her grandmother on the subject, concluded that 'she never said it'.[1] Nonetheless, Queen Victoria's supposed catchphrase stuck, suitably regal and disdainful, quite in character for a woman who spent half her life in mourning. To this day, the phrase remains firmly lodged in the public imagination, bolstering the widely held conceit that both Victoria and her subjects were, for the most part, miserable puritans.

The idea that our Victorian ancestors did not know how to enjoy themselves is, of course, nonsense. The nineteenth century was an age of popular entertainment, from the Crystal Palace to the 'palace of varieties'. True, the Victorians promoted 'rational recreation', including public parks, libraries and museums, but they also craved excitement. The Greater Britain Exhibition at Earl's Court (1899), for example, contained not only instructive colonialist exhibits, but the Great Wheel, a 300-foot-tall precursor of the London Eye, and assorted fairground rides. Further attractions included bicycle polo; the Bioscope (early cinema); the Electrophone (Walkman-style headphones for listening to music by telephone); and a re-creation of a Hong Kong opium den (without the opium). A favourite with the crowds was the Great Canadian Water Chute, like a modern log flume but in a flat-bottomed boat, which enabled visitors to 'indulge in the British pastime of shouting'.[2]

If we rather struggle to imagine proverbially dour Victorians screaming with joy and delight, this is partly an image problem. Countless hatchet-faced pictures of our great-great-grandparents suggest a rather grim, buttoned-up world composed solely of tight corsets and uptight people. We forget that presenting an unsmiling countenance was photographic studio etiquette; and that these were formal portraits, rather than attempts to capture a fleeting moment. Even when film footage survives of Victorians simply having fun – e.g. R.W. Paul's 'A Switchback Railway' at Alexandra Palace – the scenes are necessarily mute, the noise and excitement lost to posterity.[3] But there were smiles, shouts and even giddy screams. The Victorians developed their own modern forms of leisure, suited to the industrial age. Their history is the core subject matter of this book: the invention of mass entertainment.

Throughout the nineteenth century, traditional venues for recreation were upgraded, to cater for and create demand. The homely public house yielded to the more commercial, custom-built gin palace. Rooms above the pub, which once hosted convivial sing-alongs, grew into grand music halls, and then variety theatres. Quiet seaside resorts, newly served by steamships and railway lines, constructed elegant ironwork piers and palatial winter gardens. New mechanised amusement rides prospered at exhibition grounds and beside the sea, prefiguring the modern theme park. The pace of change could be dizzying. Football offers a prime example. During the 1880s and 1890s, assorted humble sports clubs, formed at the workplace, school or church, developed into profitable businesses, with grand stadiums, professional players and crowds of spectators numbering in their thousands, or even tens of thousands.

Various factors facilitated the growth of mass entertainment, not least a rapidly urbanising population. There was also a slow but sure rise in the standard of living among the working class in the final decades of the century, which gave 'the lower orders' more disposable income. This was coupled with the growth of mass media, including the sporting press, and the advertising industry. The rigid discipline of the factory also contributed to a clear demarcation of leisure time, combined with the gradual introduction of a shorter working week. This included replacing customary informal absences on Mondays (so-called 'Saint Monday') with an agreed half-day on Saturday. Railways, meanwhile, offered unparalleled opportunity for recreational travel – particularly important for exhibition grounds and seaside resorts. But the great overarching driving force behind the entertainment explosion was the quest for profit. The densely populated cities of the industrial revolution allowed publicans and other leisure entrepreneurs to become 'traders on a large scale'.[4] The Victorians *were* amused; and it could prove a very profitable business.

There was, admittedly, opposition to this new leisure world, much of it religious. The proponents of sabbatarianism and temperance were implacably opposed both to the gin palace and the music hall. There were some evangelicals who thought all music, dance and theatre distracted from the serious business of spiritual and moral improvement. As the influential Baptist preacher Charles Spurgeon sternly remarked, 'This is the age of excessive amusement: everybody craves for it, like a babe for its rattle.'[5] The truly devout damned all contemporary places of entertainment as the *loci* of criminality, intemperance and prostitution. Leisure activities opened the door to sin, whether by association with bad individuals or through exposure to insidious, immoral narratives. When the *British Mothers' Magazine* mused on the question 'May Christian Mothers Permit Their Children to Learn Dancing?', it concluded, in essence, better safe than sorry.[6] Glasgow manufacturers Campbell & Co. marketed their melodeons, a type of home organ, under the tag-line, 'It will make home more attractive, and save more expensive and dangerous amusements' (i.e. the moral dangers of the music hall). For some temperance campaigners, the merest hint of alcohol ruined any chance of useful recreation. The noisy campaign of Frederick Charrington against the People's Palace, an educational/recreational institute for the East End, was typical of this more hardline approach. Charrington himself was the scion of a wealthy family of brewers, but had turned his back on the family business after observing rampant alcoholism on the streets of the capital. When the People's Palace was first mooted at a public meeting, he stormed the stage, shouting: 'Is strong drink to be sold in the Palace and is it going to be open on the Lord's Day or not? We only want those two questions answered!'[7]

The Victorians' urge to regulate and control leisure time was also about utilitarian social engineering. Certainly, this applied to the public house, since inebriates were poor workers and, when finally relegated to the workhouse, a drain on the public purse. Likewise, prostitutes who congregated in the theatre, music hall and pleasure garden were stigmatised as carriers of sexual disease (unlike their equally contagious clients). More broadly, time devoted to leisure was economically unproductive. There were even fears that unchecked idleness produced social unrest, stimulating Chartism and radical politics. Indeed, the proponents of 'rational recreation' sought to discipline the habits of the poor and to create their own ideal social order. Social conservatism also played a part. We see this in the opposition to the gin palace in the 1820s and 1830s, which revolved around the place of women in the public house. The 'demoralisation of females' (which generally meant working-class females) was a constant, cautionary refrain in public debates about leisure.[8]

Yet, despite all this, the most influential, direct opposition to individual places of entertainment was often itself commercial. Brewers bribed the magistracy to close down independent rivals to their own 'tied' public houses, often under a cloak of moralising complaint. Victorian pleasure gardens were sometimes criticised for harbouring vice, but fell prey to land-grabbing property developers. Music halls were persecuted by theatre managers who resented the halls' popularity. Both sides formed 'protection associations' and repeatedly clashed in the courts over archaic licensing laws. Money, by and large, talked much louder than morals. Temperance campaigners themselves came to this conclusion, opening their own temperance hotels, coffee taverns and music halls to compete commercially, as well as spiritually, with existing places of recreation. They rarely prospered and did little to dent the profits of the drinks industry. The Coffee Tavern movement, which briefly flourished in the late 1870s and early 1880s, opening dry public houses, was soon acknowledged as a failure.[9] Similarly, the Royal Victoria Coffee Music Hall, opened in 1880 by social reformer Emma Cons (nowadays the Old Vic Theatre), failed to make any kind of profit and soon became more of a lecture/meeting hall, backed by charitable donations.[10]

This book, in any case, is not about the advocates of temperance or other moralists; or, at least, only to the degree that such opposition demonstrably influenced the development of particular leisure institutions. Instead, I examine the growth of the leisure industry on its own terms, mostly in London, but also wandering a little further afield, including visits to industrial Lancashire. This is not, I should stress, a comprehensive survey of the Victorians' leisure activities, geographically or topically. Rather, I am interested in documenting the new and rapidly evolving institutions that fundamentally changed the Victorians' shared public experience of leisure and recreation: the gin palace; the music hall; the exhibition ground; the seaside resort; the football club. I will also consider a couple of illuminating failures: the rise and fall of the 'casino' dance-hall (within the much-neglected topic of commercial social dancing) and the extinction of the pleasure garden. Ultimately, I hope this book provides a detailed guide to the nineteenth century's great innovations in mass entertainment; the entrepreneurs who drove things forward; and the forces ranged against them.

I

OR,

THE ABODES OF SUICIDE

THE EMERGENCE OF THE 'GIN PALACE' in the 1830s, on the cusp of the Victorian era, seems a good place to start. These alluring drinking establishments, adorned with gaslight and gilding, were highly attractive public houses, catering to the common man. Their elaborate décor, however, provoked much earnest soul-searching among social commentators. Journalists lavished countless column inches on the threat posed to public morals. Magistrates threatened to remove licences; temperance campaigners fulminated against a glamorous new enemy. Charles Dickens describes a gin palace in one of his earliest journalistic sketches, *The Gin-shop*, first published in February 1835. He recounts a visit to a public house situated on or near Drury Lane, adjoining some of the worst slums in London. Naturally, Dickens notes the stark contrast between the pub's ornate facade and the poverty of the surrounding streets; likewise, between the opulent interior and the morally dubious clientele. The character of the place is revealed in a series of droll vignettes. A cocky young man tries to seduce the worldly barmaid (she flatly rejects him, 'not remembering precisely how blushes are managed'); a pair of garrulous old women down glasses of 'rum shrub' (lemon juice, sugar and rum). Finally, the scene dissolves in a mass brawl of Irish labourers.[1]

Dickens and his contemporaries were particularly fascinated/disgusted by the extravagant ornamentation of the gin palace. Typical decoration included illuminated clocks; etched plate-glass windows; over-sized gaslights; extensive bars of polished mahogany. Behind the bar stood vast barrels of branded liquor, the likes of 'Old Tom' and 'Cream of the Valley'. The American author Theodore Sedgwick wrote back to his countrymen, awestruck, 'Everybody has heard of the gin palaces in England; few, however, can have any adequate conception of them.'[2] The superabundant use of gas was a great source of amazement: 'at one [establishment], a revolving light, with many burners, playing most beautifully over the door; at another, about fifty or sixty jets in one lantern, throwing out their capricious and fitful, but brilliant gleams'.[3] Gaslight was so integral to the modish spectacle that gin palaces themselves were often described as 'flaring', a transferred epithet, belonging more properly to their conspicuous lights, suggestive of garish vulgarity. Drunkards reportedly grew confused when other shopkeepers adopted similar illumination. One sorry inebriate, arrested after angrily demanding liquor at the local baker's, allegedly confessed to the magistrate, 'Upon my sowl, I tuck it for a gin-shop; but they light up every place now as if they sold nothing but gin.'[4]

Dickens and Sedgwick both concluded that the gin palace exercised a fatal fascination, promoting alcoholism and criminality among the working class. Throughout the 1830s, moralists queued up to denounce these newly constructed 'gin temples' as a dreadful innovation. The satirist George Cruikshank described them luring the poor and needy to gin-soaked ruin, turning them into 'sneaking, beadle-kicked, gruel-swollen paupers'.[5] The MP James Silk Buckingham, a proponent of temperance and sabbatarianism, warned of the consequences of endemic gin-drinking: 'a fiery flood of disease, of crime, and of physical and mental destruction'.[6] Some even compared gin palaces to prostitutes: 'like true nymphs of the pavé, [they] seduce and entrap the irresolute and unwary'.[7] 'Flaunting' was another much-used epithet, suggesting seduction, indecency and vice.

Specific complaints included the fact that these new premises lacked seating. Drinkers were expected to stand at the bar and quickly down their 'dram'. Landlords claimed this prevented dubious characters from lingering and fraternising. Their critics, on the other hand, argued that the rapidity of the transaction and the strength of the liquor fostered what we might now dub 'binge-drinking'. Multiple doors with smooth 'patent hinges' were also condemned: thieves and prostitutes could allegedly dart in and out of crowded bar-rooms, using these entrances and exits to evade the police. The gin palace was repeatedly damned as an unprecedented scourge. *The Times* noted mournfully that the magnificent decoration once reserved for gentlemen's clubs and hotels was now being displayed not only in London but nationwide, by greedy publicans, 'for the benefit (or rather corruption) of the lower classes'.[8] The American author Alexander Slidell Mackenzie picked out the use of stained-glass windows ('rosettes, bunches of grapes and rich devices') which surely were supposed to be reserved for the saints and martyrs in church.[9]

But was the gin palace truly such a novel threat to the nation's morals? Reading through the newspaper articles, pamphlets and parliamentary debates of the period, one might imagine that gin palaces materialised, *sui generis*, to the utter amazement of respectable society. Nothing could be further from the truth. The 'gin panic' of the 1830s obscures a long-running battle between various interested parties over the form and function of the public house; it represented a backlash against modernisation and commercialisation in the licensing trade.

To understand this hidden history, we must begin in the late eighteenth century. Metropolitan magistrates, tasked with keeping order in the capital, grew increasingly concerned about 'gin-shops'. Most vocal was Patrick Colquhoun, the merchant who famously founded the Thames River Police to reduce theft from London's docks. Colquhoun wrote extensively on crime and policing in London. His first pamphlet on the subject, composed after two years' service as a justice of the peace (JP) in Shoreditch, was entitled *Observations and Facts Relative to Public Houses in the City of London and its Environs* (1794). Colquhoun's thesis was that pubs were too numerous in the East End and needed culling by the magistracy at their annual licensing sessions. Public houses in poor districts had long been perceived as breeding grounds for dissipation and criminality. But Colquhoun was especially keen to suppress 'liquor shops which draw no beer' (also known as 'liquor-shops', 'dram-shops', 'spirit-shops', 'gin-shops' and even the euphemistic 'wine vaults' – all these phrases meant much the same thing, i.e. licensed premises primarily selling spirits). He took it as axiomatic that a busy trade in spirits produced moral and physical decay.[10]

Gin-shops, without doubt, were a meeting place of choice for prostitutes and their clients, with glasses of 'blue ruin' facilitating many a dubious transaction:

I met the prisoner in Drury-lane, whether I accosted her or she me I cannot say . . . the prisoner asked me if I would give her some gin, which I did in a gin-shop in Drury-lane, she asked me if I would go to her lodgings, which I did . . . I there gave her another glass of spirits, I made an agreement to stop with her all night, I paid her four shillings for it . . .[11]

Memories of the infamous 'gin craze' of the mid-eighteenth century also loomed large, when excessive taxation, aimed at reducing alcoholism, had led to illicit liquor flooding the capital. Gin had then become so cheap and popular that itinerant vendors roamed the streets. Pubs had famously boasted 'drunk for a penny; dead drunk for tuppence; clean straw, gratis'.[12] But the gin-shops which Colquhoun hoped to eradicate were not as rough-and-ready as the Hogarthian dens of the previous generation. If anything, they offered a somewhat upmarket and increasingly popular alternative to the traditional public house ('alehouse').

The difference between alehouse and gin-shop is key to understanding Colquhoun's objections. The former had a tap-room with plenty of seating, and sequestered side-rooms and comfortable parlours which might cater for different social classes (charging different prices according to the exclusivity of the room). There were also roving staff to take orders, ferrying drinks hither and thither.[13] There were numerous smaller, more modest houses; and so-called 'flash houses', said to be principally frequented by the criminal classes. Nonetheless, the ideal alehouse was a model of segregated social harmony. The tradesman sat happily in a slightly more select and expensive parlour, the humble labourer frequented the tap-room; and they both formed part of a temporary fellowship under the watchful eye of a convivial, respected publican. The late eighteenth-century gin-shop, however, was quite different: a smart, single room, where spirits were sold from behind a counter to a transient, socially mixed clientele. There were few or no seats; nor any traditional extras, like newspapers and tobacco pipes. Furthermore, gin-shops did not give credit. This streamlined approach was designed to maximise profit, with a quick turn-over of customers and no frills. Gin-shops were more like a retail *shop*; a departure from the alehouse, which, in the mists of time, typically began its life as a domestic dwelling, a public *house*.

Colquhoun considered gin-shops exploitative and immoral. Their proprietors, with few overheads, could undercut the regular pub trade, which had comparatively noble origins in providing rest and refreshment for the weary traveller. Colquhoun also argued that gin-shops relied on a deception. The law explicitly stated that spirits were only to be sold from licensed premises *which already sold beer*, i.e. vended by respectable publicans. In practice, gin-shop owners obtained a beer licence as a mere formality, keeping the absolute minimum of ale or porter in stock. Some did not even trouble to do this. On the rare occasions beer was demanded, they sent out for it to the nearest alehouse. Colquhoun claimed that the gin-shop was therefore an aberration, with no legal footing: the product of conniving publicans exploiting a loophole in the law, and licensing magistrates failing in their duty to protect the public.

The worthy magistrate backed up his words with deeds. He boasted of suppressing 87 gin-shops (out of 1,100 licensed houses in his district) in his early years on the bench.[14] Others followed his example. In 1800, a magistrate in Spitalfields forbade the display of spirits in pub windows (landlords placed coloured vials and jars of spirits on show, to indicate their availability). The same magistrate also prohibited any exterior writing or signs referring to gin.[15] This interference in private property, removing licences outright, or demanding alterations to the way public houses were managed, was very much out of step with the laissez-faire mood of the period. The following, from a report of the Society for Bettering the Condition and Increasing the Comforts of the Poor, written in 1805, casts some light on why magistrates were willing to take such measures:

> The *increase* of the number of *gin-shops* within the last ten years, and the disgraceful and insulting *splendor* and *elegance* with which they are decorated must have been the subject of observation to every one. A different and superior order of visitants do now haunt these *abodes of suicide.*[16]

In other words, these Georgian gin-shops were perceived as 'flaunting' their wares, long before the advent of gaslight and the epithet of 'gin palace'. They encouraged the impressionable to partake of the abominable practice of gin-drinking, 'who would otherwise be ashamed to be seen drinking spirits'.[17] This was what truly worried Colquhoun: gin-drinking was becoming popular among the more respectable members of the working class, not merely the dregs of society. Indeed, it was becoming socially acceptable and even fashionable.

This change was largely thanks to landlords' newly built premises, full of 'splendor and elegance'. The new gin-shops, in fact, took inspiration from the provision already made for the sale of spirits within the better class of alehouse: discreet little rooms, reserved 'for the sole purpose of Dram drinking'. Here the liquor was served over a counter, from a cubby-hole stock-room known as a 'bar'.[18] These small rooms within the pub (confusingly, also dubbed 'gin-shops') were rarely the object of magisterial opprobrium. But they revealed the advantages of counter service when selling spirits. The economic logic was quite straightforward. A compact space selling short drinks, on demand, was noticeably more remunerative than a rambling alehouse, where seated customers got slowly, comfortably befuddled on beer. Thus, at the turn of the nineteenth century, an increasing number of publicans were beginning to make counter service of spirits fundamental to their business. This typically involved some physical changes to their premises. Counters grew ever larger, and smart new fixtures and fittings were installed. This was, doubtless, partly to appeal to the eye of the customer, and partly to defuse fears of a return to the days of 'dead drunk for tuppence, and straw gratis'. There was, however, no standard layout for the new breed of gin-shop. Some of these new shops serving spirits over the counter were entirely independent of existing public houses; others were converted pubs, or 'partial liquor-shops' (an enlargement of an existing alehouse's cubby-hole and counter, with a separate door opening onto the street).[19] But they had one important thing in common: they looked modern and appealing and were very well patronised.

Gin-drinking had acquired a thin veneer of respectability: nothing, thought Colquhoun and his supporters, could be more pernicious.

There was little prospect of government legislation to curb this worrying innovation in retailing. Raising high levels of tax on spirits in the reign of George II had resulted in wholesale illegal distillation, endemic smuggling and violent public atrocities against government informers. Finally, a balance of licensing and moderate taxation had been settled upon. Few were in favour of disturbing this hard-won status quo. Magistrates, however, possessed wide discretionary powers when it came to licensing public houses. Justices hostile to gin-shops, inspired by Colquhoun, became increasingly dictatorial about the design and decoration of existing public houses. If it was impossible to outlaw the drinking of gin, they could restrict how and where it was sold.

Landlords began to find themselves under the threat of losing their licence at the next annual sessions unless they took practical steps to remove any hint that their house resembled a gin-shop or could be described as such. Magistrates relied upon the legal distinction made clear by Colquhoun: the law only allowed legitimate publicans to sell spirits – i.e. those whose principal business was beer. Magistrates inquired as to the volume of beer sold. They issued directions about the use of advertising; the number of doors (endeavouring to prevent easy access from street to bar); and the internal layout of the building (especially whether the tap-room, selling beer, was the principal room at the front of the house, or secondary to a bar, selling liquor). Fixtures and fittings were subjected to scrutiny, with magistrates even mandating the removal of modern touches, such as pewter-topped counters. Exterior signs showing grapes, indicative of wine and spirits, likewise had to be removed. Chequerboard decoration, the traditional symbol for an alehouse, had to be (re)painted on lintels or posts. The further a landlord strayed from the ideal of a model old-fashioned alehouse, the less likely it was that his premises would receive its annual licence.

John Bowles, a Southwark magistrate, took up Colquhoun's crusade in 1802 (both belonged to the Society for the Suppression of Vice, a Christian pressure group for the improvement of public morals). He persuaded fellow justices that any public house without a tap-room – i.e. without seated accommodation – should not be licensed. Warning notices were sent round the district. In May 1803, judges sitting at the county sessions at Guildford offered their support (Southwark fell within their jurisdiction). They bemoaned 'the increasing use of spirituous liquors among the inferior ranks of people of both sexes' and recommended licensing only pubs that sold 'a reasonable quantity of malt liquor, respect being had to its size and situation'.[20] Unfortunately, the application of these resolutions proved contentious. Some on the Southwark magistrates' bench believed that only a *disorderly house* could be closed by magistrates (i.e. a place which nurtured habitual gambling, violence or prostitution). The result was muddle and inactivity.

Individual magistrates, however, continued to target particular public houses, in Southwark and throughout the metropolis. A decade later, Bowles was still arguing his case, exchanging barbed open letters with a fellow Southwark JP, Robert Wissett ('I am by no means inclined to engage in a paper War', proclaimed Bowles airily, before doing just that). Once again, Bowles tried to persuade his fellow justices to abolish gin-shops at a stroke. Wissett, while decrying drunkenness, adopted a relaxed attitude to gin and mocked the idealised vision of a public house promoted by opponents of spirits. In reality, he claimed, the much-praised tap-room was the scene of 'boisterous and indecent language . . . to say nothing of quarrels and fighting'.[21] Bowles, on the other hand, stressed the need to protect the poor from temptation and stem 'the destructive practice of dram-drinking'.

One John Irving Maxwell, a jobbing writer of legal textbooks, penned the case for the hard-pressed publican, describing confused magistrates 'rouzed into instant hostility against *back-doors, casks, and counters*' (i.e. new-fangled features of the modern gin-shop: doors which led directly to a bar; vulgar display of liquor; and counter service).[22] These are all, of course, things that we now associate with a modern public house. Magistrates, claimed Maxwell, were abusing their powers; and publicans were placed in a no-win situation. Those owners of gin-shops who had responded to complaints by installing seating and additionally selling porter were chided for selling it too cheap and injuring the business of the local alehouse.

Some magistrates sympathised. J.T.B. Beaumont despaired of the contradictory instructions which issued from his fellow justices:

> One will have the tap-room in the front of the house, another at the back; the same with the bar. One year a man is directed to clear away all his benches and tables, that people may not sit down to tipple; another yet he is called on to provide all these things, that people may sit down to drink beer instead of spirits. In one division I have known every bench ordered to be removed from the front of road-side houses. In an adjoining one, such accommodation is approved of, a seat on which the traveller may rest while he drinks his ale . . .[23]

Beaumont had a vested interest. He himself had fallen foul of licensing magistrates when trying to set up public houses on his own real estate developments. But he had a point. It was very difficult to define the characteristics of a 'respectable' pub, whenever beer and liquor were both on sale. Was the mere existence of a bar and counter sufficient to mark a public house out as a despised gin-shop? The high constable of Holborn, obliged to inspect pubs and report back to magistrates on the 'gin-shop or alehouse' question, stated that many premises had some combination of tap-room, parlour(s) and the facility to sell gin, such that 'it is a matter of opinion which are gin-shops and which are not; there is a line to be drawn between the two, which you can hardly distinguish'.[24]

* * *

Magistrates fussing over the interior layout of pubs may seem peculiar; but the fervent obsession with the tap-room and its location had a specific purpose, beyond reducing sales of gin. The aim was to deter a distinct subset of the customers who now flocked to the dram-shop, namely working-class women. Unaccompanied women were reluctant to enter the macho environment of the tap-room, 'ashamed to pass through a room which was crowded with men' (i.e. for fear of being labelled or treated as prostitutes).[25] Gin-shops allowed single women to evade the tap-room entirely. Counter service meant that working women could quickly pop in, take a dram and leave through the nearby door to the street. JPs, therefore, were very keen to retain and promote the common tap-room as a sort of buffer zone against female intemperance. It is notable that images of gin-shops frequently show unaccompanied females standing at the bar, from Thomas Rowlandson's *A Gin Shop* (c.1808) to Cruikshank's *Tom and Jerry Taking Blue Ruin* (1821).[26] The women who appear in Cruikshank's cartoons for Pierce Egan, influential comic chronicler of 1820s London 'low-life', are largely prostitutes and criminals. The likes of 'Gateway Peg', 'Mother Brimstone' and 'Fat Peg' exchange banter with Egan's famous creations, the Regency bucks Tom and Jerry. But this was the moralist's charge against the gin-shop: that such premises harboured prostitutes, ruined the morals of more decent women and, by promoting drunkenness and sexual immorality, undermined family life and the nurture of children.

In reality, the gin-shop brought working-class women of every occupation to the bar, and that included both married and single. Colquhoun's fellow moralists did not exempt married women from reproach:

> I recollect when it was a singular thing to see a woman in any public-house, unless at a distance from home, and of course, dressed. Now, it is quite common for women to attend their husbands at their usual haunts, sit down, drink and sing in company, get drunk and swear with as good a grace as any trooper.[27]

There had always been some women, married or otherwise, willing to brave this sort of moral censure. Local ties and familiarity with individual landlords could trump the blanket presumption of 'immorality' levelled against female drinkers. It is also worth noting that there were quieter alternatives: the back rooms of chandlers' shops were spots for 'females, servant-maids and wives of the midling sort of people' to obtain a discreet 'cordial draught'.[28] Gin-shops, all the same, were making liquor more readily available and socially acceptable to working-class women, including those who might previously have only resorted to quiet, relatively concealed tippling, courtesy of the local chandler. This was not confined to the metropolis. The 'spirit-vaults' of industrial Stockport, in the north-west of England, 'fitted up in a style of great splendour', attracted troops of women from the local factories, 'that would have been ashamed of it some years ago'.[29] Likewise, a Manchester letter-writer worried that the '[gin] palaces' brought in 'respectable looking females, and the wives of working men who would be ashamed of being seen in a public house'.[30]

Yet if gin-shops provided greater opportunity for recreational drinking among working women, landlords also had to be wary. The mere presence of unaccompanied women might suggest 'immorality' to the authorities. For the interior of the pub was a highly gendered space; and the perceived problem was not solely about women consuming *more* alcohol, or even the ease with which women could purchase liquor, but the gin-shop's dramatic reconfiguring of traditional male territory. The fact that the publicans were obliged to physically remake their premises, stripping out new counters to return to the old status quo, restoring the tap-room to its traditional prominence, speaks volumes about the powerful anxieties which the gin-shop created. A good example is provided by the Adam and Eve pub in Tottenham Court Road. The house had a door to the street which provided direct access to the bar selling gin, avoiding the tap-room. Magistrates expressed concern, and an investigation took place. It was reported that in a single hour 'ten women at least, and some of them decently dressed like servant maids of the neighbourhood, went to the counter, took a glass of gin, threw the halfpence down and were out in a moment'.[31] The Adam and Eve lost its licence. Anything which 'demoralised' the female servant was patently a danger to society.

Some London publicans, however, questioned whether magistrates' ongoing moral crusade against the gin-shop and gin-drinking was entirely disinterested. The capital abounded with rumours about the influence of wealthy brewers on magistrates' decisions, and the landlord of the Adam and Eve believed that he had been singled out precisely for this reason. Brewers had a stake in the matter: growing consumption of gin was a factor in declining sales of beer and porter in the early 1800s. Rising costs and taxes had rendered these staples increasingly expensive during the Napoleonic Wars; adulteration had become commonplace;

cheaper spirits more popular. Brewers felt somewhat threatened by the rise of the gin-shop. Breweries did not own many London alehouses outright, but they often had a de facto proprietorial interest. It was commonplace for would-be publicans to obtain a mortgage from a brewery in order to purchase their lease. They were then expected to take that company's beer.[32] It was alleged that these 'tied' houses were never the subject of magisterial correction and that some licences were removed because favoured brewers had opened their own pub nearby.

A parliamentary select committee, led by the Whig reformer Henry Bennet, addressed these very questions in 1816, and pretty much confirmed the popular rumour about monopolistic practices and corruption. Magistrates' decisions on licensing were, according to the committee's final report, based on 'arbitrary discretion, varying caprices or interested bias'.[33] Bennet pushed hard for an improved licensing process. In 1817, he produced a bill which proposed increasing landlords' sureties for good conduct and handing over the business of removing licences to a jury trial. Bennet did not discriminate between 'alehouse' and 'gin-shop'. He seems to have thought the distinction between the two unworkable; or else manufactured by justices to provide an excuse for brewery-influenced interference. Publicans themselves held demonstrations, supporting Bennet's proposals and complaining of oppression by brewer and magistrate acting in concert; they raised fulsome petitions to parliament, but all to no avail. The status quo was maintained.

A surviving petition, drawn up in 1816, reveals something of the specific concerns of gin-shop owners. It is notable for its lofty but defensive tone: 'we reject with disdain the revolting and false imputation of our houses being nuisances'. Landlords are characterised as 'men of property and respectability'; selling gin is represented as a respectable calling. The petition is clearly not just about magistrates and licensing, but also about reputation and status. Ironically, it survives solely as an appendix to a pro-brewery pamphlet that ridicules the petition's demands for recognition. This was all part of the war of words waged by brewers, magistrates and publicans in the wake of Bennet's contentious recommendations. The anonymous pamphleteer sneers at gin-shop owners as erstwhile 'cellarmen, ostlers, waiters, grooms, footmen, coachmen, &c.' – somewhat ludicrously, since the owners of traditional alehouses were mostly from similar backgrounds.[34]

Did the magistrates actually have a case? Were gin-shops generally more ill-managed than neighbouring alehouses? It is hard to disentangle facts from prejudice and propaganda. Bennet's committee certainly heard several cases

where the utter respectability of individual gin-shop owners was acknowledged, even as their licence was removed (the presence of a bar serving spirits
being deemed sufficient cause for interference). On the other hand, complaints
which filtered through to the parliamentary committee were inevitably from
more reputable landlords, with a plausible grievance.

The liveliest portrayals of gin-shops and gin-drinking appear in the
picaresque works of Pierce Egan. In *Real Life in London* (1822), at one gin-shop
in Shoe Lane the protagonists encounter, among others, 'a Black Man with a
wooden leg' playing the fiddle to a cavorting blood-soaked butcher; an old
woman selling periwinkles and crabs; an Irish bricklayer; a porter; and a dustman.
Slang abounds. This is not a gin-shop but a 'sluicery'. The regulars drink not gin
but 'blue ruin', 'flash of lightning', 'white tape', 'max', 'Jacky' or 'Daffy's Elixir'.
Such caricatured accounts provide some insight into the underbelly of the early
nineteenth-century metropolis, but they were designed to titillate the middle-
class reader. While gin-shops catered principally to the working class, there is
little to suggest that they were more riotous than their beery competitors.

Real Life in London also includes a moralising footnote:

> It is lamentable to observe the avidity with which the lower orders of society
> in London resort to this fiery liquid, destructive alike of health and morals.
> The consumption of gin in the metropolis is three-fold in proportion to
> what it was a few years ago. Every public-house is now converted into
> 'Wine Vaults' . . .[35]

The upgrading of premises from old-fashioned alehouses into something more
modern and commercial clearly continued apace.

The most famous gin-shop owner, Samuel Thompson, absolutely insisted on
the respectability of his trade. He himself was an alderman of the ward
of Farringdon Without in the City of London, an ancient elected magisterial
office, held for life and carrying a certain prestige. Thompson was the principal
partner in Thompson and Coates, later Thompson and Fearon, an extensive,
highly successful wholesale and retail wine and spirits business, based at 94
Holborn Hill. He seems to have been the instigator of the 1816 petition to
parliament quoted above, and would continue actively to defend the gin trade
against its detractors. He was, behind the scenes, also the promoter of Maxwell's

defence of publicans (a document which asserts – surely no coincidence – that the wine vaults of the City of London are the most respectable in London, managed by persons of wealth, respectability and talent).[36]

The firm of Thompson and Coates was founded at the end of the eighteenth century.[37] Early advertising proclaimed the virtues of 'English Gin', whose consumption, it was noted, boosted the fortunes of British agriculturalists and the exchequer (drinking it, therefore, was virtually a patriotic duty during the Napoleonic Wars). The retail part of the establishment on Holborn Hill allegedly possessed 'perfect decorum and respectability . . . [and] no TAP-ROOM [sic] for the encouragement of idleness and the promotion of dissipation and riot'.[38] The shop was often namechecked by contemporaries as the archetypal 'gin-shop', with the working class forming a large proportion of the clientele. Thompson's shop was actually a little unusual in that it served as a retail outlet to a large-scale wholesale business at the rear. This perhaps explains Thompson's particular emphasis on respectability, for fear of alienating middle-class wholesale clients, families who might order a dozen bottles of wine or a gallon of spirits, to be delivered to their homes.

Thompson himself was an uncompromising character, a charismatic self-made man with rather radical views and a church elder in a splinter group of Unitarians called the Freethinking Christians (also known as the Church of God). He preached regular Sunday sermons at a meeting-house near the Barbican, railing against the established Church, its priesthood and the Holy Trinity. He also offered moral support to members of the sect, who were obliged to marry under the Church of England. 'Freethinker' couples would present the presiding clergyman with a pamphlet outlining their objections to his authority. Not surprisingly, they were usually met with hostility and a refusal to perform the marriage ceremony. Thompson accompanied them and offered earnest lectures to the harassed cleric on points of doctrine, before squaring up to the local magistrate.[39] Thompson's beliefs also encompassed political dissent. Press reports record him organising a much-criticised petition to the Prince Regent complaining about government sinecures, and getting up a political rally to protest about the Peterloo Massacre, demanding electoral reform.[40] Naturally, his political and religious radicalism won him many enemies, who regularly adverted to his morally doubtful trade.[41]

Thompson took comfort in his commercial success. A rival alehouse-keeper reported to Bennet's committee that he had observed over 1,400 people enter

Thompson's shop in the space of three hours. There were some complaints: a local constable believed that the busy gin-shop contributed to 'riot and confusion' arising from Sunday morning drinking around Holborn Hill (while conceding that the proprietor was 'a very respectable man, who has brought up his family very well').[42] Regardless, Thompson's trade steadily increased, rewarded with a place in popular song:

> Thompson's shop on Holborn Hill, is crowded like a fair,
> All the taps continually running out are there;
> Swing swang go the doors, while some pop out and some pop in,
> Foreigners must surely think that John Bull lives on Gin . . .[43]

During the 1820s, the company was so prosperous that it took to placing ever larger advertisements in *The Times*, directing the public to its 'vaults, warehouse and counting house'. The warehouse and bar stocked not only gin, but also wines and spirits of all kinds: port, sherry, madeira, rum, cognac, brandy, plus various cordials and liqueurs. Thompson's stress on respectability remained a constant. A report in *The Times* in 1821 describes an incident in which a drunk is unceremoniously ejected from the shop. The piece is book-ended, clumsily, by the journalist praising Thompson's practice of not serving those already intoxicated: an early example of what modern marketing people call 'native advertising'.[44]

By the mid-1820s, the reputation of Thompson's gin-shop and liquor had grown to such an extent that it had become a must-visit place for anyone passing through the metropolis:

> It was almost looked upon as an omission of duty . . . not to turn into that celebrated Gin-shop, to taste one of the famed cordials, served from the fair hand of one of four handsome, sprightly and neatly-dressed young females, but of modest deportment . . .[45]

Thus, it was in Samuel Thompson's shop that the process which had begun at the start of the century approached its apotheosis: gin-shops emerging as the new, modern type of public house, utilising counter service, and increasing in 'splendor and elegance' to attract trade. The phrase 'gin palace' had not yet been coined, but the dram-shop on Holborn Hill had already acquired sufficient notoriety and glamour to become something of a tourist attraction.

Thompson began to consider investing more money in improving the property. Meanwhile, two legislative interventions would encourage fellow 'gin-spinners' to copy his example, which in turn would spark a moral panic.

The first change in the law was a dramatic reduction in spirit duty in 1825, from 11s 8¼d to 7s per gallon, intended to harmonise rates of duty within the United Kingdom, reduce smuggling from Scotland and Ireland, and encourage trade. The Chancellor of the Exchequer blithely assured parliament that he expected there to be no great impact on consumption of liquor. After all, other nations had even lower duties and were relatively temperate in their habits.[46] The history of politicians vainly hoping that the British might adopt the drinking habits of the Continent is a long one. The Chancellor was proved quite wrong. The number of retailers of spirits would increase by 120 per cent during the next five years, and the retail price would fall markedly.[47] The exchequer, for better or worse, would receive a substantial boost to its income despite the reduction in tax, as considerably more gin was sold.[48] It is not clear how much of this was a switch from smuggled liquor to taxed; but this change seems to have provided greater opportunity for enterprising publicans.

The second crucial piece of legislation boosting the gin trade was 'An Act to Regulate the Granting of Licences to Keepers of Inns, Ale-houses, and Victualling Houses in England', promoted by Thomas Estcourt MP, passed in 1828 (aka the Alehouses Act).[49] The legislation belatedly addressed the problems identified by Bennet in 1816. The act prohibited magistrates from having any business connection with breweries, distillers or publicans, and it created a right of appeal for the aggrieved landlord to the quarter sessions (i.e. the chance of a jury trial, if only on appeal).[50] In other words, the arbitrary powers of the magistrates were, so it seemed, finally curbed. In turn, investments in gin-shops now appeared more secure.[51] One Thomas Spring, owner of the Macclesfield Arms, City Road, was typical, borrowing £2,100 to set up his two sons in their own pubs, precisely for this reason ('upon the faith of Mr. Estcourt's Bill').[52]

Samuel Thompson, now in partnership with his son-in-law, Henry B. Fearon, was similarly emboldened to employ the architect John Papworth to rebuild his entire premises between 1829 and 1832 (described in Papworth's biography as 'the earliest of the gin palaces'); he also fireproofed his warehouse and opened an additional West End wholesale warehouse at 145 Bond Street, a highly prestigious location in Mayfair.[53] Fearon estimated the cost at a monumental £15,000.[54] Other businessmen had much the same idea, ploughing money into building new gin-shops or converting old-fashioned alehouses, not always in the city centre. The Old Queen's Head in Islington, for instance – an ancient quaint tavern, with projecting bay windows and gables, and not yet surrounded by the growing suburb – was entirely demolished, to be replaced by the present building, described at the time as 'a modern "Gin-shop" upon a scale unprecedented'.[55]

This, then, was the birth of what would become known as the 'gin palace', aided by cheap gin and reform of the licensing process – not so much a radical innovation as the culmination of a trend which spanned at least three decades. The arrival of these new 'palaces', however, was not greeted with universal acclaim.

Farmers and brewers played a part in stirring anti-gin sentiment in the late 1820s. They looked at the slashing of spirit duty and demanded an equivalent for malt and hops. Beer, they argued, was too expensive, which was one of the reasons people took to gin. Large, well-attended public meetings were held, which demanded reduced taxation on 'that wholesome beverage, beer', which served as 'liquid food' for the working man. Statistics showed that beer consumption was dropping, which surely imperilled the strength of the nation. Something had to be done: 'The drinking of beer strengthened the labourer; the use of spirits rendered him weak.'[56] Why should it be only the gin trade which benefited from a reduction in tax?

Yet it was magistrates who remained the most vocal and persistent critics of the gin-shop. Sir Richard Birnie, Bow Street, complained vociferously about the scourge of cheap gin and the refitting of premises: 'Every petty public house was now being converted into a flashy gin-shop.'[57] The 1828 Alehouses Act did nothing to change the views of the Westminster bench. Birnie and his fellow magistrates simply ignored the new law and doggedly held to their old interpretation of statute. In 1829, edicts about tap-rooms and accommodation for beer drinkers, identical to those circulated almost thirty years earlier in Southwark, were despatched to every public house in Westminster and Middlesex. Magistrates in Marylebone ensured that seventeen landlords were forced to employ a small army of carpenters to restore recently converted alehouses: reintroducing seating and tap-rooms; blocking up newly opened doors; removing

new-fangled counters and bars.[58] Birnie continued to bemoan the demise of
quiet respectable public houses turned into 'flaming dram-shops': a reference to
giant gaslights and ardent spirits, and perhaps a hint of eternal damnation.[59]
There was also that old favourite, 'lamentable degradation brought upon the
female character'.[60] *The Times* took up the worthy magistrate's cause with
remarkable vigour, running a leader entitled 'INCREASE OF DRUNKENNESS
AMONGST THE LOWER ORDERS', which reported Birnie's pronounce-
ments and recorded this observation:

> On passing through Long-acre the other day, he was astonished to find that
> a little common public-house had been taken down and a building erected
> in its stead which had more the appearance of a palace than a gin-shop.
> What would be thought of a house, for the sale of gin, being built in a
> splendid style of architecture, supported by Corinthian columns?[61]

Thus, the phrase 'gin palace' entered the English language in the winter of
1829 (briefly vying with 'gin temple' before triumphing over its rival). The
style of architecture in question was the latest fashion: neo-classicism (this was
the decade, for example, that saw giant stone caryatids built around St Pancras
New Church). Looking at lithographs of actual 1830s gin palaces, as opposed
to caricatures, many appear rather plain, reserved buildings, not unlike a late
nineteenth-century bank, and not palatial in the slightest. But the wood-cuts
rob scenes of colour and light; and these new public houses were in stark
contrast to what had gone before.

There were those who pluckily defended the gin palace against the magistrates'
interference. *Bell's Life in London*, a newspaper focused on sport, with more of a
pleasure-seeking readership than many of its serious-minded rivals, decried the
puritanism of the bench.[62] A letter to *The Times* would state the obvious: whatever the law had decreed, there were still pre-existing long-standing links between
magistrates and brewers. The anonymous correspondent also accuses the newspaper of rank hypocrisy for chastising the poor while ignoring the equally unpal-
atable vices of the rich, 'excesses which are practised in turtle-eating, in
tobacco-smoking, in beer-drinking, in opium-eating, in wine-drinking'.[63]
The lengthiest rebuttal would come from Samuel Thompson himself: a
two-column advertorial (an extensive rant, appended with a list of his prices)

which he took out in *The Times* on 14 January 1830. The title of this peculiar advertisement was 'GIN PANIC', and it heaped sarcasm on the brewers, the magistracy and the newspaper itself. There was a concerted effort, he claimed, to push the brewer's agenda (cheap ale), which was cynically served by libelling the gin-shop owner. Thompson pointed out the revenue to the exchequer derived from gin and charged the Westminster magistrates with exceeding their authority. The conspicuous crowds at his own shop were, he stated, not only gin-drinkers but consumers of wine, rum and brandy. Many were servants, procuring quarts of spirits and bottles of wine to take home to respectable families.[64] As ever, Thompson stressed his shop's respectability, stating that it never supplied more than two glasses of spirits to the same person; never sold liquor to children; removed anyone who appeared disorderly; and profited from the absence of a tap-room, a species of accommodation which only ever amounted to a refuge for the dissipated. The figures given out for the number of visitors to his shop, he said, were grossly exaggerated. Besides, it only measured '11 feet 8 inches by 15 feet'. How would they all fit in? The precision of *11 feet 8 inches* is a nice touch. One gets the impression that Thompson, writing this lengthy apologia, enjoyed himself immensely.

In a sense, Samuel Thompson need not have worried. There would be no immediate *direct* interference in the gin trade, at least from central government. But there was momentum building behind the brewers' demand for reduced taxation on malt and hops. The argument that beer was healthier for working men than fiery spirits was very plausible; and thus, any measure to encourage the poor to eschew the gin-shop for the alehouse was welcomed by MPs. The political and economic ideal of 'free trade', which would amount to lowering taxation, making beer cheaper and more competitive, was also very popular. Some hoped, furthermore, that cheaper beer might help diffuse the growing social unrest among the lower orders, focused on electoral reform. The promotion of beer over spirits also appealed to a nascent temperance movement, which was just beginning to make itself heard. Beer, in this period antedating the rise of teetotalism, was still seen as something of a temperance drink. Bills bearing the slogan 'If you will be happy in time and eternity, avoid the gin-shop as you would the devil' were posted throughout the metropolis.[65]

The result was the Beer Act of 1830. This new legislation was rather radical, going further than brewers or beer-selling publicans wanted. The act not only slashed taxation, but also introduced unabashed free trade. It allowed anyone in

England or Wales to brew and/or sell beer from their own home, after purchasing a two-guinea annual licence. Magistrates could no longer exert any influence on any licensed premises that sold only beer. Taxation on beer and cider was completely abolished. The response from the public was immediate: a third type of public house appeared within days, supplementing the alehouse and gin-shop – the humble beer-shop. Within a matter of months, there were 24,000 such shops scattered throughout the country, many of them little more than kitchens or front parlours opened to the public.[66] *The Times* expressed satisfaction at the lower price of beer now on offer (1½d a pint), hoped that there would now be less consumption of spirits, and decried anyone who objected to the legislation as part of 'the school of big brewers and licensing magistrates'.[67]

The gin palace, however, proved very resilient. If anything, it prospered. Some claimed that, ironically enough, the Beer Act persuaded increasing numbers of traditional publicans to invest in upgrading their premises into gin palaces; they had to diversify and improve, or go under in the face of such widespread, cheap competition. This may well have been an incentive, but it is clearly not the whole story. The change from gin-shop to gin palace was *already* under way, ever since liquor duties were reduced in 1825 and the Alehouses Act passed (hence the likes of the Old Queen's Head in Islington). The broader shift from old-fashioned alehouse to gin-shop had been going on, in one form or another, for several decades.

One chance factor which helped the gin trade thrive was a clause inserted into the Beer Act during its passage through the House of Lords. In an effort to prevent late-night carousing, it was stipulated that beer-shops must close at 10 p.m. In practice, serious drinkers moved from beer-shop to gin-shop (which, unaffected by the legislation, generally closed at midnight). The hours between 10 p.m. and midnight were, therefore, something of a bonanza. One City of London accountant believed this was the ruin of his employee:

> I have actually noticed it in a clerk of my own; he says 'It is 10 o'clock, I shall not go home yet;' and he goes to the gin-shop, and after taking a small quantity of ale he goes and takes some pennyworth of gin, and it upsets the whole frame altogether . . .[68]

This was typical of the unintended consequences which attached to the new legislation. Worst of all was the perceived character of the beer-shops themselves. Portrayed by the supporters of the Beer Act as decent self-supporting private enterprises, beer-shops were soon criticised as dens of iniquity. They were, it was claimed, not even under the supervision of the policeman (police did not, when the legislation was first introduced, have the powers to search the premises for criminals). They were damned as the haunts of the lowest of the low, who would not dare set foot in a properly managed public house.[69] The same accusations of immorality which bedevilled the gin palace were flung at its cut-priced beery rival (namely criminality, juvenile delinquency, drunkenness). Most alarmingly, the numbers of both beer-shops and gin palaces continued to swell. Gin was still very affordable: a pennyworth, mixed with water, was considered better value than a half pint of ale.[70]

In fairness, the gaudiness of the gin palace and the strength of its liquor attracted greater criticism than the lowly beer-shop. The *Standard* had no doubts on the matter, singling out Thompson's gin-shop for 'so much immorality, poverty, crime, disease and death', the equivalent to 'one hundred beer-shops'.[71] Typically, the gin palace was portrayed by its enemies as an artificial, unnatural type of public house, infinitely more dangerous than its competitors. The beer-shop, although a government-led innovation, was seen as renewing a lost tradition of individual households home-brewing their own beer. This was an idyllic vision which, in most cases, bore little relation to the gritty reality.

The cartoonist George Cruikshank, himself a reformed alcoholic, contributed to the most prominent pieces of 'anti-gin' literature, including collaborating with John Wight to produce *Sunday in London* (1833). The booklet supported a Sabbatarian bill by Sir Andrew Agnew, but was also unsparing on the subject of gin, with a good deal of purple prose:

> . . . gin is become a giant demi-god – a mighty spirit, dwelling in gaudy gold-bespattered temples, erected to his honour in every street, and worshipped by countless thousands, who daily sacrifice at his shrine their health, their strength, their money, their minds, their bodies, their wives, children, sacred home, and liberty . . .[72]

It was in this heated atmosphere that James Silk Buckingham, member of parliament for Sheffield, called for a government inquiry into habitual drunkenness among the labouring classes. Buckingham singled out one unnamed gin-shop in Holborn (surely Thompson's) which served 5,000 customers per day. Such numbers were bad enough; but many of the drinkers were female, reportedly surpassing their male counterparts in the grossness and depravity of their demeanour. Certain premises in Manchester were said to have low counters, specifically for the sale of gin to minors, with liquor sold in 'squib' glasses for a ha'penny, or even a farthing. Buckingham persuaded fellow MPs to establish a Select Committee on Drunkenness, which began hearing from witnesses in the summer of 1834. The prospect of new government restrictions on the sale of gin suddenly loomed on the horizon.

Buckingham's committee, however, although it conducted extensive hearings – with magistrates, the police, publicans and others – had little impact. *The Times*, although resolutely 'anti-gin', swiftly ridiculed the committee's final report. Buckingham's error was simple. Full of enthusiasm for social reform, he advocated wholesale social improvements: public education for the poor and government-funded parks, libraries, museums and reading-rooms. He even hesitantly touched on the possibility of the total prohibition of liquor. The former set of proposals would have entailed untold expense; the latter would have necessitated unprecedented interference in the rights and property of publicans and brewers.

Buckingham cited the inquiries into slum living conditions which had taken place during the recent cholera epidemic of 1831–32 as his justification. The state *could* interfere with private property, he noted, when necessary. Was there not a problem with spirits, which likewise had reached *epidemic* proportions? But the local boards of health which had carried out slum investigations in 1832 were much disliked, their legal position contested; they were abolished as soon as the epidemic had passed. Buckingham, in fairness, had hinted at these wide-ranging proposals in his initial speech to parliament. *The Times* and the government, although forewarned, could not countenance such novel propositions. With the exception of prohibition, they would all come to pass by the end of the nineteenth century, but Buckingham was ahead of his time. His inquiry was mocked as 'the Drunken Committee'. Why, asked one journalist, did the number of gas burners, mahogany counters, modern doors on patent hinges, or the presence of pretty barmaids make gin any more dangerous than previously?[73]

While the press thought Buckingham had over-reached himself, there were others who contested the need for *any* interference. Again, *Bell's Life* championed the pleasures of the working man, challenging the assumption that the grandeur of the new gin palaces represented a worrying development. This was, claimed the paper, another instance of specialisation in trade, a feature of modern commerce; and, if anything, it signified improved 'public taste' when it came to choosing where to consume alcohol.[74] There were others who stated that temperance campaigns began 'at the wrong end'. There would always be a supply to match demand, unless reformers could first persuade consumers to forgo drink.[75] Some questioned whether, in any case, the government truly wanted to regulate the gin trade, since liquor brought too much profit to the exchequer.

By the time Victoria came to the throne in 1837, despite opposition the gin palace had become commonplace. Lively advertisements proclaimed the merits of the demon drink:

> Stop! stop! stop! Here you may get the regular knock-me-down, sow-me-up, do-me-brown, ask-me-how, come-it-strong, out-and-out, genuine, never-split, cream of the valley, price twopence the glass, including a rusk and a dash of carraways.[76]

There was still much hostility. Temperance campaigners regularly produced tracts denouncing gin palaces as the work of Satan; some magistrates still gave vexing decisions regarding the licensing of individual premises.

The case of Thomas Wallis, formerly of the Crown and Checkers, Borough, provides an extreme example. His pub had been pulled down to make way for the new London Bridge, which was completed in 1831; and he had been given a new site, generously provided by the City of London Corporation. He rebuilt on a grander scale, only to be informed by Surrey magistrates, the relevant licensing authority, that they would not license a 'gin palace'. He made repeated appeals between 1833 and 1836, all of which were knocked back. Wallis had spent more than £3,000 and had taken care to provide facilities which marked out a pub as respectable: a tap-room with seating and a fireplace, so that the working man could sit and 'dress his dinner' (bring a cut of meat and have it cooked). Upstairs, there were dining facilities and a coffee-room. But there was also an extensive curved counter of the sort commonly found in gin-shops. The magistrates suspected that the tap-room seating would be cleared out as soon as the licence was granted, and so they continued to refuse him.

Wallis had local supporters, and the magistrates' decision was annually jeered by spectators. But what is most striking in this example is the similarity between Wallis's struggles in the 1830s and those in Colquhoun's day: the same arguments about the function and respectability of the public house were *still* being aired, some thirty years after Colquhoun first raised the issue. Complaints about standing at the counter, access to the street and extravagant decoration continued to be a regular feature at licensing sessions. This begs an important question. Why was there such a furore in the press and parliament about 'gin palaces' in the early 1830s? The talking points were identical to those of the early 1800s; the gin palace was, plainly, nothing more than a larger, somewhat better-lit gin-shop. Why was there, as Samuel Thompson correctly identified, suddenly a full-blown moral panic?

A variety of factors contributed to the hubbub. There was probably a substantial rise in the consumption of gin after 1825, when taxation was reduced, presumably with an increase in drunken and anti-social behaviour. Thompson's partner, Henry Fearon, challenged this supposition, suggesting to the 1830 Sale of Beer Committee, which drafted the Beer Act, that the principal increase in consumption was among the middle classes, buying gin wholesale, instead of cheap wine and brandies. But this disingenuous argument suited a wholesaler who traded on his eminent respectability. The reality, on a Saturday night, was surely a little different. A local magistrate would describe a typical late-night scene to Buckingham's inquiry:

There is a gin committee in the Borough of 10 to 12 women, at the head of which is a chimney-sweeper's wife, who nightly patrol around four short streets in which walk they regale themselves with 13 glasses of liquor. There are twelve public houses in that walk and the thirteenth glass is drunk in honour of the house which sells the strongest gin.[77]

Yet, equally, the gin panic did not commence until 1829/30, five years after taxation was reduced and prices plummeted. The passing of the 1828 Alehouses Act, encouraging more ambitious investment in the pub trade, may therefore have been a factor. One other intriguing possibility is that the introduction of the Metropolitan Police in 1829, more disciplined and coherent than the old parish watch, may have brought more drunks before magistrates. This, in turn, prompted renewed soul-searching about the nature of the modern public house.

The amount of money being spent on new premises undoubtedly riled temperance advocates. Certain shops under construction even warranted individual mention in the press ('The house at present is a common public-house, and the money agreed to be paid for its conversion is 3,000*l.*').[78] Cynics suggested, however, that such reports were barely concealed advertisements, 'puffs' placed by obliging hacks. We should also question whether such lavish spending was unique to the so-called gin palace. Thomas Spring, owner of the Macclesfield Arms, admitted that he had spent £10,000 on building and fitting out his premises, but described the place as 'a beer-house, not at all as a gin-shop'. In fact, the binary division of public houses into good 'alehouses' and bad 'gin-shops' was becoming outdated and artificial, even as the term 'gin palace' came into common parlance. Glamorous architectural and illuminatory accoutrements, initially associated with gin-sellers, were gradually being adopted by publicans across the board. Counter service, likewise, was also becoming the norm throughout the licensing trade, for both beer and spirits. This was thanks to the growing adoption of the beer engine/pump, which one can find mentioned in advertisements for the sale of pub properties from the early 1800s.[79] By the end of the 1830s, the term 'gin palace' meant nothing more or less than a modern public house.

There was also a deep psychological unease lurking beneath the more obvious causes of the panic: anxiety about class and social status. The gaslight, glass and gilding used in the 1830s – the same elaborate decoration increasingly applied to all sorts of retail premises – *were* staggeringly expensive. This sort of expense normally bought the shopkeeper a degree of respectability. Yet the sale of ardent liquor was seen as morally dubious. This created a moral incongruity which could only be squared by denouncing the splendid gin palace as a whited sepulchre, a disturbing affront to decent society; vice hiding in plain sight. The gin palace's clientele posed their own related difficulty. The 'superior order of visitants' of the early 1800s, i.e. the more respectable members of the working class, were joined after the reduction of duty in 1825 by the abject poor, drowning their sorrows in liquor. The price of gin dropped as low as 2½d for a quarter of a pint, which might be shared between two or three people. Thus the caste of the gin-shop customer post-1825, even more than at the start of the century, seemed to be in inverse proportion to the grandeur of the surroundings. This had worrying social implications. It is significant that many contemporary accounts describe gin palaces' 'mock' finery and ornament:

We've seen an arched lighted roof, supported on Corinthian columns; Classic displays thickly sculptured on the walls, chandeliers of crystal and lamps of bronze suspended by thickly gilt chains; and stately mirrors on all sides reflecting the mock grandeur of the scene.[80]

The gin temple's plate-glass, gaslight, stucco, etc. were actually the same ornamentation visible in many a grand shop, the same decoration increasingly on display in London's West End. But to protect middle-class sensibilities, the 'gaudy' gin palace had to be differentiated. For the presence of the poor and ragged in the gorgeously appointed gin palace undermined the social status of more respectable retail establishments (and, indirectly, their clientele). Occasionally, someone would dare to suggest that gin palaces brought architectural excellence and taste into the lives of the poor ('these public haunts . . . have done much towards improving the architecture of our day').[81] But, for the most part, middle-class commentators refused to accept that the trappings of affluence, betokening taste and refinement, could now be purchased with the profits of a mere public house; and that the poor could or should enjoy them.

Worse still, the glittering gin palace, by its very existence, seemed to ridicule respectable society. The much-vaunted grandiose gaslights were rather subversive. Gas had long been championed as part of the march of progress. Gaslights illuminated the darkest recesses of the capital, making the streets safe for the general public. Crime dropped wherever they were introduced. The Benthamite *Westminster Review* observed, praising this panoptical moral power, 'men are afraid to be wicked when light is looking at them'.[82] The gin-shop's gaslights, on the other hand, lured the unwary to a life of misery and dissipation, like moths to a flame.

Finally, it is worth remembering that the gin palace was described as an unprecedented, dreadful innovation by writers with a vested interest. The early 1830s gin panic had a purpose. Its authors were either actively campaigning for temperance or, like Dickens, keen to make a broader point about the evils of poverty and drink. There was no mileage in pointing out that a variety of opponents had already spent wasted decades railing against fashionable improvements in pubs.

Inevitably, the panic eventually subsided. The modern public house, with its easy counter service, was here to stay. Moralists continued to rage against intemperance, but they made relatively little impact on the licensing trade. Publicans always found ways to work around the obstacles placed in their path. The 1839 Metropolitan Police Act, for example, prohibited Sunday opening before 1 p.m., a small victory for temperance and Sabbath observance. Previously, London's pubs opened from early in the morning until 11 a.m., when a drunken mob was turfed out and expected to proceed directly to church (not that many clergymen welcomed their occasional bouts of drunken piety). Enterprising landlords around the slums of Seven Dials, therefore, posted announcements on sign-boards outside their houses: 'As we are prevented by law from serving until one o'clock, PLEASE to *bring your jugs and bottles* on Saturday night.'[83]

Business as usual.

II

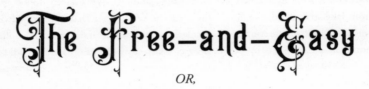

OR,

THE GLORIOUS APOLLO

THE MODERNISATION OF THE PUBLIC HOUSE in the 1820s and 1830s coincided with the first stirrings of another leisure phenomenon: music hall. The publican, having successfully invested in gaslight and gilding, looked for other ways to expand his business. Historians agree that this was something of an evolutionary process. First, landlords turned amateur pub sing-alongs into a sort of commercialised cabaret. When this proved profitable, they built ever more elaborate pub concert-rooms. The popularity of these venues, or 'music halls', ultimately led to the construction of magnificent 'palaces of variety'. The individual publican, meanwhile, who had started the music-hall boom, mortgaged up to the hilt with his local brewery, soon found himself in competition with a wider range of theatrical speculators. For music halls proved themselves a reliable investment. Indeed, it is difficult to think of a major London hall that failed during Victoria's reign. Few West End venues ever came to grief and most expanded their auditoria to meet growing demand.[1] Whenever management faltered, there was always another entrepreneur eagerly waiting in the wings. Music halls only really began to struggle with the advent of cinema in the early twentieth century. This was a little ironic, since moving images were first popularised by the halls themselves, incorporated into their programmes from the late 1890s.

The broad historical trajectory of music hall, outlined above, succinctly summarised in the late Victorian coinage 'from pot-house to palace', has been well documented.[2] Yet the early history still remains rather opaque. How precisely did the drunken antics of amateur choral societies provide the basis for the century's greatest entertainment innovation? Given that the halls' origins can be traced back to the 1820s, why was it another thirty years before music hall became big business in London? There are close parallels with the rise of the gin palace. Both institutions were established by enterprising landlords; both faced opposition from magistrates and moralists. Music hall, however, more than the gin palace, was moulded by these conflicts, particularly in the crucible of the metropolis. The boundaries established by public debate, court cases, licensing and legislation, c.1828–50, would define and delimit the nineteenth century's most popular form of entertainment. This chapter, therefore, focuses on those crucial early years.

At the start of the nineteenth century, many metropolitan public houses provided modest amusements: a skittle ground, billiard table, bagatelle or draughts. Some taverns on the edge of town also had pleasure gardens. These ranged from small back gardens to several acres of manicured lawns, gaily lit arbours, and dedicated spaces for al fresco concerts, dining and dancing. Pubs might also host a variety of itinerant musicians, and occasionally clear a space in the tap-room for dancing. Last but not least was the popular 'free-and-easy', when friends and acquaintances came together to sing, smoke and drink. These evenings were also known as 'harmonic meetings'; or, where women were included, 'cock-and-hen clubs'. They took place in the club-room, a meeting-room for hire, typically on the first floor of the public house.

The free-and-easy was essentially a social club with a choral bent. Chairs were drawn up around a long dining table. Club rules were written up and posted on the wall. Members paid a small subscription and strangers required an introduction. If this all sounds somewhat formal, note the debating society 'rules' in Rowlandson's satirical cartoon *The Brilliants* (1801):

1. That each member shall fill a half pint Bumper to the first Toast
2. That after Twenty four Bumper toasts are gone round, every [*sic*] may fill as he pleases

3. That any member refusing to comply with the above regulations to be fine[d] a bumper of Salt & Water[3]

Pub-based societies always provided an excuse to drink; and the free-and-easy was no exception.

A leading member of the club acted as 'chairman', a gavel-wielding master of ceremonies. The chairman banged his hammer, called for 'order!', and ensured that each of his comrades 'obliged' by performing a favourite song or possibly a recitation. He also led collective renditions of 'glees'. These were songs with multiple parts and hearty choruses sung by the entire room. Clubs sometimes appointed their chairman on a rotating basis, and members eagerly anticipated their turn at the head of the table. Mr Batch, a jovial baker in a 1790s musical comedy, proudly remarks: 'I'm in the chair to-day, as I told you before; big as a peck loaf, when I'm in the chair!'; and then proceeds to sing a jolly song about it ('With hammer in hand, Zounds, how I command!').[4] Waiters attended the room, keeping it well sluiced with drink. Publicans welcomed harmonic meetings precisely because of these repeat purchases of alcohol. Landlords could even be persuaded to lend their club-room gratis, on the promise that the assembled singers were a thirsty crowd. Hence, the chairman's frequent cry of 'Gentlemen, the waiter's in the room, give your orders, gentlemen!', plus toasts to the health of the monarch, the prosperity of the nation, and much else besides ('May every virtuous woman be happy, and every vicious one penitent!'; 'The immortal memory of Nelson!'; 'Drops of sorrow and draughts of delight!').[5]

These Georgian get-togethers, in short, were the fertile soil from which commercial music hall would eventually spring. Readers already familiar with Victorian music hall will recognise certain elements: performers getting up to take brief 'turns' before the crowd; communal singing; the jovial chairman dominating the room. The harmonic meeting also shared something else with its more commercial successor: accusations of immorality.

Working-class harmonic meetings, for a start, might include women. The presence of women, at what amounted to a drinking club, was deemed scandalous by magistrates and middle-class moralists. The Yorkshire Grey public house in Holborn was described as 'kept in a very bad manner', thanks to the existence of a rowdy cock-and-hen club, where the parish constable found – to his horror – not only women participating but 'a female in the chair'.[6] Working-class teenagers of both sexes also frequented their own cock-and-hen clubs. Francis Place, the working-class memoirist and social reformer, recalled a popular venue off the Strand, where local boys and girls met for 'drinking – smoaking [*sic*] – swearing – and singing flash songs', until they gradually paired off at midnight. Such encounters rendered cock-and-hen clubs highly offensive to self-professed guardians of public morals: '[places where] boys and girls meet . . . and get drunk and debauch one another'; '[where] persons of both sexes sing obscene songs and are guilty of every kind of debauchery'.[7] Naturally, teenagers themselves were very keen to attend. Several contemporary court cases describe teens stealing money for this very purpose; and some youths became rather obsessed with the heady mix of beer and popular music. One such individual was dismissed from his apprenticeship for shirking his work, preferring to lose himself in 'spouting-books and song-books' (i.e. learning popular tunes and comic monologues). The boy's mother defended him in court, telling his master: 'Well, and what of that? You go to the free-and-easy every night and sing songs yourself, at Merlin's Cave.'[8] Such fanciful nomenclature was the norm: the humble free-and-easy at the local pub might be known as 'The Cave of Harmony', 'The Nightingale Club' or 'The Glorious Apollo'.

The lyrics of certain club-room songs gave credence to accusations of corrupting the youth. Risqué ditties about sex, while not necessarily the staple fare, were familiar to the club-room audience. Most of these songs were comic in tone, but this did not appease those who cried 'debauchery'. Men-only 'song-and-supper rooms' around Covent Garden – the likes of the Coal Hole, Cyder Cellars and Offley's – were especially notorious for explicit lyrical content. Surviving bawdy song-books, full of ribaldry, double entendre and frankly pornographic detail, provide an insight into the nature of the material. We might take as an example the following verses from *Fanny Hill's Bang-up Reciter* (1835), the tale of a young fellow who has won a bantam at Croydon Fair:

Two ladies, who were in the coach,
Beheld him first on his approach —
They view'd his cock with much delight
And said, as he was so polite,
Sooner than he should not ride,
Why, he might bring his cock inside . . .

'Pray . . . what makes it look so very red,
So stiff and spruce about the head?'
'Fair lady, it is quite unruly
I'll tell you what's the cause and truly,

Before you, you have got a muff,
Which appears both warm and rough.
If you will give him shelter there,
But one half hour in your care.
He'll lay his head down quiet.'

Some singers preferred to add new filthy verses to existing songs, or swap familiar lyrics for bawdy alternatives (e.g. 'there's no love like the first love' becoming 'there's no shove like the first shove').[9]

Bawdy pieces, however, were only part of a much larger repertoire of popular music. Most commercial song-books of the period contain only earnest paeans to 'Bacchus' or 'Venus', and comic doggerel (with titles like 'The Misfortune of Buying Tripe on a Friday' or 'Dash My Vig!').[10] The Covent Garden rooms, well known for their racy material, were somewhat atypical. They were run on more commercial lines than the average free-and-easy, serving hot food and staying open after midnight. They provided a bibulous post-theatre refuge for young men about town in central London, 'reeking with a dense atmosphere of smoke, flavoured with the mingled fumes of the public-house and the cook-shop'.[11] This supper-room crowd were a self-consciously bohemian mix of young lawyers, actors, journalists, medical students and assorted would-be hedonists; they wanted their songs to be shocking.[12] The commonplace free-and-easy, on the other hand, was a more humdrum affair, with salacious material held in reserve. The chairman was expected to maintain a balance, starting off allowing only 'songs of sentiment and feeling . . . national or patriotic or bacchanalian or amatorial expression' before working up to cruder stuff later in the evening, when the company was thoroughly inebriated, and the more prudish had retired.[13] One journalist, reminiscing in the 1850s, noted that midnight marked a tacitly agreed watershed. Songs 'seldom very indelicate' then finally yielded to a 'torrent of lyrical filth'.[14] This may still seem remarkable for an era we tend to associate with prudery; but Georgian permissiveness lingered well into the early Victorian period.

The likes of the Coal Hole and Cyder Cellars have sometimes been put forward as *the* inspiration for music hall. Some writers have suggested them as a bridge between the wholly amateur amusements of the free-and-easy and the commercial halls that began to appear in the mid-century. Certainly, the supper-rooms focused on making a profit from the sale of food, and increasingly employed professional singers, many of whom would migrate into music hall proper. But the men-only night haunts of Covent Garden were part of a more general trend. From the late 1820s, publicans throughout the metropolis began to offer commercialised 'harmonic' entertainment to their clientele of working-class men and women. We know this thanks, in part, to an obscure but important court case – *Green* v. *Botheroyd*.

In 1828, a certain Mr Botheroyd, landlord of the humble King's Arms, Golden Lane, on the borders of the City of London, was accused of holding a cock-and-hen club without an entertainment licence (known as a *music and dancing* licence). These licences had originally been introduced to control disorderly suburban pleasure gardens, but the licensing law in question, the Disorderly Houses Act (1751), theoretically extended to anywhere within 20 miles of the metropolis.[15] *Theoretically* is the key word. For the prosecution of Mr Botheroyd was a curious affair. Few had ever troubled to apply entertainment licensing to petty amusements in the public house.[16]

The prosecutor, a certain Mr Green, made a speciality of such peculiar litigation. He was a 'notorious informer', which essentially meant an unscrupulous prosecutor of trivial offences. Informers made a living by discovering obscure, forgotten laws, which offered rich rewards to those bringing prosecutions. They then sought out suitable victims. One Thomas Stowell, infamous for his manifold money-making schemes, actually hired whole bands of cronies to execute his plans. For instance, he tricked all the bakers in a certain district into committing the unlikely offence of selling penny rolls before 9 a.m. on a Sunday morning. He then meticulously brought all the cases to court.[17] Mr Green, following this model, brought the King's Arms to book for illicit music and dancing, and laid twenty-six further indictments against other publicans.[18] Most of Green's victims immediately settled out of court; or, to put it more practically, bribed him to relent. Mr Botheroyd, on the other hand, defended himself before the local magistrate, and took the case to the higher court of the King's Bench. Botheroyd was quite determined to have his day in court, having made a costly investment in his property. The room in which his cock-and-hen club was held had recently been enlarged to form a 'concert-room', holding 300 people.

Botheroyd conceded in court that there were 'concerts, and singing and recitations' above his pub; that women sang (as well as men) and tuppence admission was charged. Still, this was only a 'cock-and-hen club'. He claimed that his working-class clientele was respectable enough; that the presence of ladies of 'known character' (i.e. prostitutes) was incidental, no worse than any other place of public resort.[19] The pub was a respected, long-standing family business, and even the parish vestry used the new room for their official dinners. Finally, he protested that the entertainment licensing law was an antiquated statute, designed to regulate pleasure gardens, not public houses.

Unfortunately, the court did not agree. They punished Botheroyd with a £100 fine, half of which went as bounty to his persecutor. Lord Tenterden, one of the judges, mused that magistrates had a duty to prevent working men spending their time in such places, 'which ought to be employed in another way' (although, sadly, he did not specify the wholesome activities he thought preferable).[20] The champion of popular pleasure, *Bell's Life*, declared the decision 'all cant'. This was a blatant oppression of the licensed victualler, with no purpose except to line the informer's pocket.[21] Regardless, the judgment in *Green* v. *Botheroyd* was much publicised in the press and, because it derived from a superior court, set a precedent. London magistrates would henceforth consider themselves obliged to supervise public house amusements. This was the beginning of two decades of doubt and uncertainty about the status of pub entertainments in the metropolis. During that time, decisions by magistrates and legislators, mostly without any great forethought or planning, moulded the greatest entertainment phenomenon of the nineteenth century.

One might legitimately ask why Botheroyd's club-night attracted the informer's attention in the first place. This was not, after all, the first time a publican had offered some form of organised entertainment to customers. The size of the new concert-room was undoubtedly significant, more like a small theatre than a mere club-room. There was also an entrance fee, considered a necessary condition for imposing a penalty in licensing cases. Mr Green, for his part, must have anticipated a lucrative new revenue stream. After all, this was the era of the gin palace. Throughout the metropolis, ambitious publicans were beginning to remodel their houses. Walls were being knocked through; back yards covered with bricks and mortar. Competition, innovation and investment, surging on profits from gin, were altering the size and shape of the public house; and that included new, mostly unlicensed, spaces for entertainment. Sadly, press reports contain no details of the arrangement of Mr Botheroyd's concert-room. We know that some concert-rooms of this period did contain a gallery, above the main body of the auditorium, which would become a defining physical feature of the mid-century music hall.[22]

Botheroyd's room, in short, was just one expression of a broader trend. Landlords were beginning to enlarge and monetise traditional harmonic meet- ings, at the same time as they improved and expanded their premises. Professional singers and chairmen were hired. Piano accompaniment replaced the fiddle; venues were publicised in the press.[23] The club-room sing-along began to become more like a cabaret night, with ticketing on the door, or purchase of a token which could be redeemed for alcohol. Larger audiences in concert-rooms were accommodated on multiple benches or tables. Those publicans who could not afford to construct a new concert-room installed a small podium stage. From the late 1820s onwards, the 'free-and-easy' and 'cock-and-hen' slowly but surely became a more commercial enterprise.

This change was a gradual process, and we can only speculate precisely how it played out in individual cases. Publicans began, perhaps, by offering a small commission to amateur chairmen who brought good custom to the house. One court case records an amateur handing out 'invitation cards' (i.e. flyers) to work colleagues and acquaintances.[24] We know some hard-working individ- uals actually combined the role of chairman with that of waiter, taking a percentage on every drink sold, regularly pausing proceedings to personally refill every pot and glass.[25] It is not hard to imagine how such arrangements solidified into formal employment. Landlords looked for men who would keep the concert-room crowd merry. The successful chairman was an affable, larger-than-life 'mine host' figure, known for (what passed for) witty banter ('He soon silenced a chap that was rigging him on the greyness of his hair, by saying, "leave such a subject alone, it is a *lice*ncious one" ').[26] The chairman also usually had some vocal talent, leading the communal singing, contributing the occasional solo. Contemporary advertisements for pub events in *Bell's Life* stress the inclusion of this new breed of professional: 'a professional character will take the chair'; 'a celebrated character will preside'.[27] The right chairman was clearly a 'draw' for the concert-room-going public.

Professional singers did not entirely usurp the highly popular amateur element, at least not immediately. On any given evening, some singers were full-time entertainers; some might be aspirants with a day job; the remainder were simply audience members who enjoyed belting out their favourite tunes (i.e. the traditional free-and-easy membership). But there were no fixed rules. In Dickens' *Oliver Twist*, when Fagin comes across a harmonic meeting above the Three Cripples pub, the landlord plays the role of chairman. Some performers brought sheet music; otherwise, a pianist improvised accompaniment. Singers do seem to have always predominated over other acts. There are contemporary mentions of other performers in the pub: reciters of verse; jugglers and tumblers; novelty acts, like a man singing while standing on his head, or a talented amateur playing a sailor's hornpipe 'on his teeth with the aid of his finger nails'.[28] Still, vocal music, both serious and comic, was pre-eminent. Full-time singers even began to declare themselves 'professional gentlemen', or 'pros', to distinguish themselves from amateurs.[29] If this mix of amateur and professional seems peculiar, think of modern stand-up comedy 'open mic nights', where hopefuls mingle with more established 'headliners' and MCs.

Occasional reviews/advertisements for the commercialised free-and-easy began to appear in the press, principally in *Bell's Life*:

> We were much delighted at the talent of Mr. Charles Sloman at Gaynor's Free and Easy on Wednesday. He is the best impromptu singer . . . with a rapidity scarcely conceivable, composed a song 'trippingly on the tongue' in which he touched upon every topic that had been mentioned during the evening, and brought in the names, with due measure, of every person, stranger or friend who were present.[30]

Note '*every* person' and 'stranger or friend'. Most performers in this early period were still working in relatively intimate spaces, mixing with the audience on easy terms. This close-up conviviality was part of the club-room's original appeal; and the owners of larger concert-rooms strove to retain the old-fashioned atmosphere. The professional chairman not only accepted drinks from star-struck young men but sometimes accorded them the honour of a seat at his table. Singers chatted with the audience, and similarly accepted libations from their fans. Dickens describes the performers at the Three

Cripples enjoying the spirits and water purchased for them by the audience, a mixed group of men and women. Female professionals, too, were actively encouraged to socialise and accept a drink from their male admirers, although some considered this morally questionable. As one female performer in Liverpool confessed to the journalist Henry Mayhew, albeit a couple of decades later: 'It brings company to the house, and if we did not drink with the sailors and others who invite us, we should lose our situations. We are not told this, but we know what would happen.'[31]

Performers' wages were good. Singers could make as much as 2s 6d a night – the sort of money a labourer might be grateful to earn in an entire day – and sometimes considerably more.[32] By the mid-1830s, the 'tavern singer', performing at both club-rooms and concert-rooms, was a novel, but established, profession in the metropolis. One man remarked, explaining his trade in court: 'It is an odd way of making a living, but I believe that many support themselves by it.'[33] Singers even formed a 'Harmonic Benevolent Society', a sure sign of an emerging professional identity. This was a club into which members paid monthly insurance payments, upon which they might draw for sickness or funeral expenses. There was also a record kept of members' professional engagements. This allowed the society's chosen rendezvous, the Hope Tavern, off Drury Lane, to serve as a 'house of call', an informal employment exchange.[34]

This was, in effect, music hall *avant la lettre*, with professional performers and a growing number of small, purpose-built venues. Yet the verdict in *Green* v. *Botheroyd* cast a dark cloud. Metropolitan landlords who offered some form of entertainment were left wondering whether they should attempt to obtain a formal *music and dancing* licence. There were some advantages in being legitimate – not least, freedom from the attentions of the professional informer. The possession of a licence, although annual renewal was never guaranteed, also potentially increased the value of the property.[35] Conversely, there was the risk of fines or temporary closure if the application failed and entertainments persisted. Local residents could even raise a petition against a formal application, in the hope of extorting money.[36] Publicans must have wondered whether it was worth putting their head above the parapet.

This dilemma was not confined to London. By the end of the 1830s, the 'singing-room', synonymous with the concert-room, was equally popular in northern towns and cities like Manchester, Liverpool and Preston, although often condemned as a resort of wayward youths, thieves and prostitutes, a danger to public morals. Preston developed a flourishing concert-room culture, which sparked a lengthy debate in the local paper's letters column on whether the town should tolerate newly built 'singing galleries and cheap concert rooms ... nurseries of all that is vicious and immoral'.[37] Singing-rooms attracted teenagers to the public house, with the attendant risks of alcoholism, precocious sexual encounters and criminality. The battle-lines in northern towns and cities were drawn up slightly differently to the capital. Temperance advocates had a louder voice; factory workers formed a more socially homogeneous audience. Bolton saw conflict between regular publicans and those who owned singing-rooms; and there was influence from local party politics.[38] Still, just as in London, northern publicans were obliged to weigh up potential profits from entertainment against the risk of magisterial opprobrium. Magistrates throughout the country tended to err on the side of caution. To quote a typical case from the Staffordshire Potteries: 'they considered such singing-rooms, in connection with public-houses had a most demoralizing effect, and therefore they were determined to put a stop to them'.[39]

In fact, there is little evidence to suggest that club-rooms and concert-rooms were great haunts of the 'criminal classes'. They were frequented by the working class; but the precise character of the clientele varied, as in any public house. Pierce Egan invariably paints the club-room world as chaotic, prone to violent upsets: waiters frantically darting among a standing-room-only audience; billowing clouds of smoke; rival portions of the crowd singing different melodies, 'songs without tunes – words without music – rhyme out of question'.[40] But newspaper reports reveal few violent excesses; only the occasional picked pocket. Landlords had every incentive to keep profitable rooms peaceful and orderly, after investing considerable sums of money in upgrading their premises. Even temperance campaigners conceded that drunks were excluded, 'lest they should incommode the company, and injure the custom of the house'.[41] Nor was there any special association with prostitution, apart from the corrupting tendency which puritans discerned in every public house.

Nonetheless, publicans knew full well that, if they applied for a formal licence, they opened themselves up to the unpredictable whims of whoever happened to be sitting on the magistrates' bench. Magistrates remained suspicious of club-room culture and distrusted any kind of unregulated entertainment venue.

* * *

The larger concert-room was always more likely to cause more problems than the club-room. The growth of the Eagle Tavern in Islington, during the 1820s, provides a good example. Thomas Rouse, a local builder, took on the Eagle (formerly known as the Shepherd and Shepherdess) in the early 1820s and built a new public house.[42] At first, Rouse operated a typical modest club-room above the premises. Entrance tickets were eightpence, but included 'sixpenny worth of grog' once inside. Featured artistes included 'some of the best room singers of the day'.[43] Rouse never had any run-ins with the magistracy over these performances. Likewise, when he expanded the pub gardens into a pleasure garden, hosting sporting events, balloon ascents and circus-style entertainment, he remained on good terms with the bench. Then he built a stand-alone gaslit concert-room called the Grecian Saloon in 1831, with professional vocalists and orchestra.[44] The following year, magistrates refused the saloon an entertainment licence, on the grounds that it was 'a nuisance to the neighbourhood . . . the resort of hundreds of profligate persons, where the utmost licentiousness prevailed'.[45]

Similarly, in 1834 Mr Grover, the landlord of the Rose and Crown in Bromley-by-Bow, applied for an entertainment licence after remodelling his premises, at a cost of £2,000, to include a separate venue for 'music parties'. Parish officials were already using the new concert-room for their official meetings. Mr Grover, like Rouse, presented a petition showing the support of local clergy, poor law overseers and various respectable householders. Grover was also chairman of the Licensed Victuallers' Asylum, a charity for widows and orphans, which only added to his respectability. The magistrates were evenly split. One saw concert-rooms as a sign of public interest in 'intellectual and rational amusements' (i.e. preferable to out-and-out boozing); another said that such places undermined the industriousness of the working poor; another that music and dancing always led to our old friend, 'the demoralization of females'. Finally, the licence was rejected, by ten votes to eight.[46] Investing in such high-profile ventures was a costly and risky business.

This is not to say that the loss of a licence was necessarily fatal. One could always reapply the following year; and some did not wait that long. Rouse initially attempted to circumvent the closure of the Grecian Saloon by abolishing payment on the door and relying on 'subscription' tickets, purchased in advance.[47] The following summer, although the venue was still theoretically unlicensed, he was once again openly advertising concerts every evening. It doubtless helped to cultivate good relations with influential individuals. Rouse's saloon was the location for election hustings for William Clay, elected MP for Tower Hamlets in 1832. Clay, in turn, vociferously championed the Grecian at licensing sessions. Rouse also hosted a dinner for influential JPs, and arranged a private magisterial viewing of the saloon. Publicans who could rely upon such contacts tended to prosper. Rouse also repeatedly held benefits for charitable causes, donating all profits to the charities in question, which boosted his local standing.[48]

There were some attempts to update and liberalise the metropolitan licensing system in response to the rise of the pub concert-room. Sir J.S. Lillie tried to persuade his fellow justices to demand reform from parliament. He cited the widely acknowledged abuses of informers like Green and Stowell. He noted that the relevant legislation dated back to a metropolis ravaged by gin, where riotous behaviour had been commonplace. He was overwhelmingly defeated.[49] Following a parliamentary inquiry into the licensing of theatres, the radical MP Joseph Hume proposed a bill to legitimise music and dancing in any venue, whether pub, pleasure garden or theatre.[50] The bill had some champions in the national press, but was scuppered in the House of Lords. *The Times* pompously declared itself grateful that the 'floodgates of profligacy' remained firmly shut.[51]

The question of pub entertainment, therefore, remained highly contentious. Metropolitan licensing sessions regularly featured debates between magistrates who saw pub club-rooms – and even the larger concert-rooms – as a venue for healthy, harmless amusement for the working class, and those who considered them dreadful innovations, pregnant with moral peril. The overall result was that only a handful of new *music and dancing* licences were doled out, in a haphazard fashion. Publicans who were keen to legitimately expand their business struggled to negotiate a way forward. *Bell's Life* offered a mock tavern song, satirising the puritans on the bench:

For music and dancing, indulgences vicious,
Give rise to a train of misfortunes pernicious;
Such freaks (the idea our sanctity vexes)
Bring together the youth of the opposite sexes![52]

Some publicans still pressed ahead. They noted that while magistrates remained uncertain about pub entertainments, they had grown more tolerant of the capital's so-called 'minor theatres'. The late 1830s, therefore, saw the emergence of a concert-room/theatre hybrid known as the 'saloon theatre'.

The regulation of metropolitan theatres in this period was a rather peculiar business, which requires some brief explanation.

London theatres in the early nineteenth century fell into two distinct categories: 'patent' theatres and minors. The long-established patents were the self-styled 'national theatres' of Theatre Royal Covent Garden and Theatre Royal Drury Lane.[53] They had historic legal documents (patents) granted by Charles II, which gave them a legal 'monopoly': exclusive rights to performing serious drama in the capital. The original intention of the restriction was to ensure that seditious material did not appear on stage. Their plays, moreover, were subject to censorship by the Lord Chamberlain, the government official responsible for theatrical regulation. The patents' ancient privileges were jealously guarded. Their proprietors believed that the monopoly guaranteed profits. Other 'minor' theatres, meanwhile, were only legally permitted musical and mimed entertainments – comic spoofs, melodrama and pantomime – trading under magistrates' *music and dancing* entertainment licences.

Yet the distinction between the two categories of theatre had grown rather blurred by the 1830s, precisely at the time publicans began to experiment with popular entertainment. Several lesser theatres had been permitted to open in Westminster, pretty much on the patents' very doorstep. Their managers, in turn, had exploited loosely worded licensing laws to incorporate more and more dialogue, so that in practice, many minor theatres were now performing out-and-out plays. Dialogue was spoken, rather than sung, and the only musical element was the occasional token tinkling of a piano. Covent Garden and Drury Lane had launched repeated legal actions against such infractions, but with little long-term success. They themselves were also beginning to stage the same melo-dramas which had once belonged solely to their lesser rivals, further muddying the waters. Magistrates, therefore, somewhat dazed and confused, were increasingly loath to interfere in the whole business of theatrical licensing. This reluctance only increased after an 1832 parliamentary select committee recommended abolishing the peculiar distinction between the patents and their rivals.[54]

This magisterial tolerance of minor theatre was rather encouraging for the entrepreneurial publican, and this helps explain why a new type of venue appeared in the late 1830s: the 'saloon theatre' – a purpose-built pub concert-room *with a theatrical stage*. The amateur sing-along element was largely abandoned in such venues. Pub theatricals, in themselves, were not entirely novel. Actors in the provinces banded together to put on short perfor-mances of not only theatre, but song, dancing, acrobatics, recitations or even magic lantern shows in the public house, when they had no other engage-ment.[55] But the creation of a *permanent* 'pub theatre' was an innovation.

The word 'saloon' probably gained currency thanks to Rouse's Grecian Saloon. Decades later, the theatrical impresario John Hollingshead would describe the Grecian as 'the father and mother, the dry- and wet-nurse, of the music hall' and its influence has been somewhat neglected by historians.[56] Hollingshead outlines a typical evening concert at the Grecian in the early 1830s:

> The performance always began with an overture. This was followed by a chorus sung by the entire company, about twelve in number, the gentlemen appearing in evening dress. About twelve songs, duets and glees followed, the first part of the programme finishing with a concert piece . . . The second part of the programme consisted of an 'entertainment' given by the whole company, who were seated on the platform . . . [this] generally was a mutilated farce, used principally as a vehicle for song and dance . . . No scenery was used, and the performance took place on the platform in front of the organ . . .[57]

Rouse would go on to add stage, scenery and more of a theatrical element in the late 1830s, and it is highly likely that these improvements inspired the other 'saloon theatres' that followed. The phrase was initially applied to struc-tures similar to the Grecian, i.e. separate theatre-like buildings in pub gardens, like the Royal Bower Saloon at the Duke's Arms, Lambeth, opened by Rouse's son-in-law, the scene-painter Phil Phillips. But the term soon came to be used more loosely of any concert-room, whether inside or outside the main pub building, that incorporated some of the physical trappings of a theatre (i.e. stage, proscenium arch, wings, painted backdrops). The owners of saloons drew upon both the tradition of the harmonic meeting and the light entertain-ment tradition of the minor theatres (comic sketches and songs, farces, simple balletic and operatic performances, and whatever else took their fancy). Crucially, they still sold a good deal of drink. A contemporary letter to the press from 'A Magistrate' describes saloons as 'tippling theatres . . . [a] combination of the gin palace system and theatricals'. The anonymous author notes the tables or shelves set before every seat, upon which customers could place their drinks. Publicans, he complains, have smuggled all sorts of entertainments into public houses, under the guise of 'a little music'.[58]

A rare 1839 playbill for the Royal Union Saloon, Shoreditch, offers a glimpse into this emerging hybrid world of song and spectacle. First, a couple of dozen songs, serious and comic, sung by named members of the company. Then 'A Gipsey Dance by Miss C. Cusnie', a well-known ballerina. Next, 'Daring Fetes and Classical Tableaux Vivans [sic]', courtesy of the Brahmin Brothers (acrobats in Greek costume). Then 'A Comic Combat!', performed by 'Ali and Achmet'. The principal draw on the Royal Union's bill is a complete novelty: 'The NEW ZEALAND CHIEF: An ENGLISHMAN Who has been resident in New Zealand for a number of Years, and who will portray the Manners, Customs and Peculiarities of the Natives'. The list ends with comic sketches and a couple of dozen more songs – something for everyone.[59]

The great question for the owners of saloon theatres was whether their gamble would pay off, i.e. would magisterial toleration of minor theatres be extended to this new type of venue? Could the convoluted legal position, particularly the division of theatrical regulation between the Lord Chamberlain and local magistrates, be manipulated to the publican's advantage?

Some publicans did not get the balancing act right. Samuel Lane, the owner of the Royal Union, attempted to get away without obtaining any sort of licence whatever. In 1839, the police, newly empowered to take more active measures under the Metropolitan Police Act – a wide-ranging piece of legislation, designed to improve public order in the capital – conducted a full-scale raid on the premises. The incursion was allegedly at the behest of a local resident, who claimed to have observed the presence of 'disreputable persons' (a suitably vague accusation). Police officers in plain clothes entered the building and discovered that entrance was fourpence; this secured a 'check ticket', which could be exchanged, once inside the auditorium, for a pint of ale. The saloon was substantial, capable of holding 800 people, with a 17-foot-wide gaslit stage, shifting scenery and painted backdrop. When the police entered, two men dressed as 'Jack Tars' were breaking into a sailors' hornpipe. This was considered sufficient to qualify as an unlicensed theatrical performance. Thirty constables stormed the building and chaos ensued. During the subsequent court hearing, the venue was acknowledged as 'an exceedingly well-conducted place of the kind', which had been in operation for several years. Various neighbours sang its praises, but there was no arguing with the fact that it lacked any kind of licence. Lane's wife, present in the box office, received a fine of twenty shillings; performers were fined five shillings; and sixty unlucky members of the audience, dragged to the nearest station-house, one shilling. Lane himself was spared a £20 penalty at a later hearing.[60]

A similar raid took place at the smaller Victoria Saloon, also in Shoreditch. Like many a pub venue, it was accessed via a narrow side-passage, which led to what had once been the back yard. This room, only 22 feet by 13 feet, with a small raised stage, still somehow managed to include scenery, wings and a trapdoor (which led down into a tiny dressing-room for performers). There was a mixed audience, including families with children, approximately 150 persons in total. The 'horrific and facetious' items on the bill, which was a little more theatrical than at the Royal Union, included 'The Death-blow, or the Fatal Knife'; 'The White Farm, or the Murder of Young Henry'; and 'The Lawyer in a Sack'. The dialogue was reportedly 'too obscene for publication'.[61] We can only guess what this actually meant – whether it was alleged sexual obscenity, blasphemy or profanity. The landlord attempted to argue that since no charge was made for admission, the saloon did not constitute a theatre. Police witnesses pointed out that admission was only 'free' if one purchased a glass of porter at 3d as opposed to the regular 2d. The magistrates had heard enough, and imposed a similar regime of fines.

The police's initial enthusiasm for such manpower-intensive exercises seems to have peaked in 1839. The raids in Shoreditch may well have been the result of specific complaints from the local vestry. The following month, the parish clerk of Bethnal Green would send a memo asking magistrates to reduce the number of premises licensed for music in the district, as they 'proved injurious to the morals of young people'.[62] But it was not long before an intervention by central government made a more lasting and wide-ranging impact on the vexatious issue of regulating both pub concert-rooms and the more theatre-like saloons: the Theatres Act (1843).

The Theatres Act finally enacted the key recommendation of the 1832 select committee: dissolving the antiquated distinction between patent and minor theatres. Under this new legislation, the patents' archaic monopoly, dating back to Charles II and the political turmoil of the seventeenth century, was abolished. The Theatres Act allowed all theatres to perform drama, finally providing much-vaunted 'free trade' in the field of entertainment. This would, it was hoped, enable actors and managers to improve the social and moral tone of the minor theatres. Shakespeare, Marlowe and Sheridan could finally be presented to the public, in the smallest venue, without unnecessary incidental music. The act was also an attempt to introduce government regulation into the world of the minors. The Lord Chamberlain was still the censor of plays and, with the minors' dramatic productions legitimised, the Lord Chamberlain now effectively took full responsibility for supervising productions in *all* London's theatres.

The new legislation also attempted to draw a clear line between more reputable minor theatres and places like the Victoria in Shoreditch, where 'the propriety of the performance was made a very secondary consideration to the consumption of the landlord's liquors'.[63] But this was not simply an authoritarian crackdown. Proprietors of saloon theatres were invited to apply to the Lord Chamberlain, and those deemed sufficiently proper and theatrical – including a new venture by Samuel Lane, the Britannia, in Hoxton – were explicitly incorporated into the new regulatory system under a 'saloon licence'. Provisos included that doors should not directly connect the theatre to the bar or tap-room; no smoking or drinking during the performance; and no opening before 5 p.m. Police raids, in other words, were replaced by statutory absorption into the mainstream.

Various publicans applied, but not every applicant was accepted. The Prince of Denmark in Wellclose Square, Wapping, notified the Lord Chamberlain of its ground-floor concert-room, capable of seating 200 people, which had been open since 1839. A *music and dancing* licence had been obtained the previous year. Performances included vaudevilles (short comic plays with song) and ballets, and opening hours were 7 p.m. to 11 p.m. Front seats cost sixpence, back seats threepence (i.e. this was a simple room, with no gallery). The audience was composed of locals and seamen, since the pub was located near St Katherine Docks, and, it was stressed, no young people were admitted unaccompanied. For whatever reason – no records seem to survive of the decision-making process – the pub did not win the Lord Chamberlain's approval. Similarly, the Fountain Saloon in Bethnal Green was a galleried room, built in 1841 by a pub landlord and capable of holding 350 people, being 50 feet long, 20 wide and 15 high. The landlord testified that he had built the saloon to host benefit societies (savings clubs) and stage public performances. He had, he claimed, only ever used the room for vocal and instrumental concerts; but he hoped to stage 'farces and interludes'. The only entrance was through the pub, but he was happy to build a separate entrance, if required. The audience were local mechanics (skilled workers) and sailors from the docks; admission was sixpence. There would be no smoking or drinking, and a policeman would always be present. Again, we do not know the Lord Chamberlain's reasons for rejection, but the landlord had, somewhat foolishly, conceded that his prior application for a *music and dancing* licence had been refused.[64]

Nonetheless, it was recognised that there was a genuine demand among the working class for affordable theatre. The 'saloon licence', therefore, was finally granted to a total of seven public houses which already had pub theatres: The Grecian, Britannia, Effingham, Bower, Albert, Albion and Apollo.[65] The atmosphere in these places could still be rather rowdy. Harold Hartley recalled frequent fights and scuffles at the mid-century Bower in Lambeth; hawkers selling all manner of rough-and-ready refreshments, including pigs' trotters; and being sworn at for the effete crime of using opera glasses to view the stage.[66]

Other publicans could still continue to apply for *music and dancing* licences, so long as they wholly eschewed dramatic material. The chair of the Middlesex magistrates, responsible for such licences in North London, spelled the rules out in full. He declared that the magistrates had previously quietly tolerated all sorts of pub theatricals in poorer neighbourhoods, because the working class had no access to legitimate theatre. Now that they had clear and consistent regulations, they would begin to exercise much firmer control, and 'put down with a strong hand all those public houses in which anything in the nature of stage plays were tolerated'.[67] The Lord Chamberlain would firm up the regulations for the seven saloons in 1845, after it became clear that a good deal of drink was still finding its way into auditoria, and complaints were received from rival theatres. Sales of alcohol were strictly limited to the intervals, as at theatres; and tables or stands for glasses were explicitly forbidden.[68] There was to be a clear-cut distinction between respectable drama and other types of performance. Indeed, it was not many years before the saloon licence was abolished entirely, and the surviving saloon theatres were treated as any other theatrical venue.

The Theatres Act is often cited as *the* decisive moment in music-hall history. After 1843, licensed theatres, under the aegis of the Lord Chamberlain, now definitively owned dramatic entertainment. Publicans who could not obtain the Lord Chamberlain's approval, or who preferred the financial advantages of selling drink within the auditorium, now had to rely solely on song, comedy and speciality acts. This was the case with the Prince of Denmark, also known as the Mahogany Bar, which would finally become Wilton's Music Hall (one of only two surviving mid-century music halls in modern-day London). This break between pub theatricals and light entertainment, however, was far from clean. The problem of heedless landlords and unlicensed premises did not vanish. There remained a large grey area as to what actually counted as dramatic entertainment. The attentions of the police were haphazard and many individuals ploughed on with promoting wholly unlicensed entertainment, hoping they would escape prosecution.

The gap between the intent of the Theatres Act and reality was most glaringly obvious in the case of 'penny gaffs': unlicensed makeshift theatres, which were set up temporarily in empty shops or yards, admission one penny. Their audience was typically juvenile and poor: 'ragged children of both sexes, without shoes or stockings . . . some not more than 8 or 9 years of age'.[69] Penny gaffs continued to thrive in poor districts long after the passing of the act. They were frequently condemned, like singing-rooms, as dens of iniquity. Farces and pantomimes were mixed with stories of highwaymen and murder, drawn from well-known penny-dreadful serials (e.g. 'The Mysteries of Paris') or along similar bloodthirsty lines ('The Blue Apron and the Cleaver, or The Sanguinary Butcher of Cripplegate').[70] Some 'gaffs' toured the countryside, composed of nothing more than a cartload of thin planks and canvas, which could be hastily erected into a 'theatre', shielding a few weary players from the weather.[71]

Penny gaffs have themselves been linked to the rise of music hall; but the association is rather bogus. Gaffs were part of the varied entertainments on offer in poor districts, but they did not contribute to the development of the halls. Most penny gaffs were exclusively patronised by children. Teenagers did form a decent proportion of music-hall audiences, but the penny gaffs were different. The juvenile context is clear from numerous contemporary descriptions. One has a master of ceremonies wielding a long stick to (gently?) tap the children 'if they displayed any impatience for the commencement of the performance, or hooted, or made a noise'. At another venue, an observer describes a show 'in which a number of boys stood on the stage eating rolls and treacle with their hands tied', i.e. party games interrupting the bloody melo-drama.[72] The shoeless and ragged patrons of the penny gaff were not the typical patrons of the concert-room or saloon. The promoters, likewise, were them-selves quite poor, failed actors and small-time travelling showmen.

Many metropolitan landlords, however, copied the owners of gaffs to this degree: they continued to ignore the niceties of licensing. Publicans who only maintained a small club-room and who avoided theatrical entertainments kept their heads down. Neither the Disorderly Houses Act nor the Theatres Act was actively policed, and they felt sure that their small rooms would go unnoticed amid the hubbub of the metropolis. They would be proved wrong.

Matters came to an unexpected head in 1849. The Home Secretary, Sir George Grey, became interested in unlicensed music and dancing venues. The precise reasons for this sudden enthusiasm are not clear. Recent prosecutions by Thomas Stowell, the informer, against several well-known 'casino' dance-halls (to which we return in a later chapter) seem to have piqued his interest in London's night life. Grey, in any case, despatched a memo to all metropolitan magistrates, demanding that they take action on unlicensed music and dancing, echoing a call made by the chairman of the Middlesex Sessions the previous autumn. Grey may have been influenced by contemporary fears about Chartism and social unrest; but more likely, he was just dabbling in local affairs.[73]

Magistrates dutifully responded at the following liquor licensing sessions. These were quite separate from entertainment licensing sessions, which were held later in the year; but they provided an opportunity to convey the Home Secretary's sentiments to waiting publicans. For the most part, magistrates recited the ministerial warning as they issued the usual licences. The Whitechapel bench, however, went one step further. They announced that, henceforth, breaching *entertainment* licensing rules would result in premises automatically losing their *liquor* licence. They were, perhaps, very conscious of Whitechapel's notorious dance-halls, so-called 'long rooms', frequented by sailors and prosti-tutes. Whitechapel also boasted numerous cheap and miscellaneous pub enter-tainments. Circus skills, song, dance and dramatic monologues frequently shared a single bill: 'Grand Concert held here every evening, admission 2*d.*'; 'Le petit Elisa and le belle Pauline on the tight-rope'; 'Mr. Darley will dance a horn-pipe'; 'The celebrated Mr. Towler, as the Maniac!'[74]

The Whitechapel magistrates' statement of intent came as a bombshell for local licensed victuallers. East End publicans were accustomed to occasionally settling a court case brought by an informer while still legitimately selling drink. But the Whitechapel pronouncement, promising to close down pubs for trivial entertainment-related infractions, threw everything into confusion. Virtually every house in the district employed either fiddlers or a piano player; allowed itinerant players to enter the premises; or held modest harmonic meetings. These were not saloon theatres; many did not even possess a substantial concert-room. Not one, therefore, had ever troubled to apply for an entertainment licence.[75]

There was something of a public outcry, among not only publicans but also the singers who worked the pub club-room circuit. The trade paper of the theatrical profession, *The Era*, published a lengthy letter from 'A Singer at Tavern Concerts', who noted that many tavern singers were old actors who relied on the club-room and concert-room for their subsistence. In the same issue, an indignant editorial damns the magistracy as 'old meddling foozles . . . a parcel of unpaid gentry, proud of office, and delighting in exercising their authority', and describes pub entertainment as 'rational amusement . . . an important portion of the recreations enjoyed by the working classes'.[76] Local publicans hastily formed a committee to lobby for something like Hume's act, and sought an audience with the Tower Hamlets bench. Then, when the entertainment licensing sessions finally came around in the autumn, they applied *en masse* for *music and dancing* licences, to cover themselves.

Entertainment licences for North London were granted at the Middlesex Sessions in October, rather than at the smaller local hearings which dealt with liquor licensing. The uproar in Whitechapel created an unprecedented eighty-seven applications for new licences. Unfortunately, the assembled magistrates remained split into their well-established opposing camps. Some argued that they should only concern themselves with obviously disorderly houses. A certain Mr Wilks, on the other hand, interrupted the sessions to issue a lengthy diatribe against 'debauchery' in both concert-rooms and dance-halls. These were places responsible for encouraging juvenile delinquency, corrupting morals, stimulating crime, even producing insanity (presumably through alcoholism and syphilis). Various improving institutions were being built in the East End: ragged schools; public baths and washhouses; new churches; managed accommodation for sailors – there was no need to support dens of depravity and immorality. Wilks was immediately criticised for hypocrisy – it was noted that the rich enjoyed song and dance – but his heated oratory won the day. Just two new licences were granted, even though many were just hoping to legitimise their existing piano-player or fiddler.[77]

The situation in London in 1849, therefore, was a little odd. The local magistracy, at the behest of the Home Secretary, had sternly demanded that pubs should be properly licensed. Then Middlesex magistrates (a larger assembly of JPs, drawn from across North London) had refused to actually issue any new entertainment licences. Pianos and fiddles fell silent in the tap-room and club-room. Newspaper editorials denounced the bench and demanded reform:

> Everybody knows that licensing, like kissing, goes by favour. If the candi-date can make friends enough amongst the friends of the magistrates, he obtains his licence; if not, no. If he himself be a friend, so much the better . . . There is not so much self-will, caprice, and unreasonableness shewn in the granting and withholding of wine and spirit licences, as there is in the granting and withholding of licences for music and dancing . . .[78]

The metaphor of 'kissing' is telling: the licensing system as a corrupt species of flirtation or prostitution. The whole business seemed rather perverse and contradictory.

Salvation for the publicans came in the form of the timely intervention of John Adams, a barrister and Middlesex magistrate. Adams responded to the uproar by issuing a pamphlet, 'On the Subject of Licences for Public Music and Dancing' (1850). Adams was a long-time critic of the licensing system. He condemned the Disorderly Houses Act as out of date, designed to address a licentious, profligate eighteenth-century metropolis that no longer existed. He persuaded his fellow magistrates to rethink the whole issue. Adams' solution was simple enough: a two-tier licensing system, with licences either for *music only* or for *music and dancing*. This was a proposal for reform which had been mooted on several previous occasions and, indeed, already adopted on the Surrey side of the Thames.[79] The distinction gave the Middlesex bench room to manoeuvre, without offending the Home Secretary. They could clamp down on boisterous pub dance-halls, while simultaneously licensing the humble piano or fiddle as *music only*. Legal advice was required, but magistrates concluded, after some months of doubt and hesitation, that a two-tier system was legitimate.[80]

From 1851, therefore, once the legal position was settled, *music only* licences were liberally bestowed. The following year, it was noted with satisfaction that no police complaints had arisen from these new licensed houses (most of which, in truth, had always had some modest form of music on the premises). Adams argued that the more licences, the better; that they would dilute any assembly of immoral characters by their multiplicity. The National Temperance Society wrote to the Middlesex bench, praising its sagacity in removing the 'circumstantial causes of immorality and crime'.[81] Publicans' applications for *music only* outnumbered *music and dancing* by four to one.[82] It was now quite clear that if the average publican wished to amuse his customers, he should disdain both theatre *and* dance, plumping wholeheartedly for music and other forms of light entertainment.

There is a strong parallel here with the legislation of 1828, which encouraged landlords to believe that they could expand their premises into gin palaces, without magisterial interference. For the *music only* licence, now being doled out so freely, was not just a boon to those landlords who wanted to keep the fiddler in the tap-room; crucially, it offered a legitimate avenue for those stymied publicans who had seen potential profits in building or extending a concert-room, but worried about losing their investment to magisterial caprice or the strictures of the Theatres Act. Licence applications rocketed: a combination of those only wishing to legitimise existing performances and those emboldened to invest serious money in entertainment. More ambitious landlords would apply for *music only* in the first instance, hoping to earn the trust of the bench, and would upgrade to *music and dancing* at a later stage.[83] This seemingly trivial change in policy finally created an acceptable regulatory system for pub entertainment.

There were, of course, other factors at work in the 1850s, including the highly visible success of Charles Morton's Canterbury Hall in Lambeth, which we will address in the next chapter. Meanwhile, the terms 'concert-room', 'singing-room' and 'saloon theatre' began to fall out of fashion. The growing magnificence of popular pub venues – splendid, galleried halls, outstripping the public houses which had fostered them – demanded a new turn of phrase: 'music hall'.

III

The Music Hall
OR,

HE SLEPT ON THE PIANO

THE EARLY HISTORY OF MUSIC HALL, outlined in the previous chapter, was not entirely a metropolitan affair. The rise of provincial concert-rooms in the late 1830s and 1840s mirrored developments in the capital. There is little evidence to tell us whether publicans consciously emulated the metropolis, or merely came to the same conclusions about the profitability of pub entertainment. The press occasionally drew comparisons. Reeve's Gothic Saloon in Gravesend was said to be 'upon the plan of the celebrated "Bravo Rouse's Grecian Saloon"'.[1] As early as 1840, one famous hall in Lancashire already rivalled, and possibly even exceeded, anything in London: Thomas Sharples' Star Theatre and Museum in Bolton. The Star's origins were typical: a popular free-and-easy in a public house, commercialised by the landlord. Sharples, however, built an unusually capacious auditorium reportedly capable of holding 1,000–1,500 patrons; a waxwork exhibition; and a menagerie. Details of programmes from the 1840s reveal the eclectic mix of entertainments: a 'Characteristic Yorkshire Dialect Singer'; a 'True Representative of Negro Character'; assorted acrobats and jugglers; ventriloquists and magicians; even readings from popular novels.[2] While Sharples was something of a pioneer, most large conurbations contained some sort of pub concert-room or saloon by the end of the 1840s. As early as 1842, one journalist believed Manchester possessed fifty-four 'saloons'.[3] The terminology varied from place to place, but they offered comic songs and other light entertainment, similar to venues in London. Some larger venues advertised in the local press: the Norwegian Tavern Music Saloon in Hull, opened in 1837; the Polytechnic Music Hall in Salford, opened c.1842 ('a large and commodious Music Hall . . . with stage and scenery complete'); Thomas Youdan's Royal Casino, Sheffield, opened 1849 (later renamed the Surrey Music Hall). The Shades Saloon in Newcastle was dubbed by the *Era* 'not inferior to any of the concert rooms in the metropolis'.[4] Touring circuits formed, as venues multiplied. Performers ventured to nearby cities to seek better wages; proprietors looked further afield for new talent. An 1850 court case records Thomas Youdan poaching a certain Mrs Montgomery ('The Unrivalled Characteristic Vocalist') from Manchester's Colosseum singing saloon, offering her £3 a week.[5]

Music hall, therefore, was already flourishing in towns and cities across the nation by 1850. Yet curiously, histories of the halls have traditionally bestowed the accolade of 'the first music hall' upon a London venue which only opened its doors in 1854, namely the Canterbury Hall in Lambeth. This chapter begins by exploring Canterbury Hall's somewhat dubious claims to primacy; charts how music hall was challenged by growing opposition from theatre managers and moralists; and finally, describes how it evolved into the late Victorian 'palace of varieties'.

Charles Morton's Canterbury Hall appears in countless histories of the halls as *the* hall; the ur-hall from which all others took inspiration. This is peculiar, when one recalls the plethora of metropolitan and provincial venues already in existence. Some writers have suggested that the Canterbury was the first pub concert-room to adopt the term 'music hall'. This is demonstrably false. There was a Surrey Music Hall (not to be confused with its Sheffield namesake) and a Lambeth Music Hall, both within walking distance of Morton's newly opened establishment. Morton's own venue only acquired the clarification of *music* hall some years after it opened.[6] Yet the claim to primacy is not some latter-day fabrication. The Canterbury *was* widely acknowledged as the 'first music hall' by Morton's contemporaries. They must have meant something by it.

Size was undoubtedly a factor. When it opened, the Canterbury was probably the largest and grandest concert-room ever attached to a public house in the capital, a detail sufficient to grab the attention of the press. Sharples' hall in Bolton would not have been well known to London-centric journalists. Charles Morton had actually begun his entertainment enterprise on a relatively modest scale in 1852, replacing his higgledy-piggledy, ancient tavern, The Canterbury Arms, with a modern public house and unexceptional concert-room.[7] The room proved so successful that Morton undertook a major redevelopment within a matter of months. The remodelled Canterbury Hall opened in 1854, with a 1,500–2,000 capacity (contemporary estimates vary). The public house, while still fronting the street, was now quite secondary to the theatrical space. This would become standard in the larger halls which followed Morton's lead. The *Illustrated London News* was charmed by the auditorium and 'the general propriety and beauty of its decorations', a neo-classical galleried hall, lined with lofty Corinthian columns, brimming with gaslights and chandeliers.[8] There were equally sumptuous theatres in the capital, but nothing so large and imposing under the banner of pub entertainment. The layout was quite similar to Evans' song-and-supper rooms, one of the famous gentlemen-only free-and-easies in Covent Garden (which had the usual reputation for late-night drinking and saucy lyrics, associated with the district). Morton himself acknowledged Evans' as an inspiration, but made clear that he wanted to attract a quite different clientele: a less select but respectable, mixed crowd of men and women.

In fact, the Canterbury's unique selling point was ostentatious respectability. Partly this was acquired thanks to the building's size and grandeur; but the programme was also crucial. Morton employed a small corps of professional singers who performed selections from *Lucia di Lammermoor*, *La Sonnambula*, *La Traviata* and other operas. This was not a radical move, since opera had long been popular in minor theatres. London had, only a few years earlier, fallen at the feet of soprano Jenny Lind ('The Swedish Nightingale'), and worshipped the flamboyant conductor Louis-Antoine Jullien (who conducted with a jewelled baton, facing the audience). Presenting opera at a public house concert-room, therefore, was not quixotic or unprecedented. The programme at Rouse's Grecian Saloon in the 1830s had incorporated opera and ballet. Nonetheless, it did suggest a certain level of artistic ambition. Some visitors were still determinedly unimpressed by the hall's 'half-a-dozen vocalists standing in a row in preposterous evening dress', but they were in a minority.[9] *The Times*, no less, appreciated the 'operatic selections', lavishing praise on

Morton's morally improving 'superior order of entertainment'. The newspaper noted, six months later, 'nothing to offend or displease the most delicate sensibility', and reported that 'the most perfect silence' was observed during the operatic performances by an audience of respectable artisans and their wives, and a smattering of the middle class.[10] The hall would famously host the first British airing of selections from Gounod's *Faust*. The addition of an art gallery in 1858, which cost £10,000 to build (plus a further £8,000 to purchase paintings), further set the tone. When the hall was humorously dubbed 'The Royal Academy Over the Water' by *Punch*, Morton cheerfully adopted the epithet for his own advertising.

Charles Morton also made great play of the fact that he catered for a mixed audience, providing an addition to 'the very limited stock of out-of-doors pleasures permitted to the gentler sex'.[11] Journalists noted approvingly the homely presence of wives and children (the latter superbly described as 'juvenile appendages').[12] This was certainly a contrast with Evans' male-only, frequently bawdy atmosphere; perhaps Morton felt he had to make this clear. Morton's emphasis on welcoming a mixed audience, however, was also about subtle distinctions of class. The wives of working-class men had long accompanied their husbands to pubs and pub concert-rooms (even if, as we saw in the first chapter, this could provoke consternation among moralists). Why, then, even mention 'the gentler sex' in this context? Because Morton hoped to draw in men who might otherwise balk at introducing their wives to amusements in a public house: well-paid skilled artisans and junior clerks. These putative customers were working people with pretensions to middle-class refinement and manners, including the notion of 'separate spheres' (i.e. that a woman's place was, fundamentally, in the home). Such men, and their partners, were concerned about how their choice of entertainment reflected upon their social standing; and they decidedly did not want to rub shoulders with drunks and prostitutes. Morton offered them his personal assurance that they would find nothing in the Canterbury's 'out-of-doors pleasures' – i.e. entertainment beyond the safe confines of the home – to scandalise a respectable female.

Morton's hall was not the first to appeal to a mixed demographic, whatever he said on the subject. Horace Heartwell, researching concert-rooms in Manchester in the 1840s, found that 50 per cent of attendees at one venue were working women, with the audience drawn from 'the higher class of factory operatives, silk winders, fustian cutters, and a sprinkling even of the lower class of shopkeepers'.[13] Rouse's Grecian Saloon was patronised not only by clerks and shop-boys, but by 'many stayed-looking, middle-aged personages ... decent shop-keepers ... well-dressed family parties'.[14] The Surrey Music Hall, which pre-dated the Canterbury, could also lay claim to a mixed audience:

> The lower part of the Hall is patronised chiefly by the unwashed and linen drapers, shop-boys, lawyers, clerks, and the more respectable of the street costers. Each young swain seats himself beside his girl, fronted by a pipe and a pickwick.[15]

Regardless, marketing the Canterbury as morally fit for females (comparable to reassuring modern coinage of 'family entertainment') was good for business. For one thing, it rather diminished the likelihood of magisterial interference. How many women actually turned up is debatable. In one interview, some decades later, Morton let slip that the early audience was 'mostly men'.[16]

These were the ways in which Morton differentiated his hall from everything that had come before. There were still comic songs, ballads, glees, descended straight from the free-and-easy. The likes of ventriloquists, magicians and acrobats would make the occasional appearance. Middle-class commentators fell for the carefully orchestrated publicity and willingly portrayed the Canterbury as heralding a new dawn, raising the musical and artistic aspirations of the working class. We must remember that this was the age of the Crystal Palace, the Mechanics' Institute, the Penny Lecture. Here was yet another practical new institution offering not only amusement, but moral and intellectual improvement: the first (respectable) music hall.

The Canterbury's morally unimpeachable auditorium was an oblong space, halfway between a large meeting hall and a theatre. There was a balcony level; but there was no proscenium arch; no wings; no painted backdrop to the stage. This austere 'stage' was, perhaps, another token of respectability. Performers emerged from a central recessed archway. The result was that the stage itself, although substantial, was more like a bare platform, a promontory projecting into the audience's domain, vaguely hinting at the old-fashioned intimacy of the harmonic meeting.

The audience, meanwhile, were treated quite differently to theatre crowds. They were seated at long tables, long enough to accommodate forty or fifty people, set at a right angle to the stage. The emphasis was on conviviality, consumption of food and drink, smoking, and chatter, 'a din of talking tongues, and bustling boots and jingling glasses', even if the better acts could command 'perfect silence'.[17] There was no difficulty in coming and going during performances, or promenading about the room. Waiters were continually at beck and call. Amateurs did not appear on stage, but when comic songs and glees were about to start, two boys ran round the room, distributing free copies of the lyrics so that the audience might sing along.[18] The spirit of the free-and-easy thus lingered, after a fashion, including the continuing presence of a chairman, mustering the performers.

Brief 'turns' were the order of the day, with acts often going on to perform at other venues on the same evening. Morton, who basked in the title 'Father of the Halls' in his old age, was actually credited by one late Victorian journalist with inventing the 'turns' system (i.e. rotation of a variety of acts).[19] This was clearly untrue. We have already seen how concert-rooms and saloons, like the Royal Union, already mixed theatre, music and circus acts. It was also commonplace to see speciality acts in minor theatres in the early nineteenth century. Morton himself, born in Hackney, frequented East End theatres in his youth, including the Pavilion in Whitechapel, mentioned in his biography. The Pavilion, as a minor theatre, held a *music and dancing* licence and not only featured budget Shakespearian melodrama, pantomimes and musical comedies, but interspersed them with ventriloquists, bird impersonators, ballets, tightrope walkers and minstrelsy (including the well-known American performer, Thomas Rice, appearing in blackface as 'Jim Crow'). These were exactly the same sort of performers who would provide some variety at the Canterbury.

It is impossible to provide a comprehensive account of artistes who appeared at the Canterbury; but we can look at some illuminating snapshots. Charles Sloman, for example, whom we last saw reviewed in an 1820s concert-room at the Eagle, stands out for his remarkable longevity. Sloman was a fixture on the 1850s and 1860s music-hall circuit. His career can be glimpsed in various reviews, advertisements and personal recollections. Sloman, born Solomon Sloman in 1808, was Jewish. He sang and published ballads relating to his heritage – *The Maid of Judah*, *Daughter of Israel* and *Promised Land* – but his true fame was as 'The English Improvisatore'. He came up with impromptu songs or poems on subjects proposed by the audience. Often he relied on names or occupations, presumably drawing upon a large stock of ready-made rhymes. One harsh critic noted sarcastically that his rhymes were 'upon subjects which it never could occur to him twice to celebrate – such as the highly unusual circumstance of a gentleman having an umbrella; or wearing a pea coat'.[20]

Sloman's various mentions in playbills and advertisements are instructive. He appeared at Vauxhall Pleasure Gardens, the Adelphi and other minor theatres, dance-halls, Covent Garden song-and-supper rooms, the Crystal Palace at Sydenham, and even served as musical director at the opening of Wilton's Music Hall. This gives some notion of the diversity of venues which could accommodate the more versatile music-hall performer in the mid-century. Sloman can even be found twice, thinly disguised, in mid-Victorian fiction – as 'Nadab the Improvisatore' in Thackeray's *The Newcomes*, and 'Mr Rehoboam' in John Delaware Lewis's *Sketches of Cantabs*. The latter is repulsive in its anti-Semitic cliché, but it contains a fair sample of Sloman's humour. Weak puns abound:

> Now gents, although I've got a cold,
> You'll make me sing by force,
> So if I fail, don't call me ass,
> Whereas I'm only *hoarse*.[21]

Sloman was a popular and hard-working performer. He also frequently acted as a chairman, superintending amateur and professional nights at various venues, throughout his long career. In the 1840s, he placed advertisements in the sporting press, offering to speak at 'dinners, parties, concerts &c, in town or country, as comic, sentimental and impromptu vocalist' (he could accompany himself on the piano). By the mid-1850s, he was advertising himself as 'Improvisatore! Lecturer!! and Buffo Vocalist!!!' He also offered additional services, including arranging 'Glee parties' and drafting custom-written songs, poems, essays and acrostics ('5s. each. A letter containing post-office order, with sex, name, age, single or married and general description of the person to be acrosticised, will meet with prompt attention').[22] In 1860, he produced *Bennett's Conundrum Alphabet*, an illustrated book of rhyming conundrums for children. In 1864, he was being given star billing in the advertisements of the International Music and Equestrian Star Agency (his name, unlike most of his contemporaries', appears in capitals). Yet, despite all this, financial security eluded him. The death of Sloman's wife in 1866 prompted a decline in his mental health and he died, penniless and physically frail, in the Strand Workhouse, looking much older than his actual years.[23] The new music halls of the period created a brilliant, gilded environment in which established artistes could perform; but they did not necessarily make them rich or successful.

Sloman, though famous, was never quite a 'star'. That honour went to Sam Cowell, arguably music hall's first fully fledged national celebrity, and a prominent performer in the early years of the Canterbury, so much so that some credited him with its entire success. Cowell, ten years younger than Sloman, came from a theatrical family, and spent part of his youth in the United States. He returned to the United Kingdom in the early 1840s, appearing as a comic actor and singer in Glasgow and Edinburgh, before going to London in 1844. It was comic singing that brought him the greatest success, beginning with nightly turns at Evans' in Covent Garden. His early repertoire included 'the capital new racy comic song' (to quote an 1848 advertisement), 'Are You Good Natured, Dear?', in which a naive provincial, arriving in London, cannot fathom why he keeps being asked the question (a stock greeting used by metropolitan prostitutes). But Cowell was not principally about smut. His most successful piece was 'The Rat-Catcher's Daughter', a lugubrious 'cockney ballad', wherein the eponymous heroine finishes up tumbling head first into the Thames and drowning. The hero, a street-seller of sand, proves his constancy by cutting his own throat – and his donkey's. The ballad's black humour and droll text, inevitably, reveal little about Cowell's personal comic appeal. As one reviewer put it, 'it being impossible to convey by words the inexpressible mirth which even his *silence* creates'.

Cowell was such a star that when he refused to sing at the Euston Square Music Hall in 1855 because another act had performed one of his songs, there was a near riot. Like many others in the profession, he led a rather hectic existence, often performing at several venues during the same night (including, during one season, singing at the Canterbury, then Evans', then acting at the Lyceum Theatre, before returning to Evans' for a finale). In 1857–59 he embarked on highly successful national tours, featuring 'burlesques of serious subjects, ludicrous songs in character, imitations of popular performers', with Shakespeare told in doggerel and cockney slang, plus an impersonation of

'Betsy Knubbles', a stereotypical maid-of-all-work. Two years in America followed, and when he finally returned to the Canterbury in 1861, he was feted as a conquering hero. Yet, just like Sloman, he did not retire content. The story remains a very familiar one to this day: 'unbounded applause, unwholesome living, and broken health'. Cowell died, bankrupt, aged forty-four, attempting to recover his health in Dorset, while still consuming a bottle of brandy per day.[24]

Female performers in these early years of music hall never achieved quite the same level of stardom as their male counterparts, but they were numerous and popular. The career of Annie Adams is a good example. Adams, the daughter of a Southampton publican, had a much-praised mezzo-soprano voice. She began singing sentimental ballads and opera in local pubs in the late 1850s (local press reviews praise her rendition of songs from *Il Trovatore* and Flotow's *Martha*). By 1862, she was touring the country, including venues in Ramsgate, Manchester and Birmingham. She met her future husband, a comic vocalist named Harry Wall, while on tour. He promptly abandoned his career to manage his wife. Adams then proceeded to London, having been signed to the first music-hall agent, Ambrose Maynard (himself a former comic singer). She performed at numerous venues, but found her niche at Turnham's Music Hall on the Edgware Road, and was soon famous for 'serio-comic' songs, including 'If They Only Saw Me Coming', 'Hampstead is the Place to Ruralise' and 'Riding in a Railway Train', concerning a kiss in a darkened carriage and the unfortunate loss of a vain gentleman's false moustache. Adams' career peaked in the 1870s with a tour of America, and then declined. Matters were not helped by her irascible husband punching a man who allegedly hissed her performance at a theatre in Margate. She retired in the early 1880s and died in 1905, aged sixty-one.

Some performers struggled to eke out a living. The bankruptcy hearings of Mary Annie Lawrence (aka Mary Annie Macdonald or Mary Anne Gater) shine a rare light on the harsher realities of music-hall life in the early 1860s. Lawrence, separated from her husband, supported herself as a singer and music teacher ('professor of music') in Camden, North London. She performed at various major metropolitan music halls, including the Canterbury. She also sang at provincial events, from pleasure gardens in Norfolk to local fetes in the West Midlands and Surrey. In a good week, she declared that she made seven or eight pounds (a decent weekly income for an entire middle-class family), but her earnings were highly irregular. Her finances finally became irrecoverable after she was obliged to find her own costume for a pantomime, obtaining a fashionable dress on credit. She noted, during the hearings, that she regularly incurred heavy transport costs, not only travelling across the country, but travelling by cab between two venues on the same night. An engagement at the conveniently local Bedford Music Hall in Camden had been terminated; and she had lost five weeks' income due to ill health. She was finally declared bankrupt with debts of £150, and her future earnings were tithed to pay back creditors – a mixture of local tradesmen and publicans who had repeatedly loaned her cab fares. Intriguingly, the court proceedings mention in passing that Mrs Lawrence had already fought a legal battle: to retain control of her own earnings, keeping them from her estranged husband. This was a course of action only recently opened to married women under the Matrimonial Causes Act of 1857. Music hall did not guarantee a regular income; but it could potentially provide a form of emancipation for some female artistes.[25]

The Canterbury, regardless of its debatable claims to primacy, soon had numerous, equally splendid rivals: Weston's in Holborn (1857); Wilton's in the East End (1858); the Pavilion (1859) and Alhambra (1860) in the heart of the West End; the Philharmonic Hall in Islington (1860); and the South London in Lambeth (1860). Some of these new venues were, like the Canterbury, built around or in connection with an existing public house (Weston's; Wilton's; the Pavilion). The Alhambra, on the other hand, was a conversion of an elaborate Moorish-style 'scientific exhibition' building, which had recently served as a circus. The Philharmonic and South London stood on their own merits. But they were all newly built, lavish affairs, which tried to surpass the Canterbury in both ornament and respectability. Weston's Music Hall, Morton's first great rival, opened its doors in Holborn in 1857 with the owner flanked by the brewers who had provided financial backing. Mr Weston promised to provide amusements 'with a strict regard to the decencies of life . . . the high mental enjoyment of the higher classes'. Operatic selections featured heavily, and the venture was such a success that the building was remodelled within a couple of years, incorporating such extravagances as a 'magnificent sun-burner of cut-glass . . . the largest ever made, being composed of no fewer than 27,000 pieces of cut-glass'.[26]

Morton's rivals did not adopt his peculiar promontory stage, but they did imitate the Canterbury's companionable seating arrangements, with chairs or benches set around tables (i.e. rather than theatrical stalls facing the stage). This was still very much in the style of the public house concert-room and designed to facilitate waiters serving drinks. New venues were also, at this stage, mostly in the style of a galleried, oblong meeting-room, rather than the late Victorian horseshoe-shaped theatre. Morton himself, meanwhile, purchased the Boar and Castle coaching inn on Oxford Street, flattened the pub, and replaced it with his second venture, the Oxford, opened in 1861, 'rich with Italian pillasters, coloured marbles, fretted ceilings, mirrors of prodigious size, and glass chandeliers of gigantic proportions'.[27] Morton also hired a small fleet of broughams to ferry acts between the Canterbury and the Oxford, creating a perpetually mobile company. This sort of circulation was not entirely new. The diaries of Charles Rice, an aspiring tavern singer in the 1840s, show the author engaged in a constant dash around town, rushing from one small concert-room to another to find outlets for his talents.[28] But Morton did things in a more organised and elaborate fashion, and made sure to mention the fleet of carriages to the press – anything to remain on top of his metropolitan rivals. Morton was very much the man to beat in these early years. His influence beyond London is harder to evaluate, but it is notable that a 'Canterbury Music Hall' appeared in Bristol, and an 'Oxford Music Hall' in Brighton, both within twelve months of their (wholly unrelated) London namesakes.

The new breed of halls was not universally welcome. Theatre managers panicked as venues multiplied in the West End. They feared losing their audiences to these gaudier, more popular rivals. Managers clubbed together to mount a series of legal challenges, led by Benjamin Webster, the notoriously litigious manager of the Adelphi Theatre.[29] The first sally was a formal objection to the Alhambra's licence, on the grounds that it (allegedly) provided a refuge for prostitutes and that the area around Leicester Square already had enough entertainments. Moreover, since the Alhambra's proprietor managed two other theatres, this was tantamount to a monopoly.[30] The Middlesex magistrates were unconvinced, and so another tactic was required. The following year, therefore, Webster resorted to ferreting out alleged infractions of *music and dancing* licences. Webster launched his first prosecution, relying on professional informers, shortly before the opening of the Oxford; very much a shot across the bows.

Morton had, it was alleged, permitted a dramatic performance at the Canterbury, although licensed only for *music and dancing*. The prosecuting barrister noted that music halls were adopting scenery, theatrical lighting, 'all the implements of stage property . . . in fact, everything which could constitute a theatre', but they did not possess a theatrical licence. The legal argument relied partly on a recent, obscure precedent set in the seaside town of Margate, whereby it was established that a 'duologue' between two actors constituted a play.[31] For the supposedly offending 'dramatic' piece at the Canterbury was a comic two-hander, *The Enchanted Hash*, a very abbreviated traditional pantomime, complete with the Italian characters of Harlequin and Columbine, Clown and Pantaloon. The piece was largely an excuse for amusing fast changes of costume and startling comic 'business':

> . . . the clown brings onto the stage a basket he had purloined, and while devouring a part of the contents, described as mutton pieces, the placard is changed into 'Pussy Cats', seeing which the clown becomes suddenly ill, and the pantaloon brings in a stomach pump, by means of which three or four fine kittens are extracted from the stomach of the astonished clown . . .

Morton's defence was that this was not, by a long chalk, serious drama. A decade earlier, Thomas Youdan had successfully fended off a very similar prosecution in Sheffield with the same argument.[32] But the Margate precedent, and the precise terms of the Theatres Act, left Morton exposed. The result was a £5 fine and the removal of a comic 'burlesque' (theatrical parody) from the Oxford's opening bill. Webster issued a public letter stating that theatre managers had to 'protect their rights'.[33]

Several similar cases followed, involving different proprietors and venues. Morton was targeted again in 1865 over a 'comic burlesque' entitled *Hodge Podge*. The novelty of *Hodge Podge* was the use of 'Pepper's Ghost' throughout the performance – the latest theatrical special effect, a version of which was on display in virtually every music hall in the capital. The trick relied on a large sheet of nigh-invisible glass, angled to cast a ghostly reflection, making spectral forms appear 'on stage'. The actual performers were concealed below the line of sight of the audience. Morton's barrister deployed the ingenious argument that, since nobody actually *stood* on the stage, *Hodge Podge* could not possibly constitute a play. The magistrate dismissed this casuistry, but remained highly sympathetic to Morton. He noted that he had never received complaints about the Canterbury. He reluctantly imposed a fine of twenty shillings and costs.[34]

Such fines were trivial; but the darker threat of losing the hall's entertainment licence at the next sessions hung over the court proceedings.

After several victories, the theatre managers finally over-reached themselves, when they once more targeted the Alhambra. They claimed that a dance that involved sixty ballet girls waving flowers and palm leaves amounted to an unlicensed stage play. These grand ballets had become the Alhambra's speciality; and while some considered the women's costumes and dancing a little daring, there was no precedent to suggest that a theatrical licence was required. The Lord Chamberlain had never taken an interest in *any* balletic performance, because no script could be submitted to his office for censorship. Hours were wasted in court discussing whether the floral display had 'meaning' sufficient to constitute a play, but the Middlesex magistrates unanimously ruled that the case was a nonsense.[35]

The Times, without taking sides, summarised the state of play as an economic struggle between 'protectionist' theatre managers and 'free-trader' music-hall owners, who believed in unfettered competition.[36] The latter circulated a pamphlet pointing out that the existing twenty-three London theatres only accommodated 33,000 people, and showed no sign of expanding; whereas the music halls were booming, already holding more than double that number (much more besides, if one included the 100,000 capacity of the Crystal Palace at Sydenham, which likewise held an entertainment – rather than a theatrical – licence).

The claims for and against 'free trade' would finally be thrashed out in a parliamentary select committee in 1866. The owners of music halls emphasised the respectability of their profession and demanded regulatory reform, such as putting all places of amusement under the control/censorship of the Lord Chamberlain, or abolishing theatrical regulation altogether (either of which might free them from vexatious litigation). There were obvious parallels with the minor theatres of the early 1800s, which had finally been granted parity with the patent theatres under the 1843 Theatres Act. Did not music halls deserve the same fair treatment? Theatre managers, on the other hand, declared that the 'dignity of the drama' should not be tarnished by eating and drinking in the auditorium; and that music halls' freedom in this regard provided them with unfair competition.

Some committee members were openly in favour of tree trade; and the theatre managers repeatedly met with mild sarcasm. When one manager complained that 'A man with his mouth full cannot pay proper attention to the performance', a committee member joked, 'He does not eat with his ears?' The manager of the Olympic Theatre claimed that the public only went to halls 'to smoke, drink and make appointments to see women of the town'; and one magistrate decried the presence of 'half-naked' ballet girls in flesh-coloured tights. He was gently mocked with the teasing retort, 'What part of the figure should you say was half naked?'

The content of performances was addressed. The theatrical impresario E.T. Smith, who had himself briefly served as the lessee of the Alhambra, helpfully offered an example of unwanted music-hall smut:

> Perhaps a man comes on the stage, and he has a clock under his arm, and he says, 'This is the way I wind the old woman up on Saturday nights,' and all kinds of allusions and bestialities in a mild way.

Presumably, as was so often the case in the halls, the humour (and perceived indecency) was as much in the actions as the words. The phrase *in a mild way* is significant. Throughout the lengthy hearings, no one could actually demonstrate much in the way of immorality in the halls; at least, nothing beyond mild suggestiveness and double entendre.

Nothing tangible came of the committee's deliberations. Relations between theatres and halls remained distinctly uneasy and further court cases occurred on a regular basis.[37] Both theatre and music-hall managers relied on communal funds from their respective protection societies to cover legal costs. The issue of whether comic sketches actually constituted drama remained a running sore. While prosecutions never really amounted to an existential threat, music halls and theatres continued at loggerheads over their respective rights and privileges for the remainder of the century.

The growing popularity of grand music halls during the 1860s was not only marked by theatrical opposition. A swathe of social commentary on the character of the halls, rather negative in tone, began to appear in magazines and newspapers. The original utopian vision of music hall as a vehicle for working-class self-improvement swiftly yielded to a more cynical reappraisal. There were various specific complaints: accusations of lyrical inanity and lyrical obscenity; and worst of all, allegations that the new halls effectively served as promenades for prostitutes. The first substantive criticism of music hall in the media, however, centred on a different sort of moral question: the employment of 'sensation acts'.

'Sensation' was a buzz-word of the mid-century, encompassing modernity, shock and spectacle in the arts. The books of Mary Braddon and Wilkie Collins, revolving around murder, false identities and moral transgression, were dubbed 'sensation novels' ('preaching to the nerves instead of the judgment').[38] Dion Boucicault's long-running play, *The Colleen Bawn*, with its elaborately staged, nail-biting rescue of a drowning heroine, was 'sensation drama'. The term carried a strong hint of disapproval; and some warned of the moral and physical danger of unchecked exposure to pure 'sensation'. Women's notoriously delicate nervous equilibrium was said to be especially at risk.

Music hall was dragged into the sensation debate by the performances of Jules Léotard (the great trapeze artiste) and Charles Blondin (the world-famous tight rope walker). Both Léotard and Blondin toured the country in the early 1860s. Both performed at music halls, as well as other venues, with Blondin famously wowing crowds at the Crystal Palace. Commentators in the press admired the skill but deplored the risks, and the breathless effect created in the viewing public (the very definition of *sensation*). The *Standard*, reviewing Léotard at the Alhambra, decried his 'highly dangerous antics, provocative of extremely unpleasant sensations to the audience'. The *Morning Post* talked of Blondin's 'insane exploits'. Dickens wrote scornfully of society reverting to 'barbaric excitements'.[39] Blondin pushing his daughter along a tightrope in a wheelbarrow, between the Crystal Palace's iron girders, prompted a question in the House of Commons.

The biggest problem were the numerous imitators, who found employment in assorted music halls and pleasure gardens. They were not always quite so skilled. When, in August 1862, two performers fell and sustained serious injuries at Highbury Barn and Canterbury Hall, the press rushed to denounce the 'immoral appetite' of the public and the venality of their hosts:

The question among the owners is what may create a sensation? What may draw? An immoral appetite is catered for by the immoral food it craves, and a bargain which may end like that at Highbury Barn depends on the question, how many extra sixpences or shillings this LEOTARD or this BLONDIN or some male or female imitator may be expected to draw, by offering a reasonable expectation of breaking his neck?[40]

That *female* performers were prominent – 'The Female Blondin' fell at Highbury – was deemed particularly unsavoury.

The number of serious accidents would diminish, as safety nets were gradually adopted.[41] The moral perils of 'sensation entertainments', therefore, while generating quite a few column inches in the press, caused music-hall proprietors no more than temporary embarrassment. But the new breed of halls was presented, for the first time, as posing a distinct moral danger to their audience, the proprietors condemned as venal. This accusation would resurface in various forms throughout the following decades. Music-hall proprietors would soon find themselves engaged in a constant battle to justify the moral integrity of their business.

In fact, the (lack of) intellectual and artistic content in music hall generated more negative comment than the dangers of the high wire. Leading writers in the music press were among the first to politely voice the opinion that Charles Morton, despite being thoroughly well intentioned, had created a monster. The opera in most halls was, allegedly, badly sung and poorly accompanied. The remainder of the performances were, carped the critics, stupid and degenerate nonsense. Writers also routinely mocked the speciality acts: 'gymnasts who ape gorillas . . . contortionists in crinoline . . . clowns who dance in clogs'.[42] The greatest critical disdain was reserved for 'black-face minstrels' or 'Ethiopians'. Commentators, by and large, did not object to the racism of this entertainment, in which performers blacked their skin and spoofed the supposed speech, manners and music of American slaves. Rather, they despaired of the low slapstick comedy and crude word-play.[43] The following both gives an idea of Victorian minstrelsy in action and captures the sarcastic, wearied tone of many a reporter:

> Nor were their doings a bit newer than their sayings. Jumbo artfully withdrew Mumbo's chair, as of old, bringing Mumbo with a crash to the ground, and whereon Jumbo, as of old, promptly delivered himself of an apropos, though not over delicate riddle, concerning the railway engine and the tender behind. Gumbo played the bones over his head, and under his legs, and behind his back . . . and Mumbo cried, 'Gor 'long, nigger!' several times, and in very effective style . . .[44]

The comic song, always the principal attraction for music-hall audiences, was equally derided as 'sorry rubbish', 'idiotic trash', 'pointless twaddle'. Much venom was reserved for female singers, so-called 'lady serio-comics' like Annie Adams, whose material was principally 'fast and slangy' songs. These women were allegedly failed actresses, trading on their dress and sexuality, with 'a liberal display of legs, suggestive attitudes and the utterance of double entendres, slang and sentiments unwomanly and unnatural'.[45] The music-hall vogue for female singers cross-dressing as fashionable men about town attracted similar notice. The *Era*'s critic tartly observed: 'We shall be very glad indeed to see the end of women delighting to sing in breeches, and we trust that the ladies will preserve their sexuality whenever they possibly can.'[46] This would prove a vain hope.

Much ink was also spilled about nonsense and 'clap-trap choruses': songs whose meaningless refrains became irritating popular catchphrases. Arthur Lloyd's 1868 hit, 'Immenseikoff, or The Shoreditch Toff' is a good example:

Ha, my dear friends, pray 'ow de do, I 'opes I see's yer well
Perhaps you don't know who I is, well I'm the Eastern Swell
My chamber is in Shoreditch and I fancy I'm a toff
From top to toe I really think I looks Immenseikoff.

Immenseikoff, Immenseikoff
Behold in me a Shoreditch Toff
A toff, a toff, a toff, a Shoreditch Toff
And I think myself Immenseikoff.

When the song became popular, impressionable youths declared everything 'Immenseikoff!' on a regular basis. The word also became slang for the type of fur-lined overcoat which Lloyd wore on stage.[47] This was not the elevation of public taste which Charles Morton had cleverly trumpeted at the Canterbury, and it was clear by the mid-1860s that the touting of 'operatic selections' had done little to dampen popular enthusiasm for low comedy, repetitive lyrics and catchy music. Opera, in fact, was already playing a steadily diminishing part in proceedings at most venues, although Morton's Oxford fought something of a rear-guard action. Audiences were keener on women dressed as men and on male '*lions comiques*': a novel species of comic singer, whose act involved appearing in character, dressed to the nines as a 'swell' (a jovial, inebriated dandy). George Leybourne's 'Champagne Charlie', introduced at Canterbury

Hall in 1866, was among the most popular ('good for any game at night', and ready to buy any man a bottle of 'fizz'). Leybourne became famous partly thanks to being regularly driven around London in character as 'Charlie', toasting his fans. He also famously made a hit of 'The Daring Young Man on the Flying Trapeze', a tribute of sorts to the joys of sensation entertainment.

The capacity of comic songs to cross class boundaries inordinately vexed music critics. The *Pall Mall Gazette* feared that it would not be long before the scions of the aristocracy were singing 'The Eel Pie Shop', replete with its 'harmonious bow-wow chorus'. The appearance of two *lions comiques* at an aristocratic house party fanned the flames. The Prince of Wales himself was present, enjoying the humour of John 'Jolly' Nash and The Great Vance: 'the depths of vulgarity . . . sanctified by the patronage of the aristocracy'.[48] Henry Lunn of the *Musical Times* feared that decent middle-class women were purchasing music-hall songs to play at home, lured by the colourful sheet-music covers.[49] Charles Mackay, writing in *All the Year Round*, decried songs which relied on 'the language of burglars and beggars' (i.e. slang). Modern popular music, claimed Mackay, no longer praised virtue, true love or patriotism, as in the olden days; rather, singers traded on objectionable snide, low humour.[50] The staging of a 'comic concert' of music-hall stars at St James's Hall, Piccadilly in 1869, a venue normally associated with popular classical concerts, particularly enraged serious critics. Far from elevating public taste, music-hall artistes and proprietors seemingly wanted to drag the rest of society down to their level.

It was, of course, impossible to legislate against the halls' perceived philistinism; but some went further in their complaints and argued that lyrical vulgarity descended all too frequently into obscenity.

The most obviously objectionable material was double entendre. Music-hall stars routinely denied the existence of innuendo in their acts, but this was all part of the fun. When a lady serio-comic sang sweetly of the 'charms and fancies of her Pussy', only the most naive missed the sexual frisson.[51] Songs with titles like 'I've Got Something for You, My Love' or 'Pulling My Rhubarb Out' were rendered risqué by the slightest gesture or suggestive glance, and only really made any comic sense with the suggestiveness included.

There were other elements that discomfited moralists. A transcript of a performance at Cardiff's Philharmonic Music Hall made by a hostile reporter records all sorts of purported obscenities, above and beyond sexual references:

a ditty about losing one's underwear ('the song went on to describe a misfortune he had whilst bathing'); blasphemous puns ('Hell-theries Exhibition' for the 'Healtheries Exhibition'); suggestive rhyme substitution ('Have you seen Yum Yum, With a pimple on her . . . boko?'); coarse humour ('When a little dog comes up and mistakes you for a lamppost, it is above a joke').[52]

Marital misadventures, another music hall commonplace, also featured in Cardiff, including this surreal and suggestive example:

> Beauchamp said his wife was the very falsest woman he ever knew. When she got home after the wedding, she took off her hair, and put it on the piano, then she took out her teeth and one ear, and put those on the piano. She unscrewed her left arm, one of her hips and both legs, and put these on the piano. That night, he slept on the piano.[53]

One wonders whether contemporary *audiences* – as opposed to evangelical busybodies – considered such things obscene. The house at Cardiff reportedly responded with 'roars of laughter' and 'went into convulsions'. Were they titillated, shocked or taking the material in their stride? They did not walk out.

The question of the audience's state of mind is actually very difficult to answer. There was no single, homogeneous 'music-hall audience'. The mix of social classes varied from hall to hall, and audience members responded differently to individual jokes, just as with modern live comedy. For music-hall songs *were* a species of comedy, not just popular song. Carefully prepared comic monologues, interjected between verses, often formed an integral part of the performance. Indeed, the atmosphere in a music hall was more akin to a modern comedy club than a music venue, as this description from 1889 makes clear:

> Then, again, some 'pros.' have established a reputation for making personal remarks upon such of the audience as are in conspicuous positions, and these remarks frequently serve for introductions when young men and women in close contiguity come in for some broad impertinence from the stage. The girls always seem to like it, and the young men will certainly not allow themselves to show any displeasure, whatever they may feel.[54]

Audiences, therefore, surely allowed for some pushing at boundaries and taboos; comedians have always been permitted to say the unsayable.

There was also a good deal of comedy about troublesome spouses, petty functionaries, the police, public transport, etc. – none of which remotely relied on taboo or sexual frisson. Sexual allusions, meanwhile, when they appeared, remained relatively sly and subtle. Songs like the following example, touching on extramarital sex, were declared 'immoral' by the more sensitive:

Miss Muffet once went for a walk in the Park
With Simon a simple young lad
And did not return to her home until dark
Then seemed to be awfully sad . . .
What ailed this young lady, the Ma could not tell
At length she called in Doctor Quack
Who said she'd be worse much, before she got well
He called it a bilious attack.

The above cautionary tale ('Little Miss Muffet') was said by one moral investigator to be 'full of indecent suggestions'.[55] But note that illicit sex and illegitimate pregnancy (only marginally more obvious as the song proceeds) are merely *suggested*. Performers at Covent Garden's song-and-supper rooms, in the first half of the century, would have rendered the same tale in barely concealed anatomical detail.[56] The suggestiveness and double entendre of late Victorian music hall were, comparatively, a species of decency. This was frequently acknowledged by those who remembered the 'bad old days' of the Coal Hole and the Cyder Cellars.[57]

Magistrates and local authorities, in fact, largely tolerated the music-hall song, doing little more than tut at any dubious examples that came their way. The possibility of music-hall censorship, mirroring that applied to theatres, was frequently discussed; but only the magistracy of Bolton, Lancashire, introduced a system for pre-approving songs and sketches.[58] This suggests that most authorities did not take the question *that* seriously. Likewise, very few proprietors were ever penalised for offensive material. Magistrates issued stern warnings and proprietors routinely promised to dismiss and/or fine any offending artistes; nothing more. The general public, meanwhile, were broadly content with the fare they received on stage – at least on the rare occasions they were asked.

The popular high-kicking singer Lottie Collins (of 'Ta-ra-ra Boom-de-ay' fame) actually won a libel claim against a weekly journal which had described her performance as vulgar ('not redeemed even by the singer's surprising agility and rose-red petticoats'). The crux of the complaint was a song called 'The Little Widow'. Collins portrayed an (implicitly) sexually voracious young widow, who had already seen off two exhausted husbands ('He died, all the doctors said "shortness of breath"'). Two music-hall managers, including Charles Morton, and the theatre critic of the *Daily Telegraph* volunteered that they found nothing vulgar whatsoever in Miss Collins, rose-red petticoats and all. The jury, without even bothering to retire, immediately awarded her £25.[59]

Likewise, when Edward Villiers, the manager of the Pavilion Music Hall, was accused of putting out 'foul and festering stuff . . . brayed forth every night in defiance of decency and decorum', he won a libel case against the obscure newspaper in question. A jury listened to witnesses on both sides, scoured the relevant lyrics, and found for Villiers, who received £300 in damages. Villiers' case was helped by the fact that he was shown to have actively policed content, and had banned certain performers and renditions he considered 'slightly broad . . . I will not say indecent'.[60] He was not alone in taking such precautions. The manager of the Royal Holborn (formerly Weston's) had rules for performers posted in his dressing rooms, including 'Rule 3. Any *artiste* giving expression to anything obscene on the stage will be subject to instant dismissal, and shall forfeit any salary.'[61] Some managers were more specific, forbidding offensive references to royalty, MPs, 'German princes', the police and London County Council, as well as any reference to religion or the judiciary.[62] Whether such rules were always rigidly enforced is another matter.

There was one accusation which, briefly, seemed to pose a genuine threat to the halls' existence: the charge of harbouring prostitutes. This damaging claim, frequently coupled with accusations of obscenity, would be levelled by late Victorian moral reformers, determined to 'purify' popular entertainment. The most vigorous and extensive of these puritan campaigns was waged in London. The West End, home to the largest, most profitable halls in the country, as well as to endemic, highly visible street prostitution, would become the venue for 'The Battle of the Music Halls': a showdown between self-confident champions of 'social purity' and harried music-hall proprietors.

There were earlier debates about music hall and morality. Bolton's singing-rooms were condemned as immoral haunts in the early 1840s. Joseph Hobson's Royal Casino in Leeds, opened in 1849, was likewise the object of a concerted letter-writing campaign, demanding its closure ('no female can visit the Casino without endangering her character . . . thieves out of gaol are attendants there').[63] From the early 1860s onwards, there were fears that London's large West End music halls provided a convenient rendezvous for the district's notoriously large regiment of 'loose women'. An anonymous City Missionary, visiting Charles Morton's newly opened Oxford, found 'very many depraved men and women' scattered among the clerks and shopkeepers. The world-weary diarist Arthur Munby, likewise, noted the predominance of 'whores, instead of respectable wives and sweethearts'. Respectable women, he thought, stuck to more suburban venues like the Canterbury. The critic of the *Musical World*, equally, detected worryingly high numbers of 'spicy' patrons: 'the patrician *roué* and the plebeian "fancy man" . . . members of the "frail sisterhood" '.[64] These writers were not mistaken. Freedom of movement within the venue and the ready supply of alcohol provided an ideal environment for prostitutes meeting clients. There were also ongoing claims, staunchly denied by proprietors, that some halls allowed single women free passes or season tickets, to draw in the young men who sought their company. The question of prostitution was also raised by the 1866 Select Committee on Theatrical Licences and Regulations, when it was suggested that select male customers were admitted to the Alhambra's staff bar/canteen to fraternise with off-duty ballet girls (a parallel to the long-standing theatrical tradition of young gentlemen going 'behind the scenes' to begin 'friendships' with actresses).

The idea, therefore, that music halls were the haunt of prostitutes was not novel; but it would begin to gain a firm hold on the public imagination in the late 1870s. This did not happen in a vacuum. The decade had already seen much public discussion about prostitution, thanks to a prolonged and highly publicised campaign for the repeal of the controversial Contagious Diseases Acts of the 1860s (which had introduced state inspection of prostitutes in garrison towns, while leaving their clients untouched). This went hand in hand with stirrings of a national movement for 'social purity', driven by a peculiarly Victorian mix of evangelical religion and radical feminism. Why, asked the self-described puritans (reasonably enough), should men not be held equally responsible for sexual misconduct? Puritan campaign groups, emboldened by more frank public discussion of sexual matters, began to demand greater sexual continence from *both* sexes and a wholesale reform of public morality. They concentrated primarily on 'rescue work' among the 'fallen' (i.e. guiding prostitutes into reformatories) and on shaming their clients and brothel owners. But they also talked of the manifold evils of combining alcohol with entertainment; and music halls were soon in their sights.[65]

The first well-publicised piece of propaganda about music halls and prostitution appeared in 1877 in the *Echo*, a metropolitan halfpenny evening paper with a large readership. The sensational article describes a visit to a pseudonymous West End 'Corinthian Music Hall' (Corinth being a classical byword for profligacy).[66] The author begins conventionally enough, with remarks on stupidity, vulgarity and double entendres, but then goes further, damning the halls themselves as a 'serious social danger'. He notes the presence of scores of 'loose women'. He suggests that the heated drink-sodden atmosphere is more likely to lure young men into the clutches of prostitutes than passing 'the syrens who crowd the Strand and Coventry Street' (i.e. worse than street prostitution). Finally, he blames magistrates for permitting 'this school of the devil'.[67]

There had been few things written about the halls in the popular press that were quite so damning. Music-hall artistes queued up to respond in their trade paper, the *Era*. Most focused on the lesser charge of dubious lyrical content, since the presence of *some* prostitutes was inarguable. The popular comic singer Arthur Lloyd declared, disingenuously, that harmless lyrics were 'twisted and turned by fast youths into meanings that were never intended'.[68] Another correspondent cited the smash hit song of the 1850s, 'Sam Hall', the gloomy ballad of a convicted killer on the scaffold ('And it is my funeral knell, and I'll meet you all in Hell . . . Damn your eyes!'). Surely a few jolly double entendres were preferable to inhabiting the mind of a murderer? But the image of the glamorous West End music hall as a 'school of the devil' was a vivid one. The *Echo* article rather set the tone for subsequent debate.

The first active anti-prostitution campaign began the following year. It was orchestrated by Major William Lyon, a long-serving Middlesex magistrate with a long-standing interest in curtailing immoral entertainment.[69] Halting proceedings at the annual licensing sessions in 1878, Lyon declared sententiously that music halls in general were a curse upon society; and that he would oppose every licence where there was any evidence of the building providing a resort for immoral women. Lyon then attempted to make an example of the Oxford, interrogating the ex-policeman responsible for the hall's security. He extracted the confession that prostitutes were tolerated within the building, so long as they did not actively importune.[70] This was hardly surprising: such toleration had long been practised by the West End's police. The Oxford, therefore, received its licence; but Lyon had made his point. In January 1879, he wrote an open letter to the Home Secretary, backed by half a dozen fellow JPs, complaining that the police failed to arrest prostitutes in music halls. Lyon opined that 'the police should be requested to pay more attention than hitherto to such places' and, for good measure, take 'particular note where immoral songs were sung'.[71]

Lyon's campaign was not terribly popular with the general public; and he was deluged with hate mail. The *Sporting Times* drew up a satirical timeline, in which the major's puritan crusade led to the closure of music halls, then churches ('on account of soiled doves creeping into their congregations'), then to all women being imprisoned in their own homes.[72] He was not, however, without his supporters, the most unlikely of which was the Music Hall Proprietors' Protection Association. The MHPPA declared that proprietors were unable to correct lyrical filth because comedians constantly interjected 'gag' or 'gags' (i.e. improvised humour) into their material, and it stated that something should be done. Cynics astutely suggested that the proprietors desperately wanted the authorities to put them under the direct control/censorship of the Lord Chamberlain. This, in turn, would finally free them from recurring tendentious prosecutions by theatre managers based on the interpretation of *music and dancing* licensing.

The Home Office, having allowed a decent period to elapse, refused to make any changes to the law. But there were others intent on ploughing the same furrow as the major, with even more determination. First and foremost was the East End evangelist Frederick Charrington, who embarked upon his own personal crusade against 'harlots' in the halls.

Charrington was a dynamic and driven character, the son of a partner in one of the East End's largest breweries, which, according to his biographer, would have left him heir to a personal fortune of over £1.25 million.[73] Yet, having witnessed endemic drunkenness on the streets of East London, he became convinced that the family business was at the root of multifarious social evils. Consequently, he renounced his tainted inheritance and became a fierce proponent of temperance and Christianity. During the 1870s, he busied himself in the role of 'home missionary' to the East End's poor: helping with educational projects; holding religious meetings, sometimes leasing music halls (which were closed on Sundays) for the purpose. Finally, he opened his own Mission Hall on the Mile

End Road. The choice of location would prove fateful, for the Mission Hall had something of a rival in the nearby Lusby's Music Hall. Charrington, confident in his righteousness, doubtless relished the contrast. In the summer of 1880, he effectively declared war on Lusby's, focusing on the topical question of music-hall prostitution. He claimed that a local man had told him of the moral danger of ordinary women being lured into prostitution in the hall ('those reptiles at —— ruined my wife'); and in due course, he 'rescued' several women who stated that they, too, had first succumbed to sexual temptation at Lusby's.[74]

Lyon's campaign must surely have been an influence; but Charrington believed in direct action rather than lobbying the government. Nightly vigils were held directly outside the premises; pamphlets were liberally distributed, virtually on the hall's doorstep; those suspected of being prostitutes and their clients were accosted and implored to repent. The management, Messrs Crowder and Payne, were not happy, particularly when Charrington claimed that a box within the theatre had been used for an 'immoral purpose'. They responded with threats and physical intimidation. Hostile youths, on sundry occasions, threw flour, pease pudding and red ochre at the assembled evange-lists. Allegedly, Crowder and Payne's employees finally emptied the contents of a chamber-pot on the head of their persecutor. Charrington did not relent, justifying his efforts as a struggle for the souls of the East End.

The result was at least half a dozen separate court cases between 1880 and 1885 that revolved around Charrington being a public nuisance – or, conversely, the object of threatening attention. The courts, by and large, accepted both that Charrington was a troublemaker (however moral and well intentioned) and that he was a victim of unwarranted attacks. They were, to his dismay, distinctly unwilling to endorse the accusations that he made in his vividly narrated literature:

'This is the way to the pit, Sir,' said the attendant to the theatre . . . 'Yes,' said he to himself, 'this is the way to the pit – the pit of hell . . . where Satan's seat is, where drink and lust reign supreme, where the seducer is in his glory, where the harlot walks unabashed, whose house is the way to hell, going down to the chambers of death, where the lewd and filthy song defies the mind and pollutes the heart, where the loving husband is turned into the false friend . . .

The fire-and-brimstone rhetoric did not help; but the crucial factor for magistrates was that the police described Lusby's as orderly. This was sufficient to ensure Lusby's survival at the annual licensing sessions, even when Charrington mustered a petition of 1,500 persons for its closure in 1883. The mere presence of prostitutes had long been tolerated at places of public amusement, and magistrates were not inclined to change their tried-and-tested laissez-faire approach. The traditional magisterial respect for the capitalist and his property triumphed, and they refused to interfere in Crowder and Payne's business. The prostitute and her client, likewise, if they behaved in an 'orderly' fashion, were to be left to their own business.

Ironically enough, Lusby's itself would be consumed by fire – not the fires of hell, but a more prosaic conflagration. Much to Charrington's annoyance, it swiftly rose again, reborn as the bigger and better Paragon Theatre of Varieties in 1885. Charrington's efforts, therefore, yielded no great change of habit among music-hall visitors on the Mile End Road; and he seems to have abandoned his nightly vigils in the mid-1880s. Instead, still busy with his mission work, he forged an alliance with like-minded individuals at the National Vigilance Association (NVA), a new pressure group dedicated to 'the repression of criminal vice and immorality'.

Direct action to shut down the halls had failed; but there were other ways to attack Satan's seat.

The NVA was actually created to address contemporary concerns about juvenile prostitution, child abuse and 'white slavery' (human trafficking). The immediate impetus for its foundation was the *Pall Mall Gazette*'s sensational exposé of child prostitution and trafficking in 1885: a notorious series of articles entitled 'The Maiden Tribute of Modern Babylon'. The furore around 'The Maiden Tribute' was so great that parliament was persuaded to raise the age of consent from thirteen to sixteen, amid a groundswell of popular agitation (including a 40,000-strong demonstration held in Hyde Park and composed of religious groups, trade unionists, the Women's Suffrage Association and numerous others). The NVA was formed in this heated atmosphere, dedicated to rooting out child prostitution and its causes. Founder members included the Bishop of London, Cardinal Manning, Bramwell Booth of the Salvation Army, Josephine Butler and Charrington himself.[75] It was not long before focus shifted to the more general question of 'social purity', i.e. wholesale improvement in sexual morality, including preventing *all* forms of prostitution.

Despite this mission creep, music halls were not an immediate target. Reading through the organisation's initial publications and minutes, the topic simply does not feature. But the editor of the NVA's magazine, *The Vigilance Record*, would pen an article entitled 'Public Amusements' in April 1887, which roundly condemned the halls:

> the quantity of intoxicating drink sold – the universal smoking – the low estimate of womanhood likely to be fostered by the spectacle on the stage – the shameless pursuit of harlotry – and the appeal of the whole thing to the most selfish side of human nature . . .

That editor was Laura Ormiston Chant, an ardent feminist, suffragist and proud puritan. Chant then followed up these thoughts with five investigative articles, entitled 'Amused London'. These fascinating pieces each describe a visit to an unnamed venue in the capital by 'a novice', most likely Chant herself. They capture both the atmosphere of 1880s music hall (including the different social groups in different venues) and the puritans' objections.

The first West End hall in 'Amused London' is described as 'luxuriously fitted . . . like a theatre built square' (some halls were still large, oblong galleried rooms, rather than the horseshoe shape of a modern theatre) with luxurious plush settees and shared marble-topped tables. The audience includes 'a great number of society young gentlemen accompanied . . . by ladies not in society'. Expensive boxes are filled with cigar-chomping gents and ladies in 'extremely decoltée [*sic*] costume'. The chairman sits with his back to the stage, facing the audience, using a mirror to see performers, doing little more than announcing the acts.

Putting aside the dubious females in the audience, the author predictably finds the songs smutty:

> The poor little darlings they're not to blame,
> They know that their mothers have done the same,
> So why should we blame the girl?

and the comedy vulgar:

> an immense deal of solo-burlesque dancing of a very objectionable kind, which culminated in the appearance of a man, about 6ft 6in. high, attired as a ballet girl . . .[76]

The only consolations are a highly skilled Japanese juggler and some dancing dogs.

The findings in 'Amused London' are not uniformly condemnatory. A music hall in Paddington – clearly, by its description, the Metropolitan in Edgware Road – frequented more by the working class, is praised for down-to-earth humour, 'unseasoned by vicious jests or indecent allusions'. The audience are polite to each other; and one 'character song' is even impressively moral:

> he gave highly dramatic sketches of the fate of the dishonest city clerk, the
> gambler, and the drunkard, and finally of the little actress, 'Flo', who was
> betrayed by the fine gentleman in whose promises she had put her faith,
> and who ended her life by a fatal plunge off London Bridge . . .[77]

The only offensiveness is the endemic tobacco smoke.

An East End music hall, on the other hand – probably the Paragon – is not only plebeian but 'very vulgar, the jokes low, the riddles coarse . . . [consisting] largely of noise and rough horse-play'. Songs are distastefully jingoistic ('What British pluck can do!'). Teenage girls are exploited in the ballet which, incongruously enough, portrays the Battle of Trafalgar, replete with a young ballerina as Nelson.

Significantly, however, the greatest moral obloquy in 'Amused London' is reserved for 'one of the most celebrated West End Theatres of Variety'. Variety theatres would become the focus of the NVA's campaign for 'pure' entertainment.

The term 'variety theatre' or 'palace of varieties' became fashionable among the capital's music-hall proprietors in the 1870s and 1880s. Canterbury Hall, for example, no longer in the hands of Charles Morton, was rebuilt as the Canterbury Theatre of Varieties in 1878. The actual content of variety shows was pretty much identical to music hall. Certain large West End variety theatres specialised in presenting elaborate ballets, but even these places retained a diverse programme. Looking at a typical bill from the Empire Theatre of Varieties, Leicester Square, one finds not only two lengthy 'Ballets Divertissement', but a 'siffleur' (professional whistler); a cornet player; ventriloquist; comic vocalists (including G.H. Chirgwin, 'The White-Eyed Musical Kaffir'); an opera singer; a 'Chansonette Excentrique'; 'Danseurs Excentriques';

and the 'Royal Troupe of Doughty's Dogs: As Performed before Her Majesty the Queen at Osborne'.

The word 'variety', however, indicated more than just a superficial rebranding of the music hall. It signalled a determined move away from the traditional symbiotic link between the hall and the public house. For a start, newly built variety theatres tended to be large stand-alone venues, i.e. no longer hidden behind a pub. Secondly, tables and benches, designed for communal drinking, were replaced with theatre-like individual seating. Bars still served alcohol, and there were promenade spaces where one could mingle and move around; but these newer venues were essentially *theatres*. By the late 1880s, therefore, West End variety theatres, such as the Empire and the Alhambra, were the most extravagantly decorated, profitable examples of the modern music hall. This is what made them an excellent target for the NVA.

Thus, the author of 'Amused London' discerns rank immorality lurking beneath a glittering facade of crimson and gold and superficial bourgeois respectability. The West End variety theatre is revealed as a whited sepulchre. Ballet girls cavort in 'semi-nude' costumes. The songs are full of 'immoral tone, indecency, and intentional suggestiveness'. Worst of all, the precincts of the building are the blatant haunt of prostitutes, 'nothing but an open market for vice . . . wretched painted women openly plying their horrible trade . . . guilty, foul-eyed men, seeking whom they might devour'.[78] The music hall once again as 'pit of hell' and 'palace of vice'. No wonder that Frederick Charrington found common cause with Laura Chant and her colleagues.

In fact, it is easy to see why the NVA alighted upon the music hall and prostitution, beyond any personal influence exerted by Charrington. This barely concealed evil was confined to specific locations, licensed halls and theatres, supposedly regulated by the state. The mechanisms for control were already in place; it was just a question of persuading the authorities to take their moral duties seriously. But, with the magistrates indifferent, as proved in Mile End, what was to be done?

Opportunity knocked with root-and-branch reorganisation of local government in 1888 and elections for the newly created London County Council (LCC) early the following year. Charrington himself was elected councillor for Tower Hamlets. He joined a council that was dominated by social reformers. These were 'progressives' of various hues, religious and secular, Liberal and Radical, who believed the time was right to improve the mental, physical and moral condition of the average Londoner. The LCC was the first proper local authority for the whole metropolis and, crucially for the music halls, took over entertainment licensing from the magistracy. An LCC Theatres and Music Halls Committee was established to make initial judgements about *music and dancing* licences before they were ratified by the full council. Charrington and his NVA allies rushed to fill the vacuum in the committee room.

Captain Edmund Verney, a respected war veteran and member of parliament, laid out the objectives of the social purists in an interview with the *Pall Mall Gazette*. He declared music halls themselves 'an essential adjunct of civilisation' which had been degraded by the presence of prostitutes and coarse entertainments. The remedy was for the LCC's committee to solicit complaints from members of the public, which might then be investigated. The council's new committee, implied Verney, would take a much more active inquisitorial role. The mere nod of a local policeman would not be sufficient to counteract suspicions of immorality. He admitted that he had personally visited a 'cheap concert hall' in Hackney and found it unobjectionable; but the greater moral danger was actually to be found in central London, with its great concentration of fallen women. He was at pains to stress that he was not a prude:

> I am not a strait-laced person by any means, nor should I object to tights, or a thing that even the most indifferent man of the world could regard as illegitimate. But I think it is little short of an insult to a decent working man and his wife that when they go to a place of that kind, they should be affronted by coarse obscenity and downright filth.[79]

Indeed, Captain Verney was not at all strait-laced. Two years later, he would be imprisoned for employing a French procuress to entice Nelly Maud Baskett, 'a well-looking young lady, 19 years of age', to prostitute herself in Paris ('She said I could earn 5*l.* or 6*l.*').[80] For the record, Miss Baskett said no.

Frederick Charrington, having obtained a place on the music-halls committee and fuelled by evangelical zeal, tried to lead it by the nose. He also pushed his own objectives at the main London County Council meetings. He did not make himself popular. From the very beginning, he interrupted council proceedings to inquire about the presence of loose women in the halls and to denounce 'scandalous houses such as the Empire and the Alhambra'; his interjections were repeatedly met by cries of 'Order!' The LCC's emollient chairman, the Earl of Rosebery, tactfully tried to suggest that Charrington was going beyond the temperature of public opinion. Charrington and his allies pushed ahead regardless. There followed various efforts to remove or curtail music-hall licences, on the grounds of obscenity and prostitution. A parliamentary bill for the registration of music-hall artistes (designed so that they could be 'struck off' if they performed indecent material) was drawn up and, although swiftly abandoned, augured ill for the profession.[81] Music-hall owners feared a new era of restrictive licences and closures, all thanks to the promptings of the reformers – or, as some put it, 'cranks' and 'fanatics'.

The NVA, fortunately for the owners of London's music halls, proved its own worst enemy. Charrington himself was such a nuisance that he was voted out of the licensing committee in November 1890 (he had privately employed his own inspector to visit the Empire Theatre, against LCC regulations).[82] Other members of the NVA were quite willing to take up Charrington's baton; but they, too, met with decidedly mixed fortunes.

For instance, in 1890, the NVA's secretary, William Coote, objected to a poster advertising 'Zaeo', a female acrobat in a figure-hugging costume and skin-tone tights, standing with her arms raised behind her head. The poster was allegedly suggestive and indecent because of the pose: it clearly showed the female figure, clad in tight clothing, including – the horror! – her armpits. The picture was also reportedly being 'decorated in a most immoral and indecent manner' by graffiti artists.[83] The venue in question, the Royal Aquarium, grudgingly conceded the point and removed the image from circulation. In the meantime, a quarter of a million pocket-sized photographs of Zaeo were reputedly sold to the public, all thanks to the free publicity. We cannot check this figure, but, as one sarcastic journalist noted, 'Nobody but a few high pressure, goody-goody, latter-day saints took the slightest notice of the pictures until the discussion about them was raised.'[84] The Aquarium, in fairness, had something of a reputation. A bluntly worded cartoon from the *Licensed Victuallers' Mirror*, published two years previously, shows two gaudily dressed women taking tea at the venue, and is simply entitled 'Aquarium tarts'. But the conclusion for the NVA was something of a Pyrrhic victory which 'did more than anything else to bring ridicule upon the early doings of the Council'.[85]

There was some suspicion that the complaint about Zaeo was part of an ongoing vendetta. The NVA had failed the previous year to deprive the

Aquarium of its licence on the grounds of harbouring prostitutes. The Aquarium's management, in turn, took its revenge by bringing a libel complaint against an LCC councillor, William Coulson Parkinson. He had claimed, during the Zaeo hearing, to have witnessed an 'indecent' performance of marionettes at the venue. On further examination, the indecency was said to have involved a female life-sized puppet sitting on a butterfly, as part of pantomime-style clowning. Parkinson was coyly unwilling to spell out his fears in full. He presumably either objected to any reference to the female posterior, or held darker anxieties about the butterfly's final destination. Unfortunately, it was shown that the automaton in question was male, not female, and that Parkinson, in any case, could barely see the stage. With the puppets and their actions displayed in court, the whole business made the councillor (who was obliged to find £250 in damages) a laughing-stock.

The Empire Theatre of Varieties became a target in 1894. Like the Aquarium, it was indubitably notorious as a place to meet prostitutes. These were well-dressed women who lingered on the theatre's exclusive five-shilling promenade spaces, 'astounding in their professional magnificence'.[86] Mrs Ormiston Chant personally led the charge, reporting to the Theatres and Music Halls Committee on women 'very much painted ... more or less gorgeously dressed' who frequented the theatre.[87] The Empire's ballet girls were inappropriately dressed; and she had even witnessed one instance of an indecent comic song ('he sang a song in which in the course of his singing, with a very unpleasant gesture, he tells us how a young lady comes up to his counter and says I wish to see your winter night-wear'). Laura Chant was a highly effective professional public speaker, who conducted her case with barrister-like efficiency. The LCC was convinced on the question of prostitution and effectively closed the theatre until structural alterations were made, to reduce the offending promenade areas and separate them from the bars selling alcohol.

Victory, once again, proved rather moot. The management used temporary canvas screens to effect the transformation. The screens were swiftly torn down by a gang of aristocratic young men as soon as the venue reopened. Some two or three hundred youths assembled, infuriated by the council's interference in their nocturnal fun, and revelled in the destruction. Among the riotous mob was a party of Sandhurst cadets, led by none other than the young Winston Churchill (who later proudly recounted his role in the affair). Furthermore, within a year the promenades were legally reopened, partly thanks to the flagging political fortunes of the progressives in the 1895 LCC elections. Many contemporary commentators considered the Empire affair a fiasco from start to finish. The political appetite for conspicuous moral interference was considerably diminished.

A renewed assault on the licence of the Empire in 1896 was marked principally by Coote inadvertently giving the impression that he thought a 'tableau vivant' – a living re-creation of Courbet's daring painting *La Source* – actually depicted a nude woman urinating. The tableau's nudity was, as everyone knew, a skin-toned body-stocking; the question of urination related to a trickling fountain beneath the performer's static, carefully framed body. Coote would later clarify that he had meant to imply that the 'La Source' tableau vivant was an oblique, indecent reference to woman's generative powers, and presumably her sexual organs, not urination. He was so embarrassed by the affair that he withdrew his objections. This comical episode was typical of NVA-sponsored assaults on London's music halls – much sound and fury; endless debate about public morality; no tangible result. While social purity campaigners undoubtedly set the initial agenda for the Theatres and Music Halls Committee, they did not manage to impose any permanent closures. The interference with the Empire's promenades in 1894 briefly seemed to herald an era of restrictions and interference. In truth, it was a false dawn for the puritans. Arguably, Charrington, Ormiston Chant and colleagues put proprietors on their mettle, and encouraged more 'decent' performances on stage. This was trumpeted in various pieces of election literature written by the LCC's progressives.[88] But there is actually little evidence to support this claim. The LCC committee *was* inquisitorial. Inspectors visited halls and quietly filled out brief reports about the morality of performances; and this must have put certain managers on their toes. But on the other hand, it is easy to find continuing examples of wayward performers (despite managers including notices in their programmes that asked the audience to inform them of 'any suggestive or offensive word or action upon the stage that may have escaped notice').[89]

Many acts, in truth, were already perfectly 'clean'; and some embraced the notion of purity wholeheartedly. The 1880s catchphrase of the Moore and Burgess Minstrels was 'Fun without Vulgarity'. This was not, however, a universally acknowledged maxim. The great comic singer Marie Lloyd was famously criticised by the puritans for singing 'Johnny Jones' in 1896. The song featured Marie, dressed as a schoolgirl, asking the question 'What's that for, eh?' The song was ostensibly about a father's adultery revealed by childish questioning – itself a doubtful topic. But Marie asking young Johnny Jones 'What's that for, eh?' allowed for a more risqué anatomical interpretation. It remained very hard to prevent certain comics from tweaking the nose of the puritans with such material. Lloyd, by all accounts, relished this game of cat-and-mouse.

At the same licensing sessions, the comedian R.G. Knowles was criticised by a female member of the NVA, who was subsequently cross-examined:

> With regard to Mr. Knowles, he said that when a woman went into bed she looked under it to see if there was a man there, but a man would not, as he would not care though there were twenty women there.
> – That you call obscene?
> Yes.
> – In your experience, do women look under the bed?
> I do not know.
> – You don't look under the bed?
> No. (Laughter)
> – But you are not afraid that there might be anybody there, perhaps?
> No. (Laughter)[90]

This laughter, recorded by the sessions clerk and generated by a teasing line of inquiry as suggestive as the original patter, is interesting. Most likely it came from the gallery, packed with music-hall performers and theatre folk; but one wonders if members of the committee were also smiling. The social purists were not always taken terribly seriously. Knowles himself would still be worrying the puritans ten years later, with gags like 'Marriage is a committee of two with discretionary power to add to their number. Pity is that some people haven't more discretion', interspersed with 'knowing' winks, nods and gestures.[91] If there was any reform in comic manners thanks to the NVA, it was not wholesale.

And yet, all the same, music halls *were* changing in the 1890s, becoming exactly what Charles Morton had originally promised: respectable. This change was associated not with questions of sexual morality or with vulgarity; it came about because many of the halls abandoned the sale of drink.

Late Victorian variety theatres were deliberately designed to sever the halls' traditional bonds with the public house and to present a more sober face to the world. We have already alluded to key structural changes: pub frontages disappeared; shared tables and seating were replaced by theatrical stalls. Proprietors even did away with the chairman, that totemic figure of bonhomie and booze. Prosaically, acts were announced by placing numbers on a board, relating to numbers on the programme. Drinking gradually became less a part of music-hall culture. But why did this happen?

Magistrates played a large part, issuing local diktats that restricted drinking to separate bars, rather than the auditorium; or forbade it altogether. Numerous halls, therefore, were entirely alcohol-free by the early 1900s.[92] This was not thanks to any national legislation or policy. Rather, the local magistracy in towns and cities imposed their own licensing prohibitions, and proprietors cut their cloth accordingly, even to the extent of how they (re)structured their halls. Magistrates were usually keener on temperance than on social purity – possibly because it was easier to ban liquor – and the temperance lobby could exert considerable influence. The temperance movement was at its zenith in the 1890s, with the Liberal Party actively allied to the cause, and the option of local prohibition of alcohol included in its 1895 election manifesto. This was, admittedly, the peak of the movement's national political influence, since the Liberals were soundly defeated in the polls. Nonetheless, there remained strong local support for temperance ideals. Outside London, Methodists were particularly good at rallying the troops whenever big money came to town promising to build a 'seat of Satan'. The Manchester Palace, promoted by a London syndicate, was kept dry by the lobbying of local Methodists and fellow teetotallers. The Sheffield Empire Palace, likewise part of a national syndicate of music halls, also could not obtain an alcohol licence. The local coalition of puritans included Wesleyans, the Sheffield Women's Temperance Association, the Salvation Army and the Sunday School Band of Hope.[93] Temperance sentiment was never as strong in London, but the LCC Theatres and Music Halls Committee discussed a blanket ban on intoxicating drink in 1894. The committee was disappointed to find it was *ultra vires*. The subject rested, thanks to a dip in the progressives' electoral fortunes, but was revived again in 1898. After minimal discussion, newly built metropolitan halls were no longer permitted to sell beer or spirits, as a condition of their licence.[94]

The story of the 'dry' variety theatre, however, is not exclusively about magisterial compulsion, at the behest of special interest groups. The variety theatre represented, at least in part, a determined effort to open up a new income stream: the disposable income of the burgeoning late Victorian middle class; or, more accurately, the lower-middle class. The music hall, shorn of its ties to the public house and built in the manner of a West End theatre, was more appealing to the sober, industrious clerk or shop assistant and their families. Proprietors were very keen to develop this lucrative market. The economics made sense – at least in a large theatre, which might hold multiple categories of seating. The diminished alcohol revenue was offset by a willingness to pay for more comfortable individual seats and to spend more on refreshments. This is not to say that other working-class customers suddenly absented themselves from the halls. Rather, large variety theatres were carefully designed to provide class-differentiated entrances, seating and prices. The typically Victorian goal was to cater for a broader, but meticulously socially segregated, audience, and thereby make a greater profit.

Proprietors still preferred to sell some alcohol; and the general public were never absolute teetotallers. The finances of the Palace Theatre in Manchester were supported by the management purchasing the nearby Railway Inn. Likewise, in Sheffield, the Empire Palace issued passes to audience members, allowing them to pop to the nearest public house during the performance.[95] Yet late Victorian music-hall owners were quite keen on the notion of temperance and respectability:

Our highest ambition is that our performances should include the best music of a light and bright kind . . . and that the words to which the songs are sung should be wholly free from coarseness or indecency . . . It is not the desire of the proprietors and managers of the music halls to attract a minority of dissipated or half-tipsy youths. The patronage we seek is that of the immense majority of respectable artisans, assistants and small tradesfolk with their wives and families, who, after all, are the pillars of a music-hall's propriety. The more respectably a music-hall is conducted, the greater is the profit . . .[96]

These were the words of J.L. Graydon, secretary of the Proprietors of Entertainment Association, facing the much-anticipated onslaught of the NVA in 1889. They were, we must assume, crafted to ease tensions; but they reflect the public position of pretty much every substantial music-hall manager throughout the 1880s and 1890s. The managers of large music halls embraced the notion of propriety as much as Laura Ormiston Chant and Frederick Charrington; they just set slightly more relaxed boundaries.

Some commentators have depicted the undoubted growth of the middle-class portion of the audience as an appropriation of working-class halls and their culture. There was something of a campaign by managers to reduce more risqué lyrics and dubious 'gags'. We should, however, admit the possibility that the working-class audience itself was also changing. Speaking in 1893, Graydon, owner of the historic Middlesex Music Hall, was convinced that there was 'improvement in the taste of music hall audiences . . . brought about by the refinement of public taste', citing the declining popularity of the idiocies of the 'negro delineator' as proof ('What they clamoured for twenty years ago they will hiss to-day'). Most audience members, stated Graydon, now spent more on cakes, pies and tobacco than beer, with many not drinking at all.[97] Graydon, in short, did not claim that a better class of customer now came to the halls, but rather that the original audience's tastes had changed. His argument was not that the middle classes had invaded a working-class space, but rather that the working-class audience had itself become more respectable, more temperate, more like the notional middle-class ideal; or, to put it bluntly, less vulgar. Younger audience members would now all have received primary education under the 1870 Education Act; and universal, regimented schooling may well have begun to impact upon standards of public behaviour and popular taste.

Graydon may have made his comments with a view to placating the puritans; and audiences differed from district to district. The music-hall audience in Leicester Square was decidedly not the same audience as in Whitechapel. But it is worth noting that metropolitan halls were removing companionable bench seating, the most obvious manifestation of the halls' traditional drinking culture, before the LCC even existed.[98] There was no element of direct puritanical compulsion. William Holland, the manager who had first introduced Blondin to the halls and made George Leybourne a smash at the Canterbury in the 1860s, also touched on this subject in an 1890s interview. People, he said, were now willing and able to pay higher prices, but they expected more for their money: carpets instead of sanded floors, cushioned 'arm-chairs' instead of benches, the finest fabrics, fixtures and fittings. This was, said Holland, an unprecedented 'age of luxury'.[99] We should consider the distinct possibility that customers from *all* social classes were perfectly happy to trade the more rowdy, boozy, 'traditional' music-hall experience for the luxury of the palace of varieties.

The variety theatre of the 1890s also reflected a structural change in the music-hall industry. A new breed of entrepreneurs, the likes of Edward Moss and Oswald Stoll, had begun to build national chains of venues. They opened luxurious variety theatres in the suburbs, with an emphasis on providing family entertainment (again, an echo of Morton's promises in the 1850s). They decidedly did *not* want to evoke the gritty atmosphere of the pub parlour. Extravagant new venues, like the Hackney Empire, opened in 1901 by Oswald Stoll, were specifically designed to rival the glories of the best West End theatres. Chains of such theatres also required more professional management. Thus, by 1900, the ambitious publican was no longer the sole type of owner/manager. He had rivals who were professional theatrical managers, answerable to corporate shareholders, operating within a group containing multiple venues in different towns and cities. Artistes, likewise, found themselves working in a new, more professionalised environment. Performers for Stoll and Moss were instructed to supply musical parts for at least a twelve-part orchestra; advertising copy had to be approved by senior management; and, last but not least, performances had to be 'Free from all Vulgarity'.[100] All this naturally contributed to the steady evaporation of the halls' traditional bibulous atmosphere. The fact that certain proprietors now owned chains of halls also left the artistes far less able to contradict the management. Long hours and poor pay were commonplace. This would lead to the music-hall strike of 1907, when artistes fought for improved pay and conditions – and succeeded, thanks in large part to the support of certain major performers, including Marie Lloyd.

This professionalisation of the halls was reinforced by a growing emphasis on health and safety, rigidly enforced by late Victorian municipal authorities. Smaller, old-fashioned halls, built in odd spaces behind public houses, did not meet the latest fire regulations; nor could they afford the expense of refurbishment. Faced with serious legal challenges, many simply shut up shop. It has been suggested that the NVA-dominated LCC cynically exploited fire regulations to put down more modest pub music halls, thereby taming the last remnants of a more authentic, disorderly working-class culture. The inquisitorial, puritan LCC of the early 1890s undoubtedly discouraged some applicants and reduced the number of licences. But the LCC's own figures show that this drop in numbers was only temporary. A detailed look at LCC records reveals that the treatment meted out to parish halls, working men's clubs, theatres and music halls was fairly uniform, i.e. all were at risk of closure thanks to stricter fire regulations.[101] Fire risk had exercised the authorities since the early 1850s, when the Metropolitan Buildings Office had found existing regulations for concert-rooms and saloons 'in many cases . . . neglected or evaded'.[102] The Metropolitan Board of Works had begun to address the issue in the late 1870s; and other local authorities followed suit. The LCC was continuing this work.[103]

The nineteenth century ended, therefore, with the temperate variety theatre triumphant and the old-fashioned pub music hall teetering on the verge of extinction. There were complex pressures at work. Performers, moral pressure groups, local authorities and the audience: all had some interest in the halls and exerted a degree of influence on proprietors. No single legislative change, moral campaign or economic factor exclusively shaped the transition from the pub to the variety theatre. But without a doubt, as the Victorian era turned into the Edwardian, music hall gradually became a little more corporate and a little more respectable. There was no surer sign of this change than the first Royal Variety Performance, held before King George V at the Palace Theatre in 1912. Music-hall performers were now considered decent enough to set before the King.

Marie Lloyd, rather pointedly, was not invited.

IV

OR,

THE WAY OF THE WHIRLED

At the start of the nineteenth century, the main venue for commercial dance was the assembly rooms. Jane Austen's well-to-do heroines attended such rooms in search of amusement and eligible beaux. The grander examples contained spaces not only for hosting public balls and meetings, but also for concerts, tea-drinking, reading, backgammon, billiards and card-playing. Money came mainly from the sale of seasonal 'subscription tickets' and from refreshments. There were notable rooms in London, such as Almack's in Mayfair, but many provincial rooms were equally, if not more, elaborate. Indeed, by the early 1800s, ornate neo-classical assembly rooms had become a standard feature of county towns, seaside resorts, towns associated with race meetings (i.e. anywhere that attracted wealthy visitors). Tourist guides for fashionable spa towns like Bath, Cheltenham and Leamington boast about their luxurious design and decoration ('the walls are panelled and in the upper compartments are some exquisite imitations of *basso relievo* . . . the ceiling is coved, and from it are suspended three magnificent lustres, built by Mr. Collins of London').[1] These were places for 'Society' to congregate. The origins of particular assembly rooms varied. Some were the work of individual speculators; some were built by groups of local investors who intended both to make discounted use of the facilities themselves and to turn a profit. York's assembly rooms were built on the latter basis, promising a 5 per cent return, derived from 'Rents of the Monday Assembly, Friday Consort, and Tickets to be deliver'd out for the BALLS during the RACES'.[2] Some substantial taverns, such as the Star and Garter in Richmond, also had their own suites of rooms which were hired out for public balls.

The key to commercial success was attracting wealthy, well-connected customers. This was critical for ventures by solo entrepreneurs: fashionable patronage could make or break. For instance, the proprietor of new assembly rooms at Cheltenham, a certain Mr Kelly, persuaded the Duke and Duchess of Wellington to attend his inaugural ball in 1816. This coup all but guaranteed him a profitable summer season. Kelly was presumably much relieved: he had reportedly spent between £50,000 and £60,000 on his premises. Ticket prices helped to establish the social tone. Seasonal subscription in Cheltenham cost a guinea for gentlemen and fifteen shillings for ladies, or five shillings for any individual event. These were amounts suited to the purse of the upper classes. Cheltenham also had a 'Committee of Public Amusements' which decided on the social calendar for the season and appointed the necessary master of ceremonies. The MC's role in assembly rooms was extensive: allocating tickets; maintaining order in the room; making suitable introductions between prospective dance partners; and ensuring that there was no 'improper company'.

The degree of exclusivity enforced by proprietors, committees and MCs varied from place to place. The likes of Bath and Cheltenham grew very snobbish during the Regency, when the MC was tasked with excluding not only the disorderly or immoral, but any 'clerk, hired or otherwise . . . persons concerned in retail trade . . . theatrical or other public performers by profession'.[3] Dickens' preening master of ceremonies, Angelo Cyrus Bantam, waxes comically lyrical on the subject in *The Pickwick Papers*:

> The ball-nights in Ba-ath are moments snatched from paradise; rendered bewitching by music, beauty, elegance, fashion, etiquette, and – and – above all, by the absence of tradespeople, who are quite inconsistent with paradise, and who have an amalgamation of themselves at the Guildhall every fortnight, which is, to say the least, remarkable.[4]

Dickens was not the only one to find this ridiculous. A letter to the press from 'An English Gentleman' in 1834 complains of the caprice of Brighton's high-born 'lady patronesses' who arrange 'public' balls but then refuse tickets to the gentry, a 'gratuitous exhibition of aristocratic impertinence . . . entirely out of keeping with the general intelligence of the age'.[5] Similar complaints were made of Almack's in London, where lady patronesses wielded their power with notorious severity and maintained a rigid door policy. Wellington himself was said to have twice been excluded from the premises, once for having arrived after midnight and once for wearing trousers rather than breeches.

Fortunately, not everywhere was quite so snobbish. Assembly rooms might host county balls; race balls; military balls; tradesmen's balls; charitable balls for the local orphanage, hospital or foreign refugees. Tickets for some of these assemblies, while still priced to exclude *hoi polloi*, could be purchased from local booksellers, music publishers or the assembly rooms themselves. A few public balls even bordered on the egalitarian: Sir John Malcolm recalled attending two dances in Ludlow, Shropshire, in the early 1830s, 'one being a public ball open to all classes, and the other attended only by the elite of the county'. He remembered the former much more fondly, describing it as containing mixed society, including 'one lady called the Princess Royal, for she was acknowledged heiress of the Crown (Inn)'.[6]

Assembly rooms, however, would diminish in importance during the nineteenth century. As a business, they were too reliant on society patronage and seasonal subscription money. Proprietors could not cope with a gradual withdrawal of the aristocracy, who increasingly preferred to host their own lavish house parties, rather than mix in public. This was not, therefore, fertile ground for the evolution of accessible, affordable, commercial dance-halls for the masses. While there was a tendency for assembly rooms to move downmarket, the proprietors of rooms tended to reframe themselves as multi-purpose function rooms, rather than focus exclusively on dancing. Almack's, once described as the 'seventh heaven of the fashionable world', became a rather generic set of rooms, which could be hired for 'public meetings, dramatic readings, lectures, concerts, balls and dinners'.[7] Yet people of all classes *did* dance at a wide variety of venues during the Victorian period. These have been rather overlooked by historians.

The history of music hall suggests the public house as the most obvious base from which social dancing might have evolved into a form of commercial mass entertainment. But the music-hall model of 'pot-house to palace' was not actively pursued. Dancing, as we have already seen, posed a greater risk of magisterial opprobrium, and music hall itself looked much more profitable to entrepreneurs. One exception was the Surrey Music Hall in Sheffield, rebuilt by Thomas Youdan in 1856 as a hybrid venue. This 'theatre' included not only the auditorium, but also a museum, menagerie and ballroom capable of 'dancing comfortably fifty or sixty couples'.[8]

Yet the humble public house *was* intimately connected with commercialised social dancing, even if only at a very basic level. Many an early nineteenth-century publican hired a fiddler or permitted an itinerant musician to enter the premises, so that customers could dance ('persons of all descriptions and ages from 14 to 40 . . . tippling and smoking . . . tripping it on the "light fantastic toe" to the lascivious scraping of a crazy old fiddle').[9] An article from the *Morning Post* describes a blind fiddler working in the tap-room at the Salmon and Compasses in Brooke's Market, Holborn, a miserably poor district. Money is collected, tables are dragged to the side. Then, as one customer remarks, 'when the fiddler is paid he strikes up and we jump up and dances [*sic*]'.[10]

Some landlords did take things one stage further and had dedicated dancing-rooms, or devoted some evenings to 'hops' in the concert-room, catering to a largely working-class clientele. Dancing-rooms were quite common in maritime districts, meeting sailors' insatiable demand for excitement after coming ashore from a long voyage with money in their pockets. The pubs of East London's docklands were notorious for their 'long rooms' (rectangular rooms, benches along the side, with a stage or gallery for musicians) which were principally the resort of 'seamen and girls of the town'.[11] Long rooms were regularly condemned in the press as the haunts of predatory prostitutes, but they were the principal places of recreation in the district. They were, for the most part, quietly toler-ated by the local magistracy, unless violent disorder occurred. Similarly, most port cities boasted pubs with 'dancing-rooms' or 'dancing saloons'. The Ship Inn, Hull, had a room which attained brief notoriety thanks to a fight between two local prostitutes, the marvellously named 'Pablo' and 'Cottingham Poll'.[12] Lancaster, an inland port, likewise had a weekly 'twopenny hop' at the Golden Ball Tavern, frequented by both sailors and teenage millworkers.

There were also, of course, numerous pub dancing-rooms without a sea-faring connection. The Grapes Tavern in Old Compton Street, Soho, was described in the late 1830s as one of many public houses giving 'public balls' (in a legal case where a customer tried to recover damages for a shawl stolen from the cloak-room).[13] A couple of years later, the Union public house in Southwark faced a ten-shilling fine for unlicensed dancing. The concert-room contained sixty or seventy customers dancing to a violin, violoncello and harp, 'chiefly boys and girls, some of whom were decked out in spangled dresses and wore masks'.[14] This was probably some sort of plebeian masquerade ball; but clearly these customers had dressed up for the occasion. None of these venues developed into anything more elaborate; but they were places where people paid money to dance.

We know relatively little about how such dancing was organised. Historians have tended to suggest that working-class dancing was predominantly undisciplined jigs, reels and hornpipes, in stark contrast to the upper-class ballroom. Henry Mayhew's famous description of the twopenny hops attended by coster-mongers in *London Labour and the London Poor*, focusing on clog-dancing and 'vigorous laborious capering' would seem to support this view. Still, Mayhew's collaborator, Bracebridge Hemyng, would later acknowledge the accuracy and grace of dancers in East End long rooms (albeit with the caveat 'considering the position and education of the company').[15] One can easily find passing references to ballroom dances in the most humble settings, from waltzing in Wapping to quadrilles in Miss Kirby's beer-shop, Preston ('The magistrate said it was quite time that something was done to put a stop to quadrille dancing at low beer houses').[16] The polka, likewise, which began as an Eastern European peasant dance, ironically reached the English working class via its prior adoption in the upper-class ballroom ('It has infected all the several grades of society. In our own manufacturing community, young girls leave their spinning . . . to shine as polkaists').[17] The stereotype of working-class social dancing as necessarily primitive and clunky should be treated with caution.

Beyond dances in the public house, often unlicensed and illegal, there was an array of minor independent dance-related enterprises. They had little in common, and were mostly temporary, makeshift affairs. One Jeremiah Callaghan held a club in a back-street property in the Whitechapel slums, essentially a weekly house party, where youths paid a penny admission, and a further penny to stand up and dance. Local residents soon complained:

Every Sunday evening, from seven o'clock until two or three the following morning a vagabond Irish fiddler has a juvenile ball, or 'innocent hop' as he

calls it, at which young boys and girls from the ages of 12 to 18 congregate
. . . to the amount of from 100 to 200 . . . and there is a convenient dark
recess where the novices are initiated into the mysteries which lead to their
ultimate destruction . . .[18]

A 'twopenny dancing shop' in Berwick Street, Soho, was run by a Mr
Gilbert, who played the fiddle, and his sister, 'a showy girl in Bartholomew Fair
finery', who enticed customers into the premises. The customers were principally mechanics and apprentices, young men from the local workshops.[19]
A more expensive alternative to the pub dancing-room was the 'dancing
academy'. Originally, this term referred to dancing schools for the children of
middle-class families, or those who had not obtained the accomplishment in
their younger days. Mr Allen of Golden Square, Soho, for instance, widely
advertised his academy in the early 1800s, targeting 'Ladies and Gentlemen
who have never learned DANCING or are imperfect'. Allen taught the latest
fashionable steps and 'every modern requisite for genteel company' (most likely
etiquette and deportment). There were also lessons available for the piano,
pedal-harp, violin, the broad-sword and fencing.[20] By the 1820s, however, the
term 'dancing academy' also encompassed more lowly establishments, serving
the lower-middle-class shopkeeper, clerk and artisan. Many of these venues did
not provide much in the way of instruction and were little more than slightly
more expensive – and therefore marginally more exclusive – 'hops'. This was
especially true in London, where proprietors were keen to avoid the demands
of *music and dancing* licensing. The choice of the word 'academy' was often a
means of deflecting the attention of the magistrates. A *school*, based on monthly
or termly payment, was theoretically not a place of entertainment. Yet proprietors of these so-called academies often tried to have it both ways. They claimed
exemption from magisterial oversight *qua* dancing instructors, while still taking
door money from casual punters. The Oxford Street Assembly, opened in 1825
by a certain Signor Joseph Antonio in a converted auction-room, provides a
useful example. Antonio, brought up before the bench for noise nuisance,
claimed that he not only ran an 'academy', but offered free admittance. Yet it
was soon discovered that every so-called pupil was required to buy a two-
shilling 'coffee card', supposedly entitling him or her to unlimited refreshments. Upon inquiry, not a drop of coffee could be found. Signor Antonio
received only a warning; but the rooms closed within a matter of weeks. The

licensing status of academies, genuine and fake, would remain a bone of contention, with magistrates regularly having to rule on particular examples.

The two dancing academies which appear in Dickens at least provide lessons for pupils. All the same, they are both somewhat seedy affairs. The first, from *Sketches by Boz*, is run by a faux-Italian 'Signor Billsmethi' (i.e. Bill Smith), a retired actor.[21] It is situated near Gray's Inn Lane, ironically described as a 'populous and improving' district (actually an area which contained notorious slums). The would-be student is one Augustus Cooper, heir to a local paint shop, who notices the tempting advertisement of a 'grand ball' to be held at the rooms, and promptly invests in lessons and a fine pair of dress pumps. Balls were given by dancing-masters at regular intervals, serving both as advertisement and a party for pupils and guests. Augustus Cooper pays four shillings and sixpence for the quarter, and rattles round the academy's parlour, learning the quadrille with Billsmethi's daughter ('regular warm work, flying into corners, and diving among chairs, and shooting out at the door'). He learns very little, but attends the grand event, finally allowed into Billsmethi's assembly rooms proper. Dickens mocks the ball's working-class finery: 'such pink silk stockings! such artificial flowers! such a number of cabs!' Then there is a romantic entanglement, which ends with Billsmethi falsely claiming that our hero promised to marry his daughter. Augustus's mother settles the claim for £20 4s 6d 'exclusive of treats and pumps'. Augustus himself retreats, vanquished. The story is comic; but the reader is left in no doubt that the Billsmethi family has exploited the gullible youth, and it reads as a cautionary tale.

Mr Turveydrop's academy in *Bleak House* is not such a cynical enterprise and pupils do seem to get a fair return on their investment, but Turveydrop himself is hardly appealing. He is a faded Regency dandy, whose chief claim to fame is having once been noticed by the Prince Regent at Brighton. Turveydrop is a 'model of deportment', but utterly lazy and self-absorbed, delegating his business to his dutiful, put-upon son. The academy itself is situated in Newman Street, a neglected backwater north of Oxford Street, popular in real life with dancing-masters. Turveydrop shares the house with a drawing-master, coal-merchant and lithographer, with his modest ballroom built out into the back mews: 'a bare, resounding room, smelling of stables . . . [with] forms along the walls, ornamented at regular intervals with painted lyres and little cut-glass branches for candles'.

* * *

These, then, were some of the places where one could dance in the early nineteenth century. This long list is already somewhat confusing. The upper and middle classes could resort to genteel assembly rooms and academies/balls run by superior dancing teachers. Less grand 'academies', varying in quality and social tone, catered for the lower-middle class. The public house and makeshift dancing-rooms were open to all. There were other temporary venues. Individual balls and masquerades, often held in aid of some charitable cause, took place not only in assembly rooms, but also in theatres, with the stalls/pit cleared of seating. These could be rather elaborate events. A poster for a masquerade held at Drury Lane Theatre in the late 1820s lists various appealing features to attract customers: a band of reed instruments set in a Greek temple; Indian jugglers and acrobats; a magician; ballet girls; a 'flight of cupids' ('who will distribute various Mottos, Enigmas, Charades, Bon-bon, Confiture and Free Supper Tickets'). Most importantly, the poster promises 'specific arrangements made for Quadrille Parties'.[22]

The pleasure garden also offered considerable opportunity for al fresco dancing during the summer months, and we shall return to that subject in more detail in the next chapter. Fairs, held on public holidays, were also a possibility. Larger fairs featured 'dancing booths' – canvas tents with carefully assembled wooden flooring. Such booths could be rather substantial: 'Algar's Crown and Anchor', the most famous example of the breed, was rather like a touring assembly rooms. The lamp-lit tent, approximately 60 feet wide and 320 feet in length, pitched up at fairs and racecourses in London and the home counties. There were several internal 'rooms', one of which was devoted to the sale of food and drink ('cold beef, roast and boiled, French rolls, stout, wine, tongue, ham, even fowls').[23] Such was its fame that entrance cost a shilling, whereas rivals charged sixpence. The orchestra consisted of 'two harps, three violins, bass viol, two clarionets and flute'.[24] One Canterbury local, Robert Cowtan, recalled that the temporary dance-hall, arriving in town in the early 1830s, attracted 'almost all the well-to-do male population of my native city . . . [but] no woman with any regard to propriety and decency would be seen at such a gathering'.[25] Dickens, in *Sketches by Boz*, describes the same booth at Greenwich Fair as a more innocent affair, but accompanied by a distinct relaxation of manners: 'ladies . . . dancing in the gentlemen's hats, and the gentlemen, largely clerks and apprentices, promenading the gay and festive scene in the ladies' bonnets'. He also mentions hangovers the next morning.[26]

Yet despite all these manifold possibilities, there were no straightforward commercial dance-halls open to the general public, beyond the rough-and-ready 'twopenny hop' above a pub. Balls held in assembly rooms tended to be occasional and expensive affairs for the upper classes. Pleasure gardens were only open during the summer and were situated on the outskirts of town. Dancing academies were more accessible; but they required termly subscriptions (and, at the very least, a semblance of tuition). There were a handful of small night-clubs, catering for West End 'swells', but these were places for aristocratic whoring, drinking and gambling, often mere clip-joints. The Royal Victoria Saloon in Catherine Street distributed cards advertising 'a ball every evening . . . attended by a splendid assemblage of fashion and beauty'. The reality was a room packed with prostitutes, cheap champagne at exorbitant prices and little in the way of dancing.[27] Paris, on the other hand, famously had a number of relatively respectable, lavish public ballrooms, where one paid at the door. Several were associated with pleasure gardens, allowing their proprietors to offer music and dancing to the public in both summer and winter.[28]

In short, there was nowhere reliable in central London where a young person could simply turn up on a whim, and pay money to dance to a good orchestra. Then, in the mid-1840s, came the 'casino'.

Laurent's Casino, opened in October 1846, was the brainchild of James Ellis, the proprietor of Cremorne Gardens, the famous Chelsea pleasure garden, and his musical director, Émile Laurent, well known to concert-goers as a virtuoso soloist on the fashionable new solo instrument, the cornet-à-piston. The French capital undoubtedly provided inspiration, since Ellis was keen to forge a Paris-style link between pleasure garden and ballroom. Cremorne Gardens was essentially a hybrid of public park, funfair and, after dark, al fresco night-club. But it was open only during the summer months. Ellis hoped that, by opening the Casino, he could lure the garden's clientele to his new venture in the winter. Laurent, meanwhile, whose father had managed opera houses in both London and Paris, doubtless drew upon his own experience of Parisian night-life.

Ellis and Laurent were also inspired by a recent vogue for 'promenade concerts'. These had been introduced to London in the late 1830s, with programmes consisting principally of dance music, and with prices as low as a shilling. The eccentric, dandified conductor Louis-Antoine Jullien was their most successful exponent. Jullien's concerts largely took place in theatres. The

stalls/pit were boarded over, the auditorium decorated with elaborate drapery
and artistic accoutrements, and a full orchestra placed front and centre. The
audience did not actually dance, but they could circulate and chat among
themselves. Such concerts had amply demonstrated the public's enthusiasm for
lively, populist orchestral music. Jullien had shown that there was money in
opening up concert-going to the burgeoning lower-middle-class demographic,
who were attracted by the shilling admission. Why not create a respectable
public ballroom, similarly priced, with a proper orchestra, which permitted
the same audience to listen *and* dance, for an equally modest entrance fee?

This idea was rather timely thanks to another contemporary craze: polkamania. The 1840s saw the beginnings of a ballroom dance which spread to
England from Eastern Europe via Paris, 'like a contagion': the polka.[29] The new
dance was performed by couples in a hold, like the waltz; it was relatively easy to
learn and was set to a lively 2/4 beat. Critics complained that the dance's bold
skipping movements lent themselves to wild, undisciplined capering; but this
was precisely its appeal. Men, in particular, found it was perfectly possible to 'jog
along comfortably', without being too fussy about the steps. Hitherto reluctant
young men rushed onto the dance floor. F.C. Burnand recorded the transformation in his memoirs: 'for [every] one who sat out after a quadrille and waited
patiently for another, there were now fifty who, at the sound of the polka, started
up, obtained partners and danced for all they were worth, and more'.[30] The new
dance soon made an appearance on the London stage, most notably in the ballet
La Vivandière at Her Majesty's Theatre, and a one-act farce at the Lyceum, entitled *Polkamania*, which ran for more than a year between 1844 and 1845.
Magazines described the steps to their provincial readership ('The Polka Taught
without the aid of a Master'). Fly-poster advertisements for polka-related plays,
concerts, balls, sheet music and so on covered 'every allowable inch of dead
wall ... in letters as large as your legs'. One contemporary writer jocularly
described the craze as 'the Ball-room Revolution of '44'.[31] It was hardly surprising,
therefore, that entrepreneurs tried to capitalise on this new enthusiasm.

The Casino, situated in the Adelaide Gallery, just off the Strand, was not
purpose-built: the long, galleried room had previously been used as an exhibition hall for scientific contraptions, including various automata and a steam-
powered precursor of the machine-gun. Laurent may have chosen the venue
because he himself had performed at concerts there in the early 1840s. Once
converted into a dance-hall, the space could accommodate sixty to eighty

couples. The room was somewhat narrow, but benefited from ventilation provided by the lofty gallery. Decoration was in the style of Louis XIV, with mirrored walls, artificial flowers, evergreen wreaths and Grecian statuary. Press advertisements maintained the French connection, promoting nights at the hall as 'Grandes Soirees Musicales and Dansantes'. The refreshments, likewise, were 'of the most recherché description . . . quite Parisian'.[32] Champagne, ices and coffee were on sale, but the most popular beverage was not French, but a new American cocktail, the sherry cobbler (sherry, sugar and lemon, sipped through a straw). This was considered lighter and more refreshing than the traditional ballroom negus (hot port, sugar, lemon and spice).

The Casino's programme began with an hour or so of concert music from the fifty-piece orchestra, many of whom were leading instrumentalists from the likes of Her Majesty's Theatre and the Royal Opera. This first half was essentially a promenade. Dancing then commenced after a brief intermission. A typical night included music by the likes of Musard, Strauss, Fessy and Labitzky.[33] Laurent displayed his virtuosity on the cornet-à-piston, an instrument which had become rather too ubiquitous for the liking of music critics, but was still highly popular with the public.[34] He also conducted the orchestra, very much in the exaggerated, dramatic style of Jullien. There were experiments with other types of performance at the interval and end of the evening: Ethiopian serenaders, comic singers and the 'Monster Achromatic Microscope', a mixture of microscopy and magic lantern. Dancing remained the only real attraction in what amounted to London's first popular, open-to-all commercial night-club. The band was widely praised as among the best in the capital.

The author and lecturer Albert Smith provides the best account of the Casino's male clientele. He describes slumming aristocrats, a barrister, journalists who have gained free entry on the promise of a review, shop workers, City clerks, students and 'two unmitigated Gents in white coats, and hats out of the perpendicular, short sticks, and flaring cravats, who think they are "doing the fast"'.[35] These are, in other words, typical West End 'loungers' or men about town. As for women, the *Era* suggested that the price of one shilling 'would place it [the Casino] within reach of all classes, and yet still ensure respectability' – i.e. minimise prostitution.[36] This was perhaps a little optimistic. Yet there seems to have been no notable suggestion of vice in the early years. Even the sensationalist *Paul Pry* conceded that this was the sort of place one might bring one's wife or daughter (albeit only if one could bring oneself to ignore the 'libidinous' dancing among the low-bred shopmen).[37] The same magazine's illustrated cover shows young women sipping cocktails, and raffish young men polkaing around the floor, wearing their best silk top hats, while indulging in the peculiar contemporary affectation of brandishing a riding crop in their leading hand. This was clearly a place for 'fast' young men, but the consensus seems to have been that Laurent's was, in these early years, still not terribly louche or bohemian. It was, in any case, distinctive and successful. The journalist Edmund Yates, writing his memoirs, recalled that 'such an entertainment . . . had never been seen before in London'.[38] The relatively low admission price, moreover, meant that the Casino was described as offering 'dancing for the million', i.e. affordable for the common man.

Laurent's Casino made such an impression that competitors swiftly appeared. Coleman's Casino de Venise and Bal Ridotto, which soon became known as the Holborn Casino, was opened in December 1846, a matter of weeks after Laurent's. We know next to nothing about the original proprietor, Mr Coleman, except that he was American and had hastily converted Holborn's National Swimming Baths into a ballroom.[39] Again, this was a galleried room, with a front entrance that led almost straight into the converted pool/ballroom. There were several small bars around the wings, serving wine and beer (the premises never acquired a spirits licence, but relied on an archaic 'Vintner's licence' from the City of London). There was also a 'Turkish Divan': a room reserved for smoking. As at Laurent's, it was possible to pay solely for entrance to an upstairs gallery, and watch the dancing throng. The press was not very kind on the much-touted opening night, noting 'the company, to be sure, are less select than numerous'. Part of the problem was a shortage of women; and there was also a distinct lack of the oriental luxury promised in advertisements, 'not yet very apparent in the naked walls, bare floor and odour of fresh paint'.[40] The orchestra and vocalists could not quite match Laurent's band, but the Holborn Casino ultimately proved as popular as Laurent's. There would be occasional variety acts: Bedouin acrobats; Herr von Joel and Son, the famous imitators of birdsong; Carlos Alberto, 'The Celebrated Bottle Equilibrist'. Yet, as at Laurent's Casino, these were novelties: dance was the heart and soul of the business, managed initially by an MC named Grindleigh, who swiftly had a quiet word with anyone who broke formation in a quadrille or who polkaed beyond bounds.[41] Despite this strict supervision, a newspaper reporter visiting the venue a couple of years later noted that the dancing was rather 'fast', which amounted to much tight squeezing of waists by the gentlemen. Manners were also overly familiar, with liberal use of first names. Girls, he noted, came by themselves in search of a dance partner, and sat in the refreshment room 'with their legs upon chairs, and sometimes on their particular Charley or Ned's lap'.[42] These were either prostitutes or lower-class women with no regard whatever for social proprieties (which, to the Victorian moralist, amounted to very much the same thing).

A third London casino would open in Leicester Square in September 1848. This was yet another converted space, originally Miss Linwood's Gallery of Needlework (1809–45); then the Walhalla Theatre, famous for the *poses plastiques* (human statuary, generally in skimpy classical costume) of Madame Wharton. Finally, it became a casino, known awkwardly as the Walhalla Salle de Valentino (after the Salle de Valentino in Paris) or more simply as The Walhalla. Once again, there was a pleasure-garden connection. The conductor was Herr Redl, musical director of Vauxhall Gardens. The principal director, Richard Pridmore – who claimed to have spent over £4,000 on the project – was also a business associate of Robert Wardell, Vauxhall's recently bankrupted owner.[43] The ballroom was approximately 100 feet long and 46 feet broad, decorated 'quite in the French style' and lit by a dozen sparkling chandeliers. The rather cynical paper, the *Satirist*, summoned to a press junket to promote the venture, spent more time mocking the greedy guzzling of fellow journalists, noting 'Champagne was tasted by lips that were most assuredly more accustomed to the flavour of Barclay and Perkins' (a well-known firm of brewers).[44] The same journal would later publish a mock account of a servant's observations on the casino's clientele. 'Jeames' tells the reader that there is a mix of 'the scion of *no*bility and the scion of *mob*-ility' and 'the noble mansion and the shop comes into igstrornary contact you know what I mean – all huddled together promiscous' [*sic*].[45] The Walhalla was, in other words, part and parcel of the same phase of London's night-life that could be glimpsed in Covent Garden's song-and-supper rooms, certain theatres, West End cigar shops, late-night eateries and Cremorne Gardens: shop workers, clerks, bohemians and aristocrats, all mingling together, drinking and dancing 'promiscuously'.

Casinos seemed to be a booming business. An unbiased observer looking at Laurent's, the Holborn and the Walhalla at the close of 1848 might well have concluded that *this* was the future of metropolitan entertainment, not the humble pub music hall. Indeed, such was the impact of these new ventures that the term 'casino' was briefly adopted nationwide for any type of dancing-room or even music hall, i.e. any popular form of nocturnal entertainment. Manchester's Royal Casino Promenade Concert Hall (opened 1848), the Royal Casino in Sheffield (1849) and the Royal Casino in Leeds (1849) were principally music halls, but they took their name from the new, glamorous London venues.[46]

But the London casinos, however inspirational, would soon find themselves under attack.

The initial onslaught came in January 1849, courtesy of Thomas Stowell, the notorious professional informer. He had noticed that both the Walhalla and Laurent's had never applied for a *music and dancing* licence, and swiftly drafted a case against them. The precise dates and times of the legal wrangling need not concern us, but Richard Pridmore of the Walhalla was eventually found guilty of running an unlicensed house. The venue returned to showing Madame Wharton's *poses plastiques* and London lost its newest dance-hall, barely six months after it had begun. These were the highly publicised proceedings which, likely as not, caused the Home Secretary to issue his edict to magistrates about unlicensed entertainment, and, in turn, led to the fateful adoption of *music only* licensing, critical to the development of music hall.

Stowell claimed he was acting on behalf of 'interested, licensed parties'. If true, this was probably the West End theatre managers Benjamin Webster and Charles Matthews (the same protectionists who would later hound Charles Morton). Webster and Matthews are likely candidates, since they openly protested against Laurent's Casino at the subsequent entertainment licensing sessions in October 1849. They armed themselves with a petition from the clergy of St Martin-in-the-Fields, the nearest church to the Adelaide Gallery. Laurent's Casino harboured, it was alleged, 'people of bad character . . . women of the town . . . and by its allurements the seduction of young women had been carried on in a very great extent'.[47] The defence, predictably, said the same was true of the theatres. Laurent's lost its *music and dancing* licence by a narrow vote and the venue was closed. James Ellis went bankrupt, forced also to abandon Cremorne Gardens, and set out on new ventures in Australia. The Holborn Casino was suddenly the only dance-hall in the capital.

Émile Laurent, however, found a new business partner almost immediately. This was another West End character, Robert 'Bob' Bignell, a well-known bookmaker.[48] Bignell purchased the Hall of Rome in Great Windmill Street, near modern Shaftesbury Avenue. The hall, an erstwhile theatre, waxworks and home to *poses plastiques*, was swiftly remodelled as a galleried casino. The building was christened the Argyll Rooms, in honour of the Regency assembly rooms of the same name, once situated on nearby Regent Street. Laurent fulfilled the same role as musical director and band leader, and was soon attracting the same large crowds that had flocked to the Adelaide Gallery. The awkward lack of a licence was overcome by the customary flimsy claim to be a 'dancing academy'. Further prosecution by Stowell followed, but a proper entertainment licence was granted the following year. We cannot know exactly what influence was brought to bear on the magistracy, but Bignell mustered all his aristocratic contacts from the turf, presenting a petition to the bench signed by a long list of barons, earls and viscounts and their progeny, as well as military men and members of parliament. Only two out of twenty-one magistrates dissented.

This resurrection was something of a victory for Laurent and Bignell; however, it heralded not a new dawn for metropolitan dance-halls, but rather a period of dull entrenchment. Music halls, fortified by the Middlesex bench's decision to offer *music only* licences, multiplied and prospered. The Holborn and the Argyll Rooms inspired no further rivals. *Diprose's London Guide* from 1856 lists only one other commercial venue for dancing that was open every evening: Caldwell's Assembly Rooms in Soho.

Caldwell's, which had also opened in 1849 and was capable of holding up to 600 people, actually catered more for the working-class dancer. The diarist Arthur Munby made a point of visiting and noted the distinct difference in both social class and manners, compared with the Holborn and Argyll Rooms:

Lots of young men, clerks & apprentices, dancing with young women of the same class – shopgirls & milliners – also respectable, but not very attractive. Things carried on in an easy & unconstrained but virtuous manner: for fast girls & prostitutes think the place 'slow' . . .[49]

Less kind commentators damned the place as 'dreary as a gospel hall', with its insistence on strict morality, including leaving one's hat at the door and paying a penny for the privilege (whereas the relaxed casinos, as contemporary sketches demonstrate, permitted visitors to remain casually hatted, as if wandering about outdoors). One former customer recalled:

the most sepulchral gravity of demeanour was insisted upon . . . If you smiled, a master of ceremonies frowned at you. The young ladies called you 'sir', and begged you not to talk during a quadrille, lest they should forget the figure. And certainly the figure required all their attention, being much more elaborate than any I have seen in practice elsewhere . . .[50]

The ostentatious seriousness was because Caldwell's was a slightly more plebeian version of the casino, albeit with genuine origins as a dancing academy. There was no need to subscribe to lessons (although some teaching did still take place); and admission was a mere sixpence on the door. With a more working-class clientele, it was more imperative to avoid any hint of immorality, in order to retain an entertainment licence. The venue did have trouble with liquor licensing, and John Caldwell purchased the nearby Crown and Two Chairmen public house, so that waiters could ferry beer and spirits to customers, from pub to dance-hall. But Caldwell's, overall, was treated rather favourably by the Middlesex magistrates, largely thanks to its spotless reputation. Caldwell himself also noted that, despite catering to working people, 'I do not think I saw but one man in my rooms come in with corduroy trowsers [i.e. work clothes]; the gentlemen are always dressed in black.'[51] These were not, therefore, the poorest of the poor, but artisans and tradesmen in steady employment, who could afford basic evening dress.

Caldwell's prospered in the 1850s, thanks to rigid moral policing. The reputation of the Argyll Rooms and the Holborn Casino went in the opposite direction. In 1857, shortly after the death of Émile Laurent, Robert Bignell found himself the victim of a crusade to purge the West End of prostitution. The Argyll Rooms, which closed at midnight, was condemned for supposedly spewing out crowds of drunken debauchees and fallen women, who then infested the streets around the Haymarket and Piccadilly. The late-night Haymarket was notorious, a district famous for street soliciting, riddled with brothels and drinking dens; it possessed this reputation long before the advent of the Argyll Rooms. Nonetheless, magistrates responded to a vigorous anti-vice campaign, led by the local vestry, and promptly removed the Argyll's *music and dancing* licence, a scapegoat for a wider malaise.

Bignell, unwilling to abandon the casino, was sufficiently wealthy to stay put, rather than sell up. He temporarily returned his dance nights to the

Adelaide Gallery, then contested the decision the following year. The police, who had always regularly patrolled the building, gave highly favourable reports. Sergeant Edward Castle noted that there was never any disorder. He conceded that there were usually five men for every woman; and that the latter were often prostitutes. But, he said, they were better dressed than the women who prowled the Haymarket, and better behaved. Sergeant Richard Tanner asserted that boys and young women were not admitted; and that he had seen respectable folk at the Argyll, both male and female, including 'police inspectors with their wives . . . but I should prefer not to mention their name'. A certain Mr Purdy, a teacher of music, said he had taken his wife. He recounted, to much laughter in court, that she had thought the women present were respectable, and 'had she not been told what they were, she never could have suspected it'.[52] Two magistrates even conceded that they had visited the rooms, with a party of MPs, and had seen no impropriety. Clearly, this testimony was all carefully orchestrated for Bignell's defence; and the licence was restored.

A celebratory dinner was arranged for Bignell by his numerous friends and hosted by Lord William Lennox; there he received a 300-guinea 'testimonial'. This gives some indication of the Argyll's clientele – and, more importantly, how the casino crowd radically changed under Bignell's influence. The rooms, which had begun by providing affordable 'dancing for the million', became an integral part of the 'fast' West End, catering more for pleasure-seeking aristo-crats. The admission fee remained the same, but by the end of the 1850s, a notable part of the clientele were wealthy gentlemen and their inamoratas:

> fashionably-dressed women, who usually came alone, driving to the Rooms in broughams and cabs . . . kept women . . . [who] visited the place in company with the persons under whose protection they lived and whom they met there by appointment . . .

> They come in and walk out by themselves and never join in the semblance of dancing going forward on the floor of the room. An extra charge is made to those who would obtain admission to the gallery frequented by these bedizened and brazen-faced harlots.[53]

As at the Empire Theatre of Varieties, a particular (and more expensive) upper section of the building was *the* place to meet women. The farce of 'courtesans' coming and going 'by themselves' also gives some credence to the police's repeated claim about such venues, i.e. that 'nothing improper occurred'. Ostensible propriety was maintained. Proper *conduct* was sufficient for policing purposes; motives were not a concern. This was the same wilful blindness, or admirable tolerance, which would so frustrate Frederick Charrington and Laura Ormiston Chant.

The Holborn Casino did not attract quite such an aristocratic clientele, but still acquired a similarly louche reputation. Throughout the 1860s and 1870s, both venues appear in press reports which touch on sexual promiscuity and prostitution. A woman in a divorce case is said to have 'frequently visited the Holborn Casino and the Alhambra with different persons'; a prostitute, having stolen her friend's best dress, is found wearing it at the Argyll; another is taken to the Argyll by a procuress to be introduced to gentlemen ('when either of them went home with me, she came the following day for money'). Men even taunted their wives that they could easily pick up a replacement at the Argyll or the Holborn.[54] George Hayman, an unremorseful clerk who stole funds from his employer, wrote to an acquaintance outlining his joyous week-long spending spree, including four trips to the Argyll Rooms ('took a box at the Oxford; and had two or three ladies; made them all drunk with champagne. We all went to the Argyll Rooms and then to supper, all jolly and drunk. Tuesday, boosing all day').[55] Possibly the original casino at the Adelaide Gallery had its share of such things; but by the 1860s both venues were absolute bywords for vice and dissipation. The American public speaker George Francis Train, inveighing against immorality in 1862, pointedly asked whether his listeners would take their wives and daughters to the Holborn Casino, or to dance the Lancers at the Argyll Rooms. 'No!' shouted the dutiful audience.[56]

The casinos were not unique in this regard. The Portland Rooms (aka Mott's), near Regent Street, were originally assembly rooms, a space for hire, used for occasional public meetings and balls. By the mid-1850s, they had become a dance-hall where aristocratic men could meet the leading 'courtesans' of the day, who proudly dubbed themselves 'independent ladies'. These were well-known women, who kept their own carriages and maintained something of a fan club among wealthy, impressionable youth. One famous habituée was Nelly Fowler, said to be blessed with a natural perfume 'so delicate, so universally admired, that love-sick swains paid large sums for the privilege of having their handkerchiefs placed under the Goddess's pillow'.[57] Mott's, however, never offered anything like 'dancing for the million'. Entrance was half a crown (two shillings and sixpence) and the door policy strictly limited entrance to familiar faces from among the upper classes.

We should not assume that *all* women who frequented the casinos were prostitutes; nor that all men were seeking commercial sex. The casinos were merely a venue where such connections *could* be made. As one prostitute explained to Bracebridge Hemyng, 'I go to the Holborn, dance a little, and if any one likes me, I take him home with me, if not I go to the Haymarket, and wander from one café to another.'[58] Edmund Yates recalled the Holborn Casino as quieter than the Argyll Rooms, with 'some element of respectability' among the women, and men who were more middle class, rather than West End 'swells'. They were, recalled Yates, 'young fellows from the neighbouring Inns of Court, medical students, Government clerks, with a sprinkling of the shopocracy'.[59] It was a place 'where people went rather to dance than to look on at dancing, as was the custom at the old Argyll'.[60] This is corroborated by the fact that, upon its closure in 1873, there was little fuss or triumphalism. The same could not be said of the end of the Argyll Rooms.

The 1870s saw the Argyll facing constant criticism and regularly appearing in the press. The venue barely retained its licence in 1873, after Bignell was accused of using it as a gambling den. Shortly afterwards, a fight broke out between police and off-duty soldiers who had been asked to leave the premises, with much attendant negative publicity. Frank Bayne, another errant clerk, stole his employers' money and headed straight from Chester to the metropolis, spending most of the loot on champagne, 'seven or eight bottles a night at the Argyll Rooms'.[61] The following year, the pastor of a neighbouring church opened a 'midnight mission' specifically to preach to those quitting the building. There seems to have been a concerted effort to make a mockery of this evangelical outreach. The church was soon filled with drunken men and women engaging in loud talking and laughing throughout the service/lectures; they 'appeared to enjoy their flirtations the more in consequence of the novelty of their position'.[62]

Matters came to a head at the 1878 licensing sessions, when Major William Lyon launched his campaign against West End vice, already noted in the context of music hall. Lyon mustered dozens of magistrates to appear at the licensing sessions – so many that some had to sit on the public benches. Police testified that women present at the Argyll were not street prostitutes, but rather 'kept' by men in their own homes in districts like St John's Wood, Chelsea and

Belgravia. The chaplain of Clerkenwell Prison was brought forth to make the unlikely claim that he 'constantly' was told by convicted burglars that the Argyll served as their meeting place of choice in the West End. The closure of Cremorne Gardens the previous year was cited as a useful precedent. The Argyll, finally, was refused a licence: an early victory for the puritans.

Few defended the Argyll in the press. A letter-writer to *The Times* bemoaned the lack of respectable dancing places for the young, blaming the magistracy for scaring away decent entrepreneurs. Many papers printed salacious details, including the fact that two guineas was positively the lowest sum accepted by the Argyll's women. They noted that Bignell had a splendid mansion near Kew and reportedly netted £15,000 a year from his dubious rooms. The Argyll itself actually remained open for a spell, without music or dancing, presumably on the strength of its drinks licence; but it was clear that its days were numbered. A couple of weeks after the licensing sessions, a street protest against the decision, organised by waggish medical students, descended into a riot, as police officers closed the venue and blocked off access to surrounding roads. Prostitutes cheered as drunken youths hurled firecrackers at the massed constabulary. Needless to say, this did little to endear Bignell and the Argyll to the authorities. The dance-hall closed for the final time, before briefly serving as a restaurant; it was then converted by Bignell into the Trocadero Music Hall. One reviewer of the 'Troc's' opening night noted: 'never was a tamer performance presented . . . The Middlesex Magistrates have evidently taught Mr. Bignell a lesson on propriety.'[63] Bignell himself, who died in 1888, was remembered by music-hall performers as a generous employer, who 'sat in state in the saloon bar of the Trocadero, where he loved to be every night'.[64]

The closure of the Argyll marked the end of an era. Most of its contemporaries had already vanished, including Mott's (closed c.1868); Caldwell's Assembly Rooms (1871); and the Holborn Casino (1873). This last had been successfully replaced with a grand restaurant, which explains Bignell's initial effort to move into catering. The Trocadero's final replacement of the casino is telling: music halls were a much safer investment, even as they, too, were assailed by Lyon and the National Vigilance Association.

The dubious reputation of the Holborn Casino and the Argyll dissuaded other entrepreneurs from creating more metropolitan dance-halls. Yet, while the mid-century casino experiment had categorically failed, there were still numerous other places to dance. The dancing academy still flourished, in various degrees of respectability, although defining the difference between teaching and entertainment remained a vexed question. The was not only the case in the metropolis. A long-drawn-out case occurred in Cardiff in 1888. The proprietor of the Philharmonic Hall, built above commercial premises, was taken to court for the noise and disturbance caused to its downstairs neighbour, an accountant and auctioneer named Jenkins. The latter mustered numerous points of complaint: that vibration from the 'cellar flap breakdown' (a lively jump step, popular among the working class) was damaging his gaslights; that the rough class of clientele ('artisans, such as shipwrights, apprentices and coal-heavers and also women of that class') were urinating in the shared hallway; that alcohol was illegally consumed; and that the premises were an unlicensed place of public amusement. Magistrates sided with the owner of the Philharmonic Hall after police testified to orderly behaviour, while customers asserted that there was a water-closet and that the proprietor regularly split them into groups of different ability and showed them dance steps. The venue, magistrates concluded, should have been licensed, but they would only impose a nominal fine of a shilling. It is noticeable that magistrates, although having a reputation for hostility to dance, could be quite sympathetic to certain individual proprietors. The *Morning Chronicle* once stated, with heavy irony, that aged members of the bench 'being no dancers themselves . . . [had] an instinctive dread of the effect of Hops on the lower orders'.[65] This was true when licensing magistrates felt that they had to demonstrate their moral credentials; but individual cases like Caldwell's or the Philharmonic Hall could be treated with considerable leniency.

The working-class 'dancing-room', with little or no pretension to teaching, likewise remained a feature of poorer districts. A reporter's inquiry into the 'shady side of Nottingham' in the late 1870s describes a room in the back yard of a public house on North Street charging sixpence a head, with a fiddle and harp providing the music. Fifty or so people are present, but most of the female portion are teenage girls; and the men/boys are in their work clothes. The author concedes that some present are 'sweethearts' (i.e. have come as a couple) but says that the room accustoms teenage girls to drink and excitement, a 'nursery of folly and prostitution'.[66]

Late Victorian London, meanwhile, teemed with low-class dancing venues, according to investigative reporters from the *British Weekly* (a nonconformist journal, reporting the capital's temptations for young shop workers). The magazine's lengthy report breaks them down into various types. 'Elementary dancing-rooms' are described as dull and decorous, but pupils swiftly learn steps and seek excitement elsewhere. There are rooms associated with gambling and betting clubs; and rooms associated with prostitution ('There is a sixpenny dancing-room in the vicinity of Gower Street Station, which has a wide reputation of an unenviable character'). More respectable are 'shilling dancing-rooms . . . found in every leading thoroughfare of London' (surely something of an exaggeration). The report describes one such venue, in Clerkenwell, in some detail. It is gaudily decorated with gilt ornaments, wall mirrors and gaslights. A woman stands on the staircase, before a pair of baize-covered doors, to prevent the admission of prostitutes. The dance floor is well sprung and surrounded by small booths with seating, although no alcoholic liquor is served, due to the difficulty of obtaining a licence. There is also a smoking room with easy chairs and a piano, 'and it is not unusual to see women of the mechanic class in here smoking, as well as the men'.[67] The short-lived 1890s journal *Dancing: A Journal Devoted to the Terpsichorean Art* also occasionally sent out reporters to such working-class venues. These included the Hall of Science on City Road (a hall for hire), where it found natives who, on being asked about the dance programme for the evening, replied 'Oh, the MC 'ollers out!'[68]

There were various new late Victorian venues which also permitted dancing, even if it was not their raison d'être. Grand hotels, the likes of the Savoy or the Langham, provided numerous amenities for wealthy guests, including restaurants and ballrooms. Civic buildings also increasingly served as respectable dance-halls for those a notch down the social scale. Holborn Town Hall, opened in 1880, had a galleried multi-purpose 'public hall', some 96 feet by 45 feet, which operated as a ballroom every Monday and Saturday, under the tutelage of a West End dancing-master H.R. Johnson. Elementary class was at 6 p.m., then a ball from 8 p.m. to 11.30 p.m. The balls were quaintly known as 'Cinderellas', because they were guaranteed to finish by midnight. They cost 1s 6d entrance, 2s per couple, or a seasonal subscription. One contemporary account describes the female clientele as waitresses and shop girls, keen to fill up their dance-cards (and meet potential husbands). The women, notes the reporter, wear ordinary indoor frocks, with a modest corsage. The young men are in dark suits and coloured ties. They are described as men who 'go by bus or by bicycle' – i.e. shop workers and clerks. More formal dress is reserved for special gala nights.

Town hall dances were a socially superior alternative to the potentially seedy dancing academy or low-class dancing-room. Balls at Holborn Town Hall even included a manual of etiquette, on sale for sixpence, with guidance on how to approach a dancing partner (and cope with refusal) and three degrees of bowing for different social occasions ('the profound or reverential, the medium, and the petit').[69] Holborn Town Hall also saw the first, and possibly only, demonstration of the Baden-Powell Schottische, by a Mr W.F. Hurndall, dressed as the hero in military khaki, presenting an interpretive dance of the siege of Mafeking ('Miss Dell will produce a bandage made up of a small Union Jack, and bind my wounds, whereupon I will get up and proceed with the dance, the public joining in'). This was, presumably, considered just the sort of thing to boost the morale of the humble clerks and shop men.

Smaller, respectable venues for dancing included a growing number of parish halls and temperance halls. Needless to say, they were often reserved for church and charity events; but they could also be hired out. This could sometimes cause difficulties. The owners of the Temperance Hall in Hulme, Manchester, were nonplussed to discover that the 'Manchester Pawnbrokers Association', renting the room for a ball in September 1880, was actually a front for a gay club night: the clientele was composed wholly of men, dressed in male and female masquerade costume. The feverish tabloid coverage of this same-sex dance, complete with whispered secret passwords and blind musicians, must have caused much embarrassment.

Another new type of venue which might host occasional dancing was the private working-men's club, which became a common feature of working-class districts in the 1880s and 1890s. Charles Booth would anatomise such clubs in his *Labour and Life of the People of London*. The typical East London political club, noted Booth, charged 6d a month subscription, plus 6d on the door. There was a bar, selling beer, spirits, tobacco and teetotal drinks; pub games such as billiards, bagatelle, cards and dominoes; a small library or room for reading newspapers. These were, in short, assembly rooms for the common man. The main function room might host weekly entertainment: music-hall acts, or amateur performances by members, and occasional dance nights, when members could bring their wives and sweethearts. Booth considered such clubs 'a bright and lively scene, and very attractive as compared to the ordinary homes of the classes from which the members are drawn'; but he distinguished them from 'proprietary' clubs, which refused all entry to strangers. Many of these more secretive venues, in London at least, were run by immigrants, and amounted to 'a combination of the lowest type of gambling hell with the lowest type of dancing saloon'.[70] Some were, in effect, a new breed of small night-club, and during the late 1880s and 1890s they increasingly came to the notice of the authorities. The Queen's Club in Hoxton Square, whose membership was a suspiciously low tuppence a month, was prosecuted as an unlicensed place of public entertainment in 1888. The police found that its total membership subscriptions only covered a quarter of its rent – never mind the expense of running the building. The principal money, rather, came from so-called 'guests' on the door, and sales of drink.[71] Many of these clubs were fairly temporary, makeshift affairs. In one issue of *Dancing*, the magazine's roving correspondent, accompanied by a policeman, braves Whitechapel to attend a 'Burglars' Dance' (disappointingly, only a dance at which the policeman happens to identify a burglar). The venue in question turns out to be a converted warehouse, with the first floor containing two billiard tables and a rough-and-ready bar, filled with barrels of beer and stout, and the second storey serving as a splinter-strewn dance floor, where clients could hop to the accompaniment of a piano. The men wear black outfits ('several respectably dressed . . . black-coated like myself, although, perhaps, the cut was not quite that of the West End') and women have on the outrageously plumed hats that pleased the female inhabitants of Whitechapel in the 1890s.[72]

There were also similar, but rather more upmarket, 'members' clubs' (hoping to avoid the need to apply for entertainment licensing) in the West End of the 1890s. These small night-clubs, many of which were managed by Italians and Germans, were to be found in Soho and Fitzrovia, either side of Oxford Street: the National Italian Club in Frith Street; the Eldorado Club in the Haymarket; the Gardenia in Leicester Square; the Palm Club and the Alsatian Club, on opposite sides of Oxford Street; the Victoria Supper Club in Charlotte Street. Most contained a bar, a small dance floor and a few quiet rooms for drinking and gambling. The conductor and writer James Glover, writing in 1911, recalled a police raid on the Gardenia in the 1890s:

the Inspector arrived at the psychological moment when a lady was dancing a can-can barefooted, on a table in the centre of the room, dressed in soiled spangled evening dress with a glass of champagne in one hand, and conducting the band with the other . . .[73]

Glover describes the West End clubs' male clientele as actors, musicians, music-hall artistes and sundry late-night party-goers; the female as prostitutes, actresses and kept women. None of these clubs were terribly large, but they were numerous and much frequented by theatre people, artists and other restless bohemians.

We have now sketched in full the plethora of small and medium-sized dance venues in the metropolis. Their sheer diversity, however, means there is no realistic way of gauging their combined popularity. The question of whether dancing was a mainstream commercial leisure activity remains debatable. How many people actually went dancing on a Saturday night in London in the 1890s? The figure will be nothing like the numbers attending music halls or public houses; but beyond that, it is very difficult to speculate.

We can at least state that the early promise of the casino was not fulfilled. The metropolitan casino was a dead end that failed to revolutionise the business of dancing. The experiment was swiftly concluded, although the original venues lingered on for some years. No one in London dared build palatial night-clubs that might rival the nascent palace of varieties during the late Victorian era. Potential entrepreneurs were far too wary of accusations of immorality and the implacability of licensing magistrates. The economics of scaling up dance-halls in the metropolis were also problematic: the space required for dancing on a larger scale required too much prime real estate. There was plainly more money to be made in music hall. The multi-tiered auditorium of the palace of varieties allowed one to pack considerably more people into the same-sized building.

The only places that did construct grand ballrooms for the general public, in the later years of the nineteenth century, were certain coastal resorts. Large seaside resorts, at their seasonal peak, contained a sufficiently large pool of potential customers, land was not at such a premium, and there was a long-standing tradition of dancing while on holiday. Many resorts had begun the nineteenth century with genteel assembly rooms. The larger working-class resorts, which blossomed in the late Victorian period, continued this customary holiday fun, but on a much grander scale. Douglas on the Isle of Man became well known for its 'dancing palaces' in the 1880s. Likewise, Blackpool in the 1890s, with its Tower Ballroom, and rival rooms at the Winter Gardens and Royal Palace Pleasure Gardens (which we will look at in Chapter Seven). The writer Hall Caine describes one such venue on the Isle of Man in his story *The Manxman* (1894), a vast galleried conservatory-style building:

Three thousand young men and young women were dancing, the men in flannels and coloured scarves, the women in light muslins and straw hats. Sometimes the white lights in the glass roof were coloured with red and blue and yellow. The low buzz of the dancers' feet, the clang and clash of the brass instruments, the boom of the big drum, the quake of the glass house itself, and the low rumble of the hollow floor beneath – it was like a battle-field set to music.[74]

The description fits the Palace Pavilion in the Castle Mona pleasure ground in Douglas, the Isle of Man's tourist-filled capital, although there were two other similar venues in the city. The Palace's real-life advertisements boasted 'the Largest Dancing Floor in the World, with an area of 16,000 Feet of Polished English Oak'.[75] The plot of *The Manxman*, incidentally, caused something of an outcry on the island: while watching the dancing, the lead character is propositioned by a fifteen-year-old prostitute, who claims to have been led astray by an earlier encounter with a tourist. The *Isle of Man Times* declared the author to be a desperate sensationalist: 'Our younger visitors are merry and lively, noisy and demonstrative in their mirth, and at times a trifle disorderly; but they do not go about the country seducing village girls of fifteen.'[76] Dance-halls maintained their unfortunate reputation, even at the end of the nineteenth century.

Ultimately, the dance venue that *did* sweep the nation was the interwar *palais de dance*, beginning with the Hammersmith Palais, which opened in 1919. It was American entrepreneurs who were behind that project, which followed a model already established in the United States. There were also by that time large and respectable chains of variety theatres, which provided something of an inspiration; and equally, those seaside ballrooms which continued to cater for working-class customers. Most of all, it was the craze for jazz that provided the spark for the interwar *palais*, much as polkamania had done for the casino. Dance fever had been building since 1912, with ragtime dances such as the 'turkey trot', 'bunny hug' and 'grizzly bear' crossing the Atlantic – and being banned in certain more stuffy venues. Post-war euphoria, and the growth of mass media, including the gramophone record, combined to create unprecedented enthusiasm for social dancing and dance music.[77]

V

𝕿𝖍𝖊 𝕻𝖑𝖊𝖆𝖘𝖚𝖗𝖊 𝕲𝖆𝖗𝖉𝖊𝖓

OR,

THE MIDNIGHT ROYSTERERS

THE COMMERCIAL PLEASURE GARDEN WAS not a Victorian invention. Vauxhall Gardens in Lambeth possessed a lineage dating back to the 1660s, when John Evelyn described the New Spring Garden at Fox-Hall as 'a pretty contrived plantation'. By the mid-eighteenth century, the landscaped garden contained assorted decorative additions: 'pavilions, lodges, groves, grottos . . . temples and cascades; porticos, colonnades and rotundas . . . pillars, statues and paintings'.[1] Trade was seasonal, restricted to the summer months, and the garden was open from early evening to the small hours. Visitors came to promenade, dine and listen to music outdoors. Rival gardens, large and small, peppered the fringes of the Georgian metropolis. Pleasure gardens were always situated in this liminal position, their lawns, shrubberies and arbours offering a carefully curated rusticity. Larger venues, like Vauxhall, operated as independent enterprises; smaller gardens were usually adjuncts to taverns. Some grounds also opened by day: Marylebone Gardens, although popular by night, offered breakfast with 'tea, coffee, cream, butter, etc.' and 'no improper company'.[2] The original attraction of Bagnigge Wells in Islington was its supposedly medicinal mineral waters. There were also simple 'tea-gardens' which offered afternoon tea or a pleasant supper.

Vauxhall, unlike most of its eighteenth-century competitors, survived into the Victorian era. The public continued to come to Lambeth not only for the numerous ornamental features, *trompe l'oeil*, music and dance, but increasingly for the grand spectacle: firework displays, balloon ascents and circus performers. Some, admittedly, considered Vauxhall a quaint Georgian relic. Modern-day historians have tended to adopt a similar attitude, treating nineteenth-century pleasure gardens as vestigial, doomed to failure. This dismissal is unmerited. Large new grounds would spring up in various parts of the metropolis, and further afield, *during* the nineteenth century. Pleasure gardens still seemed like a viable mass entertainment business. Some were entirely new sites, such as Rosherville Gardens in Gravesend, built in a landscaped former chalk pit (fl. 1837–1907). Others were in the grounds of existing public houses, such as Islington's Eagle Tavern (1822–82) or Highbury Barn (a Georgian tavern, which served as a full-fledged pleasure garden c.1847–71). Cremorne Gardens in Chelsea was originally a stately home, converted into a sports club in 1831, then finally into a pleasure garden (1843–77). There were only half a dozen large gardens in the metropolis in the mid-nineteenth century, and a dozen or so minor examples; but collectively, they daily (and nightly) catered for several thousand paying customers. There were similar Victorian grounds in other large cities, such as Manchester's Pomona Gardens (1845–88) and Belle Vue Gardens (1836–1980), and Birmingham's Aston Hall (1858–64).[3] The pleasure garden, therefore, was not merely a hangover from the Georgian period; and its nineteenth-century history forms a crucial part of the story of popular entertainment.

What exactly went on in the commercial pleasure garden, beyond drinking and dining? It is quite difficult to describe 'typical' pleasure-garden entertainments. The multifarious amusements differed not only from place to place, but from year to year. Novelty was very important. Managers of larger gardens could spend several thousand pounds each year, not only hiring new entertainers, but constructing entire new buildings: a different style of theatre; a new dancing platform; a more elaborate architectural folly. The press dutifully reported on these extensive alterations and improvements, and hopefully the public attended with renewed curiosity.

Vauxhall Gardens provides us with a useful initial benchmark. Indeed, such was its fame and longevity that 'Vauxhall' was often used as a straightforward synonym for 'pleasure garden': several other towns and cities – including New

York – boasted their own 'Vauxhall Gardens', named after the original.[4] If we take the 1820s as our starting point, visitors could arrive by road or via the Thames. The ground's location in South London was still relatively rural, although the bricks and mortar of the metropolis were beginning to encroach, helped by the opening of Vauxhall Bridge in 1816, which had created a convenient transport link to the West End. Vauxhall Gardens itself was an enclosed, cultivated park. The public came to saunter along its gravelled paths, down tree-lined avenues, lit by innumerable coloured oil lamps; or along canvas-covered cast-iron colonnades. One end of the gardens featured a 'dark walk' for those who required romantic privacy, but the overall impression was one of astonishing brightness and brilliance. The lights numbered in their thousands, and their sheer profusion more than compensated for the lack of modern, brighter gaslight.[5] One might come upon various talking points while taking a stroll: twin grand triumphal arches; a transparent portrait of George IV; a scene painting of a 'submarine cavern' with a real waterfall; the 'Heptaplasiesoptron' (a set of seven mirrors reflecting 'revolving pillars and palm-trees, twining serpents and a fountain of real water ... lighted by coloured lamps').[6] Throughout the site, paintings, panoramas and 'cosmoramas', which included three-dimensional effects and lighting, produced a magical, otherworldly feel. Many visitors, however, chose to inhabit the alcove-like supper-boxes along principal avenues, where groups could sit, dine and drink.

The key location in the grounds for actual entertainment was the 'orchestra', an elaborate two-storey gothic bandstand, with a built-in organ.[7] Musicians and singers performed from the open upper tier to rapt crowds. In bad weather, the music was adjourned to the gardens' circular Rotunda assembly room ('an Indian garden-room, the prevailing colours of which – scarlet, blue and yellow – are most effectively shewn by a sumptuous cut-glass chandelier').[8] Other buildings in the 1820s included a theatre where comedies and ballets were performed; an ornate platform for launching firework displays; a ballroom attached to the Rotunda; a 'hermitage' where one could have one's fortune told by the solitary inhabitant; and a gallery containing paintings on patriotic/military themes, along with a seemingly transparent 'magic clock'. Visitors could pick and choose from these diverse amusements. Concerts, both indoors and outdoors, were supplemented by variety acts: Ramo Samee, the famed Indian juggler; Mr Blackmore (stage name 'The American'), who performed nightly on the tight and slack rope while wearing a cap fitted with fireworks; Ching Lau Lauro, the acrobat and contortionist; Signor Spelterini, 'The Wonderful Italian Hercules'; and, in 1830, the peculiarly popular performance of Michael Boai, 'whose unrivalled MUSIC on his CHIN has drawn forth such great astonishment and delight'. Large open-air spectacles in the late 1820s included a firework-packed re-creation of the Battle of Waterloo and Cooke's Equestrian Circus (both were first seen at Astley's Amphitheatre, a popular venue for equestrian and circus shows, located nearby). One novel exhibition re-created James Clark Ross's expedition to the North Pole, replete with a ship entombed in faux icebergs, 'which are as large as reality, many being upwards of seventy feet high . . . seen floating on the waves . . . the whole Area of Ground appears as ONE ENTIRE MOVING MASS OF ICE'.[9] Ross's icebergs were not only elaborate and expensive to stage, but topical – the polar expedition was still very much in the public consciousness. This was, therefore, a particularly unique and extravagant display, since it could not be profitably repeated the following season.

Readers may be forgiven if they find this whirlwind tour somewhat bewildering. To a degree, the pleasure garden was a vacant space which could be filled with virtually any form of spectacle or popular amusement. Yet, picking through programmes from Vauxhall and other gardens that flourished in the nineteenth century, it is possible to discern three broad categories of entertainment. First, grand spectacles to draw in the crowds. These included novelties such as Ross's icebergs, but more typically fireworks, ballooning and tightrope walking. Secondly, musical and theatrical performances. And last but not least, social dancing.

The most common pleasure-garden spectacle was undoubtedly the firework display, rounding off the evening with a literal bang. Such displays dated back to the mid-eighteenth century and would remain a staple throughout the Victorian period. Pyrotechnics could also be incorporated into other performances, whether as a backdrop to circus acts performed outdoors, especially tightrope walkers, or during theatrical set pieces that made use of the extensive grounds, such as dramatic re-creations of famous battles. Patriotic themes for displays were always popular. During the 1850s, Cremorne Gardens in Chelsea staged its own explosive tributes to British troops fighting in both the Crimean War and the Indian Mutiny. Similarly, Manchester's Belle Vue and Pomona Gardens each had its own rival diorama of the Siege of Sebastopol, with nightly pyrotechnics restaging the onslaught.[10] Surrey Gardens in Walworth, on a less militaristic note, employed pyrotechnic and lighting effects to present the nightly eruption of Mount Vesuvius. Oriental settings were also popular, with the 'firing of the Golden Temple of Honan' playing for two seasons at Vauxhall, then transferring to Manchester.[11] Some pyrotechnicians were more radical in their choice of subject matter. Joseph Gyngell (aka 'Signor Gellini'), based at Rosherville Gardens in Gravesend, put on 'pyrotechnic ballets', which combined lights and fireworks with live performance. The 1855 season featured 'The Freaks of Will o' the Wisp', a highly topical allegory on cleanliness and public health in the age of cholera, with 'imps' representing individual epidemic diseases, vanquished by 'Hygeia', the spirit of health.[12]

The other great spectacle was the 'balloon ascent', popular ever since the Montgolfiers' first flight in 1783. Intrepid aeronauts launched themselves into the aether, accompanied by music and cheered on by a crowd of paying visitors. Vauxhall Gardens actually has its own peculiar place in the early history of aviation. The balloonist Charles Green set a long-distance flight record in the *Royal Vauxhall Balloon*, travelling from Lambeth to the Duchy of Nassau in Germany in 1836. His vehicle was promptly renamed the *Great Nassau*, and made further flights from Vauxhall and other gardens, drawing huge audiences. Balloon ascents were usually much-publicised special occasions rather than a nightly occurrence, but they were a great crowd-pleaser. Thomas Rouse, when establishing the Eagle Tavern in Islington in the 1820s, made sure to include ballooning in the pleasure garden's initial attractions. Rouse charged a shilling for entrance, which allowed a closer view of the balloon and its elaborate 'car', decorated with crimson velvet, festooned with fringes of deep green and yellow silk. A further shilling secured access to an 'inner ring' or stand, close to the launch site; and gentlemen occasionally paid a hefty premium to actually go along for the ride. The danger of ballooning was palpable, and the audience at the Eagle gasped when one aeronaut, named Harris, took along a volunteer from the crowd, one Miss Stocks, a mere thirteen-year-old girl, on an ascent in May 1824. Their fears were not unfounded: Mr Harris crashed the balloon in Carshalton, losing his life. Miss Stocks (who later turned out to be an eighteen-year-old out-of-work pastrycook 'of a romantic turn of mind') went on to become something of a minor celebrity.[13] The popularity of Rouse's balloon displays was such that surging crowds, unwilling or unable to pay a shilling, repeatedly blocked neighbouring roads and thronged adjoining rooftops. On one occasion, a makeshift scaffold erected on slum cottages behind the ground collapsed, leaving four people dead and several dozen spectators injured.

Professional balloonists toured not only different gardens in the metropolis, but different cities, too, transporting their apparatus by rail. Some were more professional than others. James Goulston (aka Signor Giuseppe Lunardini) died on the Oldham moors in 1852, with the newspapers avidly reporting his abrupt collision with various buildings and garden walls ('a quantity of blood and brains . . . another sickening splash of blood . . .').[14] He had departed from Manchester's Belle Vue Gardens, but first had travelled up by train from London. Goulston was something of an amateur daredevil, since his principal occupation was as owner of an oil-cloth factory in the Old Kent Road. He was reportedly entreated to abandon his flight because of poor weather conditions, but replied that he did not want to disappoint the waiting public.

Aeronauts also took up non-human companions. Monkeys and cats were released from airborne balloons, despatched from the heavens in their own miniature 'cars' with parachutes. This was supposedly a scientific experiment, but it conveniently also 'afforded great amusement to the children'.[15] Charles Green and others regularly ejected 'Signor Jacopo, The Celebrated Monkey' from balloons at Surrey Gardens and Vauxhall. Local residents kept a careful watch on the skies, since an attached label promised the finder £2 and free admission to the Surrey Zoological Gardens.[16] Some aeronauts took things a stage further: horses (and other quadrupeds) were tethered under the balloon, to be lifted into the air. A certain Madame Poitevin ascended from Cremorne Gardens on the back of a bull, depicting 'Europa and the Bull'. The balloon landed in Ilford, east of London, and the animal subsequently died of exhaustion and fright. However, during the Victorian period, public sentiment grew more hostile to blatant exploitation of animals. The Society for the Prevention of Cruelty to Animals successfully prosecuted Madame Poitevin and her husband, who was piloting the balloon. Cremorne Gardens' owner, T.B. Simpson, disingenuously blamed the animal's terrified demise on rowdy, unsophisticated locals who surrounded the fallen creature, remarking that a bull plummeting from the sky was 'a thing not seen every day in Essex'.[17] Frequenters of pleasure gardens could also enjoy the antics of occasional (human) parachutists, pilots of makeshift gliders and assorted 'flying machines'. Fatalities among the inventors of flying machines were predictably high. Vincent de Groof, for example, took off from Cremorne Gardens in 1874, tethered to a balloon in his winged 'machine', manufactured from cane and silk, with wings operated by levers. He had supposedly successfully piloted the device on a previous voyage on the Continent, reportedly 'flying' to earth from a height of 1,000 feet. Unfortunately, on this occasion, whether by accident or design, he detached from the balloon at a mere 80 feet. He was found dead, with multiple injuries, in the churchyard of St Luke's parish church, Chelsea.

Tightrope-walking was another death-defying feat that regularly featured in the grounds of pleasure gardens. The French tightrope artiste Marguerite Antoinette Lalanne ('Madame Saqui') set the example in 1816, descending a rope which ran along one of the main walks at Vauxhall. The rope was tethered to two giant poles resembling ships' masts, and the whole performance was carried on against a backdrop of exploding fireworks. Others, male and female, followed suit, including Selina Young, 'The Female Blondin', aka Madame Genevieve, who famously crossed the Thames on a tightrope, from the Surrey side to Cremorne, in 1861. The risks were very real. Young would suffer a crippling, career-ending fall while performing at Highbury Barn Gardens, distracted by fireworks affixed to either end of her balancing pole. Carlo Valerio fell and died at Cremorne, toppling from a rope poorly tethered between two of the grounds' ancient trees. Another 'Female Blondin', one Selina Powell, died while performing at Aston Hall in Birmingham. The tightrope walk, nevertheless, remained a pleasure-garden standard. Performing outdoors allowed for the dramatic backdrop of the firework display, and gave an opportunity to set up equipment at whatever height/distance one saw fit. Other dangerous acts could also take advantage of an outdoor space. Signor Sebastiano Botturi walked through a burning shed in a fire-proof suit which resembled 'a Polar Bear on its hind legs . . . [with] two glass eyes, or rather windows, which glared without speculation on the company'. *The Times* reviewed Botturi rather harshly: 'the shed was much too small, and the stay of the Signor within it much too short'.[18] Still, such risks could never have been taken inside a theatre.

Pleasure-garden entertainment was not all about dangerous stunts. The outdoor setting favoured the spectacular and sensational; but fireworks, rope-walkers and the rest were usually only one aspect of a larger programme of entertainment, much of which was conducted in halls and theatres that formed part of the property. There were also considerably more tame circus performers and variety acts. Favourites at Cremorne were the 'Beckwith Frogs', the family of Fred Beckwith, a champion swimmer. They appeared underwater in a specially made glass tank, performing such mundane tasks as 'smoking' a pipe or 'eating' breakfast.

* * *

The principal musical offerings differed little from performances in regular theatres and concert-rooms/music halls. Comic songs were highly popular in Vauxhall in the 1820s. Printed song-books containing the season's comedy hits could even be purchased in the gardens (for one shilling and sixpence). The great smash hit of 1823 was 'Polly Hopkins', sung by Miss Tunstall and Mr Mallinson. In the song, the self-possessed heroine tartly spurns her would-be lover's advances:

> *He* – When dead and buried, Polly Hopkins, you'll think of me, you'll think of me.
> *She* – Just as you please, Mister Tomkins, so let it be; so let it be.
> *He* – You'll fret and cry –
> *She* – Cry! to be sure.
> *He* – To think that I –
> *She* – Didn't die before.

Miss Tunstall and Mr Mallinson were not exclusively performers at pleasure gardens; nor were they from the world of the pub concert-room, which had not yet quite emerged from the harmonic meeting. They came from a theatrical background and were considerably better paid than the average 'room singer' (records from the gardens show Miss Tunstall and colleagues on £5 a week during the summer season). Mallinson had previously toured the country, appearing at various theatres – principally as a comic singer – including a stint in the north-east where he proved highly popular, until 'he sung [*sic*] a song about Adam and Eve which was considered rather too gross by the religious people of Hull'.[19] Catherine 'Kitty' Tunstall appeared at Vauxhall in 1816, 1820 and 1823–25, but she had begun her career at Drury Lane and the Olympic Theatre. Beyond the capital, she appeared in venues as diverse as the Theatre Royal, Bath; the Apollo Gardens in Yarmouth (a minor provincial 'Vauxhall'); and the Royal Amphitheatre, Liverpool (a venue principally for circus and equestrian acts). Several of these excursions were provincial tours, where she was billed as appearing with fellow artistes from both Drury Lane and Vauxhall.

Had Catherine Tunstall been born but a few years later, she might well have been part of the music-hall scene. She appeared at a benefit performance for Pierce Egan at the Surrey Theatre in 1836 with none other than the omnipresent *improvisatore* Charles Sloman. She also performed as Kitty Tunstall in the early years of the Grecian Saloon. This was not unusual. The self-same singers appeared in pleasure gardens, theatres and, increasingly, music halls, performing the same material. Pleasure-garden proprietors did not discriminate and booked whoever seemed popular with the public. The only difference was that large pleasure gardens could occasionally afford to showcase superstars. Paganini gave several performances at Vauxhall in the early 1830s. The eccentric, but hugely popular, Louis-Antoine Jullien conducted the orchestra at Surrey Gardens, although he was rather disappointed to be paid in £2,000 worth of valueless shares, shortly before the Surrey Gardens Company went bust in 1855.[20] He also took an orchestra on tour to gardens in Manchester, Liverpool and Birmingham.[21]

Theatrical performances, similarly, were rarely unique to the pleasure garden. They were, however, of a type. With so much on offer within the grounds, audiences were easily distracted. Short comic pieces, therefore, predominated. The 'vaudevilles' of William Thomas Moncrieff were typical: short comic plays punctuated by comic songs. Amusingly enough, one of Moncrieff's works, *How to Take up a Bill; or The Village Vauxhall*, features a debt-laden young man hastily improvising a pleasure garden – 'Bacchus Gardens' – in the grounds of his uncle's country villa. The garden already contains arbours for relaxing, eating and drinking; the summer house is pressed into service as 'Orchestra and Concert room'; the wine cellar is emptied for saleable alcohol; the cook is told to cut the ham very fine (the ham at Vauxhall Gardens was notoriously thin). Turnpike tickets are given out as passes to the grounds; and visitors instantly appear. The play, for all the exaggerated comedy, touches upon most of the key elements of the pleasure-garden experience.

There were inevitably some eye-catching novelties put upon the pleasure-garden stage, including shadow pantomimes, puppetry and carefully staged *poses plastiques*, first introduced at Vauxhall in the 1830s. Cremorne Gardens briefly possessed a dedicated 'Marionette Theatre', but this was swiftly converted to more general use after the puppets proved unpopular. Pleasure-garden theatres could hold anything from magicians and mesmerists to the ever-popular freak show; whatever might draw the public. The Victorians enjoyed staring at all manner of excessively tall, short, hairy and 'malformed' individuals. 'The Hirsute Kostroma People: From the Primeval Forest of Central Russia' feature in a rare surviving advertisement from Cremorne. A handbill for the Eagle Tavern in 1830 simply mentions 'The Giraffe Girl', with no further explanation. There were other anthropological objects of curiosity. Robert Wardell, who managed Vauxhall for much of the 1840s, initially took the gardens principally to showcase the Ioway Indians: a touring troupe of Native Americans, displaying their skills in archery and horsemanship, as well as their wigwams, forming a 'picturesque encampment' in the grounds. Once again, these were not performances unique to the pleasure garden. During the same season, the Ioway Indians would also set up camp at Lords Cricket Ground and perform an evening show at the Egyptian Hall in Piccadilly.

The final great attraction in larger gardens was the 'dancing platform'. These were sprung wooden dance floors, built around a showy exotic 'orchestra' (i.e. a bandstand for the musicians, like the ornate gothic construction at Vauxhall). Cremorne Gardens had an elaborate Chinese pagoda, built in 1847. Musicians performed on the upper tier, and there was a refreshment counter on the lower, with dancers swirling around it. The pagoda was further ornamented in 1857 with innumerable cut-glass droplets and festoons of gaslights, and dubbed the 'Crystal Platform'. The actual dancing provided a spectacle in itself. Crowds sat at tables on the periphery, downing their drinks and watching the whirling participants. The management also installed twin tiers of supper-boxes around the platform, where visitors could take a full meal, sip champagne and still enjoy the view. Most large grounds also had grand ballrooms for when the weather took a turn for the worse. Highbury Barn, for instance, had a 'Leviathan' outdoor dancing platform ('beautifully illuminated, and has a very handsome gaselier in the centre, representing a group of Calla plants in full blossom'), but it also possessed an equally glamorous ballroom, with sparkling mirrors, enormous gaslight chandeliers and extensive scenic paintings of Egypt and the Nile.[22]

Focusing on dance as an al fresco entertainment was the great Victorian contribution to the pleasure garden. It was not unknown before the 1840s – the Dandelion Gardens in Margate, for example, had a platform at the start of the century – but the dancing platform's scale and importance increased.[23] Platforms seem to have expanded and multiplied in response to the craze for the polka, which (as we have seen) swept the nation in the mid-1840s. In 1846, Vauxhall acquired a large new stage in front of its orchestra, which previously was more of a place for listening to music and for the occasional impromptu twirl. In 1850, Belle Vue Gardens in Manchester advertised that it had more than doubled its platform to 15,000 square feet, capable of entertaining a hundred quadrille parties. At Whitsun, three brass bands were employed 'that dancing may continue during the entire day, without interruption'.[24] The Belle Vue orchestra was later rebuilt in an Arabesque style and fixed on a revolving turntable. The table could shift the players' position to compensate for a strong wind damp-ening the sound; or alternatively, it could rotate the band more towards a larger patch of open ground, which was used for dancing whenever the platform was full.[25] Vauxhall boasted in 1851 that its platform, once again extended, could now accommodate 2,000 people, with 'the largest complete Quadrille and Waltz Band in England'. In 1853, a second circular platform was erected at the rear of the Vauxhall orchestra, 'on scientific principles, affording space for several Thousand Couples'.[26] Surrey Gardens, which began as a menagerie (Surrey Zoological Gardens) and then hosted promenading to music, finally sold off its animals and became a full-fledged 'Vauxhall' with the belated erection of a dancing platform in 1858 ('under the talented direction of Mr. Le Vete, whose urbanity of manners amongst the lady patrons is highly commendable').[27]

The social mix of pleasure-garden patrons varied a good deal from place to place. The Eagle Tavern was founded in the 1820s, on the borders of the densely popu-lated working-class East End of London. This population formed its natural demographic. The grounds included the Grecian Saloon and assorted lesser attractions, such as a mock-ruined Greek temple, backed by a scenic panorama of Tunbridge Wells Spa; and a second-hand gothic archway, first used in the coronation of William IV (which provided justification for the more grandiose – though little-used – title of 'Royal Eagle Coronation Pleasure Grounds'). Charles Dickens describes a night at the Eagle in *Sketches by Boz*. His protago-nists, Samuel Wilkins and Jemima Evans, are a carpenter and shoe-binder on a date. The Eagle's regular customers are described elsewhere as 'young shop-keepers, artisans and apprentices . . . milliners and dress makers, draper's shop-women and domestic servants . . . the unphilosophical aborigines of the City-road and Shoreditch'.[28] Cremorne Gardens in Chelsea, on the other hand, charged exactly the same price for admission as the Eagle (a single shilling) but attracted a more middle-class crowd, including more in the way of clerks and members of the professions. This, too, was thanks to its location, by the Thames, on the western borders of the metropolis. This meant there was no substantial working-class population in the immediate vicinity, and most customers had to come by public or private transport. Travel added considerably to the price of a night out. Steamboats to Chelsea from central London, the cheapest mode of travel, cost three or four pence each way. Moreover, while the Eagle granted each visitor a sixpenny 'refreshment ticket', included in the price, Cremorne was notorious for its additional fees and charges. Social balance in the pleasure garden also varied according to the day of the week and time of year. Manchester's Belle Vue Gardens was said to attract large working-class crowds on Saturday and Monday nights, because wages were traditionally paid on Saturday evenings. Wednesday evenings, on the other hand, were 'especial and favourite times for those who can afford to go any evening'.[29] More generally, the Easter and Whitsun holidays gave workers opportunity to visit such places of entertainment.

Some pleasure gardens undoubtedly grew more plebeian as the century progressed, chasing the emerging working-class mass-market. This shift was very noticeable at Vauxhall, which had once been a fashionable night-spot for the *bon ton* of Georgian London (albeit where they mingled, to a degree, with the lower orders). By the 1820s, the aristocracy was in retreat, preferring social exclusivity and only attending Vauxhall for one-off expensive charitable fetes, which might cost as much as a guinea. The grounds' regular admission price of four shillings was still intended to appeal to the middle classes: doctors, lawyers, clerks, students, well-to-do shopkeepers, merchants and their families. Profits, however, began to diminish in the late 1820s, and admission was slashed to a single shilling in 1833, finally making Vauxhall affordable for the artisan and workman. This was also a boon for young gentlemen about town, attracting working-class women looking for a night out ('All the mantua-makers' girls and the chandler-shopkeepers' daughters can come now . . .').[30] There was still a certain faux gentility maintained, even down to the signs in the gardens forbidding the smoking of cigars in public; but the class of customer changed dramatically. The grounds, as it happened, would continue to struggle financially. Multiple proprietors quit in the face of bankruptcy during Vauxhall's final two decades, and prices varied between a shilling and half a crown. Any remaining pretence that the gardens catered to the elite vanished.

Surrey Zoological Gardens, likewise, began in 1831 under the patronage of Queen Adelaide, with a list of wealthy and respectable subscribers who could obtain shilling tickets for friends and family. The gardens later acquired the patronage of the young Victoria, who was said to admire the giraffes very much. By the 1870s, things had changed considerably. After suffering financial mismanagement – and several years of closure, during which the grounds were let to St Thomas's Hospital – they fell under the management of Frederick

Strange, formerly of the Alhambra Music Hall. Entertainments now included not only operatic concerts, but Professor Brown ('The Aquatic Velocipedist'), Professor Burman (a magician), 'steam circus, shooting saloons, Cave of Mystery, Wire Walkers, Dogs and Monkies, Dagger Throwers, Cosmoramas, Wizards, Ghosts, Swings', etc.[31] The price was still a shilling, but this was no longer a place for a quiet promenade in superior company.

Indeed, during the mid-century, London's pleasure gardens began to acquire more of a fairground atmosphere. Large metropolitan fairs, such as Greenwich Fair and St Bartholomew's Fair, had been abolished by local authorities weary of annual complaints about riot, noise and crime. Pleasure-garden proprietors spotted an opportunity. Such attractions were not entirely a novelty. The Eagle Tavern, not long after it had opened in the 1820s, included 'Russian mountains', a primitive form of rollercoaster, made famous in the Tivoli Gardens in Paris. The inspiration for this experiment was probably nearer home: the incorporation of the said 'mountains' into a play at nearby Sadler's Wells Theatre during the previous summer ('with the Cars descending on an inclined Plane . . . across the Orchestra to the Back of the Pit, with the most perfect Safety').[32] Likewise, the gardens at Copenhagen House, a local rival to the Eagle, contained an 'Up and Down', a gondola-style swing consisting of four carriages, each capable of holding ten people.[33] St Helena Gardens in Rotherhithe opened a centrifugal railway, a single loop rollercoaster, in 1851, to draw some of the crowds flocking to the Great Exhibition. By the 1860s, however, the fairground attractions were more prominent and the quiet satisfaction of strolling around gravel walks was being supplanted by amusements 'not much above the level of a good country fair . . . [and] booths where you may play at losing games for prizes not worth winning'.[34]

This shift in emphasis is humorously captured in James Payn's *Lights and Shadows of London Life* (1867), a comic tale of an innocent traveller, returned from a long spell in the colonies, who is shown the nocturnal delights of London. Our hero is led to believe that Cremorne Gardens is a 'fête champêtre given in a nobleman's grounds', a select rendezvous for the upper class, but is soon disabused of the notion when he spots patrons downing 'shandy gaff' (beer and ginger beer, mixed). He dines al fresco on cold meats, pie and lobster salad. He watches couples dance waltzes and Schottisches on the dancing platform, and notes that the men drink and smoke freely, despite the mixed company. He pays an extra shilling to have his fortune told in the Hermit's Cave, another sixpence to gawp at an 8-foot 'giant', and yet another shilling to observe the 'Woolly

Woman' ('she is genuine; you are at liberty to take hold of this lock of hair and pull it – in moderation').[35] He watches a ballet, shoots an air-gun, rambles through the maze, and finally wanders home. The aristocratic *fête champêtre* is more like a fairground, with money extracted from the visitor at every turn. This rapacity was also a much-repeated complaint among real-life visitors.

Similarly, the home missionary James Inches Hillocks, writing in the mid-1860s, describes the vulgar attractions at Highbury Barn:

> The weighing machine is in full operation, at a penny a-head. The owner, anxious to gratify his female customers, while filling up the card, and giving it to the girl, takes care to assure her that she is precisely the weight of the Princess Royal previous to her marriage. This is done in such a manner as to give an opportunity for some lewd remark and a roar of laughter. There, too, were the vendors of moustaches and paste-board noses, of all shapes and colours, 'for the small charge of one penny.' The moustache and the nose serving as a kind of mask . . .[36]

This was a real metamorphosis for Highbury Barn, which had begun the 1800s as a genteel rural retreat, known only for cakes and ale, and occasional cricket matches between the local gentry. The change into a pleasure garden occurred under the managements of Archibald Hinton (1847–60) and the comedian Edward Giovanelli (1861–70). The former built a dancing platform, reduced entrance to a mere sixpence, and transformed the old tavern into a fashionable resort, with '[emptied] champagne bottles on every landing'.[37] The latter introduced music-hall acts and built a dedicated music hall and theatre. A flyer from 1870 – advertising a 'Grand Bal D'Opera Al Fresco: Derby Night!' – captures the jaunty populist tone of Giovanelli's tenure. The proprietor and two of his actresses appear in caricature as jockeys in the race, while the text below offers tips for the winning horses ('GIOVANELLI'S TIP FOR THE DERBY . . . *Come to the Bal D'Opera Al Fresco, and tell him if his is wrong!*'). Vertical sidebars promote a comedy in the grounds' Alexandra Theatre, *Bluebeard*, starring Giovanelli himself; and a 'French Eccentric Troupe' performing the 'Royal Can-can'.[38]

North Woolwich Gardens, which opened in 1851 as another working-class pleasure garden, had customers travelling from the East End by the Eastern Counties Railway. The diarist Arthur Munby found the clientele 'respectable looking artisan folk, men, wives and damsels'.[39] It, too, steadily accumulated all sorts of fairground amusements: rifle galleries, a steam-powered merry-go-round, 'punching the head of a lay figure specially constructed to try your strength', and the opportunity to receive shocks from a galvanic battery.[40] This was followed in 1870 by the introduction of a novelty: a barmaid show, which proved so popular that it became an annual event. Young women were to stand behind separate mock-bars in an exhibition hall and serve drinks to visitors over a period of six days. The women originally were judged by a jury; but in later years the public handed their preferred barmaid a ticket to register their vote. The barmaids were to dress 'plainly' but with 'a happy blending of colours'; to 'ingratiate' themselves in the most affable manner, but 'without undue forwardness or frivolity'. This must have been something of a fine balancing act. This peculiar beauty contest reportedly drew numerous young men to the gardens, although not all were impressed (one letter writer complaining 'among the 30, only two had any pretensions to personal attraction'). In 1881, for a little variety, the barmaids were housed in mock-ups of Tudor inns, and dressed according to the period. Some considered the barmaid exhibition not only the height of vulgarity, but morally dubious, concluding that it contributed to making North Woolwich 'a place where young persons might be tempted to acts of imprudence'.[41]

Unsurprisingly, the morals of pleasure-garden visitors were the subject of some scrutiny. This was principally about individual gardens providing a meeting place for prostitutes and their clients. On occasion, there were also complaints about actual al fresco sexual encounters. The long-established 'dark walk' at Vauxhall provided convenient anonymity for sexual adventures in the early nineteenth century. Licensing magistrates, pressured by the complaints of a local clergyman, made a point of requiring Vauxhall's owners to better illuminate their property.[42]

The Eagle Tavern, likewise, had a certain reputation:

the cockneys are the least particular or decent in their wooings and their cooings . . . and in certain gardens, at eleven o'clock at night, one can hardly turn a corner or cross a grass-plat without invading the *al fresco* beds of lads and lasses from the shops and factories.[43]

On one side of the place, there are a number of private arbours and boxes, so private that it requires no small effort to discover them . . . the ingenuity of man has given a spur to the agencies of vice; and here the courtesan can point triumphantly to the scene of many a guilty hour . . .[44]

The former quote, we should note, forms part of an extensive rant against the garden's plebeian pleasures; the latter comes from a magazine which 'exposed' London's nocturnal vices, principally for the purposes of titillation.[45] Unbiased evidence of sexual activity in pleasure gardens, such as contemporary court cases, is actually rather hard to track down. *Sewell* v. *Topham* (1862) provides one example: an accusation against a medical student of 'seduction' in Surrey Gardens, leading to pregnancy. This was a civil action, which relied on showing that a 'previously chaste' young woman had been persuaded or pressured into sexual relations, with the promise of marriage. Miss Sewell gave evidence in court:

I walked with him about the gardens for about three-quarters of an hour. We then sat down . . . I continued sitting on one of the seats with the defendant in a secluded part of the garden . . . [The] defendant commenced taking liberties with me, and afterwards had intercourse with me. He said I should not leave the gardens until I had yielded to him. He said nothing in particular, but I knew what he meant. He said if I got into trouble *he would get me out of it*, and if I was a good girl, he would make me his wife.[46]

The defendant claimed that the gardens were too crowded for unobserved congress, while gallantly conceding, 'It was my intention, if I had an opportunity.' The jury awarded Miss Sewell's mother £20 redress (such was 'seduction' law: 'for loss of her daughter's services').

Sewell v. *Topham* is something of a rarity. Many more press accounts exist of sexual transgression in London's royal parks than in its pleasure gardens. Researching the history of Hyde Park, one uncovers police cases involving prostitution, flashing, homosexual encounters and paedophilia. This difference may be because pleasure gardens were private property. Cases of 'public indecency' involving consenting adults may have been kept quiet, rather than rushed to the attention of the authorities. Yet we should not dismiss the possibility that pleasure gardens were, for the most part, what their proprietors claimed: well lit, well policed and relatively chaste. Some apparently verged on the morally spotless. A female journalist remarked of Manchester's Belle Vue

Gardens that they would please the most rigid puritan, given the great consumption of milk in the refreshment rooms, in preference to alcohol.[47] The grounds were hardly dry. During Whit week in 1852, Mancunians downed 150 barrels of porter within the gardens, albeit leavened by 32,000 bottles of ginger beer and 35,000 Eccles cakes (with a bakery on site to cope with demand). But minimal spirits were consumed, in stark contrast to the likes of Cremorne in London. Belle Vue's refreshments room, moreover, was built specifically to accommodate families bringing their own lunches. The gardens themselves closed at around 10 p.m., as soon as the firework display had ended, to the tune of 'God Save the Queen'.[48] This was not a place for late-night carousing.

Equally, there is no doubt that certain London pleasure gardens did provide a convenient 'place of assignation', where bargains could be struck before the parties retired to a nearby 'house of ill-fame'. Vauxhall was notorious in this regard in the early nineteenth century. A contemporary court report records the arrest of four teenage prostitutes on the premises, aged 13–17, who were forced to work from a nearby brothel, opened by their East End pimps specifically to target the gardens' clientele.[49] In 1831, on the night of a popular 'Juvenile Fete', where children's entertainment predominated, it was said that the gardens were 'as well stocked with harlots as on ordinary occasions'.[50] The temperance campaigner James Balfour, likewise, reported of the Eagle Tavern:

> No gentleman, well dressed, can promenade there without being solicited by a female to go to houses of accommodation outside, whether he be aged, middle-aged or young. I had not sat down five minutes when I was solicited twice, and told that there were houses outside for me to go to.[51]

The London City Mission, waging a war against Sunday opening in the early 1840s, singled out the Eagle for accommodating up to 5,000 visitors a night, including, it was alleged, 'nearly 1,000 fashionably dressed women of loose character'.[52] We cannot rely too much on these figures. There was a puritanical tendency to condemn working-class girls who visited places like the Eagle for social dancing, coming in groups from the workshops of nearby Clerkenwell and Shoreditch, as 'loose women' (i.e. by virtue of their very presence in such a place). Nevertheless, soliciting does seem to have occurred.

Chelsea's Cremorne Gardens, most of all, was *the* place where prostitutes were widely acknowledged to be regular customers, principally during the hours of darkness. These included many women who kept their own carriages and rented a modest house or apartment nearby. The reason was a quirk of Cremorne's history, a unique association with the 'fast' night-life of the West End, even though Covent Garden and the Haymarket lay 3 miles distant.

Cremorne Gardens was something of a one-off and had a suitably peculiar start. Baron de Berenger, also known as Charles Random, an eccentric marksman and gunsmith, opened the property in 1831, having purchased the country home and grounds of the recently deceased Lady Cremorne on the banks of the Thames.[53] De Berenger's plan was to open not a pleasure garden, but rather 'The Stadium', a subscription-based sports club/venue for gentlemen.[54] De Berenger stated that he was promoting healthy exercise, to counter what he saw as a rising tide of indolence, unmanliness and even the abuse of opium, the 'dry-rot' in the national character.[55] He therefore proposed that the government underwrite this much-needed project; but if it would not, he also offered 500 shares at £100 each. No one seems to have taken up the share offer, nor did the government intervene. De Berenger proceeded regardless.

The Stadium, unfortunately, proved something of a flop. De Berenger kept going, holding occasional gala nights, with fireworks and others spectacles; and on one notable occasion, he lent the gardens to Lord Sandwich for an 'aristocratic fete'. But he struggled to make any money. In 1843, therefore, de Berenger finally let out the grounds to a third party. The ownership of the gardens under this arrangement was rather labyrinthine, as subsequent law suits would attest. The precise details need not detain us, but three key figures were involved: 'Baron' Renton Nicholson; James Ellis; and Thomas Bartlett Simpson. Together, they would forge a unique link between the pleasure garden in Chelsea and the capital's bohemian, late-night milieu, centred on the Haymarket and Covent Garden.

The self-styled 'Baron' Renton Nicholson was already well known to the pleasure-seeking public. He ran the infamously bawdy, men-only 'Judge and Jury Club' at the Garrick's Head Hotel on Bow Street, staging comic mock trials in the pub's concert-room ('Lushington Jinks against Matilda Rose Squineye, spinster . . . will demonstrate the folly of single gentlemen who have passed the days of puberty and perfection, confiding in the fictitious passions of jilting dress-makers').[56] The Garrick's Head was the archetypal Covent Garden 'night-house': a slightly disreputable, late-night venue, beloved by students and 'flash' young men. It was also something of a tourist destination. Country folk coming up to town on holiday or business sought out Nicholson's infamous hostelry. Outlining his CV at a bankruptcy hearing, Nicholson would describe himself as not only landlord of the Garrick's Head, but 'Proprietor of the Turf Rendezvous and Appollonian [sic] Hall, New Bond-street ... Hotel-keeper, Theatrical Manager and Author ... Lecturing on Poetry and Song, illustrated by Tableaux Vivans, Female American Serenaders ... and having Booths at Fairs, Races, and Regattas'.[57] He was, in short, a larger-than-life 'character' with connections to the sporting fraternity, and well known to men about town.

James Ellis was more involved behind the scenes in West End entertainment. He was a 'refreshment contractor', with catering contracts at Her Majesty's Theatre, The Lyceum, Crockford's, the Princess's Concert Rooms in Oxford Street and the famous Hanover Square Rooms in Mayfair. He would also, as we have already noted, open the Adelaide Gallery, near the Strand, as a 'casino' to offer a winter dance-hall for his customers.

Finally, Thomas Bartlett Simpson was a publican, landlord of the Albion Tavern c.1830–50, a celebrated theatrical hostelry directly opposite the pit door of the Theatre Royal Drury Lane. He had organised a 'Neapolitan Carnival and Masquerade' at Drury Lane in 1839, and occasionally provided drinks for similar events; and he had helped Nicholson establish himself at the Garrick's Head. But this was the limit of his prior entertainment experience, before becoming involved with Cremorne Gardens. He proved to be the most financially secure of the three men, buying out Cremorne's freehold and going on to run the gardens by himself between 1851 and 1860. Again, he was very much part of the same milieu – publicans, theatre managers, owners of late-night cafés, cigar shops, restaurants, etc. – that maintained the night-side of London.[58]

Nicholson was perhaps the most important of this trio in the beginning. As the 'Lord Chief Baron' at the Judge and Jury Club, he had something of a fanbase among impressionable youth. He issued numerous classified ads simultaneously advertising both venues. But all three men had the right connections to actively promote Cremorne Gardens in the West End. The result was that the new pleasure gardens soon became a fashionable 'finish' for the habitués of the capital's night haunts. A veritable convoy of black cabs would wind their way from central London to Chelsea, containing tipsy young bucks and assorted hangers-on, who then partied into the small hours beside the Thames. Cremorne, consequently, became a noted hunting ground for London's more ambitious *demi-mondaines*, following the money. The gardens' manager in the 1860s, the theatrical impresario E.T. Smith even opened a sister restaurant in Leicester Square, trading on the gardens' links to the West End. This was the Cremorne Branch Restaurant or Cremorne Supper Rooms at 1 New Coventry Street, which offered a restaurant meal for half a crown.[59]

There were, in effect, two faces to Cremorne Gardens. By day, it was patronised by respectable families, much like Manchester's Belle Vue Gardens; whereas, as night fell, a change occurred:

> In the early evening, the gardens were crowded with family parties, servants, soldiers, and their sweethearts, small tradesmen, and country visitors. It was then that the tea and shrimps were in request . . . But, with the display of fireworks, respectable people went home to bed . . . Fast men about town came down in hansoms after the opera, and the ladies of Brompton and Pimlico and St. John's Wood drove up in their broughams . . . a miscellaneous medley of swells, betting men, kept women and common prostitutes . . .[60]

Cremorne's late-night reputation only grew worse as the years progressed. It was often spoken of in the same breath as the Holborn Casino and the Argyll Rooms. When Lord Ingestre hired the gardens for a charitable aristocratic fete in 1858, he faced a barrage of press criticism condemning him for choosing such a dubious location. Was this a fit place for the aristocracy? *Punch*, mocking the moral agonising, set out a fake flyer for the event, including: 'Regulations: 1. All Married Ladies and Widows to produce their Marriage Certificates at the door.' Radical newspapers were more serious, accusing upper-class women of dabbling in 'aristocratic Traviatism' (i.e. copying the antics of West End prostitutes).[61] The women, it was claimed, wished to see the haunts of vice, while maintaining their own social elitism. This was, in other words, a species of slumming.[62]

Cremorne, like the Holborn Casino and Argyll, featured in numerous divorce cases in the 1860s, and various tangential references to the so-called *demi-monde* are scattered through the press. One Rose Brookes, a regular in the gardens, self-confessedly 'on the town', was drawn into a legal dispute with a carriage-maker in 1865. She had ordered a miniature brougham with all the trimmings – monogrammed doors, silver-plated lamps, 'a card basket with ivory screw sockets', 'a looking glass to drop down from the roof' – but fell into a disagreement about the terms. She stated that she had chosen the company because she saw them exhibit their latest models at the gardens, and the cachet of owning a carriage would help her successfully pursue her vocation with Cremorne's wealthier visitors.[63]

The uninhibited late-night crowd could grow rather raucous. These were young men for whom 'an intimacy with some flyblown demirep of uncertain age or a brawl with a waiter or policeman at Cremorne' was considered a rite of passage.[64] Many were 'gents' rather than gentlemen: lower-middle-class youth, mocked for aping their aristocratic betters. Derby-night 'rioters' found guilty of starting a fight in 1863 included one young man of independent means from the north of England, but also an architect's clerk from Bath, a soldier on leave of absence from his barracks and a draper's clerk. They had nothing in common, except that they were young, drunk and had come to visit one of the most famous night-spots in the metropolis.

Cremorne's late-night clientele under Nicholson and his successors inevitably led to objections from local residents. In 1845, five householders of nearby Cheyne Walk complained to magistrates who were preparing to renew the *music and dancing* licence that balloon ascents were attracting dissolute characters. When this proved unsuccessful, a petition was raised against the liquor licence, led by Mrs Leicester Stanhope. She was Cremorne's next-door neighbour, and her children 'had picked up some very distressing language' over the garden wall. It was also alleged that property prices had been depressed; that there was immoral conduct; and that no one could sleep thanks to the noise nuisance.[65] A Mr Flood, formerly a Kensington magistrate, raised a new petition against the drinks licence in 1850, claiming that 'the devil dwelt on the banks of the Thames'.[66] In 1857, the same year in which a campaign was waged against Haymarket prostitution, a 'Ratepayers Association' was formed specifically to lobby the local vestry to close the gardens. The existing local vestrymen were persuaded, somewhat reluctantly, to forward complaints to the magistrates' bench. The list was predictable: noise from fireworks; noise from late-night carousing; roads blocked by cabs of the West End crowd; prostitution; and claims of a drop in neighbouring house prices and empty unlet properties. It is worth noting that these gripes were very much from a local clique, who set up their private 'Association'. One resident wrote to the papers to state that he regularly took his wife and children to the gardens, and the nuisance was greatly outweighed by the amenity. Finally, after something of a lull during the 1860s, Rev. Canon Cromwell, of the nearby St Mark's Training College, was instrumental in persuading the magistrates to strip the gardens of its *music and dancing* licence on multiple occasions. This contributed to the gardens' eventual decline and closure in 1877.

Cremorne was not unique in facing opposition from its neighbours. There was a similar long-running moral campaign against Highbury Barn in Islington, which some dubbed 'the North London Cremorne'. In 1854, a petition of 143 residents, championed by another local clergyman, the Rev. Collison, complained of the introduction of dancing at the gardens. They noted, accurately, that the proprietor, Archibald Hinton, had obtained his *music and dancing* licence supposedly for musicians to play at public dinners. Instead, there was brass-band music blasting out dance music from 4 p.m. until 11 p.m. daily. They suggested that the low charge of only sixpence was bringing in disreputable characters, including prostitutes; and, worst of all, that the noise of people leaving the gardens kept them awake at night. They succeeded in temporarily denying Hinton his entertainment licence.

Hinton, in turn, issued a lengthy apologia through the medium of *The Times* letters column. He said that he had suffered financially from the opening of the Crystal Palace at Sydenham, a rival attraction, and that he needed a fresh income stream. In deference to his neighbours, he had already changed the closing time for his 'dinner balls' and 'mechanics' club dinners' from 4 a.m. to 1 a.m. There was, he said, assuredly no licentiousness. Most visitors who danced drank lemonade and ginger beer, and his revenue from spirits was rapidly declining. The magistrates' bench, he claimed, had been packed by his opponents. Most importantly, he was there first: had not the complainants chosen to take up residence in Highbury, knowing full well that a pleasure garden existed in the vicinity?

Local hostility reached a crescendo on bonfire night 1869, when a riotous mob of Barts medical students, quitting the grounds, went on the rampage, tearing off door-knockers, smashing windows and shouting 'Fire!' Numerous householders wrote to the press, venting their frustration, and formed a 'Vigilance Committee . . . to co-operate with the police in looking after the midnight roysterers'.[67] The scandal was then compounded by another the following summer: reports of the high-kicking, underwear-revealing antics of can-can performers. The writer Nicolas Leon Thieblin (under his pseudonym

Azamat-Batuk) was despatched to investigate for the *Pall Mall Gazette*. Thieblin came to the gardens on the night of a masquerade ball and found the audience more interesting than the performers: factory-girls in both plain and fancy dress copying the exotic dancers on stage; clerks dressed as Greek gods; and others, 'swell-like dressed in fine men's clothes, but who obviously wished to suggest that they were disguised women . . . eyebrows painted . . . cheeks coloured'. These were, suggested Thieblin, admirers of Thomas Boulton, the notorious cross-dresser recently arrested for indecency: possibly homosexuals, certainly deviants. Thieblin's visit allegedly culminated in him finding himself the inadvertent recipient of pornography – a coloured sketch, thrown into his cab, 'as obscene as the filthiest imagination is capable of conceiving'.[68] This dramatic account unsurprisingly contributed to the loss of Highbury Barn's licence and its subsequent closure.

The vociferous accusations of vice which overwhelmed Cremorne and Highbury in the 1870s, however, were the exception rather than the norm. The majority of pleasure gardens were spared such disputes, operating without objection or offence. Nonetheless, the pleasure garden would fall into decline as an institution in the final decades of the nineteenth century. This was as much about money, rival attractions and changing fashion as it was about public morals.

From the 1860s onwards, the London pleasure garden was already under threat. The writing was on the wall when Edward Weston, proprietor of Weston's Music Hall in Holborn, opened Weston's Retreat in Kentish Town in 1863, only to have the project effectively stifled at birth. The site was a small one, 5–6 acres in the grounds of an Elizabethan mansion, which Weston converted into a tavern and assorted outdoor attractions. Mr Sampson Copestake, a lawyer who owned neighbouring property and who was a local churchwarden, raised repeated and successful legal challenges against granting the gardens any kind of licence (whether liquor, wine or entertainment). Copestake had support from local landowner Lord Dartmouth, whose word was presumably rather influential with the magistracy. The pleasure garden-hating evangelist James Inches Hillocks, quoted above in relation to Highbury Barn, also contributed to the campaign. Copestake successfully persuaded magistrates that the ground was, at the very least, a noise nuisance. Weston, robbed of music, dancing and grand spectacles, gamely continued with panoramas, flower shows, bowls and skittles, and assorted music-hall comedy acts. Unsurprisingly, the speculation closed in 1865. This was very much a sign of things to come. Highbury Barn closed in 1871; Cremorne Gardens and Surrey Gardens both folded in 1877; the Eagle Tavern shut its doors in 1882; and North Woolwich Gardens closed in 1887.

The massive suburban outward expansion of London was itself a significant factor. Cremorne and Highbury were vulnerable because, having begun as semi-rural resorts, they were eventually surrounded by swathes of middle-class housing. Local householders wished to impose respectability and tranquillity on their corner of suburbia, and to do away with the gardens' raucous amusements. The *Marylebone Mercury* remarked, regarding Weston's, that Kentish Town was 'a quiet retreat for business men after the toils of the day . . . residents were not invited [to Weston's] and did not wish to come'.[69] It is notable that the Eagle Tavern, despite its slightly dubious reputation, never had the same difficulties. The Eagle was situated in a largely working-class/industrial part of central London. It, too, was overtaken by suburban growth, but local residents were not so intolerant. Yet the Eagle did not survive either: it was purchased by the Salvation Army in 1882, after a 'crowd-funding' campaign by its charismatic leader, General Booth. This was very much a grand gesture on the part of Booth: 'we trust that a great many of those who have formerly been seen there seeking worldly pleasure will soon be found on the same spot rejoicing in the Lord and leading others to Him'.[70]

The growth of London was also associated with rising land prices. House builders greedily coveted pleasure gardens' green acres. Equally, for proprietors, selling up became a more profitable proposition than trying to second-guess the fickle tastes of the public and fighting endless licensing battles. In the case of Cremorne Gardens, it is striking that many of the individual voices who raised 'moral' objections in the 1870s were local rental landlords or their representatives: Mr Houghton, churchwarden and house agent; Mr Wheatcroft, a builder, with unlet houses; Mr Bradley, with seventy houses, rented for only £25 a year, as opposed to the intended £33; Mr Evans, solicitor, with forty-three houses built in 1869, but only thirty-three sold.[71] In short, the business of prostitution, with which the gardens had become indelibly associated, was bad for property prices and rents. Indeed, for several years *after* Cremorne's closure, there were still complaints that neighbouring streets harboured a disproportionate number of houses of 'bad fame'.[72] House builders did not want their growing suburb, in which they had invested considerable sums of money, becoming irrevocably tainted by vice.

There were other factors at work in the disappearance of the pleasure garden, both in London and nationally. Most obviously, the increasing provision of suburban public parks by municipal authorities created a free alternative for outdoor recreation, albeit without the spectacular amusements. One unusual suburban experiment, Willesden People's Garden Club, marked a sort of halfway point between the pleasure garden and the public park. Opened in 1871 on the north-west borders of London, this was a working man's suburban pleasure garden, built on the cooperative model. The grounds, therefore, were only accessible to subscribers, with the exception of special events such as flower shows. Facilities included extensive croquet lawns, a small theatre (hand built by shareholders), gymnastic apparatus and, it was claimed, the largest dancing-platform in Europe.[73] Unfortunately, there were insufficient subscribers to maintain this private project, which closed in 1875. Compared to the rest of the country, London was slow to include public parks within its vast, sprawling suburbs. Local authorities and philanthropists would eventually take up the baton, after the creation of the London County Council in 1887. Ultimately, not only did the public park contribute to the pleasure garden's demise, but several privately owned pleasure gardens were purchased by local authorities and municipalised (e.g. Aston Hall in Birmingham; Sydney Gardens in Bath; North Woolwich Gardens in London).

Another undoubted challenge to the pleasure garden was the rise of rival attractions, particularly the music hall and flourishing seaside resorts, easily accessible by railway. Investors in urban leisure were increasingly loath to put money into a venture that relied on a summer season and sunshine. Remunerative music halls were the obvious alternative, catering for the public all year round. The 1870s and 1880s also saw the rise of 'Winter Gardens' (indoor entertainment complexes, to which we shall return when discussing the seaside). The growing seaside resorts of Essex and Kent were a major factor in the downfall of Rosherville Gardens at Gravesend. Rosherville was traditionally a resort of Londoners, who would arrive by rail and steamboat. It had the much-publicised, cheerful motto 'A Place to Spend a Happy Day'. A comic play from the 1840s describes it as 'the paradise of milliners and straw bonnet makers'.[74] It was a rather spectacular location, built within a disused quarry, whose contours allowed for numerous romantic vistas. But why travel to a riverside resort beside the muddy Thames, when the ocean proper beckoned at Southend or Margate? The Rosherville Gardens Company, which had operated since the late 1830s, saw its business dwindle in the 1880s; it returned no profits to its shareholders throughout the 1890s and finally declared bankruptcy in 1900. There was no demand for building land or parks in Kent, and when the site was put up for auction in 1901 there were no takers. Edwardian attempts to revive the gardens met with limited success and the site was briefly used as a film set. The grounds were closed during the First World War and had a fitful post-war afterlife, gradually falling into ruin.[75]

Metropolitan gardens also faced stiff competition from a new type of leisure experience: the 'exhibition ground'. The likes of the Crystal Palace at Sydenham, Alexandra Palace and Earl's Court were very much providers of popular entertainment. As already noted, Archibald Hinton of Highbury Barn, when apologising for his dancing platform, cited the Crystal Palace at Sydenham as his greatest commercial rival. These grounds, which amounted to the commercial legacy of the 1851 Great Exhibition, form the subject of the next chapter.

More broadly, pleasure gardens fell victim to changing fashions. The gardens' outdoor amusements came to be considered passé, and the pleasure garden itself was increasingly valued more as a quaint reminder of its Georgian heyday than as a going concern. Nostalgia alone was no basis on which to run a business. The handful of gardens that survived the Victoria era as places of outdoor entertainment only succeeded because they adapted to changing leisure patterns. Manchester's Belle Vue, first opened in the 1830s – initially as a menagerie – would eventually become a twentieth-century theme park. Preston Pleasure Gardens opened in the late 1870s. While retaining areas for music and dance, it soon became more of a sports ground: bicycle racing, football and rugby were followed by speedway racing in the 1920s. The chaotic, diverse pleasures of the Victorian pleasure garden yielded to a different sort of spectacle.

VI

The Exhibition Ground

OR,

THE CITY OF SIDE-SHOWS

IN THE LATE 1840S, MEMBERS of the Royal Society for the Encouragement of Arts, Manufactures and Commerce (RSA) came up with the idea of staging a 'world's fair'. The proposal was to mount an international exhibition in London, showcasing the world's finest manufactured goods (industrial and agricultural machinery, textiles, sculpture, ceramics and more). The RSA itself had already held small shows to promote British goods and technology; and national industrial exhibitions had been regularly staged in Paris.[1] The RSA's new exhibition, championed by the society's president, Prince Albert, would serve a nobler, internationalist purpose. The global element would suggest new and improved techniques to British artisans; educate the nation about its imperial dominions ('we shall therefore probably obtain, by this means, the best practical notion of our Indian possessions'); and cement peace in Europe through the encouragement of international trade and mutual understanding.[2] The 'Great Exhibition of the Industry of All Nations' would also make a rather powerful statement about the might and resources of the British Empire, with exhibition pieces pouring in from every corner of the globe. Half the floor space would be set aside for material from Britain and its foreign possessions.

Manufacturers – home, foreign and colonial – proved keen to supply their goods for display, not least because it was a valuable form of advertisement. The process of finding a site for the Exhibition, and deciding on an appropriate type of building, was more difficult. A royal commission finally settled on Joseph Paxton's 'Crystal Palace', to be erected in Hyde Park. The building closely resembled the elaborate iron and glass greenhouses which Paxton had designed and perfected as head gardener at Chatsworth, the country home of the Duke of Devonshire. All the ironwork was prefabricated offsite, then assembled in the park. Londoners and tourists willingly paid five shillings just to enter the grounds and watch the construction process. No one had ever seen anything quite like it. The rather fanciful name, 'Crystal Palace', suggesting a magical fairyland, was spontaneously adopted by the public.[3]

The government was unwilling to commit public money, and so funding was to be partly by public subscription and partly through entrance fees. Patriotic meetings were held in major towns and cities to drum up support and raise capital. The project was presented as a national tribute to British industry and ingenuity. Despite thousands of pounds being pledged, nagging concerns about financial viability remained. These were soon dispelled when the Exhibition opened on 1 May 1851. Visitors from home and abroad flocked to London. Over a period of six months, the Exhibition's turnstiles recorded 6 million admissions. The commissioners were pleasantly surprised to be left with a surplus of £186,436 18s 6d, which, after some deliberation, was invested in a plot of land in Kensington and the construction of the South Kensington Museum. This, in turn, would lead to the creation of the museums we now know as the V&A, Science Museum and Natural History Museum, in a district sometimes fondly dubbed Albertopolis, after the Great Exhibition's royal champion.

But what was to become of the Crystal Palace itself? Paxton proposed retaining the building *in situ* as a winter garden, despite long-standing promises that it would be demolished after the event. Wealthy local residents of Knightsbridge were hostile, and the officials in charge of the royal parks were equally reluctant. One option remained (short of full demolition): the prefab palace could be disassembled and relocated elsewhere with relative ease. The commercial potential in such a move was obvious: the Great Exhibition had proved not only a magnificent trade show, but also a monumental visitor attraction. The summer of 1851 had seen the whole metropolis overwhelmed by an unprecedented tourism boom. Thousands of visitors had filled specially laid-on excursion trains, booked every hotel and boarding house, and packed out museums and galleries, venturing beyond Hyde Park. Visits to the already popular British Museum had tripled. Public visits to the military manufactory at Woolwich Arsenal rose from 17,000 per annum to 100,000.[4] Some critics were not best pleased with all the crowds, and found the Exhibition itself rather vulgar. They complained of working-class visitors who brought packed lunches smelling of 'gin and oranges', and were equally unhappy with idling members of the upper classes ('The nave is filled day after day with loungers, who appear to come there with no other object than to see and be seen').[5] The public, they noted, thronged around novel displays of machinery, such as a boy rapidly working a machine for making envelopes, while devoting only a cursory glance to the exquisite workmanship on display elsewhere. But if nothing else, it seemed obvious that there was money to be made in resurrecting the Palace.

Consequently, in 1854, a new, expanded and remodelled Crystal Palace was opened in Sydenham, South London, set in its own extensive landscaped grounds. This would be the first of various Victorian exhibition grounds to copy the Great Exhibition, while adding their own mix of commercial entertainment, education and lavish spectacle. But were these grounds a new type of educational leisure experience, or simply the pleasure garden by another name?

Without a doubt, the new Crystal Palace at Sydenham was fundamentally a commercial venture. The building was the project of the Crystal Palace Company (CPC), a joint-stock company chaired by the railway entrepreneur Samuel Laing, who also served as chair of the London, Brighton and South-Coast Railway. This railway connection was crucial, since the CPC's business model was heavily dependent on synergy with Laing's railway company, conveying thousands of visitors to the site. The principal merit of Sydenham, an obscure rural location several miles from the centre of London, was its proximity to the Brighton line. There were other advantages to Sydenham: the air was cleaner than in sooty central London, and the Palace would be constructed on a hilltop location which made it visible for miles around – 'its own advertisement'.[6] But the connection to the Brighton railway was critical.

Laing and his fellow directors, in turn, committed the railway to expanding its London Bridge terminus and constructing a new line to Sydenham, together with a new station. In addition, joint tickets – covering both transport and admission to the Palace – were to be sold by the railway company. Meanwhile, an entirely new company, which shared several directors with the CPC, was established to build a western section of track to link the Palace with south-west London and the West End (only fully realised with the opening of Victoria Station in the 1860s).[7] The Crystal Palace owed its resurrection in large part to these railway companies. Shares in the CPC seemed a good investment. Laing's period of chairmanship had seen the Brighton line become highly profitable, with five years of growing traffic, revenue and dividends.[8] The benefits were obvious: the Palace would provide a useful stimulus to further railway growth and the railway would promote the Palace. Property speculators flocked to the district, giving the scheme their tacit seal of approval. Land prices in Sydenham soared, and at the end of 1853 a Crystal Palace District Gas Company was formed, to supply both the Palace itself and its surrounds (including 'shops, inns, private mansions') and install 'public lamps which are imperatively called for in all the approaches'.[9]

Laing's vision for the project included blatantly commercial elements. He wanted the Palace to serve as a grand showcase for manufacturers of luxury goods. In a speech to shareholders, he suggested that middle-class families would no longer trawl the capital's retailers for, say, a decent piano. Rather, they would come and compare and contract the finest models on display at Sydenham. Manufacturers, in turn, would liberally pay to appear in the Palace's magnificent national showroom.[10] Yet Laing and his fellow directors were equally keen to emphasise a spiritual connection with the triumph of 1851. The directors stressed that they had a noble mission:

> To raise the enjoyments and amusements of the English people . . . to afford the inhabitants of London in wholesome country air, amidst the beauties of nature, the elevating treasures of art and the instructive marvels of science, an accessible and inexpensive substitute for the injurious and debasing amusements of a crowded metropolis; to blend for them instrument with pleasure, to educate them by the eye . . .[11]

This was to be a great spectacle, a thriving business *and* an opportunity to provide recreation and education for the common man. The original Palace had proved popular with working-class 'shilling visitors', who were admitted during the week at this cheap rate; and the new venture would likewise entice humble citizens away from the 'gin palace, dancing saloon and the ale-house'.[12]

There were, in fairness, genuine ties to the original Great Exhibition, beyond a public-spirited mission statement: Francis Fuller, prominent member of the RSA and one of the originators of the Great Exhibition, was to be managing director; the same building contractors, Fox and Henderson, were to undertake the construction work; and the extensive grounds were to be landscaped under the personal management of Sir Joseph Paxton (recently knighted). Likewise, the architect Owen Jones, who had planned the colour scheme for the Great Exhibition, was to superintend not only colour, but the fine arts and architectural displays. Many were persuaded, therefore, that the revived palace was not simply a speculation, but a serious-minded continuation of the original Great Exhibition, a 'national institution'. The Queen herself would open the site in 1854; and, somewhat controversially for a private, secular scheme, prayers were read by the Archbishop of Canterbury. Charles Dickens, not quite convinced, wrote to private correspondents that he abhorred the 'forge-bellow of puffery' (advertising) which trumpeted the Palace's national importance, manifested in a series of guidebooks to its contents, which he memorably described as 'flatulent botheration'.[13]

Those contents, however, were quite novel. First, Paxton's winter garden was realised, thanks to a basement boiler system containing 11,000 gallons of water, supplying 50 miles of hot-water piping, running under the vast iron and glass building. The heated, northern section was graced with ferns, date palms, pomegranate trees and fountains filled with tropical water lilies. There was even appropriate wildlife. A contemporary photograph shows a sign reading 'Visitors are requested not to tease the parrots.'[14] The principal areas of interest within the remainder of the Palace were a series of 'courts', self-contained zones which each provided a study in architectural history for a given historical period. The re-creation of a Pompeian villa was the main attraction in the Roman Court; whereas the other courts were themed galleries with relevant art and artefacts from a particular period, including Medieval, Byzantine and Renaissance. The experience was halfway between walking through a museum and a series of historically themed theatrical sets. The most spectacular touch was two colossal 50-foot-tall copies of the statues of Ramesses II from his temple at Abu Simbel, brilliantly painted in bright red, yellow and blue, guarding the Egyptian Court. The statues were a towering presence, even though set within such a vast structure and kept at three-quarters scale, so as not to embarrass the neighbouring winged bulls of Nineveh. The fine arts courts, taken as a whole, presented 'a grand architectural sequence from the earliest dawn of the art [sic] down to the latest times'.[15]

The 'march of progress' was hammered home by the separate 'New World' and 'Old World' natural history courts, situated at the southern entrance to the Palace. These spaces were divided into three sections, representing the world beyond Europe. The first contained the Americas and the Arctic; the second Africa, China and India; the third south-east Asia and Australia. Visitors, strolling round winding paths, were presented with not only geographically accurate flora and (stuffed) fauna from the different corners of the globe, but also life-size painted models of 'primitive peoples'. One might encounter gangs of 'Red Indians engaged in a war-dance, and surrounded by the trees and shrubs indigenous to North America' or 'a large group of Caribs, some using blowpipes, others shooting fish with bows and arrows'.[16] There was, undoubtedly, a serious ethnographical intent; but the presence of these painted 'natives' also served as a didactic counterpoint to the 'civilised world' which lay beyond. Notably, there were no comparable tableaux in the fine arts courts – merely reproductions of sculpture (in addition to four dedicated sculpture courts in the centre of the building). Visitors were, in effect, invited to imagine themselves as the 'civilised' human element in Pompeii, Moorish Spain, medieval Europe and Renaissance Italy. The Palace created a series of vivid historical worlds for its customers to briefly inhabit.

There were other things to see and do. Manufacturers contributed their merchandise for public display, albeit not quite with the enthusiasm Laing had anticipated.[17] The scent manufacturers Rimmel installed a fountain which flowed with their 'toilet vinegar' ('far superior to Eau de Cologne . . . a reviving perfume, a pleasant Dentifrice, and a powerful Disinfectant'). The Great Exhibition's 27-foot-high glass fountain, manufactured by Osler's of Birmingham, was resurrected in Sydenham. Other courts contained a collection of minerals; musical instruments; an assortment of modern household goods. The Stationery Court included a giant working press, ready to stamp out commemorative medallions. There were numerous busts and portraits of famous figures throughout the ages. Listed chronologically in a contemporary guidebook, they began with Homer and ended with Prince Albert. There was also considerable space set aside for the sale of refreshments. Cold meat, lobster and other salads cost two shillings; sandwiches cost only sixpence. Lemonade and ale were both likewise sixpence. An initial pledge to prohibit the sale of alcohol, following the temperance example of the Great Exhibition, was abandoned long in advance of the opening day. Sherry, claret, bottled ale and stout vied with the humble pint. It was recognised that refreshments were potentially a very lucrative part of the business.

The final great attraction was 200 acres of landscaped gardens, descending down the slope from the Palace. This included Paxton's grandest design: a system of giant fountains, with 90-foot-high central jets, together with associated basins and cascades. The explicitly stated intention was to create an English rival to the gardens of Versailles. The fountains were actually ridiculously expensive and overly complex – and hence not fully operational until 1855. The gardens also included something which could not be found at the French palace: man-made lakes and rockeries designed to illustrate geological strata, containing giant models of extinct animals. These models of 'saurian lizards' and other extinct beasts were also not entirely finished until 1855, but they were a startling feature – the first sculptures of dinosaurs ever constructed. They were based on guidance by the influential palaeontologist and zoologist Richard Owen and modelled by the sculptor Benjamin Waterhouse Hawkins. Famously, they were inaugurated by a celebratory dinner in the belly of the iguanodon mould on New Year's Eve 1853.[18] The event was a lively one, and Hawkins reportedly grew 'indisposed'. The dinosaurs – which were beautifully restored in 2002 – provided the final element of the Palace's sweeping (if not entirely coherent) historical tour, typifying the attempt to blend 'instruction with amusement'. Visitors could progress from the low-lying swamps of prehistory, to the twinkling vision of modernity up on the hill.

How did the Palace fare, once the public was free to roam its courts and grounds? The question of whether it was principally a place of instruction or of amusement always loomed large, and few believed that it successfully married these functions. Harriet Martineau was among the early public commentators, writing for the *Westminster Review*.[19] The opening of the landscaped gardens to the general public, the sort of space normally associated with stately homes, struck Martineau as an unalloyed boon ('luxuries requiring money, knowledge and taste for their formation are [now] within the reach of the poorest'). This had been achieved by a joint-stock company, validating her opinion of the merits of laissez-faire economics. For Martineau, Paxton's gardens were a sort of capitalist utopia, all thanks to 'perfect freedom of partnership'. Yet, on the other hand, Martineau doubted the capacity of the working class to appreciate fully what had been done on their behalf. The common people, she discovered, lacked any pre-existing historical education. She was shocked to find visitors who knew nothing whatsoever of Pompeii prior to their arrival. They were also ignorant of middle-class manners, not rising from their seats when the band struck up 'God Save the Queen' ('and the few who do rise are supposed by the rest to be going away'). Martineau was hopeful that the people could be educated; but doubted that gazing on antiquities would suffice. She also noted that the general public, working class or otherwise, had stolen many of the dinosaurs' teeth for souvenirs. Letter-writers to the papers commented on the bad manners of the common man at the Palace, which included forming 'dancing parties' on the grass ('which we are so rigidly forbidden to cross') and playing 'kiss in the ring'. The latter, a courting/chasing game much enjoyed by young working-class men and women, 'continued to scandalise decent ladies till nearly 9 o'clock'.[20] This was the sort of behaviour associated with days out in the fields or at a fair. It signified a failure to intuit the appropriate level of respectable conduct.

Arthur Munby, the barrister/poet diarist with a peculiar sexual fetish for muscular working women, was a regular visitor, looking forward to Mondays, 'the people's day, and the sandwiches and porter and the prentices and strapping servant maids'.[21] Monday was a plebeian day because many of the working class took it as an informal occasional holiday, so-called 'Saint Monday'. This allowed them to take advantage of the Palace's weekday shilling admission (as opposed to half a crown at the weekend). Munby himself participated in the sport of 'kiss in the ring', no doubt much to the disapproval of more self-conscious passers-by of his own class. Like Martineau, he, too, wondered whether working people took away any real benefit from the courts:

They are not refined, but blunted and vulgarized still more by eating sandwiches (and they will eat sandwiches) on the tombs of Kings, and drinking pots of porter in the Courts of the Alhambra; these are mighty influences for good, wasted altogether by being exercised upon those who have never been taught to feel them. Today I heard a wench exclaim, standing by the avenue of Sphinxes, before the statues of Ramses the Great, 'Come on Bill, let's cut: I'm sick of this place – there's nought to do . . .'[22]

Munby was something of a curmudgeon. He likewise condemned audiences at the Palace's Handel Festival for occasionally quitting their seats in search of ice cream and bottled stout.[23] Nonetheless, the educational value of the fine arts courts would continue to be much debated. The journalist Henry Mayhew described the artisan class as treating the original Crystal Palace as 'more of a school than a show', reverently studying every object.[24] Few commentators noted the same dedication at Sydenham, and the management of the Palace soon realised that the courts' cultural offering was insufficient to draw repeat visits from the general public. The Great Exhibition had been open for only six months and was an utter novelty; its successor, by contrast, had continually to attract custom. The company, which initially offered a respectable 5 per cent dividend to shareholders, found itself only able to pay out 2 per cent by 1860. New and additional attractions were urgently required. These, in turn, would put the Crystal Palace, whatever its mission statement might suggest, on a very similar footing to the London pleasure garden.

The educational element was never entirely abandoned. This included not only the displays in the courts, but public lectures on art, geography and science. There were also adult education classes. These were divided into a 'School of Art, Science and Literature', aimed principally at local middle-class women, and a 'School of Engineering' for young men, which would eventually offer the chance of obtaining a diploma from Cambridge University. These schools consistently turned a modest profit, but they were only a small entry on the company's balance sheet. The Palace could only prosper if it attracted thousands upon thousands of visitors.

From its early days, therefore, the CPC reached out to tour groups and meetings of public bodies. The Palace regularly hosted events for friendly societies (the likes of the Ancient Order of Foresters, the Odd Fellows, the Co-operative Society), as well as choral societies and charities, to which it offered discounted train fares and admission. Likewise, various types of public display and competition were staged, including flower shows and exhibitions of cats, dogs, canaries, pigeons and poultry. This was all very much pleasure-garden fare. Cremorne Gardens was known for its flower shows; Manchester's Belle Vue was famous for events like 'The Great Northern Tulip Show'.[25]

The CPC also sought out technological marvels that might attract the public. These included a display of velocipedes and steam engines, managed by enthusiasts of the marvellously named Imperial Velocipede and Loco-Machine Committee; a chess tournament played by telegraph; and several electrical exhibitions. Music, however, was the most remunerative attraction. Weekly operatic concerts, held in a specially constructed arena within the Palace, were always fairly profitable. An additional opera theatre was built in the early 1870s and was also used for staging plays and pantomimes. The greatest musical success was the triennial Handel Festival, which began in 1857 and drew huge audiences. The massed choir consisted of 3,000 choristers from the Sacred Harmonic Society, an amateur choral society which only ever demanded a modest cut of the profits.

There were continuing attempts to assert and retain the venue's iconic national status. For instance, at the close of the Crimean War, the management commissioned a replica of Carlo Marochetti's war memorial at Scutari, a 100-foot-high granite obelisk, supported by colossal angels, to be unveiled by the Queen. Elaborate fetes were held in honour of royal birthdays, as well as for visiting national heroes and foreign dignitaries. These included not only foreign royals, such as the Sultan of Turkey and the Shah of Iran, but returning imperial figureheads like Sir Robert Napier, after the Abyssinian expedition of 1868, and even Ferdinand de Lesseps, the French diplomat who developed the Suez Canal. The Palace offered a suitably dramatic backdrop against which to entertain the great and the good.

Yet the CPC could not survive on its national status, educational merit or even the weekly musical programme. More populist amusements, therefore, were introduced around public holidays (Christmas, Easter, Whitsuntide – and later the new bank holidays established in 1871). These were precisely the sorts of thing that could be experienced at Cremorne Gardens or Highbury Barn, including the staples of balloon ascents and elaborate firework displays. The Palace was often advertised side by side with the London pleasure gardens in the press. Nelson Lee, the manager of the City of London Theatre, staged such shows at the Palace, advertising comic ballets, dwarves and giants, 'the Nepalese Blondins', 'Ethardo the Spiral Ascensionist', as well as all the fun of the fair: 'Gymnasium, Roundabouts, Swings, Invigorators, Rifle Shooting, Archery, Bowls, Cricket, Boating on the Lake, Steeplechasers, Steam Carousel, Quoits, Croquet, Camera Obscura, Cosmorama, Mechanical Working Models, Marriott's Working Bees, the Hairless Blue Horse'.[26] As early as 1860, the central transept was temporarily yielded to a Mr Rarey, who charged half a crown to demonstrate his 'System of Subduing Wild and Vicious Horses'. Blondin himself strung his high-wire above the nave in the early 1860s, astonishing the public by pushing his young daughter across in a wheelbarrow, and cooking an omelette on a carefully positioned camping stove. Readers will remember that his exploits also graced numerous music halls. A shareholder complained that such shows tended 'to lower the Crystal Palace to the level of a fair booth', but they were popular with the public.[27] General Tom Thumb appeared in the winter of 1864, as did Wombwell's Menagerie of Wild Beasts, with a covered walkway from the main building to the circus ground. The following summer, visitors were treated to Pulleyn's Grand National Cirque and Hippodrome, featuring a 'Grand Steeple Chase' of ponies ridden by trained monkeys. Particular attractions or shows were usually run by touring proprietors, who paid a percentage of takings back to the CPC management. This general practice at the Palace of contracting out could lead to conflicts of interest. In one notable court case, the CPC's refreshments contractor sued the company because another concessions holder, running a well-attended roller-skating rink, was not letting his customers into the main grounds to purchase food and drink.[28]

Unfortunately, while the Crystal Palace incorporated the rollicking fun of the fairground and pleasure garden, it did not really prosper. By the early 1870s, share dividends rarely exceeded 1 or 2 per cent; and then they vanished altogether. There were several issues of preference shares and debentures over the years to raise more money, but these weighed down the business with ever-increasing debt. Groups of new investors, again and again, willed the grand national enterprise to succeed. Rather than being rewarded for their trouble, they found they were thanked for their patience ('the Directors desire to express their thanks to the Debenture Stockholders for their self-sacrificing liberal spirit').[29] Visitors, to their dismay, found that individual attractions within the grounds increasingly came with an admission fee. One disgruntled shareholder noted that taking a child to the Palace on a 'shilling day' actually cost more like eight shillings, with pennies charged for petty amusements (visiting a 'stalactite cave'; entrance to the aquarium; seeing an automaton chess player) and two shillings and sixpence for reserving seats at the grand concert, and again at the fireworks display.[30] It will be recalled that similar complaints were levelled against Cremorne Gardens. The struggling CPC, reconstituted in 1877, was left on the brink of bankruptcy in 1887; although it did not make an actual operating loss until 1899, it remained heavily indebted.[31] Roughly a million people a year still paid money at the door, and there were several thousand season-ticket holders; but this was never quite enough to service the debt and reward investors.

There were brave last-ditch efforts, including a greater focus on sporting events. The Palace hosted the FA Cup Final from 1895 (although it was glumly noted that this was the only football fixture that brought in a profit). A short-lived cricket club was founded in 1898, and the following year W.G. Grace was persuaded to become manager and secretary. By the early 1900s, the writing was on the wall and the business was finally wound up in 1909. The Palace was saved by being bought for the nation by the Earl of Plymouth, only to succumb finally to the infamous conflagration that occurred in November 1936.

The Crystal Palace was not an outright failure. It stayed open, without public assistance, for over fifty years. But it did suffer protracted financial decline and repeatedly let down investors. There was not one overarching explanation for the Palace's failure to attract sufficient custom to pay off its debt, but it is possible to discern key factors. Angry shareholders regularly accused the directors of amateurism and incompetence. The Palace never seems to have found a successful presiding genius to promote and manage the diverse amuse-ments. Talented entrepreneurs were probably more attracted by the lucrative possibilities of the refreshments contract, rather than the daunting prospect of managing the whole affair. Notably, the one person associated with the early management who went on to greater things was a caterer: Frederick Strange. He began his career working in the well-known Cheapside chop-house Simpson's, before opening the London Restaurant on the corner of Chancery Lane in 1857. He then swiftly progressed, with his partner Frederick Sawyer, to managing the refreshments at the Crystal Palace in 1858–64. He then moved to become sole proprietor/manager of the Alhambra Music Hall, establishing it as a leading West End venue for both music-hall acts and lavish ballets.[32]

There were undoubted problems with the original design of the site. Paxton's gargantuan water features proved incredibly costly and unreliable; and the company was soon faced with bills for major structural repairs to the main building, including strengthening the flooring. Published accounts from 1858, only four years after opening, show £20,000 – almost a quarter of annual expenditure – going on maintaining the building, gardens and waterworks, and this percentage figure remained pretty constant.[33] Gales in 1861 and a calamitous fire in 1866, which destroyed much of the tropical section, also ate into the company's bank account; the north wing never was fully restored.

As for entertainment, only music proved a reliable money-spinner. The Handel Festival saved the company from going into the red on several occasions; but even this was largely thanks to the goodwill of its 3,000 amateur choristers. There was continual debate within the company about the value of what were dubbed 'special attractions', i.e. shows, festivals and fetes beyond the Palace's regular offering. The Handel Festival, always profitable, went unchallenged; but everything else was up for discussion. The problem was straightforward. Special attractions potentially drew more visitors and generated considerable income, but they were also very expensive to stage. The company was open to ideas, discussing various 'permanent special attractions', which included an aquarium (opened in 1871) and (unrealised) swimming baths. Permanence, unfortunately, was hard to square with the public's demand for novelty. The difficult balance of mixing familiar popular elements with (expensive) novel attractions was nothing new, and pleasure gardens faced precisely the same dilemma. But there had never before been so much competition and choice for the seeker of amusement. The Palace always seemed to underperform, amid a host of rival metropolitan attractions. The shareholders variously suggested to the directors that it was too upmarket or too downmarket, but no one seemed able to keep things on an even keel.

For the *Era*, trade paper of the theatre and music hall, the basic problem with the Palace remained its ongoing failure to square the twin functions of education and amusement. It was neither one thing nor the other, neither a pleasure garden nor an educational institute. The *Era*'s editor, writing in the 1880s, suggested that this was, in any case, a stuffy, old-fashioned mid-Victorian notion, rendered redundant by the introduction of state education. The Palace was, quite simply, not fun enough:

> It dabbles in frivolity, in a feeble 'half-and-half' way, with its morning performances and fireworks; but its heart is with the antediluvian animals in the grounds, the stuffed specimens in the galleries, and the cheap microscopes . . . It must look for its financial support to the masses. As a correspondent truly says, 'popular music, popular songs, and the popular element generally is not considered at all; so popular support is not found'.[34]

This was a little unfair. During holiday seasons, the Palace was as lively as any of its rivals. The Whitsun fete of 1885 featured Harvey's Royal Midges ('the smallest people in the world'); Mr Douglas Gifford's talking parrot, 'Pretty Green Boy'; a variety show with trick cyclists, jugglers, acrobats and performing dogs; a plate-spinner; a ventriloquist; a 'water bicycle'; a bicycle versus horse race; a balloon ascent; fireworks; and the band of the Scots Guards. Throughout the year there were more upmarket dramatic performances, often by companies from leading West End theatres; assorted concerts and variety shows; ballet and opera; military bands. The fine arts courts, admittedly, were becoming something of a museum piece in themselves. Electric lights were installed in 1887 with the aim of 're-establishing them as one of the leading features'.[35] But by this period, few truly believed in the capacity of the Palace to elevate and educate the masses. This prevailing scepticism runs through George Gissing's well-known account in *The Nether World* (published in 1889) of a rowdy visit to the Palace by the 'slaves of industrialism' on a bank holiday (although the author allows his characters a brief moment of repose and quietness while listening to the band playing inside the 'great ugly building').[36]

Finally, the Crystal Palace's much-vaunted national status could actually prove a liability. This was the case when it came to the contentious issue of Sunday opening, which was forbidden by the company's royal charter, in deference to religious sentiment.[37] Rival pleasure gardens generally came to some accommodation with the magistracy on the issue of Sabbatarianism. Typically, this involved free entrance on Sundays and no stage performances, but the retention of profits from the sale of food and drink. The CPC, on the other hand, was somewhat hamstrung by its self-professed moral standing. The Crystal Palace's iconic position precluded its taking a blatantly anti-Sabbatarian stance. A shoddy compromise was eventually reached, whereby the grounds were opened on Sundays gratis, but only to shareholders (i.e. in the manner of a private club). This was supplemented by the promotion of 'share-clubs', where members of the public saved up to buy single shares, and were afforded the additional chance of winning tickets for Sunday admission during the process.

The Palace's cherished national status, moreover, did not exempt it from competition. Further international expositions and more amusement-oriented exhibition grounds were opened in the metropolis, belated offspring of the Great Exhibition.

The 1862 International Exhibition of Industry and Art was held on the site of the present-day Imperial College and Natural History Museum in Kensington.

There had already been several international exhibitions held abroad, copying the original Great Exhibition of 1851.[38] But this was the first London successor, supported by the Royal Society of Arts, funded by private subscription and managed by a new royal commission. Entrance included admission to the newly opened gardens of the Royal Horticultural Society, which adjoined the site. The principal aim was to show how British craftsmanship had improved. The internationalist message of peace and prosperity through trade was played down, seeming rather naive in light of the Crimean conflict of the mid-1850s and the outbreak of war in Italy in 1859. There was also the small matter of the ongoing American Civil War, which starved the Lancashire cotton industry of raw materials. Plainly, the industrial exposition could only achieve so much in international diplomacy. The focus was more on the quality of goods and workmanship on display. Paintings, excluded from the original Hyde Park exhibition (because they were not 'manufactured'), were now permitted. New mechanical wonders included a calculating machine based on Charles Babbage's Difference Engine.[39]

The project was somewhat ill-starred, overshadowed by the untimely death of Prince Albert in December 1861 and the Queen's mourning, which ruled out her regal patronage. The exhibition building, designed by Captain Fowke of the Royal Engineers, was derided by critics as the utilitarian product of an engineer, lacking architectural grandeur. The structure was largely built of brick, albeit with two massive iron and glass domes at either end. *Blackwood's Edinburgh Magazine* mocked it as an unsightly hybrid of 'agricultural barn, the purely practical and mercantile factory, and the middle-age cathedral'.[40] The opening ceremony was mired in controversy, thanks to the rejection of a cantata composed by Verdi, allegedly submitted too late to be learned by the orchestra. The fiasco was widely ascribed to professional jealousy on the part of Michael Costa, the conductor/composer in charge of the proceedings. *Punch* joined in, gently poking fun not only at Costa but also at the whole enterprise, suggesting that the rules for public admittance and policing should include injunctions against young persons engaged in flirtation; that members of the public should be positively forced to inspect *every* exhibit; and that 'nothing whatever is to be said about the Crystal Palace'.[41]

Financially, the 1862 exhibition was not a failure, but nor was it a great success. Takings of just under £460,000 matched outgoings; there was no profit. Six million visitors arrived in Kensington – similar to the numbers in 1851. Yet London had expanded considerably in the intervening decade and had more than tripled its capacity to bring visitors by rail, and so this was not quite so impressive.[42] The directors of the Crystal Palace, in response, attempted to persuade exhibitors at Kensington to bring examples of their goods to Sydenham and to use that site as a more commercially oriented saleroom. They also hoped that increased metropolitan tourism would boost their own takings.[43] This seems to have been the case, since 1862 was something of a rare bumper year for the Palace, with a 3 per cent dividend for shareholders and repayment of much of the previously accrued debt.[44] The CPC's directors would not be so lucky in the future, and the Crystal Palace would face increased competition from other London exhibitions, diluting its own appeal. Aside from the likes of the International Exhibition, more commercial exhibition grounds also presented a threat. In fact, the first commercial rival would be a virtual mirror image of Sydenham, set on a hilltop in North London.

The idea for a North London 'palace' was an obvious one, and was raised soon after the Crystal Palace at Sydenham was opened. Crossing central London was still something of a chore in this period, requiring a journey on foot, by cab or by omnibus. Therefore, a northern 'palace', connected to either Euston or King's Cross, would be more convenient for large numbers of tourists. All that was needed was to find a good location next to a railway line, and to avoid the over-spending that Paxton's waterworks had entailed in South London.

The first attempt was made in 1858. The rural site chosen was the Tottenham Wood Estate in Muswell Hill, which would connect the venture to the Great Northern Railway, which was already building a station in the vicinity. The land was purchased and a prospectus published for a 'Palace of the People', which was to offer much the same fare as its South London rival. The building, with a central glazed dome and a long nave on either side, was to be constructed after a design by Owen Jones, who had been involved with both incarnations of the Crystal Palace. From the top of the hill, on a clear day, one could spy the Crystal Palace glittering on the other side of the Thames valley. Visitors were promised entertainment and education, focused on displays of English history, geography, ethnography, astronomy, geology and mining. The originators of the scheme hedged their bets by setting aside two-thirds of the 450-acre site as potential building land, hoping to sell to builders as local land prices increased (a similar financial safety net had been utilised by the CPC). Predictably, directors included several individuals with interests in the Great Northern Railway. Yet nothing whatsoever came of the initial company. The promoters sought to raise £600,000 from shares and debentures, a figure similar to the initial estimate for the Crystal Palace. Potential investors may have noted that the famous South London original had eventually cost the CPC over a million pounds. They stayed away.

The project lay dormant, but was revived in 1862, when it was proposed that considerable money could be saved by adopting another CPC strategy: recycling. Captain Fowke's much-maligned building for the 1862 International Exhibition was purchased and was to be rebuilt at Muswell Hill. A new company was formed to create what was now to be known as the Alexandra Palace and Alexandra Park, in honour of the new Princess of Wales. The park itself was opened for archery competitions and various other minor amusements. Yet, once again, few chose to take up the share offer and the Alexandra Park Company was bankrupt within two years. The building itself was left half-finished.

In 1866, a new Alexandra Palace Company took up the baton, but fared little better. The principal investors were the London Financial Association (LFA), venture capitalists whose main business was investing shareholders' money in railway schemes, and the Palace's builders Kelk and Lucas. Another attempt at a share issue in 1869 flopped, with no public interest. Two years later, Francis Fuller, erstwhile managing director at the Crystal Palace, made the novel proposal of issuing shares in a tontine: shares would be converted to regular shares after a decade (i.e. no dividends in the meanwhile). To make the wait endurable, the scheme included incentives: free admission to the new enterprise and prize draws from an Art Union.[45] The idea was that sufficient shareholders would die during the decade, so that surviving investors would inevitably profit. Fuller's scheme likewise received little patronage, and the few subscriptions were soon returned. The only positive step in this period was the opening of a racecourse on the lower reaches of the park in 1868, which would turn out to be the site's one reliable source of profit.

Both the London Financial Association and Kelk and Lucas saw the park principally as an investment. They had no desire to get their own hands dirty and operate it as a business until, quite unable to find partners or shareholders, they were all but forced to take the plunge themselves. The Alexandra Palace building was finally completed and the site opened fully to the public on 24 May 1873. Unfortunately, sixteen days later it burnt down. The culprit was a builder's brazier left unattended and burning on the roof. A cynic might have suspected some sort of insurance fraud, but actually the Alexandra Palace was woefully underinsured. Two years of rebuilding and more debt accrual followed before the Palace reopened, only for the company to enter liquidation the following year. New lessees were found over the next two decades, but none survived much more than one or two seasons.

The reopened Palace was not devoid of attractions. The main building incorporated a 3,000-seat theatre; a 3,500-seat concert hall; a 12,000-seat 'great hall' with a gigantic steam-powered organ; exhibition spaces for small stall-holders selling expensive knick-knacks; an 'Egyptian Villa' and 'Moorish House'; a palm court; picture galleries; and a roller-skating rink. Plays, opera, ballet and variety performances were all staged within the building. The theatre became well known for its pantomimes, but it also hosted opera and drama. The grounds contained ornamental lakes; Swiss chalets; horticultural gardens; a cricket ground; a banqueting hall; an open-air swimming pool; a mock-up of a Japanese village; a circus ground; and the racecourse, with its grandstand, trotting ring and stabling. Yet, unlike at Sydenham, no one seemed able to consistently run the day-to-day business at a profit, let alone generate sufficient income to pay off the freeholders' debts.[46] Sir Edward Lee, manager during the mid-1870s after the disastrous fire, blamed an executive committee obsessed with penny-pinching; it supposedly interfered with his work and slashed the advertising budget. But in truth, the problem persisted throughout multiple changes of management.[47] The London Financial Association, meanwhile, lost a legal battle in which it ingeniously attempted to show that it did not possess the legal *bona fides* to have purchased the freehold in the first place. The company hoped that this would extricate it from various financial obligations and allow it to recover money from its partners Kelk and Lucas. The complex legal case was hugely expensive, and only made financial matters worse.[48]

The Palace's archives contain a remarkable list of ideas for generating income, hinting at ongoing managerial desperation. Among practical thoughts – about ensuring honest operation of the turnstiles, improving advertising and offering discounted railway tickets – an anonymous manager (possibly Sir Edward Lee) jots down anything and everything that comes to mind:

Offer prize for the best £10 piano. Also for Girl Pianists.
Trade Contests – Bartenders, Bricklayers &c

THE GOOD OLD-FASHIONED PUBLIC-HOUSE.

EXTERIOR OF A GIN-SHOP, No. 2.

1, 2 & 3. Illustrations from *The Gin Shop* (1836), a temperance penny magazine, demonstrate the difference between a homely, respectable 'good old-fashioned public-house' and the enemy of temperance: i.e. a purpose-built modern gin palace with extravagant gaslights and neo-classical architecture. These simple drawings are unusual, in as much as they offer a clear impression of the early gin palace exterior, without caricature. Note also the rural setting for the 'good' public house, whereas gin palaces represent a pernicious urban innovation.

4 & 5. The first illustration, from Pierce Egan's *Life in London* (1821), *Tom and Jerry taking Blue Ruin after the Spell is Broke up* by George Cruikshank (1792–1878), shows not only the Regency bucks Tom and Jerry but various signifiers of low-life vice: women brazenly enjoying liquor; a barefoot child collecting drink to take home to his family (in a gravy boat); an emaciated drunk, dead on his feet; a woman giving gin to an infant. In terms of layout, this a typical 'gin-shop' of the early 1800s. The second illustration, *The Gin Palace* (1842), also by Cruikshank, displays the decorative elements of the gin-shop that became more prominent in the 1820s and 1830s. There are common elements in the two scenes: both establishments have large branded casks of liquor on prominent display and bar service via pump and tap. But the more modern gin palace has a rounded bar to maximise counter space, ornate classical decoration, a clock and mirrors. The room is also well lit with a high ceiling and a stone-flagged floor, rather than straw-strewn wooden boards.

George Cruikshank fec

The Gin Palace.

The Surrey Music Hall.

6 & 7. These rare sketches featuring two early music halls appeared in the salacious and gossipy magazine *Paul Pry*, c.1856. The Surrey (above), or 'Preece's Music Hall', was situated on Southwark Bridge Road and opened in 1848, then was rebuilt in 1849 to contain two levels of seating and an adjoining picture gallery. Advertisements promised 'song, music, characteristic dancing, or any novelty fleeting on the wing of time' (*Morning Advertiser*, 26 April 1849). The more famous Canterbury Hall (below) in Lambeth, run by Charles Morton, first opened in 1852, then was rebuilt on a grand scale in 1854 and, similarly, was supplemented by an art gallery in 1858. The drawings show the contrast between the Surrey's typical, small theatrical stage and Morton's unusual platform for performers which hosted, in the Canterbury's early years, operatic performances as well as comic singing and other turns. Morton publicised his hall as being highly respectable and this carefully cultivated reputation, along with its unusual size and magnificence, garnered it the highly misleading accolade of 'the first music hall'.

CANTERBURY HALL, LAMBETH.

THE
RATCATCHER'S DAUGHTER

WITH EXTRA VERSES BY CHARLES SLOMAN,

THE MUSIC COMPOSED AND SUNG BY

SAM. COWELL.

The Musical Treasury, No. 749-50. ———— Ent. Stat. Hall.

LONDON: DAVIDSON, 19 PETER'S HIL', DOCTORS' COMMONS.

8. Sam Cowell (1819–64) was arguably music hall's first superstar. He came from a theatrical family and rose to prominence as a comic actor in Glasgow and Edinburgh before coming to London in 1844. He was the star turn at the men-only Evans' song-and-supper rooms in Covent Garden and then progressed to Charles Morton's famous Canterbury Hall in Lambeth. Much of his material focused on working-class and street life, including his most famous song 'The Ratcatcher's Daughter', a darkly humorous 'Cockney ballad', which ends with the heroine drowning and the hero cutting his own throat. Cowell toured both the UK and America in the late 1850s but died in broken health, suffering from alcoholism, in 1864.

9. Marie Lloyd (1870–1922) was music hall's greatest female star. She often appeared dressed as an 'innocent' child who stumbled upon adult sexual misdemeanours in songs like 'There They Are – The Two of 'Em on Their Own' and 'Johnny Jones' (a.k.a. 'What's that for, eh?'). She was much criticised by the social puritans of the National Vigilance Association for her use of risqué gestures and double entendres. Lloyd reputedly once turned the tables on moral investigators who had come to assess her performance by giving her regular material 'played straight', then finishing with a highly suggestive version of the staid drawing-room classic 'Come into the Garden, Maud'.

THE DRUNKARD'S CHILDREN.

PLATE III.—FROM THE GIN SHOP TO THE DANCING ROOMS, FROM THE DANCING ROOMS TO THE GIN SHOP, THE POOR GIRL IS DRIVEN ON IN THAT COURSE WHICH ENDS IN MISERY.

10. George Cruikshank's illustrated temperance tract *The Drunkard's Children* (1848) shows a working-class 'dancing room' which will inevitably lead unwary females 'to the gin-shop … that course which ends in misery'. The advertising bills on display hint at other demoralising popular entertainments, from a theatrical performance of *The Vampire* to *poses plastiques* and a 'Judge and Jury' show featuring 'Slang v Sootbag' (a bawdy, comical mock-trial). A notice to keep good order in the ballroom asks 'gents' to remove their hats before dancing, not to smoke during the dance and that 'no two gents … dance together'.

THE CAKEWALK AT A SHILLING HOP. HOLBORN TOWN HALL.

Tom Browne

11. This sketch by Tom Browne (1870–1910) from Robert Machray's *The Night Side of London* (1902) shows a 'shilling hop' or 'Cinderella ball' (i.e. finishing by midnight) held at Holborn Town Hall. The clientele, according to Machray, is mostly comprised of shop assistants, who are dressed in regular clothes rather than evening wear. The exception is the 'Professor of Dancing' who leads them in the new novelty dance of the 'cake walk' but, Machray informs his readers, they much prefer the more serious business of waltzing.

12. Phoebus Levin (1836–1908) painted this evocative scene of the dancing platform at Cremorne Gardens in Chelsea in 1864, showing the pleasure garden by day, whilst strongly hinting at its notorious nocturnal reputation. The seated solitary woman revealing her ankles, right, may be presumed to be a prostitute. In the top left, we can see the end of the tier of raised 'supper-boxes' which offered an excellent view of the dancing, particularly by night as a gas-lit spectacle, and the dimly-lit confines of which also reportedly facilitated many a sexual liaison.

13. A coloured photograph of the entrance to the Egyptian Court at the rebuilt and remodelled commercial incarnation of the Crystal Palace at Sydenham (1854–1936). The giant figures are the Egyptian pharaoh Rameses II, copied from his temple at Abu Simbel, which dominated the northern transept. The colouring shows Owen Jones' decorative scheme not only for the statues but for the Crystal Palace itself, including sky blue for the topmost iron girders.

14. A coloured lithograph of the Pompeian Court at the Crystal Palace, Sydenham, taken from a photograph by Philip Henry Delamotte (1821–99). This was a souvenir print which could be purchased by visitors ('Published by Authority by Day & Son, in the Crystal Palace'). The Pompeian Court was the only themed zone within the Palace which created a fully immersive experience for the visitor, as if they were standing inside a real Roman villa.

15. The official opening of the 1862 London International Exhibition, painted by Edward Sherratt Cole (1817–1905). The exhibition building stood on the site of the present-day Natural History Museum in Kensington. The design by Francis Fowke (1823–65) was much criticised as inferior to that of its predecessor, the 1851 Great Exhibition in Hyde Park. *Blackwood's Magazine* mocked it as an unsightly hybrid of 'agricultural barn, the purely practical and mercantile factor, and the middle-age cathedral'. The exhibition building would be recycled by its builders, Kelk and Lucas, to construct Alexandra Palace in north London, which finally opened in 1873, only to burn to the ground sixteen days later.

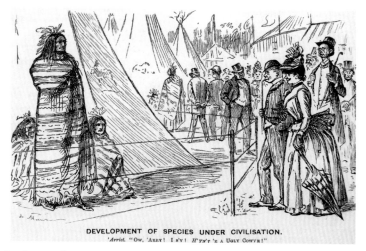

DEVELOPMENT OF SPECIES UNDER CIVILISATION.
'Arriet. "Ow, 'Arry! I s'y! If yn't 'e a Ugly Cowye!"

16. A *Punch* cartoon by George du Maurier depicting Native Americans at the American Exhibition at Earl's Court. They performed in Buffalo Bill's Wild West Show – defeated by cowboys nightly in the ground's open-air arena – and, along with their tents, formed a sort of human zoo which could be inspected by the public. The cartoon's title, *Development of Species under Civilisation*, alludes to evolutionary theory and suggests that uncouth working-class visitors, depicted with monkey-like features, are equally if not more 'primitive' than those placed on display, who possess a rather patrician mien.

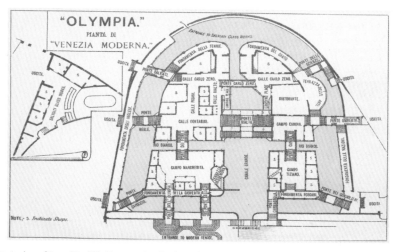

17. A plan of Imre Kiralfy's *Venice in London* (1889), a re-creation of Venice, replete with canals, gondoliers and three-quarter-size gondolas, in the annexe of the exhibition hall at Olympia. Visitors could stroll round the theme-park-like 'city', exploring shops and cafés, and could even observe a glass-blowing workshop, before attending the main musical pageant in the adjoining flooded exhibition hall, entitled *Venice, the Bride of Sea*.

18. Imre Kiralfy made sure his name was prominent on all advertisements for his theatrical and exhibition projects. Many programmes and bills also feature his likeness, but this particular example, from the India and Ceylon Exhibition of 1896 at Earl's Court, prefers to trumpet the glories of Empire. Britannia appears as a benign embodiment of British rule, with India and Ceylon personified as willing handmaidens. She gestures towards the orientalist fantasia of Kiralfy's exhibition ground, identifiable by its famous Ferris wheel. Kiralfy's international exhibitions consistently sold an entertaining, positive image of Empire to the British public.

19. One of the more unlikely side-show attractions at Imre Kiralfy's 1899 Greater Britain Exhibition at Earl's Court was the re-creation of a 'Hong Kong Opium Smoking Parlour'. Advertisements which promised 'full working order ... living Chinamen ... demonstrations constantly given' were, however, rather misleading. Visitors who paid sixpence found nothing more than a waxwork tableau.

20. The 'Witching Waves' amusement ride at Imre Kiralfy's White City, introduced in 1909, had previously entertained an American audience at Coney Island. The cars were simply on castors, but the canvas underneath undulated, thanks to electric-powered rollers, which kept them moving round the track. Film footage of this and other White City attractions can be found in *Farmer Jenkins' Visit to the White City* on the BFI website (https://player.bfi.org.uk).

21. A postcard of Clacton Pier, opened in 1871, charging the usual penny admission. We can see features common to many seaside piers, including the pavilion (opened 1893); moorings for steamers and other boats; and a booking office for coastal excursions, and another for the sale of season tickets. There are also modest bathing facilities. Signs forbid the presence of hawkers, musicians, stall-holders and dogs.

A QUIET DRIVE BY THE SEA.
A Brighton Bath-Chairman's Idea of a Suitable Route for an Invalid Lady.

22. *A Quiet Drive by the Sea* appeared in *Punch* on 19 April 1890, drawn by E.T. Reed. A serene 'bath-chairman' pulls an invalid along the Brighton seafront amidst numerous noisy catchpenny performers who compete for the tourist's attention. The list includes a fire-eater in oriental costume; a blackface minstrel; a blind man reading from a braille book; and a man costumed as if he was the popular cartoon character Ally Sloper riding a horse.

23. The Blackpool Winter Gardens opened in 1878 accompanied by lavish civic ceremonies laid on for invited officials from other English towns and cities, designed to publicise both the new attraction and the resort as a whole. During the 1880s, the site prospered under the management of music hall and pleasure garden impresario William Holland. The Ferris wheel, only the third in the world after Chicago and Earl's Court, opened in 1896 as a 'sky sign' attraction to rival the Blackpool Tower. The entertainment complex increasingly struggled to compete with the Blackpool Tower Company, who finally bought up the Winter Gardens in 1928.

24. The 1890s saw entrepreneurs attempt to build a British equivalent of the Eiffel Tower at Douglas on the Isle of Man, Morecambe, Wembley, New Brighton and Blackpool. Only the towers at New Brighton and Blackpool came to fruition, with the former, too costly to maintain, demolished after the First World War. Blackpool Tower, opened in 1894, cost £300,000 to build and incorporated a circus, restaurant, dancing pavilion and menagerie at ground level, as well as the existing adjoining aquarium. The famously opulent Tower Ballroom, designed by Frank Matcham, was opened in 1898 to compete with the Empress Ballroom of the rival Winter Gardens.

25. Paul Martin (1864–1944), a wood engraver who became a professional photographer, took candid snapshots on Yarmouth Sands with a disguised 'detective' camera in the mid-1890s. The images reveal relaxed working-class couples cuddling on the sands, as well as the obligatory stalls supplying food, drink and entertainment.

ASSOCIATION FOOTBALL : THE FINAL CUP TIE AT THE CRYSTAL PALACE ON APRIL 15.

26. The *Illustrated London News* depicts the 1899 FA Cup Final between Sheffield United and Derby County. The page mixes comic accidents – fans falling out of trees and a photographer hit by a ball – with action sequences and even a statistic ('Foulkes: Goal Keeper for Sheffield: Heaviest Football Player, Weighs 19 stone 7½ lbs'). The *ILN* was not a sporting paper and such a feature in a mainstream magazine reveals how the game had progressed from an amateur's hobby to a professional sport and national obsession, all within the space of two decades.

Sell fruit and cigars at Telegraph Office.
Big strong aviary Macaws flying about. Bear pit.
A Rabbit Warren. An Alligator Pond.
Exhibtn. Burglars Implements & means to outwit them.
Get paintings by Princesses?
Grow cucumbers & sell them, letting Public cut them.
Chess with living men.
Advt at bottom of Tumbler glasses seen as one drinks.
Find out about Water Shoes to float people across lake.
Big collection of Chimpanzees.[49]

One of the more peculiar schemes from this period – a fox hunt within the grounds – actually came to fruition. Predictably miserable scenes ensued when a notably lethargic fox was released, lay down to rest and was swiftly torn to pieces. In truth, the Alexandra Palace never laid much claim to an educational or moral purpose, unlike its South London rival, and the fact that a race-track was tolerated within the grounds was itself sufficient to put off the more religious visitor. Any lingering hint of a moral/educational mission surely died with the unfortunate fox. The end result was an RSPCA prosecution and a promise never to repeat the experiment.[50]

There were still some interesting spectacles. Hansom cab racing and cricket matches played by clowns and music-hall stars amused the crowds. Performing animals of every description, including monkeys, came and went. As ever, the foreign and exotic loomed large – from a 'Nubian Camp' of North Africans and their exotic animals to the 'Catschaacoomawaugh' refreshment bar, with 'peculiarly dressed attendants' (presumably a Native American theme). An ageing Blondin came out of retirement and still proved a big attraction. A band of 'woodland players' attempted Shakespeare in the park. Mexican Joe's Western Wilds Company displayed horsemanship and sharp-shooting. And one Professor Baldwin executed numerous faultless parachute jumps from a tethered balloon. Temporary static exhibitions included a whaling boat, which had been crewed solely by a married couple and piloted across the Atlantic. In 1882, the management arranged for competing photographers to take pictures of the crowds. The best photograph was awarded a prize; but the audience was also invited to pay sixpence for a copy posted direct to their homes, so that they could spot themselves somewhere in the hordes of humanity (a forerunner of the endless photo opportunities at modern theme parks). An electric tram was introduced to the hilly grounds in the late 1880s, for the comfort and convenience of visitors. There was even, briefly, a creche for 'mothers wishing to leave babies under the care of nurses while they spent the day in the Palace', although only a handful of women could be induced to do so.[51] None of these attractions was sufficient to rescue the dream of a northern palace. The London Financial Association, which still owned the site, finally went bankrupt in 1895.

The ultimate demise of the LFA was no great surprise. It had spent the best part of two decades trying to sell the site for building land, but it had consistently struggled to find buyers at auction, with the reserve price never met. The estate was also burdened by a legal clause which stipulated that a certain acreage had to be retained for recreational use. This public-spirited caveat had been introduced to sweeten a parliamentary bill permitting a branch railway onto the land. The Alexandra Palace and its grounds would finally be bought up, at a knock-down price, by a collective of North London local government authorities for use as a public park. The building was to be retained and leased to whoever could find a use for it: most famously the BBC in 1935.

While the Alexandra Palace failed to establish itself as a profitable amusement ground for North London, there were others still willing to speculate in exhibition grounds in a different part of the capital. From the mid-1880s, West London would provide a new, more convenient locus for Londoners seeking varied indoor and outdoor amusement.

Kensington, of course, was the original home of the Crystal Palace, and government-supported exhibitions continued in 'Albertopolis' during the 1870s and early 1880s, on the same site as the 1862 International Exhibition. These included a series of more modest, annual International Exhibitions (1871–74). Only the first made a profit, thanks to discounted access to the adjoining, newly opened Royal Albert Hall. Subsequent years all resulted in rapidly diminishing returns.[52] The idea of annual Kensington exhibitions perpetually keeping the public abreast of the latest developments in manufacturing, science and industry was reluctantly abandoned.

The managers of the Kensington estate, however, found a new purpose with a series of themed exhibitions in the 1880s. These included the International Fisheries Exhibition, 1883 (featuring 'attractive Fish Culturing Operations, large and well stocked Aquaria, Lifeboats, Life-saving and Diving

Apparatus');[53] the International Health Exhibition, 1884 (with displays including a pair of model 'Sanitary' and 'Insanitary' houses); and the Colonial and Indian Exhibition of 1886 (a mixture of imperial self-congratulation and trade show to promote Indian products and industry).[54] These three events were all a great financial success. The Fisheries Exhibition and the 'Healtheries' (a humorous name that was widely adopted) both made around £15,000 profit. The rather more exotic and exciting Indian Exhibition ('Colinderies') made a surplus of over £30,000. This money went towards building the new Imperial Institute on the site of what is now Imperial College, Kensington.

When, however, the Albertopolis site was given over wholly to the Imperial Institute and the Royal College of Music in the late 1880s, it seemed as though the age of the exhibition might finally have ended.[55] As it happens, this merely opened the door to a new series of commercially run, themed expositions a mile further west, in Earl's Court. These late Victorian exhibitions would serve as de facto trade missions, historical and ethnographical education, theatrical spectacular and imperial propaganda, with a dose of the fairground for good measure.

Earl's Court was the brainchild of John Robinson Whitley, the son of a Yorkshire engineer who had taken his father's manufactured goods on tour to international exhibitions in Paris, Moscow, Lyons and Vienna in the 1870s, and so had some idea of the exhibition business. He had made his own fortune selling Lincrusta-Walton wallpaper, based on Frederick Walton's patents. He had, according to one interviewer, 'been everywhere, seen and known everybody', had a marvellous facility for languages and organisation, and an anecdote for every occasion.[56] In 1884, he came up with a new idea for hosting thematic exhibitions in London: they would represent the arts, science and manufactures of a single foreign country. To get the ball rolling, he began to plan an American exhibition. The project was put on hold the following year, for fear it might overshadow the Colonial and Indian extravaganza at Kensington. Whitley claimed that this was thanks to polite arm-twisting on behalf of the Colonial Exhibition's patron, the Prince of Wales. The delay, whether demanded by the Prince or not, cost him many of his US backers. He recovered by persuading William 'Buffalo Bill' Cody to bring his Wild West show to London, as part of the exhibition (which, continuing the now-established tradition, was dubbed the 'Yankeries' by the more whimsical elements of the press).

Earl's Court itself, the site for Whitley's American exhibition, was a patch of neglected ground between three railway lines. It was rented from the Midland and District Railways. The land itself required extensive building work, including several bridges across the tracks, before an outdoor arena, main exhibition building and various other adjuncts could be constructed. Nonetheless, it was estimated that over 600 trains per day already stopped at nearby stations, and so the initial investment seemed worthwhile. The site finally opened on 9 May 1887. Certainly, in terms of publicity, Whitley's expectations were justified: the Wild West and the larger-than-life Cody proved an instant sensation, even if the exhibition's more traditional instructive displays of American arts, inventions, manufactures, products and resources were somewhat neglected. This was hardly surprising. Cody's action-packed show featured over 200 Native Americans and 'scouts and cowboys', 166 horses, buffalo, deer, antelope and elk, all brought over from the United States. The performance, held twice daily, took place in a custom-built outdoor stadium within the grounds. There was seating for 15,000 people, in front of an arena backed by a three-dimensional sculpted 'mountain range' designed to hide the nearby rooftops of West London (although some claimed still to be able to see 'chimney-pots growin' out').[57] Various exciting scenes were enacted, including 'an attack by Indians on an emigrant waggon'; an 'attack on the Deadwood stage coach by Indians'; and 'a realistic representation of Indian camp life'.[58] The *Era*'s critic was full of enthusiasm, although he wondered whether the show's three 'Indian attacks' might be one too many. He respectfully suggested the introduction of a 'little scalping', complete with fake wigs and scalps dripping with blood, for variety.[59] William Gladstone, the Prince of Wales and various other notables were given special preview performances. The Queen herself attended the royal box in the first week and exchanged pleasantries with the renowned sharp-shooter Annie Oakley. There were other attractions in the exhibition grounds, including a rollercoaster, a 'toboggan ride' and a grand panorama of New York painted by Bartholdi (sculptor of the Statue of Liberty). But it was the Wild West show that made the first Earl's Court exhibition popular.

Whitley was also rather innovative in his exploitation of celebrity patronage. He carefully cultivated a long list of patrons who might serve as the Earl's Court 'Welcome Committee'.[60] This amounted to dozens of authors, aristocrats, journalists, politicians, businessmen, etc. who were not only invited to the opening ceremony, but were offered membership of an exclusive 'Welcome Club'. The club building, also situated within the grounds, was essentially a well-furnished gentlemen's club (women were only allowed as guests). Members could wine and dine at the club, meet foreign dignitaries, even rub shoulders with 'Buffalo Bill' himself. This was a clever way of enticing the elite trend-setters of Victorian society to Earl's Court. The location was novel; the building itself resembled a rather upmarket hunting lodge; and it offered the sort of class and cultural distinction which eminent Victorians appreciated. This, in turn, doubtless generated many positive column inches in the press. Whitley actively promoted his exhibitions as a means of fostering international trade and business deals. This was the carrot that might induce foreign governments and institutions to supply items for public display in future. The club, there-fore, was tangible evidence of Earl's Court's networking benefits.

Whitley's second project at Earl's Court was an Italian Exhibition, held the following year. This had a rival in the Anglo-Danish Exhibition at Kensington, a last hurrah for Albertopolis as an exhibition ground (making use of the Albert Hall's galleries, conservatory and the modest patch of land that had not yet been dedicated to the construction of the Imperial Institute). The Anglo-Danish Exhibition was to celebrate the silver wedding of the Prince and Princess of Wales and to support a charitable cause, namely rebuilding the British Home for Incurables. Various entertainment elements crept in, including a rollercoaster and a toboggan slide, just as at Earl's Court. Whitley's Italian extravaganza, however, was on a considerably larger scale, staged with the enthusiastic support of the Italian Chamber of Commerce and Italian royalty. The exhibition space was reportedly oversubscribed by manufacturers, and additional attractions promoting Italian industry included displays of food products; a 'Blue Capri Grotto' (with water trickling over plaster stalac-tites); café and restaurants in the style of various Italian buildings; and a glass workshop demonstrating the skills of workers from Salviati's of Venice.

The fences around the gardens were replaced with paintings of Italian scenery, to create a more complete illusion. The rollercoaster (kept from the previous year) was remodelled with an Alpine backdrop and with boarding and exit gates that resembled a Swiss and an Italian railway station, respec-tively. The New York diorama was replaced with the Bay of Naples. The central gardens contained an 'Italian marketplace', with women in peasant costume selling fruit and flowers. And nearby was a mock-up of the Roman forum.[61]

Finally, the outdoor arena that had hosted the Wild West show was remade as the Colosseum, built to roughly the same footprint as the Roman original (albeit with fewer tiers). To preserve the effect, the section opposite the main audience contained two front rows of actors in togas, backed by rows of painted canvases of seated plebs. This was said to be an excellent optical illusion in the evening show, when the arena was selectively illuminated by electric light. There was also a separate seating area for (living) versions of the Emperor Titus and his court. Displays within the arena included the grand entrance of the emperor; athletics; chariot racing; an 'Amazon Contest' featuring female athletes; mock gladiatorial combat with net and trident; and a lengthy procession of Roman soldiers, Gauls and Britons, slaves, vestal virgins, etc. The Colosseum, strangely enough, only opened two months after the main exhibition: Whitley claimed to have been chastened by press reports that Cody's exploits were the 'tail that wagged the dog' in the American Exhibition. This, he explained, was why he had delayed the Roman spectacle – so that the public was not distracted from the other exhibits (though almost certainly the excuse concealed some failure of funds or organisation). There were complaints that the grounds were still under construction several weeks after opening ('the sounds of the hammer are still to be heard in various directions').[62] It would have been peculiarly reckless to delay the opening of such a major attraction, since the open-air site was only viable for a limited summer season.[63]

Whitley took a break the following year, although there was a Spanish Exhibition run by his business partners, which proved something of a flop. Despite rumours of a bull-fight forming the principal attraction in the arena, no such spectacle was forthcoming. There were, likewise, few exhibits on display, except for paintings, since the Spanish government was more committed to the 1889 Exposition Universelle in Paris, under the shadow of the newly built Eiffel Tower.

Whitley returned to stage a French Exhibition in 1890 (with a 'Wild East' show, populated by native inhabitants of French Algeria), with financial backing from the Metropolitan District Railway; and a German Exhibition in 1891 (with a show displaying 'an historical representation of four important periods in the military development of the [German] Empire').[64] He then quit the business, claiming to have done much for international relations. But he was a poorer man than when he had begun. One business partner would later claim that the much-feted American Exhibition lost Whitley and his backers

£70,000.[65] Regardless, Whitley remained a wealthy individual, and went on to found the Anglo-French seaside golfing resort of Le Touquet. He had, at the very least, laid the groundwork for the man who finally turned a reliable profit from latter-day exhibitions: the theatrical producer Imre Kiralfy.

Imre Kiralfy was an impresario who first came to London in the 1860s, aged twenty-one, as part of a Hungarian dance troupe. The Kiralfy family were much-praised virtuosi who specialised in Hungarian folk dancing, and Imre served as both dancer and choreographer.[66] The troupe did well in England, but sailed to America in 1869. And it was in the US that Imre and his brother Bolossy (Balázs) began to produce complete theatrical shows (as opposed to dance interludes) at various theatres on the East Coast. Early successes included a stage version of Jules Verne's *Around the World in Eighty Days* and Manzotti's allegorical ballet *Excelsior*, a tribute to human invention, scientific advancement and international unity, with nations brought together by the (electric) light of progress. Imre split with his brother in the late 1880s, but remained a noted theatrical producer/director. He became associated with a particular type of entertainment: huge outdoor spectacles, featuring massive sets and hundred of performers.

These were not entirely original entertainments. Kiralfy based his early projects on the lavish biblical/classical pageants which were being staged annually by the city of Cincinnati. Indeed, his first outdoor extravaganza was in conjunction with Cincinnati businessmen, who took the scenery from a Cincinnati production and restaged it in New York. They were known, rather marvellously, as the Fall of Babylon Company. Kiralfy produced/directed both *The Fall of Babylon* ('The Colossal Open-air, Historical, Scriptural, Musical, Martial, Spectacular Creation') and *Nero; or, the Fall of Rome* on Staten Island, New York, in 1887 and 1888, respectively.[67] The spectacles boasted a stage nearly 500 feet wide, hundreds of colourfully costumed performers, and processions of elephants and camels, all set in an amphitheatre that could accommodate up to 30,000 spectators. *Nero* was described by Kiralfy as neither a play, drama, pageant nor opera, but a novel blending of all these different elements. The spectacle consisted of various highly animated scenes, including revels inside the emperor's palace; a naval battle in the Circus Maximus; gladiatorial games and chariot racing; and finally the destruction of Rome by fire (and the divine salvation of some early Christians). The sheer scale and vibrancy of the proceedings – the cast was said to number around 2,000 – was more important than the plot. In any case, it was the outstanding success of his *Babylon* and *Nero* that led Kiralfy back to London.

Kiralfy was initially hired by Phineas T. Barnum, the famed showman whose *Greatest Show on Earth* three-ring circus had been booked to appear in the Olympia exhibition hall in the autumn of 1889. Olympia, which opened in 1886, was an empty iron-and-glass-topped hangar in West London, whose vast interior could be remodelled to various uses. Seating, which could be removed, potentially created a Circus Maximus-style arena, with a semi-circle of tiered seats at either end; expensive boxes along one side; and the other side a promenade. Barnum was providing his usual circus extravaganza: clowns, acrobats, animals, freaks, magicians, etc.; but the second half of the performance was to be a revised version of Kiralfy's most successful spectacular, now entitled *Nero, or the Destruction of Rome*. More than a thousand handsomely costumed gladiators, soldiers, singers, dancers, charioteers and athletes appeared before the public in a serious of five tableaux. The size of the venue, once again, left little scope for dialogue, but the lively orchestra and mime conveyed the minimal story, which could also be easily followed with the aid of the programme. Various sequences of action were perfectly timed by Kiralfy triggering electric bells backstage. The show, in short, proved an immense success. The capital had never seen anything on quite such a scale, and it ran for six months.

Kiralfy then began to plan his own unique show for Olympia, backed by a small group of British investors. They were all men involved in the refreshments business: Harold Hartley of the Pure Water Company; Joseph Lyons of the famous catering company; and Montague Gluckstein, a wealthy tobacco merchant, but also a founder of Lyons. Hartley had some personal experience of exhibitions: as a young man, he had worked as a 'commissioner' for the 1872 Vienna Imperial Exhibition, touring the country, persuading English manufacturers to buy up exhibition space and advertising in Vienna. But Kiralfy's new show was to be quite different from the traditional expo of arts and industry, or even the 'national' exhibitions that were being produced at Earl's Court by Whitley. Kiralfy would not only stage another massive pageant – entitled *Venice, the Bride of the Sea* – but would re-create Venice itself. The show, naturally, involved a staged Venice and presented a grand aquatic spectacle, with the main arena flooded to represent the Grand Canal. Various tableaux, fully utilising the water, were paraded before the public: the launch of a ship; a Venetian marriage; a fortress under siege by land and water; scenes from *The Merchant of Venice*. Such aquatic performances were not unknown in Victorian theatre, albeit rarely seen on such a grand scale. However, the unique feature was *Venice in London* in the exhibition's adjoining annexe. This was what might now be called a 'visitor experience' – a magical three-dimensional walk-through stage set, open to the public throughout the day. The various buildings were separated by a series of waterways seamlessly connected to the 'Grand Canal' in the main hall. Again, this was not absolutely original. There was a precedent in the construction of an 'Old London Street' at the 1884 International Health Exhibition. This was an enclosed Tudor-themed space, which was theoretically intended to show the capital's cramped and unhygienic 'olden days' but ended up rather more sanitised and charming. *Venice in London* was somewhat more elaborate in its pathways and canals, but similar in size and effect.

Kiralfy's Venice featured numerous bridges, facades of famous palaces, and strolling Italian musicians, along with working restaurants and cafés.[68] For sixpence, one could even take a gondola ride through the whole experience, staffed by real gondoliers who had been hired in Italy. The boats themselves, likewise, were authentic Italian originals, made especially for Kiralfy, although reduced to three-quarter scale to accommodate the modest diameter of the London 'canals'. There were other attractions, including, once again, Salviati's glass workshop and a bazaar selling sweets and trinkets, run by 'damsels, Venetian in costume, if not in accent'.[69] But it was the unique immersive space of *Venice in London* that set Kiralfy's production apart. The Crystal Palace at Sydenham could boast a Pompeian villa; the Alexandra Palace a 'Moorish House'. But the twists and turns of 'Modern Venice in London' let visitors believe they were in the actual city itself. Some of Olympia's well-to-do clientele had visited the original in Italy. Hartley joked that the gondoliers were 'a splendid lot of fellows who met many of their old patrons in London'.[70] Such visitors were reportedly as delighted with the fidelity of the scene as those for whom it was a species of vicarious tourism. The critic of the *Era* pointed out that the representation was unrealistic in only one aspect, being 'more bright and beautiful than the reality . . . [with] the advantage of being free from the disgusting smells of the city itself'.[71] The show was so popular that it spawned an imitator in Birmingham, situated within the city's 'Winter Gardens', an iron pavilion from a partially completed hotel and shopping development, which had previously hosted concerts and a roller-skating rink. Kiralfy sued the promoters, but failed to establish any kind of fraudulent attempt to link *Venice in London* to *Venice in Birmingham*, even though it was clearly a blatant copy.[72]

Kiralfy had not bought into Olympia itself, and had no connection with the management of the building. He took 40 per cent of the profits from *Venice in London*, which ran from Boxing Day 1891 to January 1893, and then returned to the United States. He staged another highly successful theatrical spectacular, *America*, in Chicago during the famous Columbian Exposition of 1893 (also known as the World's Fair). But he returned to the metropolis in 1895 to found London Exhibitions Ltd, which took over the running of Earl's Court.

The exhibition ground at Earl's Court, opened by Whitley in 1887, had never made a profit, and the quality of its exhibitions had been flagging ever since Whitley quit the business. Kiralfy would revive it, remodelling the grounds and buildings, incorporating a 'Gigantic Wheel' (a Ferris wheel, as first seen in Chicago) and mounting his own spectacular theatrical show in an indoor arena, the Empress Theatre. Kiralfy was now backed by Lyons' rivals, Spiers and Pond. His relationship with the catering company was a close one. Paul Cremieu-Javal, the firm's managing director, was also on the board of London Exhibitions Ltd, and Kiralfy's share prospectus for London Exhibitions was first distributed among Spiers and Pond's shareholders. The caterers ploughed £15,000 into the business when further cash was needed to get things off the ground.[73] By way of compensation, Spiers and Pond received the refreshments concession, which included free advertising throughout the Earl's Court site, and all profits from the ground's 'automatic supply boxes' (vending machines). Spiers and Pond also had a further indirect interest, since they served as the refreshment contractor for the Metropolitan District Railway. If the new venture prospered, it would boost the fortunes of the railway company, ferrying the public to and from Earl's Court.

Spiers and Pond's faith in Kiralfy proved wholly justified. After a hesitant start, the London Exhibitions Ltd, on average, paid 10 per cent dividends to its shareholders for nigh on a decade.[74] The Olympia exhibition hall, by way of contrast, struggled to remain solvent during this same period. When London Exhibitions Ltd finally fell on harder times in 1908, it was only because Kiralfy himself had opened a larger, rival venture in Shepherd's Bush. These exhibition grounds were known as 'White City', a name borrowed from the famous

Chicago exhibition of 1893. Kiralfy himself died in 1919 with an estate worth over £130,000, after twenty years as the leading exponent of 'great exhibitions'. But what was it that Kiralfy did differently from his predecessors at Earl's Court and the Crystal Palace?

We should not underestimate Kiralfy's personal attributes as a general manager. He had worked in the theatre since he was a child; and before arriving at Earl's Court, he had a decade's experience of successfully staging and promoting theatrical spectacles. John Whitley and the original promoters of both the Crystal Palace and Alexandra Palace were businessmen, but with minimal experience of showbusiness. This is not to say that Kiralfy was a great innovator: most of his signature successes were borrowed ideas. Taking on Earl's Court, for example, he continued Whitley's practice of staging annual themed exhibitions, and maintained the Welcome Club. But he was a skilled organiser and the Kiralfy brand provided the perfect blend of continuity and novelty. Every season there would be some sort of new spectacle for the public to enjoy; but it would always be a *Kiralfy* spectacle. Programmes and guides always had 'Director General: Imre Kiralfy' emblazoned on their colourful covers. His pre-existing international reputation as a theatrical impresario underwrote the whole business.

The annual Earl's Court exhibitions held under Kiralfy's active management were:

1895 – Empire of India
1896 – India and Ceylon
1897 – The Victorian Era
1898 – International Universal Exhibition
1899 – Greater Britain
1900 – Woman's Exhibition
1901 – Military Exhibition
1902 – Paris in London
1903 – International Fire Exhibition.[75]

These annual themes were, in theory, reflected across the Earl's Court site. This included the traditional exhibition element of showcased manufactured goods, but also grand Kiralfy spectacles in the Empress Theatre arena; lesser theatrical shows scattered around the grounds; and themed restaurants and side-shows. In practice, the themes were not that rigidly applied. The first year's Empire of India Exhibition was probably the most 'thematic' exhibition, with various attractions relating to the subcontinent: a 'working' mosque; an indoor re-creation of an Indian jungle; Burmese and Indian entertainers, including jugglers and acrobats strolling the grounds; a re-creation of an Indian bazaar; and a curry house ('here the Anglo-Indian visitor may refresh his inner man with his favourite Eastern dishes, prepared by a staff of Indian cooks and placed before him by native servants'). Likewise, the Empress Theatre contained a typical Kiralfy pageant, an 'operatic historical play' which offered a potted, Anglo-centric history of India, culminating in Victoria declaring herself empress.

Later years were not so consistent. Various novelties soon appeared on the site which bore little relation to the year's supposed subject matter. In 1896, a panorama of Ancient Rome found its way into the attractions of the India and Ceylon Exhibition, itself a somewhat lazy rebranding of the previous year's amusements. Likewise, a display of the latest sensation, Röntgen Rays, where one could pay a few pence to acquire an X-ray of one's foot or hand. There was always space for new technology. This included 'infant incubators' ('a perfect magnet to lady visitors');[76] various types of early cinema (including the Theatrograph, Pantomimograph and Vieograph); the electrophone (streaming of live concerts in London by telephone line); and theme park rides. The grounds opened with both a giant Ferris wheel and switchback railway (roller-coaster). And in 1899 they acquired a 'Canadian Water Chute' (log flume). In theory, this was part of the Greater Britain exhibition and represented the watery exploits of Canadian loggers; but it was a popular ride and was retained for years afterwards. This was also the case with other popular attractions, such as 'Picturesque England', an enclosed street of mock-Tudor gabled buildings. These were constructed during the Victorian Era Exhibition of 1897, as a novelty setting for shops selling British merchandise. They harked back to the 'Old London Street' of the International Health Exhibition, but they also made some (modest) thematic sense as part of a retrospective of national history and were retained for the next four seasons. Carrying over such amuse-ments created some odd contrasts, but it seems to have served Kiralfy well. Some attractions were merely repainted or redesigned to create a semblance of novelty. The rollercoaster was enlivened by a vast painted backdrop of Windsor Castle in 1897; this was replaced by a depiction of the Rock of Gibraltar two years later and Balmoral in 1901. The rifle range went through various annual incarnations, according to the whim of the proprietors. These generally represented some famous imperial battle or siege (1895 'Chitral Rifle Range'; 1898 'Khartoum Rifle Range'; 1900 'Transvaal Rifle Range').

Empire, in fact, was the golden thread which ran through the diverse Kiralfy exhibitions at Earl's Court. It is impossible to say whether the stress on imperial pomp was a crucial factor in Kiralfy's success; arguably, it was simply the spirit of the times. Eastham Pleasure Gardens in Liverpool, for example, had a 'Transvaal' shooting range installed in 1900, with Winchester rifles and figures of Boers (who flipped over when hit to reveal a white flag of surrender).[77] The stress on Britain's imperial greatness at Earl's Court, in any case, was pervasive. The 'international' character of exhibitions in the 1850s and 1860s was as much about trade with rival foreign powers as flag-waving. Kiralfy's internationalism, on the other hand, consistently highlighted Britain's imperial supremacy. The much-expanded British Empire was now very much front and centre. This was obvious in various parts of the grounds, from taking pot shots at Boers in the rifle range to the pageants in the theatre. The latter included not only 'India' in the 1895 and 1896 exhibitions, but a 'grand naval spectacle' in 1898, with scale models in a flooded arena, 'to demonstrate . . . how our ships would behave in action';[78] the 'Savage South Africa' show of 1899; and 'China; or The Relief of the Legations' in 1901, which depicted the end of the Boxer Rebellion (i.e. with the Chinese revolutionaries defeated by allied Western forces). The same year, during the Boer War, Earl's Court also featured the 'Recruitograph': a lecture on military life, accompanied by lantern slides and moving pictures, sponsored by the War Office ('The lecturer is assisted by music and a charming woman singer renders patriotic songs').[79]

It is also worth noting that the orientalist architecture of the outdoor zones in the grounds was retained throughout Kiralfy's tenure (originally built for the Empire of India Exhibition). This, too, was a nod to Britain's imperial status, although it could lead to some peculiar conjunctions: the onion domes of Mughal India formed an unlikely backdrop to the Tudorbethan street of 'Picturesque England'. This became an even more peculiar sight during the International Universal Exhibition, a generic 'International Exhibition' revolving round the goods of a dozen countries. The exhibition ground's Tudor street was plied by Japanese rickshaw men, taking visitors to the Gigantic Wheel or the nearby Moorish Camp. There, in the shadow of the Ferris wheel,

Moroccan musicians, dancers and entertainers amused the general public. Earl's Court, then, was nothing if not eclectic, offering Londoners the world in miniature. But it also presented that world, beyond Europe, as a 'Greater Britain'. The exotic architecture, the culinary delights, the exhibition halls of manufactured goods, the very people of Asia and Africa: all were subsumed and subservient to Kiralfy's project of (imperial) instruction and amusement. As one modern scholar has noted, the late Victorian exhibition served to both 'glorify and domesticate Empire'.[80] There was perhaps an element of cultural exchange, but it was all rather one-sided and tended to resemble a stock-take of foreign possessions and peoples.

Nowhere was this more apparent than in the 'human zoos' that were quartered within the site. Their inhabitants were generally on display in tents or huts brought from their 'native habitat'. They also took part in live shows. For example, the 1899 exhibition saw Zulus brought from South Africa to re-enact scenes from the Matabele War and live in a 'Kaffir Kraal', a specially built enclosure. This, too, was a staged performance and it is unlikely that the 'natives' inhabited their living space when the exhibition ground closed for the night.[81] The Zulus included women, one of whom was heavily pregnant. The 'Basuto baby', born while her mother was a performer at Earl's Court, proved a popular attraction.[82] The 1900 Woman's Exhibition, in turn, featured a re-created East African village, populated by 'actual natives from the Fashoda district and fifty Amazons from the Dinka country'.[83]

The public inspection of these faux domestic spaces did not always go smoothly. The Matabele were accused of begging money from passing tourists, drunkenness and over-familiarity with female onlookers. English women, simultaneously, were condemned in the press for undermining the very foundations of empire by their own lax behaviour, 'passing their hands over the shoulders of the savages . . . and holding their children up for kisses'.[84] An absolute divide between black and white – and insistence on racial inferiority/ superiority – justified Britain's imperial project. Any kind of 'mixing' was a dangerous business. The *Daily Mail* campaigned to close the Zulu village, posting various articles on 'The Black Scandal', highlighting the case of one of the performers, Prince Peter Lobengula, who was actually found to be in a relationship with a white woman, Kitty Jewell ('unions between savages and civilised women are never happy').[85] Kiralfy and London Exhibitions Ltd hastily closed the 'Kraal' to female visitors to avoid the bad publicity. They were able to successfully distance themselves from any embarrassment, since the 'Savage South Africa' show was run as a concession by a separate company, which had brought performers from Africa and paid Earl's Court 20 per cent of its takings. Subcontracting out amusements like this was a good way of minimising financial risk; and here it also helped reduce reputational damage.[86]

It perhaps remains questionable whether Kiralfy's undoubted managerial skills and exploitation of imperial themes provide us with an adequate explanation for his unprecedented success. He was not terribly original in the species of entertainment he introduced to the public, as already noted. The human zoo, for instance, had a long history: Ioway Indians were, after all, camped out in Vauxhall Gardens in the 1840s (see Chapter Five). And the Great Exhibition was complemented by a small 'Chinese Exhibition' in nearby Knightsbridge, which featured not only Chinese goods, but a Chinese family in 'national' costume, along with an interpreter. When Kiralfy began at Earl's Court in 1895, the Crystal Palace was already hosting 'Somaliland in London' or 'The East Africa Exhibition', with fifty-three Somali men, six women and six children in a 'native village'. Every afternoon and evening, they would lose a battle with marauding brigands, only to be saved by the arrival of European hunters, bringing the Pax Britannica to their troubled land. In fact, pretty much all the amusements at Earl's Court had already been seen elsewhere in pleasure gardens and exhibition grounds. The site had more in the way of fairground attractions than previously. The *Era* ran annual reviews of the 'Side-shows at Earl's Court', which suggests that the fairground atmosphere was an important aspect.[87] But the same sort of attractions had appeared at Cremorne Gardens, Crystal Palace, etc. since the 1860s – and indeed, as noted in Chapter Five, the Eagle Tavern's pleasure grounds boasted a primitive rollercoaster as early as the 1820s.

Kiralfy's success, I would suggest, actually owed a good deal to how he structured the Earl's Court site. The grounds, thanks to the intersecting railway lines, had three principal zones: the Queen's Palace and Court, set around an artificial lake; a narrow central strip containing the Empress Theatre, colonnaded Imperial Court, bandstand and side-shows (a region dubbed 'Elysia'); and finally, the Western Gardens. By 1899, each section had its signature theme-park ride (the chute, wheel and switchback railway, respectively). Programmes and guides tended to group the further amusements by zone. For the Military Exhibition of 1901, the Queen's Court featured 'A Trip on the

Canton River', motor boats, 'The Great Chinese Dragon' (a passenger boat with a snaking movement, styled as a dragon) and a display of wireless telegraphy. Elysia included distorting mirrors, 'Caricature Photography', a miniature railway, a 'Boer Farm', moving pictures, a rifle range, a re-creation of a Cairo street and an 'American Vaudeville Theatre'. The Western Gardens, aside from the rollercoaster, contained a 'Moving Stereorama' and 'Magic Doll'. This zoning was very much like a modern theme park. The three zones were each a distinct experience in themselves; three experiences for the price of one. They were also more like giant theatre sets than the open parkland of the Crystal Palace or the Alexandra Palace. While they were not quite in the wholly immersive style of *Venice in London*, they were self-contained worlds. The ornate buildings, laid out around the edges of the three zones, hid the suburban housing beyond. Where no buildings stood, Kiralfy carefully erected fake backdrops and screens.

The overall effect at Earl's Court, in other words, was a city within a city. Whereas the likes of the Crystal Palace at Sydenham still followed the old pleasure-garden model of *rus in urbe*, Earl's Court now offered a more modern, highly commercial alternative: to coin a phrase, *urbs in urbe*. Kiralfy's microcity was not cluttered by traffic or the pressures of working life: it offered the weary only pleasure and amusement. Again, this was not entirely novel. Kiralfy undoubtedly drew inspiration from the Chicago World's Fair of 1893, which created its own idealised cityscape. He would go on to dramatically expand this vision in building White City in Shepherd's Bush in 1908, a name which specifically referred back to the pristine facades of the Chicago exposition.

As it turned out, before Kiralfy had finished preparing his new project at Shepherd's Bush, he was pipped to the post – at least in the choice of name: a 'White City' opened in Manchester in 1907. Interestingly, the share prospectus describes the site variously as a 'pleasure garden' and 'amusement park', as if the terms were interchangeable.[88] The site contained a small exhibition element, with the first year promising space for exhibits on colonial cotton-growing (relevant to Manchester's textile heritage) and domestic electric lighting. The park was formerly the city's Royal Botanical Gardens, leased out for a couple of thousand pounds a year. Consequently, the developers were also required to maintain the existing glass houses and continue the Botanical Society's annual flower shows. Most of the 16-acre grounds, however, was devoted to theme-park rides, in the manner of New York's Coney Island or, closer to home, Blackpool Pleasure Beach. There was also the addition of a ballroom and a skating rink. The admission price of sixpence suited the working classes, who were accommodated with a novel transport feature: parking facilities for 2,000 bicycles. The promoter was Chicago-born John Calvin Brown, who had a background running mechanised theme-park rides in the US. He promised Manchester's great and good that there was 'no intention of Americanising the place', but this was essentially an American-style theme park, relying on amusement rides for its principal business.[89] Brown billed it in the press as 'The First Amusement Park in Europe' (a somewhat ambiguous phrase, conveniently ignoring Earl's Court and Blackpool). Calvin would later go on to take the lease of Earl's Court, and to open parks in Barcelona and Paris, creating a short-lived international leisure empire, which he abandoned in 1912.

Kiralfy, therefore, came second with his 'White City' in London; but his new scheme was built on a massively larger scale, and would still incorporate annual themed exhibitions, à la Earl's Court. Kiralfy's White City was like a giant version of Whitley's original Earl's Court project, but constructed in a more symmetrical, logical fashion, unconstrained by the railway lines which carved up the rival ground. There was also an element of Kiralfy's early Venetian triumph at Olympia, with a network of ornamental canals around the central 'Court of Honour', which visitors could tour using electric boats in the shape of swans. Kiralfy, likewise, borrowed the tried-and-tested Mughal style from Earl's Court for the most impressive exhibition buildings around the Court of Honour, even though the first exhibition of 1908 – the Franco-British Exhibition – was actually a celebration of the *Entente Cordiale*.[90] Some areas were dubbed 'gardens', but they were not the mock sylvan groves of the pleasure garden. Rather, these were neat, manicured lawns where one could loll in a deckchair and listen to music from the nearby bandstand, as in a public park.

The white buildings, with their oriental-style carvings, domes and pagodas, looked particularly striking at night, illuminated by thousands of electric lights. The sheer size of the site allowed for numerous exhibition spaces, cafés and restaurants, stalls, fairground attractions and rides (with titles like 'The Glacier Slide', 'The Dingle Dongle' and 'Sir Hiram Maxim's Flying Airships'). These mechanised amusements were given more prominence than previously, and it was reported that 40 of the 146 acres of land at White City were given over to 'side-shows and novel devices'.[91] There were also, as ever, human zoos – aside from Africa and Asia, Ireland was represented, in the shape of a village named 'Ballymaclinton'. This was more of a novel promotion for Irish manufacturing, although it rather resembled the typical ethnographic display. One could observe weaving and other handicrafts, and then tour the assembled 'Irish cottages'. The village was sponsored by McClinton's Soap of Donaghmore, and featured a re-creation of the cottage of US President McKinley's Irish grandfather ('a special attraction to those from across the Atlantic'), as well as a vegetarian restaurant with 'winsome Irish lasses garbed in green and red, short-petticoated and full of the native wit'.[92] There were other sponsored buildings, including the Moët and Chandon Pavilion. This featured a pictorial and dioramic tour of the history of champagne manufacture, and the opportunity to sup the finished product on a roof terrace. Moët made sure to note in its advertising that the building and its lawns immediately adjoined the Royal Enclosure.

The inaugural 1908 Franco-British Exhibition at White City was a huge success. This was hardly surprising, for the exhibition was supported by the British and French governments, not to mention King Edward himself. There was also the additional draw of the 1908 Olympics, for which Kiralfy constructed a stadium within the grounds (something of a last-minute inclusion, after Rome reneged on its commitment to hold the games). For his pains, Kiralfy took 75 per cent of the gate receipts from the sporting events.[93] The public flocked to White City to watch the games, stroll round the grounds, visit the exhibition halls and enjoy the mechanised fun-fair rides. The *Daily Mail* dubbed it the 'City of Side-Shows' and highlighted what turned out to be the biggest attraction: the scissor-like 'Flip-Flap'. Two pendulous iron-caged carriages were attached to two 150-foot steel beams, which rotated through 180 degrees, crossing in the middle, to give visitors an unparalleled view of West London and of the city-within-a-city sprawling beneath them. There was no actual 'flip' – the carriages hung down from the beams, remaining perpendicular – but the effect was nevertheless spectacular.

The promise of providing 'instruction and amusement', first made in 1854, had now definitively tilted rather heavily towards the latter. Whitley's template for geographically themed exhibitions now held sway even at the Crystal Palace. While the Franco-British Exhibition was in full swing at White City, an exhibition of 'Products, Industries, and Resources of Mexico' provided colour at struggling Sydenham. This included 'genuine natives at work and play', with cowboy-style 'Mexican lasso and lariat manipulators'. The Crystal

Palace, however, was on its last legs. Tiny newspaper advertisements for the Mexican extravaganza were buried beneath several column inches advertising the delights of White City. Even the 1908 Hungarian Exhibition at a faltering Earl's Court could afford considerably more space in the 'Exhibitions, Amusements &c.' sections of the paper.[94]

Kiralfy, as it happens, may finally have over-reached himself with White City. The 1910 Japan–British Exhibition was a great success, following the model of 1908. As well as attracting a curious public, it served as a valuable forum for international diplomacy, and Japanese royalty and military leaders were closely involved. But part of the site would be sold off to housing developers in 1911, and revenue would drop dramatically.[95] Any hope of a revival was cut short by the First World War, when the fun abruptly ended. The ground's great halls were turned over to military manufacturing, and then the site fell derelict after the end of hostilities, eventually becoming home to the BBC's iconic Television Centre in 1960. Manchester's White City actually lasted longer than its London namesake, only closing in 1928. The Manchester park was demolished and replaced with a sports stadium, which initially hosted greyhound racing and speedway. It is now the White City retail park, marked only by a solitary relic: the Edwardian amusement ground's neo-classical stuccoed entrance, which stands forlornly by the side of the main road.

VII

OR,

A TRIUMPHAL CAR FOR NEPTUNE

DURING THE EIGHTEENTH CENTURY, the supposed medicinal advantages of sea-bathing and drinking seawater were much promoted by doctors. Wealthy visitors, in turn, began to seek out pleasant and conducive locations to carry out doctors' orders. The result was the growth of coastal alternatives to the well-established inland spa towns. The likes of Brighton and Margate began to compete with Bath and Tunbridge Wells.[1] The sea air was said to be good for the constitution, and the ocean provided the perfect cure-all. As one wag noted, the sea could accommodate anyone – thin and fat; young and old; 'debauchee' and 'antiquated virgin' – all were advised to try seawater for the benefit of their health.[2] Local entrepreneurs, meanwhile, swiftly provided not only elegant bathing facilities, but the same entertainment venues one might find in the spa town: assembly rooms, ballrooms, libraries and reading-rooms. The Georgian seaside resort became a place for both health and sociable amusement. Some came for the water; others, just as in Bath, came solely to be seen among the fashionable elite of society.

Naturally, the same concerns about social status that dominated the spa towns, a desire only to mingle with the 'select', also applied by the sea. One of the advantages of visiting the seaside was a certain relaxation in manners ('a decent freedom and innocent hilarity . . . not discoverable at your stately balls in the atmosphere of St James's'), but the *bon ton* still had a horror of meeting the lesser orders upon anything that resembled equal terms.[3] Hence, when London tradesmen began to take the sea air at Margate, they faced the 'scornful sneer of more improved travellers'.[4] Isaac Cruikshank's 1803 cartoon *A Meeting at Margate* exemplifies this discomfort: an aristocrat is mystified by a vaguely familiar face on the promenade; the man turns out to be his wealthy tailor, wearing equally fine clothing as his lordship. This is not to say that there was complete social segregation. An article in *The Times* records comical games on the sands, organised for the benefit of tourist spectators: donkey races, gurning and pig hunts (youths chasing a greased pig), watched with amusement by the Duchess of Cumberland and 'all the fashionables as well as *non-fashionables* of Margate'.[5]

The balance between 'fashionable' and 'non-fashionable' visitors, however, would change dramatically as the nineteenth century progressed. Two transport revolutions – the steamboat and then the railway – slowly but surely democratised the seaside experience. Some resorts retained a measure of aristocratic custom, or prospered as middle-class health resorts. For others, the transformation was wholesale. Margate, where a lord might accidentally rub shoulders with his tailor in the early 1800s, soon began to attract visitors from lower down the social scale. Blackpool started the nineteenth century as a mere village beside the sea, consisting of fifty houses scattered over a mile, of which six were 'appropriated for the reception of company'.[6] By the end of the Victorian era, it served as a vast pleasure-ground for the factory workers of north-west England (including an amusement park that mimicked the attractions of New York's Coney Island). But how exactly did the seaside shift from the refined delights of sea-bathing to the mechanised fun of Blackpool Pleasure Beach?

To understand the growth of the Victorian seaside resorts, one first needs to look at their immediate predecessors. Margate, as already hinted, was numbered among the leading Georgian resorts, and provides a useful starting point. While it remained a working port (principally shipping corn between Kent and London), during the second half of the eighteenth century it also increasingly served as a seasonal retiring place for the upper classes.[7] This was thanks to its relative proximity to London and an extensive sandy beach. Like

Brighton, it also benefited first from eighteenth-century doctors' active promotion of sea-bathing, and then, later in the century, from the travel restrictions imposed by the Napoleonic Wars, which confined the wealthy to holidaying in their own country. At the turn of the nineteenth century, the town regularly appeared in journal articles, travelogues and guidebooks as a major tourist destination, and during the summer season, local gossip was reprinted in the London press. Good transport links with the metropolis helped maintain a steady stream of visitors. The town was accessible both by stagecoach and, more cheaply, along the Thames by taking a cabin on a tourist boat or a 'hoy' (a cargo-carrying sailing ship running along the coast).[8] These ships made quicker progress than the coach, but respectable folk were warned about the lack of social segregation, which might upset 'persons of delicacy'. Contemporary cartoons show the 'cabins' as little more than a series of curtained bunks around a shared mess hall. The same drawings also show the majority of passengers reeling from sea-sickness.[9]

Bathing remained the main leisure activity. Regency Margate was popular enough to sustain seven different bathing-rooms. These commercial establishments possessed both indoor baths – which could be filled with warm or cold seawater – and outdoor bathing-machines. These were a key element for any resort: wooden sheds on wheels, with steps at the front and back, which could be towed down into the sea, so that respectable customers could discreetly disrobe inside the vehicle. Bathers then emerged, stepping down the front steps directly into the ocean. A muscular attendant could be hired by those fearful of drowning, including female attendants for women. Bathers had the additional option of using the machine's capacious pull-down canvas hood, for complete privacy. This hood, also known as an umbrella, had first been introduced at Margate. It was the invention of a local Quaker, Benjamin Beale. He was concerned that tourists' hand-held telescopes were being trained on naked flesh (men bathed nude in this period, as did some women). The hire of a machine ranged from ninepence for two children, to one shilling and sixpence for a male bather with an assistant. Back in the bathing-rooms, warm baths were more expensive, at three shillings and sixpence. Bathing-rooms also provided free newspapers, and some rooms even had a piano, so that visitors could while away the time in an agreeable fashion, while they waited their turn in the baths.

The rest of Margate's amusements were typical of any genteel Georgian resort, whether coastal or inland. There was an assembly room complex, which offered ball-, tea- and card-rooms, coffee and billiards. This was kept by a Mr Kidman, owner of the Royal Hotel. There was a rival York Hotel (which also had warm marble seawater baths); a Prospect Hotel, which occasionally gave firework displays; and assorted lesser inns and taverns, plus houses to rent, whose terms varied according to location, season and 'style of living'.[10]

Margate also possessed a modest Theatre Royal, built in 1787. It was visited by a travelling provincial company, part of a circuit along the Kent coast. There were several reading-rooms/libraries, where cards and dice could be played, and where raffles were held. Visitors could occupy themselves with excursions to other Kent ports, sea-fishing trips and visits to a pleasure garden named Dandelion, a mile and a half south-west of the town. Set in the grounds of a ruined medieval manor, the site included a small dancing platform, bowling-green and Vauxhall-style 'alcoves' for drinking and dining. One could take public breakfasts on Wednesdays, tea in the afternoons, or spend the evening dancing.[11]

What was it actually like to holiday in Margate in the early part of the nineteenth century? A diary written by the James family from Croydon in 1828 provides a fascinating personal account of a holiday in Ramsgate, Margate and Broadstairs. The journal is co-authored by several family members, and was a collaboration designed to be sent abroad as a letter to a relative in the East India Company. It records what seems to have been a pleasure trip, rather than a tiresome medical cure.[12] The various accounts describe daily bathing in the ocean ('delightful' and 'delicious'); feeding an infant daughter sweetmeats on the beach and taking her on donkey rides; an excursion up the Thames to Woolwich Arsenal; visits to a subscription library with dice games and a billiard room. Bathing-machines are used by the ladies, but not the men (the machines available could be either 'skeletons', which provided only minimal cover, or full-priced examples with the canvas hood). Shells are collected on the beach; assorted trinkets, including a fossil, are purchased from a lighthouse keeper. Hats are tied with ribbons under the chin, to avoid losing them on the blustery pier.

What is quite remarkable is how much of this early account tallies with both the archetypal Victorian and the twentieth-century experience of the seaside holiday, from over-indulgence in sweet stuff to fretting about the weather. The family also quests in vain for 'ices' at a pastrycook's and spends a good deal of time people-watching. But the latter entries include a note of caution:

The place is filling fast, they say, it appears to me already full, certainly not of genteel company, but I believe since the Steamers have frequented it the company has very much fallen off.

The steamboats, which began serving Margate in 1815, were incredibly popular. By 1820, an estimated 40,000 visitors came to the town by steamer. By 1830, this number had risen to almost 100,000.[13] These were very much tourist boats: backgammon tables, draughts and chess boards were provided (presumably rather challenging in choppy waters); a band played; and food and refreshments were readily available.[14] The 60-mile journey from London took only six or seven hours, twice as quick as a coach or a sailing ship (with the latter, of course, being always at the mercy of the weather). Four-guinea season tickets allowed regular visitors to spend weekends in the town over the course of a summer. These were typically businessmen who would rent a place for their family in Margate, but work in London during the week. Thus the Saturday evening steamer was known as the 'husband's boat'. Such commuters were, naturally, relatively wealthy; but they were increasingly joined by those with less wherewithal, once competing steamboat companies engaged in price-cutting wars, with fares sometimes falling as low as a couple of shillings.[15] Margate, in short, grew ever more accessible. The result was that the resort seemed to be heading downmarket in the eyes of the James family. The fictional Mrs Tuggs in Dickens' *Sketches by Boz*, a grocer's wife full of social pretension, has a similar opinion: 'Gravesend was *low*. Margate . . . Worse and worse – nobody there but tradespeople.'[16]

From the very beginning, some believed Margate was a victim of its own success. As early as 1769, the *Kentish Gazette* reported that the town was too full, with the few remaining beds being let at half a guinea a night.[17] In 1800, *The Times* noted that tourists had to content themselves with 'any hole they can be thrust into, in expectation of amusement', while local shopkeepers, tradesmen and stable-keepers charged extortionate rates for basic services. Then, complained the paper, these same money-grubbing locals used their profits to build new housing for the tourist market, which they let out for the summer at eye-watering rates.[18] But there was a fundamental shift in the tourist demographic brought about by the steamboat. The result was that by the 1830s, the aristocracy might still patronise Brighton, but they now eschewed Margate as too plebeian.

A popular journal classified the remaining Margate tourists into three categories: prosperous tradesmen who, in London, kept their own carriage; less well-heeled members of the middle classes, who might only have a 'horse and gig'; and 'foot company', i.e. the carriage-less, including some from the artisan class.[19] Satirical pieces in the press increasingly focused on the amusingly 'common' comings and goings of the latter (note the cockney pronunciation of 'v' for 'w' as a signifier of class):

> We are full to an overflow . . . of tag-rag from Whitechapel and bob-tail from Blackfriars . . . cavalcades of tailors in dust-slippers, Belcher handkerchiefs and 'vite casters [sic]', 'vith their vives', bloated with 'heavy', in straw-coloured cotton gowns, green boots and blue bonnets, who infest the pier at low water . . . dozens of the swell mob are down here doing a little business . . .[20]

The arrival of the South Eastern Railway in 1846 (from London via Ramsgate) – to be followed in 1863 by the more direct London, Chatham and Dover Railway – only hastened the shift towards catering for not only the tradesman, shopkeeper and City clerk, but also the labouring classes. A good comic account of the town and its contemporary clientele appears in *Fun* magazine in 1865. Mrs Brown, a recurring character in the journal, enjoys a couple of days in Margate. Among other things, she dances at the assembly rooms ('where I've heard my dear mother say the fust in the land did use to dance') and is scandalised by nude male bathers ('full-grown Englishmen a-forgettin' of all decency . . . savages . . . disgustin' beasts').[21] Mrs Brown is a former servant, wife of a Lambeth engine-driver, i.e. a representative of the more comfortable sort of upper-working-class family, with a skilled wage-earner. These were the sorts of people who could now afford to take a holiday beside the sea.

Naked bathing was, in fact, rather a topical question for the town in 1865. While women now generally wore a loose flannel bathing costume – and in many cases hid beneath the hood of a bathing-machine – many men still followed the Georgian fashion. The continued acceptance of the custom at Margate became the subject of a series of angry articles in the *Observer* newspaper during the summer and autumn. The paper's editor objected partly to nudity in principle and partly to the proximity of male and female bathing-machines, which allowed for briny fraternisation between the sexes. But worst of all was the flagrant interest which women on land took in viewing nude bathers, gazing through opera glasses and telescopes, which should have been trained on distant shipping. It might be tempting to dismiss the latter as a prurient fantasy. But telescopes were commonplace at the seaside, and earlier references to people spying on naked bathers at Margate are numerous, including Rowlandson's *Summer Amusement at Margate* (1815), showing lecherous men spying on naked females. Conversely, the *Satirist*, in the early 1830s, mocked, with gentle ribaldry, women gaining 'knowledge . . . which may materially influence their susceptible feelings in the choice of a husband'.[22] Telescopes were not always requisite. A writer to the *Illustrated London News* in the 1850s complained of naked men at Margate:

> the Wader species who, without a stitch of clothing, stalk coolly about knee-deep within a few yards of a crowded promenade . . . gambolling like sea-calves in shallow water, and so prodigally displaying their charms to passers-by . . . [but] not in general the models of grace and vigour that might have supplied the eclectic for the Belvedere or the Farnese Hercules, but the fattest and baldest and most inelegant of their species.[23]

The town authorities finally felt obliged to act in 1865, having been repeatedly hammered by the *Observer*'s thundering editorials. They introduced poles at a certain depth along the shore, which demarcated an area where bathing costumes were mandatory; and they employed a policeman in a rowboat, 'to see that the new regulation is observed'.[24] The image is a comical one, but Margate could no longer afford to be blasé about such negative publicity. For a start, there was new housing just being built at Cliftonville, a mile from the town centre, which looked poised to become a respectable middle-class enclave.[25] The development promised to create a new suburb beside the sea, away from the hurly burly of the town centre, 'a class of houses combining handsome external appearance with every internal comfort'.[26] A press campaign against nudity, therefore, was hardly calculated to attract the sort of residents for whom Cliftonville was intended. More generally, by the mid-1860s, Margate also had to be watchful of its position relative to other seaside towns. There were increasing numbers of coastal resorts competing for tourist custom, buoyed by the growth of railway travel and increasing numbers of both middle- and working-class visitors. The seaside holiday had become big business.

Who developed new and expanding resorts? This is a more difficult question than one might first imagine. The seaside town, even in the early nineteenth century, already functioned as a sort of picturesque self-contained commercialised world, catering at every turn for the tastes of the tourist. The natural and built environment – the shoreline, the narrow lanes, shops selling trinkets, the lodging houses, hotels and taverns, the unique vistas of the sea, cliffs, ships in the harbour – combined to create a holistic experience. Strolling along the marine parade, taking in the air, was itself a key part of the holiday; merely being there was to be pursuing leisure and recreation. Therefore, one might argue, anything which contributed to the physical growth or economic success of seaside towns could be considered part of the seaside leisure industry, from the interference of aristocratic local landowners (e.g. the Duke of Devonshire's careful curation of his Eastbourne estate) to speculative builders hastily constructing new lodging houses, down to the Punch and Judy man on the seafront.

The railway, however, more than any other factor, was key to booming Victorian resorts, where coastal towns were relatively close to dense urban populations. This was not solely about connectivity, with new lines allowing large numbers of passengers to reach seaside destinations. Railway companies themselves soon identified the potential of coastal tourism and actively exploited it, principally via cheap excursions. Discounted day trips by rail, although often linked by historians to the tourist bonanza around the Great Exhibition, were readily available even in the early 1840s.[27] These often included seaside trips, which would also sometimes be combined with steamboat travel. The South Western Railway, for example, ran 'special trains at greatly reduced fares' for day trips to Southampton (which then linked with a steamboat excursion to Ryde on the Isle of Wight) during the summer of 1843.[28] The following year, the York and Midland Railway advertised a 'Cheap Pleasure Trip to Hull – Sea Voyage', departing from Leeds. Third-class passengers paid two shillings, with the option of paying a further shilling for a steamboat trip to Bridlington Bay. The third-class carriage of this period was essentially an open wagon with bench seats, but this did not put off paying customers. Year on year, new railway stations created fresh opportunities for excursion traffic. Dover station was opened in 1844 and soon hosted metropolitan day-trippers. Trains departed from London Bridge at 7.15 a.m., with the option of returning either the same day at 7 p.m., or the following evening. Day-trippers from London could also visit Southampton or Brighton. The latter cost five shillings for a third-class excursion ticket and proved immensely popular.[29] By 1850, 'cheap trip' holiday destinations from Manchester included a railway/steamboat combination to the North Wales coast and the Isle of Man, as well as trains to Southport, Blackpool, Fleetwood and, a little further afield, Scarborough. Moreover, the Lancashire and Yorkshire Railway, which ran some of these routes, allowed a return journey of anything between one and ten days after departure.

Some excursion tickets were sold direct by the railway companies; others via travel agents as intermediaries. Both the railway companies and agents pitched group outings to 'Conductors of Sunday and Day Schools, Managers of Mills, Institutions, Benefit Societies &c.'[30] The appeal to business owners is significant, for industrial towns in Lancashire had 'wakes' in the summer, when mill owners' employees decamped *en masse* on works outings ('Mr. Bashall's and Mr. Eastham's hands, number 950, for Blackpool; Mr. Paley's, Mr. Dixon's and the Park-lane mill hands, for Fleetwood, to the number of 1,800; Messrs. Birley's hands, for Morecambe . . .').[31] In the 1840s and 1850s, admittedly, the amusements on arrival were usually fairly basic. A journalist's account of Mr Paley's excursion tells of simple fun: races run by both sexes for items of clothing as prizes ('amid much laughter, the crinolines being hoisted upon a large pole'); 'gingling matches' (a sort of inverted blind-man's buff, where all players but one are blind-fold, and the odd man out rings a bell); donkey races and horse races. This was all managed by a factory supervisor, who 'never left the pleasure-seekers for a moment during any part of the day' (i.e. kept them from peeling off to drink at the local pub or otherwise disport themselves in an immoral or anti-social fashion).[32] But these growing crowds of visitors, larking in the fields or on the beach, were swiftly recognised as a money-making opportunity. Victorian entre-preneurs, therefore, began to develop new seaside attractions which might entice more tourists and make a healthy profit. First and foremost was the pleasure pier.

Regular piers were appropriated by tourists long before the Victorians. During the eighteenth century, wooden or stone piers, while providing a safe mooring for boats, were also used for promenading. When not in use by fishermen or shipping, they provided panoramic views of the coastline, combined with a romantic proximity to the deep. Unsurprisingly, therefore, some new piers built in the nineteenth century began to be designed with an eye to the tourist trade. Ryde Pier, arguably the first pleasure pier, built in 1813–14, was a 1,740-foot-long timber construction. The pier both allowed tourist boats to land comfortably on the Isle of Wight and provided a convenient promenade. There was nothing else to do on the pier, apart from sit in the small shelters dotted along its length; but visitors were happy to pay a penny for the privilege of taking a walk above the rolling ocean.

Margate Pier, rebuilt in stone between 1810 and 1815 following a design by John Rennie, was ostensibly a more practical affair, providing a solid, gently curving harbour wall and a safe berth for shipping. The owners were a joint-stock company, run by a powerful local banker and brewer, Francis Cobb. The pier was an expensive investment, costing around £90,000, and reflected the growing town's economic confidence.[33] The principal income was to be derived from a wharfage tax on people (mainly tourists) and cargoes. But the pier also had a raised perimeter section specifically built as a promenade, for which the company charged a penny admission. This upper part of the pier was built to entertain the public, and it even included a projecting section halfway along, for a band to play music to passing customers.[34]

The owners were said to be somewhat over-officious in their management, and there were several legal disputes, with petty officials hauling visitors before the magistrate for refusing to pay the toll, particularly when waving off friends and family on a departing vessel. Yet, by and large, the pier functioned rather well as a place where trade and amusement combined. For instance, when the town was first lit by gas in 1824, twenty-four lamps illuminated the pier up to the lighthouse at its far end. This both rendered the harbour more visible to shipping and provided an attractive evening promenade. The venture proved highly profitable. The company turned over £10,000 annually during the 1820s, and paid out £3,000 a year in dividends. Yet Cobb and his fellow directors were always keen to present it more as a species of public works. In 1829, they erected a commemorative tablet, with a lengthy text on copper plate that framed the pier as key to the social and physical improvement of the town. This proud inscription, among other things, listed a series of landmark dates which heralded Margate's growing independence and prosperity. These included the appointment of local magistrates in 1812; the macadamisation of the roads in 1825; and consecration of a new church in 1829.[35]

This role for the pier, as visible signifier of local prosperity and progress, would be repeatedly emphasised by pier promoters in resort towns in subsequent decades. The nineteenth-century seaside pier would become something of a statement building, with its length and ornamentation a self-conscious testimony to rising municipal greatness. Margate's Regency pier, therefore, fulfilled similar functions to its Victorian successors: a commercial venture, symbolic of local independence and achievement, providing a berth for ships and a promenade for tourists, offering some space for entertainment. There was just one crucial difference: Margate's pier was built of stone. The typical mid-Victorian pleasure pier would be cheaper and lighter: ironwork, supported by cast-iron piles, with a deck of wooden planks, and largely devoted to the tourist trade. Margate itself would be the first resort to build such an iron pier, opened in 1855 and fully completed in 1857 (replacing a timber jetty, another landing site supplementing Rennie's pier, which had been built in the 1820s). Within a decade or so, these novel iron structures, relying on the latest engineering and manufacturing technology, would become *the* iconic feature of the Victorian seaside.

There were precedents for this mid-century shift from stone and timber to iron. Brighton's Chain Pier was opened in 1823, built on the suspension-bridge principle, with metal chains hanging from Egyptian-style towers, supporting the deck. The Chain Pier, modelled on a less imposing predecessor in Leith, was designed to serve continental passenger traffic; but it was also an attraction in itself, highly ornamental and an exclusive promenade. King William IV numbered among its admirers. The suspension model did not catch on, but Brighton showed that piers could be constructed according to new, modern methods, and could provide a unique decorative addition to the resort town. During the 1840s and 1850s, railway architecture and associated engineering advances contributed to a growing interest and expertise in both the structural and the decorative potential of iron.[36] Southend Pier, for example, was extended in the mid-1840s, with cast-iron piles supporting its main wooden superstructure, to counter the damage caused to waterlogged timber by molluscs.[37] The design of the Crystal Palace was also inspirational. Mid-century pier projects were also boosted by the introduction of limited liability for companies in 1855. Promoters of piers could now offer a financial safety net, something important to timid small shareholders in the local community. Investors in pier schemes, especially in these early years, were usually small shareholders from the local area – another reason why the link between pier and municipal progress was ostentatiously emphasised.[38]

Southport in Lancashire provides us with a good example of a mid-Victorian pier project. In the early nineteenth century, the town was a rapidly developing tourist resort. In 1835, an extensive marine parade was constructed, partly to check shifting sand dunes, but also very much in the spirit of municipal improvement and attracting tourists. New hotels and commercials baths soon followed, and the arrival of the railway from Liverpool in 1848 brought more tourists and commuter traffic. When another railway line to Manchester was mooted, leading figures in the town, including four magistrates, a local builder and the local priest, put together a prospectus for a joint-stock company to build a pier. The proposed capital was £7,000, and £1 shares could be bought for a shilling's deposit. The prospectus stressed the forthcoming new connection to Manchester, which might bring tourists from both Lancashire and West Yorkshire. Furthermore, it noted the existing holiday-related annual income from the likes of donkey and donkey-carriage hire (an astonishing £3,200), sea-bathing in machines (£510) and the hire of sailing boats (£360). Tourist-filled piers, such as those at Lowestoft and Ryde, noted the brochure, already made a good profit, and Southport might similarly benefit.[39] This was, then, a local venture, but with a wary eye on similar seaside developments elsewhere in the country.

As it happens, this first Southport company, proposed in 1852, came to nothing; but the idea was revived with more success in 1859, after the arrival of the Manchester railway. Following Margate's lead, Southport became the second resort with a new iron pier. Seventy-two sets of three pillars, linked by lattice girders and strengthened by iron crosstrees, supported a timber deck that extended 3,600 feet into the Irish Sea. The opening of the pier was attended with enormous fuss and ceremony, and the pier itself was described by the *Bolton Chronicle* as 'of vast importance to the future prosperity of the town'.[40] Some 4,000 excursionists arrived by specially chartered trains, encouraged by free entrance for the day (normal rates on the pier being a penny a day; various season tickets were also available, including one costing seven shillings and sixpence for a whole year). There was a formal procession of local officials and members of the Pier Company from the town hall along the principal streets, accompanied by the band of the Royal Lancashire Militia. Buildings in the town were covered with flags, banners and floral arrangements, and the parade passed through a temporary triumphal arch topped with a portrait of Queen Victoria. The director of the Pier Company praised Southport as a 'model town' and the pier, which had cost £8,700, as its new crowning glory. The pier would assist the many invalids who frequented Southport to take the sea air. More generally, he noted, it would bring grateful tourists closer to the ocean, since, thanks to the area's peculiarly flat topography, the sea receded a considerable distance at low tide. A speech by a local clergyman, Rev. Charles Hesketh, noted that the pier enhanced the town's attraction over the rival local resorts of Blackpool and Lytham, and also enabled increased steamer traffic *between* these resorts on the Lancashire coast. Indeed, day-trips between neighbouring resorts along the same stretch of coast would become a regular feature of the Victorian seaside.[41] The only fly in the ointment at Southport was that the inaugural Liverpool steamer found itself unable to reach the new pier, since the tide was too low at the time of the ceremony.

For all the excitement, Southport Pier was only a promenade. Some minor tweaks would follow. Within a couple of years, it was agreed to install 'refreshment rooms' (café/restaurant), 'waiting rooms' (toilets) and a man-powered tramway, so that visitors could be pushed to the pier-head and back in small carriages. In 1864, the initial section of the pier was widened and the tramway converted to a steam-powered cable system. Various further changes were effected in the mid-1860s, including widening and extending the pier-head into a broad platform measuring 90 feet by 30 feet; adding an illuminated clock; and opening two shops 'well adapted for a light fancy trade' (i.e. selling small items to tourists).[42] In 1870, a brass band was hired, and a stage was built on which it could perform.[43] By 1875, £45,000 had been spent on maintaining, improving and beautifying the pier – and profitably so, since the company continued to pay out 7 per cent dividends to shareholders.[44] This model of gradual additions and improvements would be followed by many other resorts that built a pier in the mid-century. Generally, these ventures proved quite remunerative. Most of the money came from charging a penny for admission and tolls from tourist steamers; but there were other lesser sources of revenue, including from advertising boards, rents on shops and even the hire of bath-chairs.[45] Some companies stuck to the basic promenade; but those that added sundry features and adornments generally found it worth their while.

New additions to the pier were intended to keep tourists interested; but, as more resorts obtained piers, there was also an element of ostentatious inter-resort rivalry. This included the staging of entertainment, above and beyond hiring a brass band. Blackpool's South Jetty Pier, opened in 1868 (later renamed the Central Pier), took the novel but highly popular step of offering all-day dancing to its largely working-class clientele from 1870. There was a dedicated space screened from the wind on the pier-head, as well as a capacious open-air dancing platform (380 feet by 153 feet) in the middle of the promenade. More typically, pier companies built grand pavilions, which served as venues for concerts and theatrical performances.

There was generally a lag between the opening of a pier and the construction of a pavilion – the company first needed to feel sufficiently confident of its financial prospects. Some piers, however, included pavilions within the original specification. The oriental-style ornamental houses which graced Brighton's West Pier (opened in 1866) began the trend, although they were only small, decorative structures, suitable for refreshment rooms, shops or shelters. Hastings Pier (1872) had a much grander ironwork pavilion as its central feature, creating a 2,000-seat concert hall. Other resorts soon followed suit. Blackpool North Pier extended its pier-head in 1877 with two wings: on one side was the Indian Pavilion, a concert hall seating 1,500; on the other, a bandstand between a restaurant and shops, including a stationer, jeweller, confectioner, tobacconist, hosier, music-seller and photographer, as well as various artists.[46] The principal amusement in the pavilion was vocal and instrumental concerts, with an admission fee over and above the regular pier toll for evening concerts. Variety entertainers made the odd appearance. In the 1880s, during the day Mr J.B. Johnson and his niece regularly staged a 'swimming entertainment' in a tank on the stage. There was also ventriloquism, and 'comic, humorous and sentimental songs'.[47]

While most piers remained local projects, the profits in pier development encouraged one Joseph Ellis to think bigger. He was owner of Brighton's Bedford Hotel and chairman of the town's West Pier Company. In 1880, he established a Marine Piers Company 'for the purpose of constructing promenade and pleasure piers at watering-places on the coasts of the United Kingdom and elsewhere'. Piers were usually promoted by local businessmen and trumpeted as a civic endeavour. Some directors and shareholders might also come from the resort's natural catchment area: Blackpool's pier projects, for instance, attracted investors from Lancashire and West Yorkshire. But Ellis's scheme was more ambitious. The services of the leading pier designer/engineer Eugenius

Birch were secured, and the company entered into an arrangement to build piers already planned at Plymouth and Torquay, including grand pavilions.[48] The company also applied to parliament to build a pier at Folkestone, since new buildings on the foreshore generally needed government approval. Unfortunately, Ellis's dream of a national (or even international) pier-building concern faltered within a couple of years. Failing to attract enough share-holders, he hoped to build the Plymouth pier largely on credit, and then sell it on to a local company at a profit. Instead, the business was wound up in 1883. The pier itself finally opened in 1884, without a pavilion. It had cost £40,000 and was burdened with a huge debt. The pier-head was used as a roller-skating rink in winter, but it remained a failing concern. Three years later, it was sold to a local fish merchant, Walter Kay, for a mere £12,000. The seaside pier, then, was not an absolute licence to print money. Nonetheless, Kay would successfully reinvigorate the business in 1889 with the promise of building a pavilion; free season tickets were promised to anyone who bought £10 worth of shares.[49] Again, investment from small local shareholders proved crucial. Admissions still provided the principal income, but it was noted that there was also money to be made from the rental of refreshment kiosks; advertising; steamship tolls; skating; access to the pier for the local yacht club; use of the landing-stage's lower level by swimmers; and fees from toilets and vending machines.[50]

Weston-super-Mare's Grand Pier (opened in 1904) was another project that formed part of a grander design which did not go entirely to plan. The company was promoted by the directors of the P. & A. Campbell steamship company and the Cardiff Railway Company. They planned to profit, in the usual manner, from building a pleasure pier and pavilion. Their prospectus noted the healthy financial returns from piers at Llandudno, Southsea, Brighton, Blackpool and Great Yarmouth. But they also wanted to establish a steamer route between the railway company's newly constructed (transport) pier in Cardiff and the seaside resort. This link, reliant on a new pier at Weston, meant that steamers could theoretically cross the Bristol Channel, regardless of the tide, in a mere thirty minutes. Not only would this boost Weston's tourist industry (and even carry some modest freight), but it would trump the rival Great Western Railway's existing land route via Bristol and the Severn Tunnel.[51]

Unfortunately, the continuing difficulty of navigating the Bristol Channel's treacherous currents at low tide meant that vessels struggled to reach their destination. The pier's extensive 1,500-foot-long low-water landing jetty was decommissioned at the end of the First World War, though the main pleasure pier itself survived.[52] The principal profits came from admissions, but there were secondary sources of revenue. The company's prospectus promised to grant a concession for displaying adverts, rental of shops, sale of refreshments and, as at Plymouth, the provision of 'automatic machines'.[53] These doubtless included vending machines, which had been used at railway stations and other public places for the sale of cigarettes, matches, sweets, postcards, etc. since the 1880s. By this period, however, there would also have been more entertainment-oriented slot machines. Edwardian piers not only had postcard/photograph dispensers (including pictures of contemporary celebrities; more generic glamour girls; and grotesques of 'mothers-in-law'), but also early forms of moving pictures, such as the 'mutoscope' and the 'autocosmoscope'. There were also machines to test your grip; 'horse-racing' games; and numerous other mechanical wonders.[54] These were not unique to the seaside pier, but they became a quintessential feature in the busier, less genteel resorts. When the Chain Pier in Brighton was demolished in 1896, one writer bemoaned the average seaside pier's transformation from a landing-stage for steamers and a graceful promenade to its modern condition, with '[that] excruciating apotheosis of vulgarity, the Pavilion . . . an amphibious music hall with slot-machines and fly-bitten buffets'.[55]

Part of the appeal of the pleasure pier for entrepreneurs, of course, was that it became an enclosed commercial world, much like the pleasure garden or exhibition ground. An essentially captive audience, already bent on amusement, provided endless opportunities for the extraction of money. For the tourist, spending a few pennies on trinkets or penny slots became all part of the fun, albeit sometimes bordering awkwardly on the obligatory. Richard Marsh's 'The Girl on the Sands', a comic story in the *Strand* magazine, captures this perfectly. The hero, a penurious clerk, meets a mysterious young woman on the beach and offers to take her onto the pier, which, he earnestly informs her, is 'much more classy'. She is finally revealed to be that Victorian magazine cliché, an incognito aristocrat, but not before her enthusiasm for penny slots induces considerable anxiety in her suitor – 'she was game for a go at every blessed machine on the pier!' When the young lady wants to have another try at the cricket machine – 'which was supposed to return your penny if you hit a boundary' – the hero is forced to pretend that he has no remaining coppers. With rising panic, he then faces a bill of four shillings and eightpence in the café, thanks to the heroine's unfortunate penchant for donating cakes to passing children. Comic exaggeration aside, this was the fundamental dilemma of many a Victorian shop or office worker who treated his sweetheart. The pennies soon added up.[56]

The pier did not stand alone as a commercialised zone on the seafront. The beach and promenade themselves became highly commercial environments, at least in the larger resorts that catered more to working-class tourists and excursionists. This was thanks largely to travelling hucksters and stallholders. The American author Nathaniel Hawthorne, who lived briefly in Southport in the early 1850s, complained of the town's itinerant nuisances: organ-grinders; a man with a bassoon and a monkey; guitarists; Punch and Judy; and a bagpiper ('squealing out a tangled skein of discord, together with a highland maid who dances a hornpipe').[57] Three decades later, things had not changed much. *Punch* magazine ran a story in 1887 entitled 'Some Notes at Starmouth', a comic tale of a pretentious clerk aspiring to write a best-selling play while on holiday. The extensive description of a fictional popular resort provides a valuable insight into business on the shoreline. We learn that the archetypal beach at Starmouth is packed not only with tourists, but also with itinerant hawkers and fixed stalls: every sort of roving musician, from concertina to penny bagpipes; blackface minstrels; vendors of seafood; shoe-blacks; conjurors; travelling chiropodists (common on Victorian beaches); operators of electric-shock 'galvanic machines'; photographers; and amateurish theatrical types ('Open air music hall, where comic songs are shouted from platform by dreary men in flaxen wigs to harmonium . . . always crowded'). Most popular of all are the phrenologists on their own makeshift platforms, offering public 'readings' for the crowds. The emphasis is on the client being a good enough sport to have 'predictions' about his personal life and character read out before his friends ('"He is cheerful and social . . . In fact, if he were a little *less* social, it would be better. Destructiveness, small; this is not a gentleman who will do very much damage." – "You 'aven't seen 'im of a Saturday night," interrupts some vulgar brute').[58] The sheer numbers of tourists at larger resorts like Blackpool, Brighton and Great Yarmouth (presumably the inspiration for 'Starmouth') created boundless opportunities for such low-level entertainment. Blackpool Town Council would attempt to crack down on shoreline amusements in the late 1890s, including phrenologists, palm-readers, chiropodists, mock-auctions, vendors of trinkets, confectionery and photography; but it was something of an uphill struggle.[59]

Smaller towns tended to be somewhat more conservative. Late Victorian Aberystwyth – which earnestly styled itself a 'health resort' and 'The Biarritz of Wales' – had a Punch and Judy, and two council-licensed Pierrot troupes (a cut above the older tradition of roving blackface minstrels), but little else in the way of beach entertainment. The town's strict by-laws covered the licensing of cabs and sailing boats (a common practice), but also stipulated a minimum age of thirteen for driving donkeys. The council also outlawed goats drawing carriages, on the grounds of animal cruelty (the 'goat chaise' was a popular novelty for children). Residents were even strictly forbidden to beat carpets on the beach between May and October.[60] There was always much anxious talk in the local press about avoiding the Blackpool-isation of the sands, with the larger (and infinitely more prosperous) rival described as 'a showground of the worst order'. At the first sign of a rogue ice-cream man or seller of oysters, local journalists raised the dread spectre of Blackpool and its numerous 'catch penny institutions'.[61]

Blackpool's vulgarity, however, was not necessarily as bad as it was sometimes painted. The author of one promotional piece about the town stressed that Lancashire tourists were much more sober and better behaved than 'the 'Arry and 'Arriet element, with the catcalls and "what-cheers" of the Cockney holiday maker . . . a hustling, howling boisterous crowd, which is common enough nearer London'.[62] Perhaps this was just some suitable copy for an advertorial; but it is not hard to find similar endorsements.[63] The popularity of the temperance movement in northern England may help to account for the difference. Blackpool also still managed to attract middle-class custom to its more upmarket North Shore and its elegant 'hydropathic hotels', trading on the traditional health-giving properties of the seaside. Thus there was a middle-class side to the town, although the different classes did reside in different districts. The town even had a bathing inspector, armed with a telescope, to ensure that male and female visitors did not indulge in any form of unfortunate contact.[64]

Beyond the beach, there was far more to late-Victorian Blackpool than the sum of its hawkers and beach entertainers. By the early 1870s, the town could already support two piers operating at a profit. The North Pier, opened in 1863, charging tuppence, was more the resort of the middle classes. The South Jetty Pier (as noted above) opened in 1868 and charged only a penny. It became known as the 'People's Pier' and was a firm favourite with the working class, largely thanks to the dancing and cheap steamboat excursions. These were innovations introduced by the manager, Robert Bickerstaffe, a house builder and hotelier, who was a leading figure in the town. He had begun his leisure industry career rowing boats out to sea for tourists. He had then been joint proprietor of one of the town's first bathing-machines, before he purchased the Wellington Hotel on the seafront. Bickerstaffe and others could see that there was scope for further leisure developments in the rapidly growing resort (which would become a municipal corporation, with its own mayor and town council, in 1876). Three new commercial ventures would attempt to capitalise on Blackpool's popularity in the 1870s: the Raikes Hall Pleasure Gardens (later the Royal Palace Gardens), opened in 1872; the Aquarium (1875); and the Winter Gardens (1878). The history of these three institutions provides a valuable insight into how entrepreneurs were eyeing up the seaside as a potentially lucrative frontier for experiments in entertainment.

Raikes Hall was the least novel of the three developments. There had long been small pleasure gardens clustered around seaside resorts, often as extensions of rustic public houses. Blackpool had several in the surrounding countryside, such as the Cherry Tree Gardens and Belle Vue Gardens, as well as a popular beauty spot on the cliffs known as Uncle Tom's Cabin. Raikes Hall was a larger enterprise altogether, a joint-stock company established by a group of businessmen from Blackpool and Halifax.[65] The site was set back about 500 yards from the seafront, on the edge of the town's ribbon development, and was very much in the mould of a traditional pleasure garden like Vauxhall or Cremorne. Standard admission was sixpence, discounted to fourpence for pre-booked excursionists. Sixpence would become the default pricing for all the town's principal attractions, suited to the purse of working-class visitors (a shilling was the norm in London). The pre-existing mansion at Raikes Hall was converted into a 'hotel'. This was not so much a place of accommodation as a large venue for refreshments, with rooms for dining, tea and coffee, and billiards. There were 35 acres of gardens, a pavilion for concerts and shows, a racecourse, sports ground, dancing platform, conservatory and a lake used for boating and swimming matches. Fireworks, predictably, were a regular attraction. The first manager was one John Fish, who had experience of working in Belle Vue Gardens and Pomona Gardens in Manchester.[66] It was Fish who convinced the company that it needed an outdoor space for dancing and also bars, beyond the hotel, 'to sell refreshments to an almost unlimited number of people'. There was some anxiety that dancing might attract the opprobrium of the devout, but the directors deliberately put the dancing platform in a location away from the entrance, 'abandoned all scruples, and determined to act upon the suggestions of Mr. Fish'.[67]

The indefatigable Blondin performed in 1873 and the site hosted a quarter of a million visitors during this, its first full summer of operation.[68] There were frequent amendments and additions over the next two decades. In 1876, an asphalt roller-skating rink was opened in the conservatory, and there was a new grand pavilion to host 'music-hall celebrities and other caterers for the public amusement'.[69] In 1880, the management constructed a hippodrome for travelling circuses, with a central circus ring surrounded by a race-track, which could also be turned to bicycle, foot and 'chariot races' in the Roman style. Raikes Hall played host to the county's Agricultural Show, brass band contests and a mix of variety performers; and it provided the home ground for Blackpool Football Club, established in 1887. That same year, the site was rebranded as the Royal Palace Gardens, in honour of Victoria's golden jubilee. Then management experimented with a 'Great Indian Fair: Our Eastern Empire', with attendants in exotic costume selling 'foreign articles and curiosities of all Nations'.[70] Further additions to the grounds included a monkey-house and aviary, grand ballroom, seal pond, tricycle racing track and a handful of amusement rides. Visitors could enjoy a switchback railway or toboggan slide (the same attractions as at Earl's Court); a 'wheel of fortune' (which involved being strapped into a wooden tub and rolled down a steep track); merry-go-rounds; a miniature 'Lilliputian Railway'; and an aerial car (carriages running down an inclined rope on a pulley).[71] In 1893, a new theatre was opened, dubbed the Grand Opera House. The following year, Blondin returned, still performing at the age of seventy. He sustained a back injury and was nursed to health by one Katherine James, a twenty-five-year-old barmaid at the nearby Station Hotel, whom he married the following summer. Raikes Hall, in short, rivalled the great London pleasure gardens at the height of their popularity. The initial financial success was such that several of its directors, within a couple of years, attempted to develop copy-cat gardens, first in the inland industrial town of Blackburn, and then at Morecambe, a smaller resort on the Lancashire coast. Both projects were short-lived failures, but the mere fact of the attempt gives some idea of the confidence which the profits at Blackpool instilled.[72]

Unfortunately, Raikes Hall's success in the 1870s and 1880s, with annual 5 per cent dividends for shareholders, marked something of a last hurrah for the Victorian pleasure garden as entertainment institution. While the company was still investing in expensive novelties in the mid-1890s – a 'fairy fountain' pumping 100,000 gallons of water per hour through 190 jets (1893); a 360-degree cycloramic painting of Niagara (1894) – the arrival of the glamorous Blackpool Tower Company in 1894, conveniently located on the seafront, proved fatal. We shall return to the Tower in due course, but it is enough to note here that Raikes Hall recorded its first annual loss in that same year, and was bought by a land development syndicate in 1896. This syndicate was headed by John Bickerstaffe, Robert Bickerstaffe's son, who was also chairman of the Tower Company. The pleasure gardens were gradually wound down, though they continued to host popular events, including numerous sporting fixtures. There was some local speculation that the gardens might still be saved by new management. And for a brief month or two in 1898, Imre Kiralfy's son Charles looked poised to add the grounds to his father's entertainment empire. The local authority approved a deal and the newspapers made educated guesses that Kiralfy's new gardens would be a 'Venice in Blackpool', mixed with the Indian-style exhibition halls of Earl's Court.[73] The plans fell through within a matter of weeks, for reasons unknown. The only link to Earl's Court was that the grounds would provide a home to 'Savage South Africa' in 1900, after the show had outstayed its welcome in the metropolis. After an abortive attempt by locals to persuade the council to buy the site as a public park, the gardens seemingly found a new saviour in the shape of John McLaughlin, an American showman. He promised spectaculars *à la* Kiralfy, but went bankrupt shortly after reopening the grounds. Finally, predictably, the site was sold off for housing development.

Raikes Hall, therefore, did not provide a template for future resort developments. Subsequent seaside gardens tended to be smaller and largely ornamental in character, such as the Edwardian seafront strip of promenade gardens and lakes built by the local authority in nearby St Anne's. Such ornamental gardens were sometimes dubbed 'pleasure gardens' but they offered little in the way of outdoor entertainment beyond the ever-present brass band.

Raikes Hall was based on an existing formula, but the other two great institutions that opened in Blackpool during the 1870s – the Aquarium and Winter Gardens – formed part of a new trend in seaside entertainment.

The idea of building public aquariums originated in the mid-century, symptomatic of the Victorians' growing interest in natural history. London's Zoological Gardens opened the first public aquarium in 1853, and other cities in Europe and America followed. There were discussions about a possible commercial aquarium in Brighton, designed by Eugenius Birch, as early as 1866. Unfortunately, negotiations about the site, which required the town's Marine Parade to be widened, dragged on interminably. Consequently, the Crystal Palace Aquarium Company pipped Brighton to the post, opening the country's first commercial aquarium in the winter of 1871, in part of the northern section of the Palace (the area that had been destroyed by fire five years earlier). There had been an earlier 'aquarium' in the main body of the building, but this only amounted to a single large octagonal tank, containing chub, bream, carp and perch. The new building, on the other hand, held thirty-eight tanks of sea creatures, including sea-anemones, lobsters and octopuses, and associated plant life, spread over three rooms. Twenty thousand gallons of seawater, brought by rail from Brighton, were kept in constant circulation by steam pump (as were a further 80,000 gallons in twenty-two storage tanks of specimens kept behind the scenes). Admission was sixpence, on top of admission to the Palace grounds. The public, at least in the venture's early days, responded enthusiastically.[74]

Brighton Aquarium finally opened the following autumn – a larger, more lavish affair, costing £50,000 (five times the cost of its London rival), even though the building's exotic Indian-style turrets, a typical orientalist touch by Birch, were sacrificed along the way. Visitors were greeted by an appropriate biblical quotation inscribed on the frieze in the entrance court: 'And God said, Let the waters bring forth abundantly the moving creature that hath life'. The tanks were set into the walls – an effect we now take for granted, but which *The Times* described as like framed living pictures.[75] The rubber sealant strips, which allowed the glass to flex with the shifting temperatures (also used at the Crystal Palace), were likewise noted as a useful innovation. Another experiment, tying in with the seaside as a place for rest and recuperation, was the provision of wheelchair ramps for 'invalid and bath chairs'.[76]

The country's next commercial aquarium could easily have been at Raikes Hall, since the business was originally christened the 'Raikes Hall Park, Gardens and Aquarium Company'. For some reason – probably on the grounds of cost and complexity – this potential attraction never materialised. A letter from 1874 suggests that the company was also put off after hearing about a private speculator opening his own aquarium on the nearby seafront.[77] This may well have been a factor, because the individual in question was William Henry Cocker, a founding father of Victorian Blackpool. Cocker was a surgeon by profession, but was very active in local government, being a local magistrate and chairman of both the Board of Health (the de facto local authority in the 1860s) and the Blackpool and Fylde Agricultural Society. He would become Blackpool's first mayor when the town was incorporated in 1876, and went on to hold the office again in the 1880s. In terms of entertainment, he was already a director of the Arcade and Assembly Rooms and of the South Jetty Company. Cocker was a rich man: having opened his aquarium, he arranged for the transport of new specimens on his very own steam yacht. He was an influential figure and doubtless held some sway with the directors of Raikes Hall.

Surprisingly, there is little trace in the press of the opening of Cocker's Blackpool Aquarium in 1874. Cocker himself seems not to have troubled to court newspaper publicity for this venture, although he frequently opened the venue gratuitously to excursionists connected with charitable causes. His reticence is peculiar, given his involvement in subsequent, much-publicised projects. The reason may have been that the aquarium was set up by converting part of the town's existing, relatively unprepossessing 1860s Market Hall.[78] Thus there was no grand architectural novelty to parade before assembled journalists, nor was the idea of an aquarium any longer terribly innovative. In fact, the only significant newspaper account of the aquarium is an 1876 report in the *Preston Herald*. It describes three circular seal ponds in the open court-yard outside the building; inside, the reporter finds himself admiring the sea anemones, a giant sturgeon and conger eels. Cocker would take over the rest of the market buildings in 1877, adding a menagerie and an outdoor bear pit.[79]

Cocker's next entertainment project was on a much grander scale and was far less publicity shy: Blackpool Winter Gardens. The phrase 'winter garden' originally meant a conservatory; but by the mid-1870s, it had become short-hand for a novel type of entertainment experience. The winter garden was typically a compact, urban version of the Crystal Palace, often at a seaside location. Winter gardens dispensed with the 'exhibition' element and focused exclusively on concerts and other forms of entertainment. They often promised to incorporate aquariums and roller-skating rinks (a fashionable amusement of the 1870s). But Blackpool was not the first resort to have a winter garden. That honour went to its local rival Southport, a few miles to the south along the Lancashire coast.

Southport had yet to be outpaced by Blackpool in the 1870s, and could still lay firm claim to being the leading Lancashire resort, in terms of its fixed population.[80] The Grand Pavilion Winter Garden and Aquarium, the first such complex of its kind, opened in 1874. The project was developed, much like Southport's pier, by a local joint-stock company of leading townspeople, keen to attract more tourists. The lavish buildings, situated in a prime seafront location, cost nearly £100,000 and were described as 'Crystal Palace-like both in its external appearance . . . and in the rich variety of its interior attractions'.[81] The principal sections of the 9-acre site were a basement aquarium (including three performing seals and two crocodiles); a baronial gothic promenade hall; a 2,000-seat concert pavilion; and a massive iron and glass conservatory with tropical plants (the most obvious 'Crystal Palace' element). There was also a reading-room on the first floor, with tables for draughts and chess, and a balcony with a sea view. The aquarium offered a degree of 'instruction and amusement', just like the Crystal Palace; and the sea view provided a suitably grand natural backdrop for the palatial buildings, offering a maritime equivalent to Sydenham's beautifully landscaped grounds, but at no cost to the developer. The public was charged a shilling admission, with a further sixpence for the aquarium and additional charges for evening concerts. This was, in other words, a venue hoping to attract middle-class custom.

It is worth noting that, despite the name, the *winter* garden was designed for both summer and winter, not only creating a new concert venue but also offering a convenient alternative to the pier or beach during bad weather. Many seaside resorts tried to cultivate a winter season by making claims to temperate conditions (in the hope of appealing to wealthy invalids); but winter gardens could only succeed financially if they also attracted summer visitors. There were, therefore, outdoor gardens in Southport around the building, with picturesque caves, fountains, rustic grottoes and ornamental rock bridges, shielded from sea breezes by landscaped hillocks. By way of further attraction, a roller-skating rink was added to the grounds in 1875. Roller-skating – on marble or asphalt rinks – had become very popular in the 1870s, being dubbed 'rinkomania' by the press. Rinks, replete with orchestras and refreshment bars, were popping up in most large towns and cities. The managers of the gardens wanted to extract maximum commercial benefit from the site.

Southport's experiment proved incredibly influential. During the following decade, ten other resorts would acquire their own commercial winter gardens; and many more were proposed. Southport provided the template for winter garden projects in a range of resorts, including Bournemouth, Great Yarmouth, New Brighton, Morecambe, Tynemouth and, as we shall see, Blackpool. They did not all include aquariums. The winter gardens at Rhyl, opened in 1876 by a Manchester-based company, offered virtually identical attractions to Southport, right down to the basement aquarium; but the proprietors soon abandoned the latter as too costly. More surprisingly, since entertainment innovations tended to come from the capital, the Southport Winter Gardens also influenced the Royal Aquarium in Westminster, opened in January 1876. This was a long brick building, roofed with glass and iron. The layout was essentially a promenade lined with palms and tropical plants, with aquarium tanks along the walls and, on one side, a stage for a large orchestra. There was the obligatory skating rink and a 1,300-seat theatre attached. This was, despite its name, very much a 'winter garden'. In fact, the aquarium element was poorly managed and little patronised by the public. The company also had initial pretensions to supporting opera and fine art, but swiftly yielded to more populist fare, including music hall, circus acts and side-shows. Within only a couple of years, it was reported that the aquatic displays were ignored, whereas 'public concerts, the trapeze, the industrious fleas, and especially the restaurant, are heavily patronized'.[82] Readers will recollect that it was the Royal Aquarium, in this guise, which attracted the early attentions of the National Vigilance Association in the 1890s.

The Royal Aquarium was not the only inland venture inspired by Southport. The Sutton Coldfield Crystal Palace, Aquarium and Skating Company promised something very similar, set in Sutton's Promenade Gardens, an existing and popular pleasure garden near Birmingham.[83] The trend for winter gardens, including the combination of aquarium and skating, provided the impetus, even though the parkland setting meant this was pretty much equivalent to a provincial Sydenham. By the time the venue opened in 1879, the proposed basement aquarium (just as at Rhyl and Raikes Hall) had been abandoned. The promotional benefits of claiming to build an aquarium were clearly more important than the costly practicalities of actually doing so. The company, in any case, would be declared insolvent two years later. Several of the seaside winter gardens fared equally badly. The Margate Aquarium Company was established in 1874, with plans for a building with facilities similar to Southport's, but with the addition of an outdoor and indoor swimming pool. While work on the building continued, an outdoor roller-skating rink was opened to the public in 1875; measuring 170 feet by 60 feet, it was reputedly the largest in England.[84] But the company failed to attract sufficient share-holders and was sued by its creditors, Claridge's Patent Asphalte Co., which had laid down the skating rink. The rink itself survived until 1881, but the main building was never finished. There were complaints to magistrates about the insanitary condition of the grounds and about a 'tin pot band' that trav-elled round the town, 'to get all the rough people after them, and let them into the rink on buying a refreshment card for 3d.'[85]

Thus, when the Blackpool Winter Gardens opened in 1878, they were not the first of their kind, but followed an existing trend. The building cost much the same as Southport's, and similarly provided a space for promenading and concerts/theatrical performances. The entrance was via an iron-and-glass-domed Floral Hall, with flowering plants and numerous plaster busts and statues (as at the Crystal Palace); this led to the grand concert pavilion. This galleried concert space included an outer walkway, which could either be sepa-rated from the auditorium by revolving wooden shutters, or alternatively left open for promenade concerts. There was also the now customary roller-skating rink in the grounds, surrounded by landscaped rockeries and flower beds, which were illuminated at night by coloured lamps, and a fernery and orna-mental lake. But what really distinguished Blackpool from rival resorts was a growing confidence and flair for publicity. The fact that the town was now, post-1876, its own municipality seemed to engender a positively buccaneering spirit. This was obvious in the massive promotional spectacle which attended the Winter Gardens' inauguration.

Mayor Cocker, a director of the Winter Gardens Company, invited fellow mayors from dozens of English towns to the opening ceremony, putting them all up for a week at the luxurious Imperial Hotel. To mark the occasion, the assembled civic dignitaries then proceeded through the town in a torch-lit procession led by the Lord Mayor of London in his ceremonial coach, as if about to swear fealty to some new power in the land. There followed a 'masquerade procession' along the promenade watched by Cocker and his guests from the balcony of his Aquarium. Floats and characters included:

> the Blackpool life-boat converted into a triumphal car for Neptune; Britannia waving the British Union Jack; a Ghost and a Fire King . . . the hostile armies of the Czar and the Sultan; with our Prime Minister, portrayed in a transparency, high over all, and with the Mayor of Blackpool and the Lord Mayor of London supporting him.[86]

Blackpool, in short, was cheekily portrayed as no less important than the capital. Southport, which was somewhat more oriented towards the middle-class visitor, would never have dared anything so exuberant. But Blackpool had already celebrated its incorporation with extravagant public parades and fetes, and the town's councillors were well aware that such displays were good marketing. They would also manage to obtain legislation that allowed a twopenny rate to be levied on householders, solely for the purposes of advertising the resort.[87] The town's subsequent extensive poster campaigns at railway stations and on urban hoardings, which appeared even in rival resorts, would become legendary. Such advertising was not entirely unique. The Isle of Man had an Advertising Board in the 1890s that spent money on advertisements in magazines and newspapers, posters, flyers and leaflets. The board also supported more unusual ideas, such as lending magic-lantern slides of scenic locations to travelling lecturers, and, keen to build up London custom, it paid for electric-light advertisements at Earl's Court.[88] Nonetheless, Blackpool, thanks to its twopenny rate, always had more funds at its disposal.

Cocker and his fellow councillors believed in making a big splash. Consequently, the Winter Gardens' opening fete lasted two full days. Other entertainments laid on included a steamship cruise, paid for by the Lancashire and Yorkshire Railway Company, with a sumptuous on-board champagne luncheon. The mayors were also taken to Raikes Hall, listened to a concert in the North Pier's Indian Pavilion and witnessed an aquatic show by J.B. Johnson. The message to the mayoral elite and accompanying journalists was not 'come and visit the Blackpool Winter Gardens', but rather 'come to Blackpool'. The town had begun to market and publicise itself in a way no other resort had yet attempted.

The finances of Cocker's aquarium, a wholly private speculation, remain opaque. The Blackpool Winter Gardens, on the other hand, had shareholders and annual general meetings, and so we know that it began rather shakily, barely breaking even, but grew more profitable under the judicious management of William Holland (1887–95). Holland was previously the guiding spirit of the North Woolwich Gardens, London, and had thirty years of experience in theatre management. He had been credited with restoring the faltering fortunes of both the famous Canterbury Hall and Weston's Music Hall in the 1860s. At Woolwich, he had styled himself the 'People's Caterer'. He was a typical mid-century music-hall manager, 'a gentleman of geniality, enterprise and impressive rotundity'. Blackpool legend has it that, when he told a friend that they had installed expensive carpets at the Winter Gardens, the acquaintance exclaimed, 'What, spend a hundred guineas for a carpet for trippers to spit on!' Holland then reportedly advertised 'Come to the Winter Gardens and spit on Bill Holland's 100-Guinea carpet!'[89] Several local histories also suggest that Holland popularised the Winter Gardens' rather middle-class programme of entertainments.

Unfortunately, both of these claims about Holland are somewhat implausible. Respectable late Victorian theatre managers did not encourage spitting among visitors – not even in jest. Moreover, the late 1880s was the era of the grand palace of varieties: no one would have batted an eyelid at the opulence of the Winter Gardens' carpeting. On further investigation, it turns out that Holland actually told the anecdote about spitting with reference to the Canterbury Hall of the 1860s – a time when 'spit and sawdust' were still a feature of life in the halls.[90] Similarly, the idea that the Winter Gardens began as 'posh', but were then reluctantly given over to the working class, smacks of latter-day folk memory and myth-making. The fact that the Winter Gardens' initial entrance fee was only sixpence should, at the very least, raise some doubts. Acts performing in the opening season of the Winter Gardens in 1878 included 'Selbini and Villion, Royal Velocipede Equestrians, Jugglers and Somersault Act Riders on Bicycle' and Lulu, the 'girl' trapeze artiste who had recently been revealed to be a young man, but who was still highly popular. The winter of 1879–80 included a touring opera company, but also the musical comedy of the Paggi Family and the famous music-hall comic 'The Great Vance', as well as the mind-reading act of Professor Heriott and Little Louie. This mix of entertainers was typical late Victorian variety, similar to the bills of the better type of London hall. Holland's own summer programme in 1888, meanwhile, mixed up ballets, pantomime, high-wire acts and patriotic odes to the British Empire, along with selections from Gounod's *Faust* and Wallace's *Maritana*.[91] William Holland was skilful in his programming and did make some changes; but his tenure was not obviously marked by an abrupt shift from 'high culture' to low-brow music-hall acts. His tenure *was*, however, marked by improved dividends. Unfortunately, his death in the final days of 1895 came at an awkward time. For the Winter Gardens had a new competitor – an even more novel type of venue.

The Blackpool Tower, opened in 1894, imitated the triumph of the Paris Exposition of 1889: the Eiffel Tower. Indeed, it was initially known as the 'Blackpool Eiffel Tower'. The iron-and-glass roof-spans of the Crystal Palace-like Winter Gardens were now challenged by a new, more modern entertainment icon. The Tower was a vertical analogue to the ironwork pier – a 'statement building', but far more visible: tourists could spot it from the train as they approached the town, and knew that the fun was about to begin.

The original owner of the Tower site was none other than our old friend William Cocker, who had set up property development companies in the 1880s to profit from rising land prices in the town.[92] Cocker, in short, put together a site for development which included not only his aquarium and menagerie, but also the adjoining market buildings, shops and the neighbouring Beach Hotel. The idea was to sell this prime block of seafront real estate to the highest bidder. This was finally accomplished in 1891. The transaction was originally between Cocker's company and the blandly named Standard Contract and Debenture Corporation (SCDC). The SCDC was already promoting various projects in Douglas on the nearby Isle of Man, including a Douglas Eiffel Tower. Indeed, it is likely that the proposed scheme in Douglas – a rival resort to Blackpool – prompted the whole Blackpool enterprise. But the SCDC was run by a slightly shady financier named William Darker Pitt and was never a substantial concern. Like many other speculators in seaside developments, Pitt may have hoped to get in early and sell on the Blackpool site at a profit. The Douglas Tower, in any case, was never built, and when the SCDC ran into serious financial difficulty, John Bickerstaffe's Blackpool Tower Company took over the planned project in Blackpool.

Bickerstaffe, like his close friend Cocker, was a leading businessman in the town, and also held the position of mayor in 1891. He was the proprietor of two hotels, a director of the Blackpool Electric Tramway Company, part owner of the *Bickerstaffe* steamship, and a large shareholder in both the Winter Gardens and Raikes Hall. He was therefore very well placed to attract further investment. Cocker himself, predictably, was one of the so-called 'founder' shareholders in the Tower Company, where he was joined by a long list of magistrates, MPs and owners of railway companies and banks. Most came from the north-west of England. The name of John Hollingshead, the London-based writer, theatre historian and theatre manager, also appears in the prospectus as a 'founder'. He was, at the time, manager of both the Paragon Theatre of Varieties and the Canterbury Theatre of Varieties in the capital.

The design of the Tower was rather clever, with entertainment space elegantly slotted in between the building's four giant legs. There was also a surrounding set of buildings at street level that linked to the new complex, including Cocker's aquarium. Blackpool Tower opened in May 1894. There was still a considerable amount of work to complete, but a single lift could take 500 people an hour up to the observation decks at 400 and 420 feet above the ground. Visitors could then ascend an additional set of spiral steps to the 500-foot-high 'Crow's Nest' summit. Back on the ground, the 5,000-seat Tower Circus was opened to paying customers. A second lift was brought into operation and, within the next twelve months, the Tower Company also opened a palatial restaurant, menagerie and dancing pavilion, 'a vast hall, rivalling in its proportions the Palace at Douglas . . . big enough for eighty sets of quadrilles'. Here, a fifty-piece band played predominantly waltzes and Schottisches and the Lancers. The orchestra was conducted by one Oliver Gaggs, poached from the Derby Castle ballroom on the Isle of Man, and reportedly a man 'whose name is a household word in Lancashire'.[93] On the first floor (the level from which the lifts ascended), the company built, bizarrely enough, an Olde Englyshe Village, with various shops and stands, similar to the mock-Tudor shopping street which would appear at Earl's Court in 1897.

The final cost of the building was enormous – over £300,000; but the Tower thrived as a business, consistently paying shareholders a 6 per cent dividend in its first decade of operation. John Bickerstaffe was said to stand sentry at the turnstiles, mixing with the crowds and listening to holiday-makers' delighted comments about what he called his 'Wonderland'.[94] When Bickerstaffe effectively bought up and closed down Raikes Hall, the main competition then came from the Winter Gardens. Throughout the late 1890s, the two manage-

ment teams engaged in friendly one-upmanship, with the Winter Gardens ultimately choosing to build over much of its exterior garden space in order to
provide a broader range of indoor amusements. The company also constructed
a Ferris wheel (the third in the world after Chicago and Earl's Court) both as a
novel entertainment and also as a 'sky sign for the Winter Gardens' – i.e. its own
highly visible landmark.[95] William Holland, shortly before his death, was sent
to America in search of new attractions, and the Winter Gardens Company,
having noted the popularity of dancing in the Tower's pavilion, constructed its
own Empress Ballroom, which opened in 1896. The Tower Company responded
with Frank Matcham's equally lavish Tower Ballroom, opened in 1898.

There were other rival attractions, most notably the Alhambra on the
seafront, opened in 1899. This complex contained a theatre, circus, ballroom,
restaurant and café, replacing the existing Prince of Wales Theatre and Prince
of Wales Baths, where lavish aquatic displays had been staged since the late
1870s. It was intended as an alternative to the Tower, but swiftly sank into debt
and was purchased by Bickerstaffe's company in 1903, then remade into the
Palace Theatre of Varieties and Palace Ballroom. A cinema was added in 1911,
and then an underground walkway in 1914, linking the Palace to the Tower.
The Tower Company grew ever more dominant, and the Winter Gardens
would eventually succumb, swallowed up by its more profitable, voracious
neighbour in 1928.

It is easy to forget that there were other 'tower' projects, since none was even
remotely successful. For a short while, 'Eiffel Towers' looked set to become as
popular as the winter garden. Some never left the drawing-board. The Douglas
Tower never progressed beyond its foundations. Sir Edward Watkin's scheme
for a 1,200-foot-high London tower at Wembley, taller than Eiffel's, was halted
by subsidence, lack of funds and Watkin's death in 1901. Only the first stage
was completed. The four great stumpy ironwork legs and platform, mocked in
the press as 'Watkin's Folly', were demolished in 1907. The surrounding pleasure garden and sports grounds survived until they were used for the site of the
British Empire Exhibition of 1924 and Wembley Stadium.

Two other towers were attempted in north-west seaside resorts. The
Morecambe Tower also ended up incomplete. The highly eccentric Moorish
design, with a spiralling helter-skelter-style ramp, was sketched by the architect
Tom Bradley in 1898. The skeleton of Bradley's ironwork cone was completed,

but the company involved swiftly ran out of funds. The scheme was revived in 1911, to the extent of building a Moorish pavilion, ballroom and shops below; but the crowning edifice never fully materialised. The iron framework would be recycled for munitions during the First World War.

New Brighton, across the Mersey from Liverpool, fared better than Morecambe. The New Brighton Tower Company used the same engineers as Blackpool, but the tower was built 50 feet higher than that at the rival resort, to win the title of highest structure in the UK. John Hollingshead, pursuing his interest in seaside towers, was the first manager. The elaborate gothic buildings at the base contained a 3,000-seat theatre, a ballroom fit for 4,000 dancers, a billiard saloon, restaurant, menagerie and conservatory. The surrounding 33-acre gardens included a 14,000-square-foot dancing platform, switchback railway, football ground, athletics and cycle track, a water chute, tennis courts, 'Japanese tea-room', 'Algerian Restaurant' (both of these referring to decoration, rather than foodstuffs) and 'numerous refreshment buildings for the multitude'.[96] When the grounds first opened in 1897, they hosted a demonstration baseball match 'between teams of American ladies', as well as boxing and Graeco-Roman wrestling.[97] When the Tower itself opened the following year, the public was surprised to discover that the conductor Granville Bantock had replaced the anticipated brass band with a hundred-piece symphony orchestra. Bantock's classical concerts would go on to win much popular and critical acclaim.[98] The business itself did not fare so well. Calvin Brown, of Manchester's White City, took over in 1908, styling it 'The Tower and Fun Park'. But there was little improvement. The company's annual report from the following year noted mournfully that no dividends had been paid for eight years.[99] The Tower itself would be demolished after the First World War, afflicted by rust and too costly to maintain. The ballroom below survived until a fire in 1969.

Blackpool Tower, therefore, saw its principal architectural rival defeated, and no one was inclined to risk the vast sums required to build another similar landmark. New leisure complexes tended to be less extravagant. For example, the Southend Kursaal (a word originating from German spa towns, literally 'cure room', but coming to mean a public entertainment hall), first opened in 1899. The Kursaal was a low, two-storey complex containing a circus, theatre, arcade, shops and a 'Nineteenth Century Hall of Marvels' (which the manager filled by advertising for 'Freaks, Living Curiosities, Museum Subjects &c.').[100] The building still survives and includes a decorative central dome, raised atop a square Corinthian-columned base; but the overall effect is not terribly striking. Both Blackpool and Southend, however, would be leaders in the final stage in the evolution of seaside entertainment: the amusement park.

The Victorians possessed some seaside amusement rides. Blackpool's Raikes Hall, as already noted, had several, but the grounds were set back a good way from the seafront. Elsewhere, some resorts allowed speculators to build rides along the beach. John Bratby, a builder of switchback railways, erected a roll-ercoaster on Folkestone beach in 1888.[101] At Brighton, Magnus Volk opened the Brighton and Rottingdean Seashore Electric Railway in 1896. Popularly called the 'Daddy Long Legs' this resembled a mobile section of pier, topped with an enclosed waiting-room-style carriage. The peculiar contraption, standing on 23-foot-high iron legs, glided on tracks along the shore, as passengers waved to passers-by from the open upper deck. The tracks were covered at high tide, when the railway presented a remarkable spectacle.

The full-blown amusement park, however, only arrived in the Edwardian era. Blackpool Pleasure Beach and Southend's Luna Park are prime examples. They had different origins, but their promoters reached the same conclusion about the best way to extract money from seaside tourists: highly visible American-style rides on the seafront, where one could attract large crowds, and visitors could see the resort stretching out beneath them as they whirled and spun through the air.

The famous Pleasure Beach, still trading to this day, was founded by William Bean on the southern edge of Blackpool, something of a hinterland where the promenade expired. By 1901, there was already a simple fairground on the sands, with a switchback railway and swings, and advertisements for private land to be let 'for stalls, shows, roundabouts &c.'[102] Bean bought up 40 acres of rough ground and began to advertise for concession holders looking for American-style rides, the sort that were thrilling visitors to Coney Island in New York. By 1906, the site contained attractions including 'River Caves of the World', 'Maxim's Flying Machine' and 'Sea Circus', with a 'Great Canadian Water Chute' under construction. Advertisements noted that the South Shore Pleasure Beach was 'the only site in Blackpool for Open-air Attractions', i.e. a brisk and bracing alternative to the carefully managed delights of the Tower Company.[103] These were precisely the sort of mechanical rides that Imre Kiralfy would shortly introduce at White City. The following year, Bean narrowly won election to the town council, in a by-election that was fought, in part, on 'whether or not South Shore looked with favour upon this popular pleasure resort' (i.e. whether local residents approved of this somewhat raucous funfair).[104] Bean capitalised on his new position, and in 1913 negotiated a deal with the local authority, whereby he gave up some of his seafront property for a municipal extension of the promenade. In return, he received an exemption from planning permission for future developments within the park. Attractions now included 'The Famous Velvet Coaster from Chicago', the marvellously named 'House of Nonsense', and an 'Old English Village of Side Shows'.[105] The Pleasure Beach would continue to grow and grow.

Southend's Luna Park, on the other hand, was originally a pleasure garden. The town's Marine Park had been opened as a commercial garden in 1894. Tourists from London's East End were the prospective clientele and the principal attractions were a 15,000-square-foot sprung dancing platform, switchback railway, 'aerial flight ride', boating lake, bicycle track and swings. Admission was sixpence. The park was like a smaller version of Raikes Hall, but it had the advantage of being pretty much on the beach. Live acts on the opening day were 'De Rosa's lady dancers; Lieut. Taylor, with performing wolves and boarhounds; Miss Mary Wallace, with impersonations', as well as J.B. Johnson of Blackpool North Pier fame.[106] The Marine Park was floated as a public company in 1897 as the Southend-on-Sea Tower and Marine Park Co., but the putative tower complex was never built. Instead, the Kursaal opened on the site in 1899. The grounds were then purchased in 1910 by a Lancashire businessman named William Hilton. He renamed them Luna Park, after the famous park on Coney Island, and filled the space entirely with amusement-park rides. Comparisons were immediately made with both Blackpool and Kiralfy's White City. Hilton himself held Luna Park for five years, but, like his predecessors, never made a success of it. The site was then bought by Clifton Morehouse, an American industrialist, who finally turned a good profit.[107]

The seaside amusement park marked the culmination of a century of coastal leisure developments. Amusements parks appeared in Blackpool and Southend, of course, because these resorts already catered for huge numbers of tourists. The densely populated working-class catchment areas of industrial north-west England and the East End of London were the resorts' life-blood. Promoters, in turn, felt confident of hundreds of thousands of customers coming through their gates. But lesser resorts were not immune to the growing appeal of mechanised fun, even if this only meant a few basic fairground rides. Sedate Aberystwyth acquired its own 'Luna Park' in the early 1900s, atop Constitution Hill, reached by the funicular railway that had been opened in 1896. These small gardens were lit by Japanese lanterns and included a café, bandstand, camera obscura, dancing platform, wooden concert hall and some very modest fairground amusements.[108] Visitors hoping for Coney Island would have been rather disappointed.

But despite this mechanical leisure revolution, the fundamental appeal of the seaside resort did not really change. Lounging on the beach remained a great attraction, as did excessive consumption of food and drink. Nor did the seaside lose its intimate association with health, even in the bigger and brasher resorts. The 'hydropathic hotel' remained a stalwart feature of late Victorian and Edwardian resorts, trading on the supposedly curative properties of the ocean. These were generally elegant, rather expensive establishments with a range of spa treatments, as well as ballrooms, tennis courts, billiards and other sports-related leisure facilities. For those further down the social scale, resorts increasingly marketed the supposed free health benefits of their town. These included not only the watery delights of taking a dip in the sea, but even the cold winds which relentlessly battered many a holiday destination. There was much talk of 'bracing' gusts of sea air and so-called 'ozone', making a virtue of necessity. 'Breezy Blackpool', a pamphlet published by the local authority in 1899, trumpeted 'the recuperative and healthful qualities of the ozonic resort'. An advertorial in the *Sheffield Daily Telegraph* a few years later put it more succinctly: the Lancashire resort had 'champagne air'.[109] Merely to breathe in the Blackpool air, in other words, was a luxurious treat.

In truth, Blackpool was unique not for its miraculous sea air, but for the depth of its pockets and the superior quality of its marketing.

VIII

The Football Field

OR,

TO BRUTALISE THE GAME

AT THE START OF THE NINETEENTH CENTURY, the game of football was disparaged as a rather old-fashioned, rough-and-tumble amusement, suitable only for fetes and local festivals. Yet during the mid-century, it would increasingly find favour in the public schools, prized as a character-building sport.[1] Amateur clubs then began to emerge, principally composed of middle-class men who had enjoyed playing the game in their school days. Unfortunately, there were no commonly agreed rules, since each school had its own footballing tradition. Some amateur clubs, therefore, played the more physical 'Rugby game', including handling and running with the ball, while others preferred the 'dribbling game', which emphasised ball skills. The Football Association, established in 1863 to draw up a set of definitive rules, preferred 'dribbling clubs', facilitating the birth of modern soccer (as well as, indirectly, the emergence of rugby as a distinct sport). By the First World War, major soccer matches attracted tens of thousands of paying spectators. Players were well-paid professional sportsmen, and Football League clubs were highly profitable businesses. This chapter examines in detail how the humble game of football became a commercially oriented, lucrative spectator sport.

* * *

Public schools were undoubtedly the principal exponents of the game of football at the start of the Victorian era. Schoolmasters had come to consider it a
healthful and manly recreation for their young charges. Hence, when the
Queen Dowager paid a royal visit to Thomas Arnold's Rugby School in 1839,
she asked 'to witness a match at foot-ball at which game Rugby has long been
known to stand unrivalled'.[2] This was, broadly speaking, the game to which
the school would ultimately lend its name, including scrums, drop-kicks,
running with the ball, and freedom to grab an opponent during a tackle.
Running with the ball, although cherished as a distinctive innovation by
Rugby, was a relatively recent innovation.[3] 'Hacking' – essentially kicking an
opponent's shins – was also a legitimate tactic to stop runners. There was also
no limit on the number of players. The Queen Dowager, therefore, watched a
lively match between the 'School House' (75 boys) and 'the rest', totalling
some 300 players.[4]

The Rugby version of the game, however, was one variation among many.
Football matches were generally played according to local custom and practice
(unlike cricket, for which the Marylebone Cricket Club had established itself
as the overarching law-making body). Pupils attending other schools, therefore, played by their own local rules. Rugby pupils drew up a written code in
1845 for their own benefit; rival educational establishments continued with
their separate traditions. Eton's 'field game', in particular, did not permit
handling of the ball (although it did include 'bullies' and 'rouges', similar to
scrums and tries in the Rugby game). There were commonalities between the
public school variants and, even where rules differed, they were often trying to
achieve the same effect: multiple versions of the offside rule all attempted
to address the same issue, i.e. players planting themselves by their opponents'
goal for the duration of a match. But there was no agreement on what constituted the laws of football. For the sake of practicality, therefore, when teams
occasionally visited other schools, the home ground's rules were adopted by
both sides.

The public schools did not, by any means, have a monopoly on the sport.
Several towns incorporated football into their Shrove Tuesday and Ash
Wednesday public holidays. This tradition was far from universal, but places as
diverse as Richmond in Surrey, Derby and Ashbourne in Derbyshire and
Alnwick in Northumberland held annual free-for-all matches which served as
the focus of public festivities. The ball was thrown up into the air in the market

square. The assembled men of the district, formed into opposing teams, would then try and move it to distant locations, serving as goals, on either side of the town, by any means possible. The teams were named after parishes or parts of the town, suggestive of local loyalties, and hundreds of 'players' sometimes took to the streets. Shops were routinely boarded up for the duration, and the timid avoided public thoroughfares altogether. The match in Derby often climaxed in dozens of men wading through the River Derwent, scrambling for the ball, while wives and sweethearts egged them on along the sidelines ('Like the German women so finely described by Tacitus . . . to stimulate them to every effort of strength').[5]

This Shrove Tuesday saturnalia, however, while undoubtedly a grand spectacle, was also something of a public nuisance. Some locals relished the carnival-like atmosphere and the beery celebrations which followed. The footballers of Kingston-upon-Thames were said to include not only an ebullient working-class crowd, but the principal tradesmen and 'several of the gentry of the neighbourhood'. On the other hand, a Derby resident claimed that decent folk only supported the tradition 'through fear of either having their property damaged or their persons insulted'.[6] By the early 1850s, the latter view tended to prevail among the middle classes. Street games were considered a pretext for riot and drunkenness. The magistracy, who might once have contributed to beer and prizes, shifted from support/toleration to active suppression. Magistrates in Derby, having failed to lure sufficient numbers to out-of-town athletic events planned as an alternative, finally read the Riot Act to the assembled football crowd. The Duke of Northumberland, on the other hand, successfully eased local tensions in Alnwick by providing a spacious lawn on his estates for Shrove Tuesday matches, offering a prize of five sovereigns to the winning team. By hook or by crook, Shrove Tuesday football was altered or outlawed. Where it persisted, locals generally negotiated safe passage of the ball from the town centre to some more peaceable location.[7]

There were less contentious football matches played in towns and villages during the first half of the century. Some were similar annual events, such as the contest between colliers and sailors in the port of Workington in Cumbria.[8] Local newspapers also mention inter-village Shrove Tuesday games, played for cash prizes; and other local matches, sometimes for fun, sometimes for prize money.[9] Many of these prize matches seem to have been organised by publicans, who doubtless recouped their outlays from the sale of alcohol. For example, an 1848 rugby-style match between 'eight picked lads of Holmfirth against a similar number of the "elite" of Hepworth' (i.e. labourers v. gentlemen) was laid on by a local brewer. Four years later, Holmfirth men played Enderby, a small town some 60 miles distant, meeting in Hyde Park, Sheffield. Again, there was a £5 prize, sponsored by a local publican.[10] We only have brief and sporadic accounts of these local contests, and so their frequency is impossible to gauge: lesser matches, without cash prizes, may not have been considered sufficiently interesting to appear in the press; or else local football matches may just have been an occasional novelty. But generally these local games appear at least to have been relatively organised affairs, with a designated field or pitch and equally sized teams, i.e. they were not merely a village version of Shrove Tuesday free-for-alls.[11]

As for the metropolis, several comments from the 1820s and 1830s imply that the growth of London put paid to team sports on its periphery:

> All the fields and waste grounds – west, north, and south – which used to be crowded every afternoon with cricket and foot-ball players even so recently as 20 years ago, are now built over.[12]

> Until about 20 or 30 years ago, the fields around London . . . were alive with players at cricket, trap-ball, too-ball, prisoners' base, and other healthful and inspiring amusements.[13]

Similar anxieties were expressed about the enclosure of common land in the north, where the poor could hitherto 'enjoy the exercise of cricket or of football'.[14] There were, regardless, still some unenclosed green spaces even in London, and it is unlikely that casual games of football ever became wholly extinct in the capital. The *Morning Advertiser* records a Christmas morning match on Kennington Common in 1823 between tailors and whitesmiths from the Borough, who then returned to a pub for roast beef and plum pudding. This was a rugby-style match with 'several of the party . . . bruised by kicks and falls, and of course covered with mud'.[15]

There are also numerous accounts of football played at festive events organised by landowners, employers and charities. A public fete for the Marquis of Chandos's birthday at Stowe included donkey rides, wheelbarrow races, climbing a greased pole – and football. A 'gipsy party', organised by Ashford's, a Birmingham whipmaker, took workers to the fields and allowed them to participate in 'the old rural game of football'. Likewise, the youthful members of London's Shoeblack Brigade were taken to Richmond Park for a day out, which included cricket, football and 'other boyish amusements'.[16] Football was considered a very convenient way for large groups to entertain themselves at fairs and festivals. This was, perhaps, a function of the game's relative simplicity and lack of codification – one did not have to trouble too much about the precise rules – and the minimal equipment required. But there was also a definite sense that football was not something to be taken seriously, a light-hearted boisterous romp, where young men could release surplus energy. During the early years of Victoria's reign, one repeatedly finds football described as a game for either schoolboys or 'rustics':

> Football, besides being a favourite game at our public schools, is much practised by rustics, who blow out a bladder, and put peas or horse-beans therein, which causes a rattle as the ball is kicked about.[17]

It is notable that *Pierce Egan's Book of Sports* (1836) lists its subject matter as 'horse-racing, hunting, milling, cricket, sailing, boxing, angling, shooting &c' and only acknowledges football, in passing, as a game played by apprentices in twelfth-century London. Football, seemingly for Egan, was a rustic game, not a sport. But this rather widely held, dismissive attitude would begin to change around the mid-century, as the game gathered more adult, middle-class enthusiasts.

The 1840s and 1850s saw variants of football flourish in the public schools and among former pupils who had progressed to the universities of Oxford and Cambridge. The coming together of players from different footballing traditions, naturally enough, caused some problems. Two ex-Shrewsbury pupils, Henry de Winton and John Charles Thring, persuaded some former schoolboys of Eton and Winchester to join them and form a university club at Cambridge in 1846. They struggled to agree on common rules.[18] H.C. Malden of Trinity College, trying something similar two years later, likewise noted that 'Eton [men] howled at the Rugby men for handling the ball.' He convened a meeting of Cambridge undergraduates from Eton, Harrow, Rugby, Winchester and Shrewsbury, where attendees brought copies of their schools' football laws. They hammered out a set of Cambridge Rules, which were pasted up on the local playing field.[19] These included forbidding handling of the ball, i.e.

favouring the Eton and Harrow systems, rather than that of Rugby. Malden's rules had no immediate impact beyond the university, but they were a small milestone in the progress towards soccer becoming a distinct, organised sporting activity.[20]

Both de Winton and Thring went on to become clergymen. Thring would then become a housemaster at Uppingham school in 1859, run by his brother, where he encouraged the playing of football (but not in the Rugby fashion, which he abhorred). Malden, likewise, returned home to run his father's preparatory school in Brighton.[21] This is a noteworthy career path, since sport, religion and education formed a heady brew in the mid-century. Thring and his contemporaries were, in fact, part of a rising generation of educators who believed in 'muscular Christianity', which included the notion that sporting teamwork, self-sacrifice and discipline provided not only healthy exercise, but also a vital moral framework. Schoolboys, therefore, were informed that physical fitness and sporting activity bordered on a righteous duty, preparing one for the literal and metaphysical battles of life. Team games were good for both body and soul. This was the same sentiment later expressed in Newbolt's poem 'Vitaï Lampada', with its famous refrain of 'Play up! play up! and play the game!' For Newbolt, the lessons of cricket prepared young Britons of the officer class for the onslaughts of the toughest of imperial enemies. The hard knocks of football, similarly, strengthened not only the sinews, but also nerve and moral character. J.C. Thring's progress from Shrewsbury school to Cambridge University, back to Uppingham school, via holy orders, exemplifies the career of the enthusiasts who embedded team games in the English public school system. The result was that a judicious mixture of Christianity, athleticism and team sports increasingly came to be considered fundamental to a good education.

There were also practical considerations which supported the growth of football in the universities: it provided a very useful winter replacement for cricket. Christ Church College, Oxford, for example, began to use its cricket pitch for football training in 1855, supervised by a Mr Rixon from the Marylebone Cricket Club.[22] Similarly, many a military garrison also hosted football matches to occupy its bored young men during the winter months. Captain R.F. Mountain of the Royal Artillery at Woolwich paid £5 towards setting up both a cricket and a football club for his men 'to keep them from those pests of vice and disease so prevalent in large garrison towns'.[23] Cricket and football conjoined provided continuous sporting activity throughout the year.

Football, then, by the mid-Victorian period, was being played in various institutional contexts, and was a suitable game – morally and physically – for schoolboys, students and soldiers, who both played within their own institutions and also formed teams to play occasional matches against other bodies. But the late 1850s saw the emergence of something new: the independent, amateur football club.

Many of the first amateur football clubs seem to have evolved from cricket clubs. The Holmfirth v. Enderby match, cited above, took place in Hyde Park, Sheffield, home of the Sheffield Cricket Club, and the players may well have been existing cricket teams. George Sills' 'Dingley Dell' team, which initially drew on Cambridge graduates for its membership and which competed in football matches in and around London in the late 1850s, took its name from Dickens' famous fictional cricket match.[24] Searching for the very first amateur team is rather like looking for the first music hall: there must inevitably be numerous minor short-lived examples which left no imprint on the historical record. Nonetheless, Sheffield Football Club has an undisputed claim to preeminence among recorded amateur teams, dating from 1857. The club was formed by former students of Sheffield Collegiate School who had previously played cricket together in Sheffield Cricket Club. Members were elected by ballot and were mostly well-to-do professionals and industrialists.

Football flourished in Sheffield, but by the early 1860s London also possessed a dozen or more amateur teams. Some were similarly associated with former membership of a particular school, but others had links to an institutional employer (e.g. the War Office) or a particular district (including clubs based in Barnes, Blackheath, Crystal Palace, Leytonstone and Kilburn). The membership of all these early clubs was principally ex-public schoolboys and other middle-class gentlemen, but the concentration of organised, amateur clubs within the metropolis marked a growing interest in the game among adults generally. It also posed a very familiar problem: agreeing common rules. The chief areas of divergence were 'hacking' (which some considered too violent) and the preference among certain clubs for 'dribbling' (i.e. moving with the ball at one's feet, as opposed to handling). Visiting footballers, as at public schools, obeyed the laws of the home team; but these could be contentious and, even when agreed, potentially put visiting teams at a distinct disadvantage. In a match between Charterhouse school and a school team from Tunbridge Wells, *Bell's Life* noted of Tunbridge Wells 'the main reason of their defeat is to be attributed to the fact that they were unaccustomed to "dribbling" and indulged in too many long kicks'.[25]

As teams began to play more fixtures against each other (as opposed to organising games within the membership of a single club), the question of standardising the rules became more pressing. The matter was aired on several occasions in the sporting press. In response to a letter in December 1858, the editor of *Bell's Life* suggested that all teams should adopt Eton's printed rules. A Rugbeian promptly replied that Rugby's rules were also printed, but the fairer system would be to form a committee of public school men to finally decide the matter. This idea received the blessing of Frederick Lillywhite, the well-known sporting outfitter ('one code of laws . . . would be a great benefit to all, as in the case with cricket').[26] An Etonian objected to the 'shinning' in the Rugby game, and asserted that Eton would 'conform to no other rules than its own, which are now adopted at the universities and by the officers of several regiments'.[27] The correspondence lasted for a month, but grew so acrimonious that the editor drew it to a close, noting that letters from public schoolmen were 'so mixed up with abuse of each other that we consider them better unpublished'.[28]

A similar debate was started in the *Field* sporting journal in late 1861. J.C. Thring, who devoted a good deal of thought to the game, also championed a convocation of public schoolmen to establish rules for the growing 'national winter sport'. He made clear, however, that he considered the Rugby version of the game anathema, because of its aggressive elements.[29] The following year, Thring published his own set of rules in a pamphlet entitled 'The Winter Game' (which *Bell's Life* found interesting, but dismissed as 'only likely to add to the confusion').[30] Thring remained engrossed by the subject and would write to the *Daily Telegraph* the following winter, yet again reiterating the need for common rules, established by a 'parliament . . . with sufficient authority to issue a new code of laws'. Thring's call to action, on this occasion, had an impact. Two men from London amateur clubs swiftly replied that they would happily attend a meeting of London-based team captains, and draw up definitive laws of the game. They were Ebenezer Cobb Morley of Barnes Football Club and Arthur Pember of N.N. ('No Names') Kilburn FC.[31] After further anonymous comments were exchanged in *The Times*, and just as the *Field*

launched its own series of articles on the subject, Morley and Pember inaugurated the Football Association.[32]

The first members of the FA were relatively young men, who had been playing
in the new London-based clubs and wanted to bring them together to agree
upon rules and encourage more and better competition. Pember, president of
the newly formed Football Association, was twenty-eight years old; Morley,
the honorary secretary, was thirty-two. Pember was a stockbroker, who would
leave the UK in 1867 to forge a career in journalism in New York; Morley was
a solicitor and an accomplished oarsman, who replaced Pember as president.
Morley is remembered as a 'founding father' of the game, along with Charles
W. Alcock of the Forest Leytonstone club (later the Wanderers), who joined
the FA's committee in 1866. The Harrow-educated Alcock, aged twenty-four
in 1866, principally occupied himself with sport, becoming the FA's secretary
(1870–95) and secretary of the Surrey County Cricket Club (1872–1907).
His 1890s reminiscences provide a good idea of the state of amateur London
clubs in this period. The beginnings of his own club, he recalled, were a handful
of old Harrovians in the north-eastern suburbs of London, who fancied 'a kind
of "punt about" rather as an exercise'.[33] They were soon joined by former
members of the nearby Forest School. This led to the creation of Forest
Leytonstone (also known as the Forest Football Club), playing both among
themselves and against any other teams they could find. The club, in time,
grew more organised and drew upon a wider pool of talent, as more rivals
began to appear within the metropolis. In practice, this also often amounted to
leading players appearing for multiple clubs. Alcock himself would appear for
half a dozen teams in the late 1860s and 1870s.

The newly formed FA initially attempted to please everybody, with many
rugby-like elements in its first set of football rules. But after only a few meetings, a Blackheath contingent of clubs abandoned the project, alienated by the
opposition to hacking. This walk-out by supporters of the 'Rugby game' set
the FA on the path to the creation of soccer (although the game would be
known as 'Association football' or simply 'football', with 'socker'/'soccer' only
gaining a degree of popularity in the 1890s). Neither Morley nor Pember had
been to public school, and so on the face of it they had no axe to grind. Yet
from the start, they had a clear preference for the dribbling game. When the
FA finally abolished catching the ball for a free kick, a couple of years later, a

clear divide between Association football and rugby was firmly established. The creation of the Rugby Football Union in 1871 would make this separation permanent. (Henceforth, in this chapter, the term 'football' indicates the post-1863 game of Association football.)

The omens for the FA's codified version of football, however, were not terribly propitious. The public schools were seen by many as custodians of the game (however it might be played), but they spurned the organisation; and even FA member clubs still happily played against sides that kept to their own rules. After a low turnout for a meeting in March 1867, Morley suggested that the FA should be dissolved, since by this stage there were only ten teams still actively involved.[34] Alcock rallied the meeting, cheerfully noting that football was becoming ever more popular: 122 clubs were now engaging in 'foreign' matches – i.e. against other clubs – as opposed to only a couple when he had begun at Forest Leytonstone. They also had the encouraging presence of a member of the recently formed Sheffield Football Association, which represented fourteen clubs in that city (although it would be another decade before Sheffield teams adopted FA rules).[35] The Football Association, Alcock suggested, had made a modest difference, but there was still much work to be done.

The organisation survived by the skin of its teeth. Letters were written to all the clubs in the country to seek new members; these persuaded Westminster and Charterhouse public schools (among others) and trebled membership. The first county match was played on 2 November 1867 (Middlesex v. Surrey & Kent). When Alcock became secretary, his drive and enthusiasm further reinvigorated the Association. Crucially, Alcock would organise the first England v. Scotland match at the Oval cricket ground in March 1870, and the first FA Cup – a knockout tournament held in the winter of 1871–72. The early years of the Cup were rather London-centric, largely attracting metropolitan and public school teams. But the introduction of a national team and a structured annual competition provided the game with a massive boost. The Cup also helped firmly establish the rule that teams should consist of eleven men. There were undoubtedly other factors that helped develop the game in these early years – not least the activity of the Sheffield FA, formed in 1867, and the Scottish FA, formed in 1873 – but Charles Alcock's tireless enthusiasm was crucial.

No one in the FA, however, conceived of football as anything like a professional sport (i.e. in which player could or should make a living from playing the game) or as a commercially oriented activity designed to generate a profit.

That said, there were some peripheral attempts to make money from the new sporting phenomenon. Frederick Lillywhite's and John Wisden's Cricketing Outfitters (opened at 2 New Coventry Street in 1855) began to advertise the sale of other sporting equipment in 1858, including footballs. The following year, *Lillywhite's Guide to Cricketers* advertised that it included the 'laws of football', i.e. the various public school rules, listed by school, along with the rules of rackets, golf, bowls and boat-racing.[36] Frederick Lillywhite also sold a printed copy of the FA's initial rules for sixpence (or on a 'sheet varnished with rollers for the Club Room' for one shilling and tuppence).[37] He would also sell Football Association-approved balls, which cost twelve shillings, and in 1868 launched an officially sanctioned Football Annual, with the latest rules and summaries of matches.[38] There were other paraphernalia and mementoes sold to fans. After England v. Scotland matches began to be played in 1870, the London Stereoscopic Company sold souvenir photographs of the English team for six shillings and sixpence.[39] But the game itself remained an amateur affair, in both senses of the word. The FA was, on principle, opposed to professional players, believing in gentlemanly amateur amusement. Clubs themselves, meanwhile, often relied on rather *ad hoc* arrangements, such as matches played in public parks. Even the first county match in 1867, due to some confusion about booking grounds at Lord Ranelagh's Beaufort House, required the teams to hastily decamp to Battersea Park. There was no serious dedicated football infrastructure. The Oval at Kennington, home to the Surrey County Cricket Club, would serve as the default venue for the FA Cup Final until the 1890s. But by the end of the 1870s, a more professional and commercialised future was looming on the horizon. Alcock himself noted a 'serious and almost business-like' element creeping into his cherished game. He already felt nostalgic for a period when 'football had not grown to be so important, as to make umpires necessary, and the "gate" the first subject for conversation'.[40] The 'gate' was 'gate money', income from ticket sales. The question of how such income should be used by supposedly amateur clubs would dominate the next, most formative decade of the game's development.

There were a few entrepreneurs from other fields tangentially involved with the game in its early days. Thomas Youdan in Sheffield, the music-hall and theatre impresario, was also a sports enthusiast and sponsored the Youdan Cup in 1867. This was the first formal football competition in the country, played among local teams and won by Sheffield Hallam. But it was the growing numbers of fans who were willing to pay to watch a good match that drove a shift from an amateur game to a more professional and commercially driven sport. Clubs realised that there was money to be made from ticketing, and that investing that money in the club's facilities, players and connections with other teams (e.g. starting new county associations and cup competitions) would both improve the quality of the play and bring more fans/profit, creating a virtuous cycle.

This is not to say that taking money from spectators was an innovation. During 1863, for instance, the Nottinghamshire County Cricket Club took £163 from members' subscriptions and £204 gate money, while spending £335 on 'matches, scoring, telegraph, mowing machine and general expenses'.[41] Nor was taking gate money at football matches – rarely more than tuppence or threepence admission in this period – terribly contentious. The FA, although it possessed a very strong amateur ethos, never prohibited clubs from charging. This was because, for most clubs in the early years, the sums involved were relatively small and there were clearly necessary outgoings to be met, such as paying for grounds, kit and travel. Reading FC, for example, formed in 1869, took £11 or so from matches in 1878–79 and spent £8 on necessities (including a nominal sum to rent the grounds of the local cricket club). Nonetheless, some self-conscious amateurs in the club were still embarrassed by even this modest degree of commercialism, and one respectable member felt obliged to state that the gate money was not 'mercenary', but was 'to keep order and to get a *quid pro quo*'.[42]

Some clubs were more ambitious than others, and were positively keen to make good use of any modest profits. The expenses of Cheshire's Northwich Victoria FC in 1877–78 included:

£6 5s 1d for new goal posts, flags, fencing &c
£3 18s for footballs and repairs
£9 8s 1d for printing, advertising &c
£9 12s 10d for expenses of [sending] teams to matches
£1 10s for damage to field[43]

The club had £14 subscription money from seventy-two playing members and £27 in gate money. This left £15 in hand. It was immediately proposed to establish a county-wide Challenge Cup competition, which Northwich could dominate and thus obtain extra revenue from important matches. Thinking strategically about what opponents to play and how much income that might bring in was one way in which clubs could prosper and expand. This was still, of course, not a very serious business: the amounts involved were fairly trifling. The following year, the club made only £21 on the gate (blamed on bad weather) and suddenly had to find £10 rental for its ground, which had previously been gratis (presumably the landowner had heard of the club's healthy finances). Northwich was also let down by clubs in Macclesfield and Hanley, which the team had visited, but which failed to turn up for the return matches. Balancing the cost of visiting other towns against future gate money from the return visits was very important. Indeed, travel costs were a major factor that forced even the most reluctant clubs to think along more commercial lines.

Another (albeit controversial) way to invest money, whether it came from ticket sales or wealthy club patrons, was to buy in professional players. This was nothing new: cricket clubs had utilised professionals for decades, often bringing in working-class men with strong athletic abilities. Professional cricket players, however, were kept at arm's length from the gentlemen amateurs who made use of their services, with social interaction kept to an absolute minimum. They were even described as 'servants' of the respectable amateur; or, more artfully, as 'servants of the game'.[44] For the upper and middle classes, there was something slightly disreputable about the idea of playing sport for money, as a trade, rather than for amusement. A gentleman might play for a wager, but not to earn a living. Muscular Christianity, with its emphasis on the moral value of sport, further entrenched the gentleman/player distinction. The first members of the Football Association, therefore, as middle-class amateurs, had an ingrained hostility to the professional player and only wanted amateur clubs in their organisation: the working-class sportsman, paid for his skills, was not welcome.

This began to create real problems, as football gained more enthusiasts in the industrial north. For by the late 1870s, football was 'as national a pastime in its season as cricket', with more working-class men taking up the game.[45] Amateurism, which was cherished by middle-class clubs in London, meant much less to new clubs with more working-class roots – or at least when the managing committee consisted of mill owners, lawyers, accountants and other business-minded professionals who cared more about results than abstractions of gentlemanly conduct. A toast had been raised after the first game played under Association rules: 'Success to Football, irrespective of class or creed.'[46] But the class distinctions which had exercised the FA at its inception were between the public schools who spurned the organisation and the rest of its solidly middle-class membership. It had not anticipated the rapid take-up of the game by the working class. This proletarian enthusiasm was not universal, and only happened initially in certain parts of the country, particularly the industrial north-west. Nonetheless, the attitude of northern clubs to professional players would change the future of the game.

Football, beyond the metropolis, was highly popular in Sheffield, Scotland and, by the mid-1870s, East Lancashire, centring on Blackburn, Preston and Bolton. The establishment of a Lancashire County Football Association in 1878, along with the Blackburn Football Association and then a County Challenge Cup in 1879, reflected the burgeoning of strong local teams in the district. Local rivalries ran deep and stimulated ever-increasing interest in the game. When Blackburn Rovers played Darwen mid-week to settle a Lancashire Cup match that had resulted in a draw the previous Saturday, mill-hands asked their employers for time off. This was refused, but sufficient workers absconded to close down most of the town's factories.[47] An 1880 county cup match between Darwen and Blackburn Rovers reportedly attracted more than 10,000 fans.[48] This match would also become notorious for finishing shortly after half-time, thanks to a fight breaking out on the pitch. The key factor in the fracas was the presence of Fergie Suter for Blackburn. A Scottish professional, Suter had played for Darwen the previous season, but – following the money – had changed team after only a year. His presence on the pitch riled his former teammates. But the whole episode placed Suter at the heart of a much bigger row that was brewing in Lancashire: the role of professional players in an avowedly amateur sport.

Darwen, Suter's first club, had told the press that he had come down from Scotland to seek (non-sporting) employment and that the club had snapped him up. But this was the standard excuse for using imported talent: clubs would go to considerable lengths to find players a real or nominal position in a local factory – or even a pub tenancy – to establish them as legitimate migrants. The aim was to avoid awkward questions from the national or county association about professional players. Yet by the early 1880s, as more Scottish players like Suter began to appear on Lancashire sides, no one really doubted that these were professionals masquerading as amateurs. Various systems were in place to keep the business *sub rosa*. Money was left discreetly in a player's coat, or excessive 'expenses' were agreed without question. Wages were taken from the gate money before the total amount was entered in the books. Some clubs even went to the trouble of forging their accounts and keeping two sets of books. Working-class professionals with a 'day job' (fake or otherwise) might need to ask employers for time off to attend training or matches and could, therefore, also claim that any dubious payments were compensation for lost hours. And while the most obvious indicator of professionalism was when clubs acquired players from distant parts of the country, this did not in itself amount to hard proof. Tensions grew between the adherents of amateurism and those who accepted closet professionals. The ever-growing numbers of professionals meant that the strategy of quiet concealment could not last for ever.

The first real public crisis of professionalism occurred in Yorkshire. It was a curious affair, because the team in question was something of a novelty: the Sheffield Zulus. The Zulus were a bunch of leading local players, put together for a charity match in aid of British widows and orphans of men killed in the 1879 Zulu War. To add drama, they arrived at the Sheffield FC ground in a convoy of hansom cabs, their faces blacked up with cork, wearing black jerseys and stockings, and carrying Zulu weaponry, rented for the occasion and said to be genuine war trophies. The spears and shields were dropped for the actual match, but the feather head-dresses and white beads were retained. This unfortunate spectacle had a self-consciously comic air, leading to a 'considerable amount of amusement' among the 2,000 spectators.[49] Minstrelsy was still very common on the music-hall stage, and this mixture of serious football and light entertainment was cheered by the audience.

As the Zulus began to play more games, touring throughout the country, it was suggested to the Sheffield FA that they were receiving payment for their efforts. This resulted in players receiving suspensions and considerable local acrimony. Fans grew frustrated when Jack Hunter of Heeley FC, one of the Zulus, was dropped from a North v. South match against London. A subsequent match between Heeley FC and Sheffield Wednesday in January 1881 was disrupted by barracking and insults – 'remarks of a character not calculated to enhance football in the minds of the gentler sex' – largely directed against the Sheffield FA's secretary, who was then jostled by Hunter's supporters after the game.[50] The Zulus were hardly a typical football team, providing something of a theatrical spectacle; but they pointed towards a future where the amateur ethos counted for little against amusement of the paying public. Sheffield FA's treatment of Hunter also provided him with an incentive to quit the city and seek pastures new. He would follow Fergie Suter's example and take up a position as player and coach at a Lancashire club, Blackburn Olympic. There, he helped craft a team whose success would edge football one stage nearer to full acceptance of professionalism.

Blackburn was a populous mill-town and, as already hinted, something of a hotspot for football. The *Blackburn Standard* boasted at the start of the 1879 season that neighbours Blackburn Rovers, Darwen, Eagley and Turton were all down to play first-class teams with a national reputation, including the Old Etonians and the Scottish clubs Vale of Lever, Glasgow Rangers and Glasgow Partick.[51] Blackburn Olympic was omitted from the paper's 1879 roll of honour, since it was a newer team, formed the previous year from the ashes of two other local clubs. But it had won the Blackburn FA's competition in its first season 'through perseverance and scientific play', and was already attracting thousand-strong crowds to its own rented ground beside the Hole-i'th'-Wall pub.

What was distinctive about Blackburn Olympic was that it was composed solely of working men, supported by the owner of a local iron foundry. This is not to say it was unique. Nearby Darwen had reached the quarter finals of the FA Cup in 1879 and was a similar working-class club, as well as being the first northern team to scale such heights in the national cup. To cover the travel costs of playing the Old Etonians in London, the team had been obliged to send a collection tin round local mills and workshops.[52] Still, Blackburn Olympic, along with Darwen, represented a new type of football team, providing a distinct contrast to local rivals Blackburn Rovers – a more middle-class club, which Olympic fans considered 'not by any means representative'.[53] Even before Jack Hunter's arrival in 1882, 'The Olympic' were growing in confidence. The club had spent £100 on enlarging, draining and levelling its pitch, and had built a grandstand, for which the public had to pay double the regular admission.[54] Olympic's balance sheet for 1881–82 reveals a club operating on a considerably higher level than the likes of Reading or Northwich. Gate receipts for the year amounted to £445 and books of season tickets brought in £61. Meanwhile, £73 went on railway and bus fares, travelling to other clubs; £87 on printing advertisements; and £28 on refreshments.

With Hunter on board, the club felt emboldened to enter the 1882–83 FA Cup. This would prove a fateful decision. The Football Association was already growing rather concerned about paid professionals and 'imported' players, like Suter and Hunter. Blackburn Olympic would make the issue impossible to ignore. This was not so much thanks to Hunter's self-interested move from Sheffield (although he was condemned in some quarters as a closet professional).[55] Rather, the club would do something which southern amateurs found even more unforgivable: it would go on to actually win the FA Cup.

Blackburn Olympic, in fact, was not packed with 'foreign players', but there were some who questioned whether *any* team composed solely of working men could be 'amateur'. After all, covering expenses for lost working time was still a form of payment for services rendered. There were also always rumours that the clubs went considerably further, providing large cash bonuses. Olympic's various published outgoings for 1881–82 included £32 'field expenses', £25 'grants to members out of work and sick' and £27 marked down, without further explanation, as 'for players'. These were not vast sums, but some of these loosely defined payments were probably entering certain players' pockets, whether as regular pay or as bonuses. There may well have been further payments behind the scenes.

As the 1882 season commenced, the Football Association, facing mounting criticism about northern clubs' professional players, appointed a commission to investigate. The Sheffield FA, keen to offer its support, then ostentatiously refused to field a team against Lancashire unless their rivals removed imported players. They also circulated a letter to all Sheffield clubs, reminding them that the Association had resolved to forbid any payment for matches after the Zulu affair. Sheffield stated bluntly that it was determined 'to strangle the professional element in its own ranks'.[56] The Lancashire FA, in turn, responding to press enquiries, drafted a carefully worded reply that it had 'no official knowledge of professionals playing in any of the Lancashire teams'.[57] Unofficial knowledge was another matter.

The Lancashire Football Association was actually in something of a bind, since it both represented and regulated a number of clubs containing de facto professionals like Suter and Hunter. Thomas Hindle, one of the Lancashire FA's founders, had actually already tried to introduce rules prohibiting imported Scottish players from participating in the Association's County Cup. Lancashire FA, therefore, was well aware of the issue and fairly hostile to professionalism; but collectively, it also had no desire to crush the prospects of the clubs under its supervision. When the national FA's inquiry began, both Hindle (an accountant by profession) and the secretary of the Sheffield FA examined the books of Bolton Wanderers, Great Lever, Halliwell, Darwen, Blackburn Rovers and Accrington.[58] Their investigation found nothing suspicious, but the lack of a smoking gun did little to appease critics.

Blackburn Olympic would fight its way to victory in the FA Cup Final, which took place at the Oval on 31 March 1883, defeating the Old Etonians. Jack Hunter and a Sheffield colleague, George Wilson, were the only 'foreign imports' on the team, but that did not really matter to disgruntled amateurs among the commentariat. The triumph of a northern club in the Cup was deeply symbolic, marking the end of an era when former public schoolboys had been dominant. This was, to quote one journalist, 'a trial between the old and new system of football', and the gentleman amateur had fallen short.[59] Indeed, there were various ways in which the Olympics were decidedly *not* gentlemen amateurs, whatever the true state of their financial affairs. They were, obviously, of a lower social class than their opponents, including as they did a plumber, weavers, a picture-framer and iron-moulder; but they also played differently. The press accused them of tackling from behind, grabbing shirts and making cynical accusations of handball against the Old Etonians.[60] Not only did the team play more aggressively (to put it charitably) on the pitch, but more importantly, it also adopted a coordinated passing game. The amateurs of the 1860s and early 1870s had generally relied more on individual dribbling skills rather than targeted long passes. Journalists waxed lyrical about the 'brilliancy and dash' of the old-fashioned game, versus 'skilful combination [team work] and dextrous "passing"', which they considered rather too 'scientific'. Yet it was now quite clear which system was more successful.[61] Jack Hunter, famously, also laid on a special training camp for his teammates at Blackpool, with a strict exercise and dietary regimen. A 6 a.m. start and 3-mile walk (fuelled by port and raw eggs); then breakfast of porridge and haddock; legs of mutton for lunch; porridge and milk for tea; and six oysters each for supper.[62] This was innovatory and, whether the men of Blackburn Olympic were paid or unpaid, such detailed preparation was not considered amateurism. There were, one suspects, double standards at work here. It is unlikely that the Old Etonians made no preparation whatsoever for the match; but any effort on their part would always be considered 'amateur'. The distinction was always as much about pre-existing social status – and, in the case of Scottish players, even race/nationality – as about anything specific. This becomes obvious when one reads some of the contemporary press reports. One journalist, condemning the introduction of Scottish players among northern clubs, noted that such players were 'distinguished neither for refinement of manners or language'. A writer for the *Athlete* was more blunt in his racialised antagonism: 'employment of the scum of the Scottish villages has tended . . . to brutalise the game'.[63]

The success of Blackburn Olympic, in any case, was a watershed. Similar clubs would inevitably follow suit, from Lancashire and elsewhere; and the questions posed by the existence of professional players in an amateur association could no longer be ignored. The FA finally made a definitive move in November 1883. Accrington FC was disqualified from the FA Cup and banned from playing with other clubs because it had hired James Beresford, whom the press had long marked out as a professional. Later in the season, a complaint was lodged by Upton Park that Preston North End had fielded professional players in its fourth-round cup tie (the various kinds of post-match 'protests' against results were a wearying feature of football in this period). The Preston club, which regularly fielded a side including nine Scots players, was also promptly expelled from the competition. The following season, the FA began a further clampdown, sending out a survey to all clubs about players' residential status, occupation and salaries in their (non-footballing) previous and current workplaces. The FA, moreover, insisted that two years' residence was required to enter a player into an FA Cup team. This was a hardline approach. Unfortunately, if the Football Association expected such tactics to finally eradicate the professional footballer, it was in for a rude awakening. The Lancashire clubs refused point blank. They would, they announced, quit the FA and form their own British Football Association.

It was Charles Alcock who forged a compromise and narrowly averted a serious split in the game: the FA would back down and recognise professionals, but under certain conditions. These were, first, registration of professionals with the FA; second, players were forbidden to switch clubs within the same season; and finally, a two-year residence qualification. Professionals were also forbidden to sit on FA committees, which reassured amateurs about the future of the Association. Alcock's peace-making still heralded the beginning of a new professional and commercialised age. There was some irony in this, since Alcock was the very definition of an amateur player; but he was astute enough to realise that the FA could not turn back the clock to the halcyon days of the early 1860s.

The FA's demands, including that players should not change loyalty mid-season, were not wholly unwelcome among the clubs. None relished rival teams poaching their talent. Yet there were potentially damaging consequences arising from the new settlement. These were not so much on account of the FA's strictures, but rather because of the very nature of the now legalised professionalism. Richer, well-supported teams could now legitimately attract all the best players and the smaller clubs would inevitably struggle to compete. This was an issue before 1885, but creating a legitimate structure for professionals only accelerated the process. The successful professional clubs also faced increasing wage bills, as players could confidently bargain on the strength of their value on the open market. As one club secretary noted in 1886, the overall bill for wages could easily amount to £1,000 per annum.[64]

The problem of finding reliable and *profitable* 'friendly' fixtures with other clubs, outside national and local cup ties, also became pressing. There was, remarked E.S. Morley, chairman of Blackburn Rovers and vice-president of the FA, 'too much football' in Lancashire, i.e. clubs took on too many commitments, not all of them remunerative.[65] Participating in knock-out cup competitions, although very popular with the public, was also inherently unpredictable. Teams found themselves unable to realistically plan their commitments for the season. Clubs that progressed further than they had anticipated often cancelled other fixtures, or fielded below-par second teams. This, in turn, meant reduced gate money for jilted opponents, leaving secretaries desperately scrambling to arrange new matches. Larger clubs, as they invested more money in the business of football, needed regular serious matches, which the various knock-out cups could not guarantee – or which they even undermined. Cancelled matches or uncertainty over who would actually turn up damaged both finances and reputations. One man proposed an answer to this difficulty: William McGregor. A Scot who had settled in Birmingham, where he opened a drapery business, McGregor was fascinated by football and became involved in the management of Aston Villa FC. Citing county cricket as his inspiration, McGregor suggested that the problem was not the quantity of matches, but their quality. He proposed, therefore, that a small, elite group of clubs should band together to establish a fixed set of home and away matches between each other, throughout the season. McGregor canvassed support from various clubs, and his efforts led to the foundation in 1888 of the Football League, containing only twelve members.

This small number was crucial for quality control. By way of comparison, 130 clubs competed in the first round of the FA Cup in 1885 (as opposed to thirty, ten years earlier). The League would be tightly focused on the best clubs, with a policy of including only one club from any given town or city, in order to stimulate competition and popular enthusiasm. The League was not explicitly intended to vie with the Football Association, although many saw it as a useful counter-weight to the powerful national and county associations. Its primary function was to ensure a steady succession of high-quality matches between members. Emphasis was placed on clubs fielding their best players. McGregor had hoped that clubs might split gate money at each match, but it was decided to give the bulk to the home team and only £12 to the visitors. The clubs wanted to profit from however much local support they could muster 'at home', rather than rely on travelling fans (or on persuading their supporters to travel). A scoring system was required, and the League settled on two points for a win and one for a draw; if teams were equal on points, the outcome was to be decided by goal average.

The Football League soon proved, as predicted, a highly effective vehicle to maintain interest in matches throughout the season, guaranteeing supporters an entertaining experience and producing good financial returns. The idea was swiftly copied, including by the short-lived rival Football Alliance (1889–92), the more durable Northern League for teams in Northumbria (founded in 1889, initially a mixture of reserve teams and amateurs) and the Southern Football League (founded in 1894), not to mention many more local leagues for lesser clubs. The FA finally gave in completely to the logic of professionalism and abolished its residence qualification in 1889, which resulted in a new influx of Scottish players and growing profits for League clubs. By 1890, the League was confident enough to make sixpence the minimum admission for all its matches. The initial twelve clubs were expanded to fourteen in 1891, then sixteen in 1892; and a second division of twelve clubs was launched. The League further expanded to twenty in each division in 1905. League clubs, as profits swelled and they invested money back into their teams, came to dominate the final rounds of the FA Cup.

Who were the winners and losers after the creation of the Football League? The nascent League was undoubtedly fatal to certain existing clubs outside the charmed circle. Blackburn Olympic was already struggling. During the 1886–87 season, the club took only £275 in gate money (as opposed to £445 in 1881–82).[66] By 1888, Olympic had lost several key players to wealthier clubs, including Jack Hunter, who would have a short career at Blackburn Rovers. The acceptance of Blackburn Rovers as the town's sole representative in the Football League – inevitable, since it had two successive FA Cup wins in 1884 and 1885 – was the final straw. Lacking money to pay them, Olympic cut loose all its professional players in January 1889; and facing the inevitable, it was wound up in the autumn. The final humiliation was the sale of the 'woodwork' from its pitch at auction ('the whole of the boarding round the enclosure, the grand-stand, the dressing-tent and the turnstiles'), purchased for £100 by the Hole-i'th'-Wall's landlady, who planned to let the ground to the more workaday Blackburn Railway Clerks.[67] The dominance of the northern League clubs would also hold back the progress of football in the south. The Southern League, founded in 1894, mixed amateurs and professionals and provided an inferior pool of talent to test the first southern professional clubs. Finally, it is worth pointing out that membership of the Football League did not absolutely guarantee a rosy future. Stoke City, founder members, went bankrupt in 1907, failing to generate enough revenue to compete with its well-financed rivals. But the majority of League clubs prospered. A brief portrait of a couple of the leading clubs, Blackburn Rovers and Aston Villa, both of which remained in the first division of the League for the next two decades, will provide a useful snapshot of the growth of the big late Victorian clubs in this new, prosperous professional ecosystem.[68]

Blackburn Rovers were founded in 1874 by young men who had been pupils at Blackburn Grammar School (i.e. had the typical origins of a pre-1880s club). The team also included several alumni of Malvern College in Worcestershire. From the late 1870s, Rovers' managing committee of local businessmen showed a genius for obtaining good fixtures ('the first club to have a really representative list of fixtures . . . their enterprise set the whole football world talking').[69] They also had a ruthless streak, not only persuading Scottish professional Fergie Suter to move from rival Darwen in 1880, but repeatedly attempting to poach Olympic's players. Similarly, when wrangling with the Lancashire FA over professionalism, the club refused to let its own best players attend county matches, giving priority to its own more profitable fixtures.[70] The club, in short, operated in a very business-like fashion. A glance at the club's finances in 1886 provides an insight into how far the club had already come from its amateur roots. Stands, refreshment tents and grounds were valued at £500. Gate money amounted to £927 for the previous year, with a further £136 from season tickets and £581 from a prize draw among fans. The club's annual overall income was £1,853. More than £150, however, was spent on advertising; £90 on entertaining visiting teams; £358 on travel expenses; £73 on kit and footballs; and, by far the greatest individual expense, £615 on players' wages. All in all, therefore, the club was barely breaking even, after the acceptance of professionalism. The arrival of the Football League changed matters dramatically. Gate receipts during 1888–89 doubled to over £2,000, and even with the erection of a new stand the club was £576 in profit by the end of the season. By 1895, gate money had almost doubled again to just under £4,000. Costs, of course, rose as well. Players' wages doubled between 1891 and 1895, and there was considerable investment in the club's ground at Ewood Park (including £2,500 on buying the freehold). In 1897, the club became a limited liability company, and was soon paying out 5 per cent to its shareholders. By 1906, total receipts were over £8,000; by 1914, that figure had risen to over £20,000.[71] There were ups and downs, but the League brought the club considerable prosperity.

Aston Villa was another club founded in the mid-1870s, this time by youthful members of a Wesleyan chapel in Birmingham. Church-related socialising was a common beginning for many clubs in this period. Legend has it that founders subscribed two shillings each to purchase a ball. The team was knocked into more professional shape by the arrival of Glaswegian George Ramsay, who introduced training and persuaded players to learn the modern passing game. By 1888, the club had £2,739 income, but it was also spending money very freely: £908 on players' wages and £529 on training, travelling and hotels. The club also spent £500 on a new pavilion, baths and dressing rooms for its ground (on a site rented at £80 per annum).

As it happens, the Football League did not boost Aston Villa's income in its opening 1888–89 season. William McGregor still urged his club to become a limited company, pointing out that large sums of money had long been passing through its hands, yet 'no member could enforce an investigation into the club's affairs, or an examination of a single book'.[72] The club's committee devoted some considerable thought to the question. Some members of the Villa committee were hostile to establishing an ostensibly commercially oriented organisation, even if only to limit financial liability, and the club president, James Hinks, resigned. The arguments on both sides make interesting reading. Some suggested that it was better to keep Aston Villa a 'sporting club' for 'social and moral reasons'. McGregor pointed out numerous quirks in the existing committee administration, including the fact that players only made contracts with certain members of the committee (rather than with the club as a legal entity). He is reported to have summed matters up thus:

> [the proposal for limited liability] was not brought forward for the purpose of making money, but merely to place the club on a sound, orderly financial basis . . . Members had asserted that the club was set up to encourage a national pastime and to provide healthy recreation for the masses. He denied it. The club was established for the purpose of enabling its members to enjoy a game of football amongst themselves, but had grown into a business concern . . . salaried directors – players, umpires, referees, and secretaries were paid, and paid directors were better under the control of the club.[73]

Any talk of a 'sporting club', he implied, was now mere sentiment. Things had moved on.

In a nutshell, the progress outlined above was the trajectory of every successful Victorian club. The traditionalists, however, held some sway at Villa. The club initially resolved to incorporate in a manner which would exclude payment of dividends. Apart from funding other sporting activity and giving to charitable causes, it would plough all profits back into the club itself.[74] But the club's management committee would soon come under fire for poor administration and for buying costly players 'without satisfactory results'.[75] Aston Villa became a regular company, with dividends for shareholders, at the start of 1896. The club also moved to a sports ground in Aston Park. Villa took the lease and created a new stadium, which opened in 1897 with a 40,000 capacity. One side contained a tiered grandstand, but mainly the crowd stood on banked slopes around the pitch. The club was wealthy enough in 1912 to take up the option of buying the freehold, which cost over £11,000. The club, like Blackburn, was now taking over £20,000 on the gate. Two years later, Villa drew up plans for a stadium with a capacity of 104,000, though the First World War intervened.

* * *

Large clubs, then, by the early 1900s were 'business concerns'. This included not only the payment of players, but increasingly signing-on bonuses and transfer fees. There were also improvements in infrastructure. Clubs which originally had merely roped off a playing field began to build dedicated stadiums. They also secured gate money with the introduction of recently patented 'Rush Preventive' turnstiles, which could not be held open for one's friends. The progress from field to stadium was generally an evolutionary one, but often very rapid. Tottenham Hotspur, for example, first introduced wooden duckboards around the pitch for people to stand on in wet weather in 1892; then it built a small wooden grandstand for a hundred spectators in 1894 (replacing a parked wagon which had served until that point). The club also erected hoardings to obstruct the view from an unofficial stand a short distance from the ground, to which a local landowner was charging tuppence admission. In 1899, the club, facing overcrowding at its existing ground, secured a site at White Hart Lane. Tottenham relied at this point on mobile wooden stands, which could accommodate around 2,500 spectators in total. By 1905, the ends of the ground had both been banked up to provide slopes for standing. In 1909, the club employed prolific stadium architect Archibald Leitch to construct a 5,300-seat main stand, containing 550 tons of ironwork, the largest stand in the country (although concrete would become the preferred material in stadiums). Growing numbers of spectators, in short, reliably led to ever larger facilities being constructed. As one commentator put it, 'football is now as sordid a concern of commerce as Pears' soap, or the electric light . . . all the teams strive after "big gates" as the highest good'.[76]

Yet it is important to note that the FA still acted as a rather peculiar financial regulator, determined to keep in check the worst excesses of professionalism. From the early 1890s, therefore, it insisted that any new incorporated clubs limit their dividends to a maximum of 5 per cent, considered a fair and unexploitative return (one might also think of social 'model' housing companies, building flats for the working class, which offered potential investors so-called 'five percent philanthropy'). This principle was fully enshrined in FA regulations in 1899, along with the further rule that directors of football companies should not receive any remuneration, beyond holding shares.[77] The FA also introduced a maximum wage of £4 per week for League clubs in 1901, to check rising wage bills – a point on which the clubs were somewhat ambivalent. No other leisure institution was regulated in this way, limiting dividends and payments. The FA, at the same time, continued to shape the actual rules of the game, with penalties, (goal) nets and referees on the pitch being introduced in the early 1890s.

Football had its critics – often over issues which resonate to this day. Players were accused of being pampered, overpaid, housed in luxury hotels, transported in their own railway saloon carriages, and far too famous for their own good ('they cannot move in their native streets without receiving ovations enough to turn the head of a Prime Minister').[78] They were also traded by agents, with ever-increasing transfer fees becoming the norm, in catalogues that smacked of the cattle-market:

> No. 163 – Right or left full back. This is one of the most likely youngsters I have ever booked. He gives reference to a well-known pressman, who has repeatedly seen him play, and knows what he can do, and has a high opinion of his abilities and future prospects. Just note – height 5 feet 11 inches; weight, 12 stone; aged, 20. There's a young giant for you . . . this is a colt worth training.[79]

Fans were reportedly too much caught up in fevered emotion, leading to over-enthusiastic use of expletives and abuse of the referee; they watched games with 'malignant anxiety . . . ungenerous one-sided enthusiasm . . . an almost carnivorous expression on their passion-deformed faces'.[80] They were criticised as passive observers, for whom 'sport' only meant standing still on the terrace, watching a game. Professional football was damned as 'a show, not a game . . . played for the pleasure of the spectators, not of the actors'.[81] It was even claimed that it was precisely this sort of thing, along with the other ills of late Victorian industrialism, which contributed to physical degeneration of the species.[82] Temperance-minded journalists also criticised the pub culture associated with northern clubs. A brief glance at the likes of *The Football Field and Sports Telegram* – an 1880s Lancashire-based sporting paper, whose existence testifies to a burgeoning culture of football journalism and fandom – reveals numerous public houses claiming connection with local teams. In 1886, Dannie Friel's Footballer's Arms, near to Burnley's ground, declared itself 'The Home of Football Chat' and offered fans 'the choicest Cigars in the District on the way to Turf Moor'. The Britannia Hotel proudly boasted that it was 'THE RECOGNISED HOUSE OF THE BOLTON WANDERERS'. The Swan,

Accrington, was run by George Haworth, captain of Accrington FC. Sundry pubs advertised 'football gossip', 'sporting papers taken' and 'football parties catered for'.[83] Contemporary criticism of working-class fan culture, however, not only reflected genuine anxieties about alcohol, but also a degree of resentment about professional football's triumph over pure amateurism. There was a growing feeling in the early 1900s that the FA no longer had the interests of traditional amateurs at heart, and had capitulated to commercial interests. This would eventually lead to a split and to the formation of the Amateur Football Association in 1907. This catered for the southern amateur clubs, which had never come to terms with professionalism, including many public schools (although the AFA clubs would reaffiliate with the FA in 1914).

There was, at least, no arguing with the numbers, even if one disputed the morality of the commercialised pleasures on offer. The 1901 Cup final, held at Crystal Palace between the London team of Tottenham Hotspur and Sheffield United – the sort of 'north v. south' competition that fans relished – attracted a staggering 110,000 spectators.[84] The number of football clubs affiliated to the FA rose from 1,000 in 1888 to 12,000 by 1910. Football had shifted from being a 'punt about' on local fields to become a spectator sport on a scale previously unknown – and arguably the most popular communal leisure activity of the Victorian age.

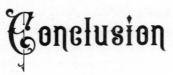

Conclusion

OR,

THE MURDERER OF THOUGHT

THE UNDERLYING CONDITIONS THAT ALLOWED all these new commercial forms of mass entertainment to flourish have long been recognised. The bustling, densely populated cities of the industrial revolution and a burgeoning consumer culture created a vast potential customer base for purveyors of goods and services, including entertainment. The Great Exhibition was particularly eye-opening, demonstrating that millions were willing to travel to the metropolis – and not only for edification, but also for recreation and amusement. The Exhibition's highly popular discounted 'shilling days' also revealed that skilled workers, with money in their pockets, were something of an untapped market. Purveyors of other leisure experiences took note, and began to think big. The metamorphosis of the music hall 'from pot-house to palace' provides a prime example; but we might equally cite the rapid development of Blackpool as a seaside resort, or even the rise of Aston Villa FC. These were all, in a way, responses to the same social circumstances and economic opportunities. The Victorians wanted to be amused, and were willing to pay for the privilege. Arguably, Imre Kiralfy's fantastical White City, an urban wonderland covering some 120 acres, marked the zenith, the ultimate in mass entertainment. This was amusement on an industrial scale, using industrial methods – from the toll-gate to the bevy of mechanised rides. White City had its roots in the fair and the pleasure garden, but with neither the transience and unpredictability of the former nor the faux rusticity of the latter. The public now had something infinitely more modern to divert them, tripping happily, a little dazed and dizzy, from the Flip-Flap to the Dingle-Dongle.[1]

There were numerous other factors which contributed to the nineteenth century's entertainment explosion. The growing advertising industry, and the wider dissemination of newspapers and magazines, helped businessmen pitch commercialised leisure to the masses. There were also useful specialist publications: theatre and music-hall artistes could peruse the likes of the *Era* and *Entr'acte*, where a good deal of business was conducted via advertising columns ('Wanted, Lady for Eccentric Comedy Part, Must have Elegant Wardrobe'; 'Wanted, Leg-mania Artiste, good Knockabout. Sing a little. No amateurs'; 'Wanted, a Good Low Comedian. Sobriety Indispensable').[2] Developments in transport and communications infrastructure also played their part. The railway network created boundless new opportunities for the proprietors of both exhibition grounds and seaside resorts, as they ferried customers from far and wide. The railways also proved very useful for entertainers themselves on provincial tours or one-off engagements. Mary Annie Lawrence, the failing music-hall artiste who was bankrupted in 1862, listed her income from both regular gigs in the metropolis and occasional appearances in the provinces ('received from Aston Park *fete*, two days, £6 . . . Vauxhall Gardens, Yarmouth, for three days, £7 10s'). The railways also materially aided the rise of roving professional football clubs, playing away fixtures in distant towns and cities. By the 1890s, of course, League football teams could afford their own exclusive saloon carriages.

As for the consumer, economists agree that the working class saw an overall rise in real wages from the 1870s onwards. Working conditions also improved, with reduced hours and more formally agreed holidays. This was not universal, and there were some notable local and national economic downturns; but overall, workers could afford to spend more time and money on leisure and entertainment. It is no coincidence that the Factory Act 1874, which guaranteed a Saturday half-holiday for textile workers, was contemporaneous with the sudden growth of football in the Lancashire mill-towns. There was now a convenient, shared time for this popular recreation, whether as player or spectator. The expansion of neighbouring seaside resorts, like Blackpool and Southport, also owed much to the growing purchasing power of the Lancashire millworker, combined with the bank holidays and half-holidays established in the 1870s.

This background will undoubtedly be familiar to anyone who has already studied nineteenth-century social history. 'Victorian leisure' itself is well-trodden historical territory. Nonetheless, I hope even the most knowledgeable Victorianist will have found something new in the pages of this book. I have tried especially hard to make deeper inroads into the origins of the gin palace and music hall, whose early years (to me, at least) have always seemed rather mysterious. The former, as it turns out, has a long history that stretches back to the very beginning of the nineteenth century, though this is rather obscured by the coinage of the phrase 'gin palace' in the 1830s. There was little to choose between the 'gin-shop' and 'gin palace': they were both modern, purpose-built public houses, varying only in scale and ambition. The origins of music hall, likewise, can be traced back further than is often allowed, to the first purpose-built pub concert-rooms of the late 1820s and the influential Grecian Saloon. The chapters in question, I hope, clarify early music-hall chronology; the meaning and importance of the 'saloon theatre'; and explain Charles Morton's somewhat dubious claim to primacy.

It is a complex, slippery history. There is always the feeling that one has mustered – to misquote a latter-day music-hall act – 'all the right facts but not necessarily in the right order'. Readers must judge for themselves. The fresh discovery in this timeline is undoubtedly the Home Secretary's injunction to metropolitan justices to clamp down on unlicensed entertainment, in early 1849. This little-noticed interference seems to have been prompted by professional informer Thomas Stowell's prosecutions of the casinos, guided by the shadowy hand of West End theatre managers. The fact that the Home Secretary addressed a single moralising communiqué to London magistrates might initially seem trivial. On closer inspection, the unanticipated results were critical to the halls' development. An over-reaction by Whitechapel magistrates provoked a public outcry against unfair licensing practices, resulting in John Adams' reappraisal of the licensing system. This, in turn, led to *music only* licences being more freely distributed by Middlesex magistrates. This provided a reliable regulatory infrastructure, which underpinned the capital's music-hall boom of the 1850s. These were unintended consequences, and there were other forces at work, but we can now make out how one thing led to another. We can also relish the irony that Benjamin Webster and his fellow theatre managers, prosecuting the casinos, accidentally instigated the changes in regulation under which their fiercest rivals, music halls, would prosper.

The Home Secretary's overlooked intervention, unfortunately, also points to something of a glaring historical blind-spot: namely, our ongoing ignorance about the motives and manoeuvring of licensing magistrates (as regards both liquor licensing and entertainment). There is no doubt that, for the supplicant publican, they occupied a unique position of immense power and authority. They were also frequently said to be corrupt. But how can we adequately judge the veracity of that claim, or how corruption played out in practice? We face the additional problem, particularly with entertainment licensing, that magistrates who attended the Middlesex sessions were a peculiarly diverse, changeable group. The *music and dancing* sessions, covering North London, were heard by whichever metropolitan magistrates chose to turn up on that day at the Clerkenwell Sessions House. Justices were often rumoured to be partial; they took most decisions in secret; and they rarely offered an explanation as to why any pleasure-ground, concert-room or music hall should (or should not) receive a licence. The lobbying of individual magistrates to make an appearance or put in a good word was commonplace.[3] A search within the attendance records for 1830s and 1840s *music and dancing* sessions reveals anything from ten to forty-two individual JPs sitting on the licensing bench. Compiling data from the period 1834–50 shows that only a handful attended more than ten sessions during this period, and the names of numerous magistrates – 66 out of 166 individuals – only appear once in the records.[4] The system was undoubtedly chaotic and highly susceptible to bribery and persuasion, if not downright crooked.

Some of the leading figures, i.e. regular attendees, do become clear from court documents and press reports, which sometimes recount exchanges between particular magistrates and applicants' barristers. Who were these more assiduous attendees? Like most magistrates, wealthy, older, middle-class gentlemen; although perhaps not always as self-interested as their critics suggested. Henry Pownall, who frequently acted as chairman, was a staunch Conservative; he would also be remembered as an ardent abolitionist and as someone actively involved in numerous charities. He was one of the founders of Exeter Hall, the great meeting place on the Strand for religious and philanthropic bodies.[5]

Sir Peter Laurie, likewise a regular attendee, obtained his knighthood thanks to his campaigns against the spectacle of public hangings and the mistreatment of prisoners. He was a self-made man: he opened a saddlery business on Oxford Street at the turn of the century and acquired lucrative army contracts, before building up his social connections via the Saddler's Company of the City of London.[6] James Whiskin, another stalwart at the sessions, was also originally in trade, although less of a philanthropist. He may well have attended so frequently in order to secure and bolster his social standing. Originally a plumber, he made money from erecting jerry-built working-class homes (and a pub) in Clerkenwell in the 1820s. The name Whiskin Street – if not the buildings themselves – survives to this day. He then became a director of the Mutual Life Assurance Society and the London and Croydon Railway, one of the earliest railway companies. Whiskin was a very upwardly-mobile individual: a parish vestryman in 1815; JP in 1835; Deputy Lieutenant of Tower Hamlets in 1846. He died in 1859 at his home in comfortable Bedford Place, Bloomsbury.[7]

A full investigation of magistrates' lives and interests would be very useful, if highly labour-intensive. What we can say is that the politics and prejudices of such men, and probably their social and business ties, played a key role in the development of both the public house and the music hall.

The one area where we can see the hands of metropolitan magistrates above the table, actively at work, is on the question of female drinkers in the early 1800s. Sir Richard Birnie of Bow Street, and many others involved in alcohol licensing, repeatedly required publicans to physically unmake changes to their premises, removing the trappings of the 'gin-shop' to preserve the sacred masculine space of the tap-room. This was not because there was anything resembling planning law in this period. Magistrates simply demanded these structural reversions in return for renewing the liquor licence. This intervention reveals a good deal about women's perennially contested position in the nineteenth-century city and the pressure to conform to certain ideals of feminine morality. But it also demonstrates that working-class women *were* increasingly entering the new public houses, with their relative anonymity and accessible counter service. The efforts of Birnie and his colleagues were a rear-guard action.

Women were also very much present in early music halls. Histories which describe the early halls as exclusively male assume that they were descended directly from the bawdy song-and-supper clubs of Covent Garden. The pub concert-rooms and the saloon theatres were more numerous, and were frequented by men, women and family groups. There were women at Botheroyd's cock-and-hen club (hence the name); and women sometimes bordered on a majority in Horace Heartwell's survey of Manchester's 1840s 'saloons' ('at least one half of audience consists of women . . . the higher class of factory operatives').[8] Young working-class women, unencumbered by maternal or family responsibility – particularly those in regular, relatively well-paid factory work – had recreational choices. The 'gin committee', which was led by a chimney-sweep's wife and supposedly terrorised the Borough, may have been exceptional; but young women were clearly capable of boisterous nights on the town. Scouring contemporary newspapers, one also finds numerous instances of young women enjoying themselves, above the public house, in social dancing. They did not always scurry demurely from factory or workshop to the family home, but went out looking for fun and, perhaps, sexual and/or marriage partners. This was not the chaperoned ideal of female complaisance increasingly promoted by middle-class commentators; and indeed, such women were often written off as prostitutes or 'fallen' by judgmental moralists. But this was the reality of working-class life. Moreover, the clean, warm, beautifully decorated, modernised pub, and later the music hall, provided rather appealing venues in which working-class women could enjoy themselves. The pleasant conditions were often in stark contrast to the domestic alternative, and offered a new sort of social freedom, however limited. They attracted the kinds of women to the pub and concert-room 'that would have been ashamed of it some years ago'.[9] Nor did women vanish from public houses as the century progressed. A 1907 London police survey of twenty-three London pubs in working-class districts found that, on aggregate, nearly 40 per cent of customers were female (in two examples, presumably near large female-dominated workplaces, men were substantially outnumbered).[10]

Middle-class women could also step beyond the confines of cramped gendered expectations when it came to leisure activities. The masculine world of football was surprised to find advertisements being placed in the press, in the autumn of 1894, for a women's club in North London. The venture was the brainchild of Nettie Honeyball, a twenty-year-old upholsterer's daughter from Crouch End, assisted by the sponsorship of notable feminist Lady Florence Dixie. Honeyball put together a team which toured nationally, playing a series of exhibition matches. The reception of the short-lived British

Ladies Football Club was predictably sexist ('let them look to their hop-scotch and skipping ropes and leave cricket and football to the boys') and occasionally even hostile, with violent incidents marring a Scottish tour in 1896. The team was then dissolved; but a marker had been laid down for future generations.[11]

Social class, of course, crops up repeatedly in any study of nineteenth-century leisure. We have seen how the gin palace's so-called 'mock' finery challenged the social status of other retail establishments and, indirectly, the social position of their middle-class clients. Likewise, how Charles Morton attempted to neutralise this problem when he promoted the respectability of his newly built Canterbury Hall. Respectability was a very useful notion, a way of claiming parity and community with those higher up the social scale. Men and women without wealth or birth could still be 'respectable' (even if, in truth, respectability was perceived fundamentally as a middle-class value). Canterbury Hall might be a place for working people, but licensing magistrates could rest easy: they were all respectable and well behaved.

That said, Charles Morton's intimations of respectability implied that he was seeking a certain class of customer. A self-conscious aspirational respectability was increasingly part of upper-working-class and lower-middle-class identity. This was how people now liked to see themselves: not terribly wealthy, but still respectable, moral, temperate, decent. Respectability, however, was not always given the recognition it demanded. For instance, the clerk and the shop assistant, no matter how much they practised their morality and manners, were regularly mocked for their social and sartorial pretensions ('scribbling in an old coat all day at his office . . . [he] now puts on a cheap Taglioni, or one of the "Gent's new horsecloth envelopes," dons a cheap pair of gloves, sticks a cheap cigar in his mouth, and imagines that he is "rather the Stilton" ').[12] These young men, in the eyes of many middle-class commentators, were trying a little too hard to rise above their station in life. They wanted to dress and behave like gentlemen, but they could only ever become 'gents', a cheap, affected imitation of the original.

Class distinction and class segregation were articles of faith for most of those who had any say in the management of Victorian society. This was one of the principal reasons why leisure institutions received such attention from moralists and magistrates: they could break down both class boundaries and conventional morality. Robert Cowtan's account of uninhibited carousing at the Crown and Anchor dancing booth at Canterbury Fair is a case in point.

Readers may recall that 'well-to-do' men flocked to the booth, but 'no woman with any regard to propriety and decency' would attend. The female dancers, in other words, were largely working-class girls, whose morals were called into question by their very presence. Some of these single women were probably prostitutes; but it is likely that others sought some mix of fun, flirtation, casual sex and/or courtship. Cowtan himself recounts how, at only fourteen years of age, he entered into a brief relationship with just such a girl, after dancing with her in the booth. She was his social inferior: Cowtan was the son of a book-seller/stationer; she was the seventeen-year-old daughter of a horse-breaker. She was also a single mother, deserted by a soldier who had promised her marriage. Cowtan tells how on several occasions he met the girl's parents, who did not countenance 'anything of an improper nature' (i.e. did not know the couple were having sex). Cowtan does not give details of how this teenage affair ended, except that his father decided it was necessary to find him employ-ment in London, away from the entanglement. But Cowtan makes clear that the girl he met at the fair was not a prostitute. She had been jilted by her original 'seducer' and, if anything, was looking for a long-term partner. He writes that he blames himself, as much as her, for their sexual transgression; and he implies that her parents had hopes of the relationship blossoming into an advantageous marriage. Cowtan's father, on the other hand, a former mayor of Canterbury, could not countenance such a relationship, across the class divide, with a 'ruined and degraded' unmarried mother. This was the sort of social chaos that made dancing seem so dangerous, to both the nineteenth-century paterfamilias and the authorities. The middle class mixed too freely with the working class; and the respectable with the ruined.[13]

We can also see a desire to 'firm up' boundaries between the classes in the aristocracy's retreat from the assembly room and pleasure garden. This was largely a matter of personal choice, a preference for conspicuous display at home and a wish to avoid the dangers of mixing with the riff-raff. This was, after all, an age that was becoming increasingly concerned with epidemic disease, as well as with more abstract notions of social purity and moral pollu-tion. Yet it is worth noting that there are also clear instances of the 'masses' pushing out the upper classes from their familiar haunts. We see this in the transformation of places like Margate, where disgruntled aristocrats began to stumble across their tailors on the marine parade, and did not return the following season. We even see something similar in London in the late 1830s, when the upper class began to abandon the song-and-supper rooms of Covent Garden. The rooms had become too famous, descended upon by 'all the shop-boys in the metropolis', i.e. far too many 'gents' and not enough gentlemen.[14] The pillorying of Lord Ingestre for hiring Cremorne Gardens for an 'aristo-cratic fete' in 1858, irredeemably tainted by its association with socially indis-criminate late-night partying, shows how far the manners of the upper class had changed by the mid-century. The likes of Vauxhall Gardens had once been considered a louche but still perfectly acceptable fashionable retreat for the *bon ton*; those days were long gone.

The middle class, meanwhile, beat its own retreat by withdrawing from the public house, heavily influenced by the proponents of temperance. To be seen drinking in public was no longer good fellowship, but a sign of dangerous self-indulgence. This would pose a problem for the proprietors of late Victorian music halls, who wanted to broaden their customer demographic, but came from a tradition associated with bonhomie and booze. The answer was to cut down on alcohol sales and provide a wide range of differentially priced zones, with varying levels of comfort. The Royal at High Holborn (formerly Weston's), for instance, offered a range of private boxes, costing £2 2s, £1 1s and 10s 6d, as well as three-shilling orchestra stalls, two-shilling regular stalls, one-shilling balcony and lounge, and a mere sixpence for entering the body of the hall. Palaces of variety, more theatre-like than the old communal halls, were designed to cater for everyone in society, carefully stratified, providing a perfect, profit-able, orderly solution. The social classes could be both apart and together at the same time; this was the Victorian ideal of social harmony.

Football was perhaps the only arena in which an outright battle took place between different class-based conceptions of leisure: the amateurism of the FA and early southern clubs versus the win-at-all-costs attitude of the northern professionals. But it is misguided to see this as a 'class' divide, or at least as 'working class' v. 'middle class', as it is so often painted. The professional clubs' managing committees consisted largely of educated, professional men and men of business: doctors, lawyers, accountants, solicitors, industrialists. The ques-tion was more about how far one adopted the public school ethos of amateurism; and if it was a class struggle, it was more 'public schoolmen' versus the rest.

While gender and class form two of the great fault-lines that lurk below the social history of the nineteenth century, there is another: race and empire. The instances of colonialist narratives and racial oppression that appear in these pages are not revelatory, but they are grimly indicative.

It is instructive to note that commentators uncritically accepted the racial travesty of the blackface minstrel, an astonishingly popular comic entertainment in the mid-century, while simultaneously being highly critical of the 'low' slapstick comedy. The latter was considered an insult to an educated audience; or a telling indictment of the uneducated crowds who found it amusing. The idea that blackface buffoonery might constitute an insult to those it portrayed does not seem to have registered or much mattered. For all the human sympathies elicited by the cause of abolitionism earlier in the century, there were still relatively few prepared to suggest that black and white were equally worthy of respect. The spectacle of the Sheffield 'Zulus' also reveals precisely how unproblematic 'blacking up' seemed to contemporaries.

Similarly, although the various 'natives' who performed in human zoos at Earl's Court and elsewhere were a sort of stage performer – there were contracts with managers and the payment of wages – they were also treated as mere objects for display. We have no reason to think that any were conscripted into performing, although we might note that the 'natives of Formosa' (Taiwan) who appeared at the 1910 Japan–British Exhibition, were overseen by a Japanese intermediary, Kumaji Oshima. This was a loan of Japan's conquered imperial subjects, a symbol of its dominance, whatever agency the individual performers may have possessed. They were, at least, to be provided with food and accommodation free of charge, and paid a yen per day.

The living exhibits always remained of interest to the general public beyond their daily performances. Some 'natives' acquired the status of minor celebrities as they explored the wider world, generally portrayed by the media as harmless fish-out-of-water *naïfs*. They were taken on tours around London, which allowed them to express suitably primitive wonder at the great imperial capital. This was also very good advertising. Harold Hartley, who managed the foreigners for Earl's Court, took whole contingents of Indian performers, some 200 of them, to Windsor, Hampton Court, Kew and Richmond ('dressed in their native, highly coloured and picturesque costumes . . . a splendid advertisement'). His only anxieties were refreshments ('somewhat difficult . . . owing to their castes and tastes') and some of the young girls taking an impromptu bath in the Thames at Hampton Court. More generally, Hartley also, to his surprise, found himself having to provide facilities for halal slaughter and obtain a regular supply of ghee ('an evil-smelling greasy stuff which they preferred to our good butter').[15]

The cheery tone of the press, focusing on culture shock and the natives' 'child-like' wonder, could swiftly turn nasty. The *Daily Mail* initially amused itself with droll commentary on Prince Lobengula's urban wanderings, dubbing him 'Lo Ben' and portraying him as an amiable simpleton from the Dark Continent. When it was discovered that the star of 'Savage South Africa' was pursuing a relationship with a white woman, the humour was instantly replaced with less kindly headlines. Reports of women visitors to Earl's Court supposedly becoming overly familiar with the inhabitants of the 'kraal' made things even worse. Letters appeared from Englishmen abroad, quite frank in their appraisal of the bulwarks of the British Empire and how Lobengula's relationship might bring them tumbling down. The white race, they suggested, had to portray itself to its subjects as untouchable and god-like: 'they believe in our superiority and it is fear, and fear alone, which holds them in check'. The consequence of news spreading in Africa about the proposed mixed marriage would be terrible retribution: an uprising of the African people, leading to mass rape and murder ('the innocent white women in Africa will expiate the folly of their sisters in England, in ways it is no good to think of').[16] While the positive vision of 'Greater Britain' displayed at Earl's Court and elsewhere served to 'glorify and domesticate empire', these brutal fantasies of wholesale sexualised retribution – and blunt assessment of imperial power – were the freely expressed, unalloyed opinions of its gatekeepers.

Naturally, the one thread that runs throughout this book is money. Speculation, questions of profit, loss, debt and bankruptcy appear in every chapter. This is not an economic history, but it is about institutions whose raison d'être was to make a profit. I have therefore tried to engage with these commercial entities on their own terms. The Crystal Palace at Sydenham, for instance, has all too frequently been dismissed as a footnote to the momentous events of 1851. While the Great Exhibition has received fulsome scholarly attention for its undoubted national symbolism and cultural significance, far fewer people have troubled to look so intently at Sydenham; and even fewer at the causes of its desperately protracted economic decline. Likewise, the Victorian pleasure garden remains very much in the shadow of the more famous Georgian gardens, and tends to be viewed largely, if not exclusively, through the lens of Victorian debates about vice and prostitution.[17] My aim, therefore, has been to bring these important institutions out into the light, and consider the factors which helped and hindered their development, *as businesses*. They are certainly worthy of attention in terms of scale and ambition. The expenses of James Ellis between 1846 and 1849, for example, as he struggled to keep Cremorne Gardens afloat, give some idea of operations in Chelsea, with over £2,500 spent on sponsoring balloon ascents; £1,000 on fireworks; nearly £6,000 on printing and advertising; and over £9,000 on the wages of musicians and performers.[18] By 1849, Ellis had spent £20,000 – the equivalent of a million pounds in modern money – more than his takings. Little wonder, then, that after he was finally declared bankrupt, he quit London for Australia.

Did these various new leisure institutions actually amount to a 'leisure industry'? They were, for the most part, substantial businesses, requiring considerable investments of capital, and collectively patronised by millions of customers. And so we must answer in the affirmative. The only exception is commercial social dancing, although we should not discount the great ball-rooms at Blackpool and Douglas. The history of commercial dance is diverse and surprising. I had thought, writing this book, merely to flesh out the history of the Victorian casino (usually only discussed as a footnote to the history of music-hall or West End prostitution). But, as well as the casino, I found a seemingly endless variety of small commercial dance-halls. These ranged from fake 'dancing academies' (which sought to evade magisterial oversight and licensing fees) to thoroughly respectable 'Cinderella balls' at Holborn Town Hall. I discovered that young working-class women in spangled dresses swirled gaily above public houses in South London, or practised the quadrille in Miss Kirby's beer-shop in Preston. Gentlemen from Kent polkaed at Algar's Crown and Anchor, and Mr W.F. Hurndall re-enacted the battle of Mafeking at Holborn Town Hall through the medium of interpretive dance. All these things were thoroughly new to me, and I suspect will come as a surprise to many readers.

The growing use of joint-stock companies to fund ventures via share offerings (and from the 1850s to limit directors' liabilities) also clearly points to how leisure became a business proposition. Such companies increasingly appeared at the seaside, as well as running football clubs, music halls and pleasure gardens (although neither de Berenger nor Simpson could ever persuade the public to buy shares in Cremorne Gardens).[19] Shares issues were often used to transform and upgrade existing businesses. Weston's Music Hall, which had begun as publican Edward Weston's challenge to Canterbury Hall, backed by his brewers, was relaunched as a public limited company in 1886, with a plan to almost double the size of the auditorium to 2,500 seats, with £70,000 in share capital. The directors included John Hollingshead, the noted theatre manager (who would go on to be involved with the Blackpool and New Brighton towers, among many other ventures); the existing proprietor W.T. Purkiss, who claimed to have been the first to use electric light in the halls; Sir Lewis William Molesworth, Baronet; and Samuel Adams, former manager of the Philharmonic in Islington. The company was a flop, becoming bogged down in the reconstruction work, and was soon struggling to pay off two mortgages. But others would do better.

The other revealing fact suggesting that leisure was an industry is the freedom with which managers and proprietors moved between different branches. Some began as publicans; some as restaurant managers; some as theatrical refreshment contractors; some as theatre managers. And many moved quite seamlessly between the worlds of the pleasure garden, exhibition, pub, theatre and music hall. If we take Edward Tyrell Smith as an example, we have possibly the most restless theatrical/entertainment impresario of the mid-century. Born in 1804, he was the eldest son of Admiral E.T. Smith, but rejected a career in the navy (reportedly at the urging of his anxious, doting mother). We have little detail about his early life, but we know he worked as a policeman, then an auctioneer and a publican. He took the lease of the Marylebone Theatre, 1849–53; then successfully revived a somewhat down-at-heel Theatre Royal, Drury Lane, in the 1850s, where E.L. Blanchard credited him with introducing theatrical matinées to London. Beginning the 1860s as proprietor of Cremorne Gardens, Smith also converted the Royal Panopticon of Science and Art in Leicester Square into the Alhambra (initially an equestrian circus, then a music hall). Further ventures *during* his tenure of Cremorne included two years managing Her Majesty's Theatre, as well as spells in charge of Astley's Amphitheatre, the famous circus, and the Lyceum Theatre. With the exception of Drury Lane (1852–62) and Cremorne (1861–69), Smith flitted between projects every couple of years. He was reported to carry a £1,000 banknote in his pocket to reassure his creditors – except that it was hired at £1 a day from a moneylender.[20] Smith also opened the Cremorne Branch Restaurant or Cremorne Supper Rooms at 1 New Coventry Street, Leicester Square, which offered a restaurant meal for half a crown. He finished his career in the early

1870s, bankrupt after a bad run at the Surrey Theatre and Highbury Barn. Smith's history, therefore, encompassed the management of two pleasure gardens, two circuses, multiple theatres, a restaurant and music hall.

The connection between food and drink caterers and the management of music halls, pleasure gardens and exhibition grounds was always strong. We have noted already Frederick Strange's progress from Simpson's chop-house, to his own restaurant, to catering at the Crystal Palace, to the Alhambra Music Hall. We might also refer again to Weston's Music Hall, which, after the joint-stock company's failure, was bought by a syndicate led by the landlord of the Star and Garter public house at Kew, and Messrs Ellis Brothers, wine merchants. There was good money to be made in selling food and drink at places of entertainment, and therefore a long history of food and drink sellers getting into the entertainment business. The managers of Vauxhall Gardens in the 1820s, Messrs Bish, Gye and Hughes, leased the gardens in the first place in part to sell the produce of their unsuccessful London Wine Company. At the opposite end of the century, large commercial caterers made similar calculations on the useful synergies when combining catering experience with the management of entertainment. Hence, Joseph Lyons and his famous catering company were a major backer of Olympia; and Spiers and Pond helped finance Whitley's Earl's Court.

For some Victorians, it must be admitted, commercial leisure was always something to be avoided. The preacher Charles Spurgeon spoke for the more religious, the obsessively temperate, the vigilance societies, when he described time wasted on such idle frivolities as inherently sinful and vicious: 'Pleasure so called is the murderer of thought.' He was speaking in the year that saw the inception of the Football League, and made a point of condemning what he called 'silly sports'.[21] Some late Victorian socialists similarly believed the likes of football to be an empty amusement, taking up valuable mental real estate which might be better occupied with musings upon the class struggle.[22] But the truth is that the serious and solemn scored few victories over the leisure entrepreneurs and the pleasure-seeking public. The only exception might be the ideals of temperance being extended by magistrates to the late Victorian/Edwardian music hall; and even here, it seems there was no great backlash among proprietors or any revolt among the general public. Some customers were undoubtedly in sympathy.

As for the rest, well, they quickly nipped out to the pub.

Endnotes

Introduction

1. James Payn, *The Talk of the Town*, Chatto & Windus, 1885, p. 219: 'There was once a young gentleman who was endeavouring to make himself agreeable as a raconteur in the presence of Royalty. When he had done his story the Royal lips let fall these terrible words: "We are not amused."'; see *Huddersfield Daily Chronicle*, 2 January 1888, for an early attribution to Victoria; Princess Alice, Countess of Athlone, quoted in a 1977 BBC interview: *Victoria, Queen and Empress – The Princess Alice Interview* (1977). See: http://explore.bfi.org.uk/4ce2b88629eda
2. Emanuel Walker, 'At Earl's Court', *The Idler*, January 1900, p. 123.
3. *R.W. Paul: The Collected Films 1895–1908*, BFI, 2006 (DVD).
4. '[T]he publican is following the course of all other trades and falling into capitalists' hands. The gin palaces keepers are merely the traders on a large scale – the Swan and Edgars of their trade' (*Manchester Times*, 15 February 1840).
5. C.H. Spurgeon, 'Sown Among Thorns, delivered on Lord's Day Morning, August 19th 1888', *Sermons on our Lord's Parables*, Passmore & Alabaster, 1904, p. 476.
6. *British Mothers' Magazine*, 1 June 1848.
7. *East London Observer*, 13 November 1886.
8. Magistrates often expressed the fear that licensing pubs for entertainment led to the venue's female clientele being 'demoralised' (i.e. corrupted, losing their morals). For example, 'Mr. Ballantine opposed the application on the general ground that music and dancing always led to the demoralization of females' (*London Courier and Evening Gazette*, 18 October 1834).
9. Andrea Geddes-Poole, *Philanthropy and the Construction of Victorian Women's Citizenship*, University of Toronto Press, 2014, p. 108.
10. For a full history, see Denis Richards, *Offspring of the Vic*, Routledge, 1958.

I The Gin Palace

1. *Evening Chronicle*, 19 February 1835.
2. Theodore Sedgwick, *Public and Private Economy*, Harper, 1836, p. 199.
3. ibid., p. 200.
4. *The Times*, 11 January 1837.
5. George Cruikshank, *Sunday in London*, Effingham Wilson, 1833, p. 16.
6. *Hansard*, House of Commons Debates, 3 June 1834, Vol. 24 cc90–126.
7. *The Gin-shop*, No. 1, 12 November 1836, p. 2.
8. *The Times*, 24 September 1842.
9. Alexander Slidell Mackenzie, *The American in England*, Richard Bentley, 1836, p. 161.
10. Patrick Colquhoun, *Observations and Facts Relative to Public Houses in the City of London and its Environs*, Henry Fry, 1794, p. 34; see also the expanded 2nd edition, 1796, pp. 37ff.; and Colquhoun, *A Treatise on Indigence*, J. Hatchard, 1806, pp. 288ff.
11. See www.oldbaileyonline.org/browse.jsp?id=t18100411-63&div=t18100411-63: a very typical pickpocketing case from 1810 in which the woman immediately absconded with the man's watch.
12. Much cited in the early 1800s. See, for example, Robert Wissett, *Letters to John Bowles*, Shaw, 1815, p. 24.
13. William Baker, for example, a West End publican, charged 4½d for beer sent out to private homes in customers' own mugs; 5d for beer consumed in the main body of his house; and 5½d in the superior 'parlour'. William Adams Larby, with a pub in the City of London, charged 6d for the parlour because he offered 'a very respectable place and many respectable merchants come and take their steak there' (1830 *Report from the Select Committee on the Sale of Beer*, pp. 41, 45).
14. 1816 *Report from the Committee on the State of the Police of the Metropolis*, p. 50.
15. *Morning Post and Gazetteer*, 3 September 1800.
16. Society for Bettering the Condition and Increasing the Comforts of the Poor, *Report of the Society*, 1805, p. 11.
17. Colquhoun, *Observations and Facts*, p. 27.
18. 'Now it is well known that every Public House or Alehouse is a Gin-shop, has its Bar or a small Room separate from the Public Drinking Room for the sole Purpose of Dram drinking' (*Public Advertiser*, 6 November 1783). The 'bar' originally meant a small room where liquor was stored. Counters were placed in front of 'bars' for convenience, and, as pubs evolved, the 'bar' came to mean the counter itself.
19. Colquhoun, *A Treatise on Indigence*, p. 288.
20. Quoted in a review of John Bowles, *A Letter to Robert Wissett*, Rivington, 1816, which appeared in the *Anti-Jacobin Review*, March 1816, p. 240.
21. ibid., p. 245.
22. John Irving Maxwell, *The Victuallers Advocate*, Hughes, 1804, p. 6; revised and expanded as *Wine Vaults Vindicated*, Hughes, 1816.
23. J.T.B. Beaumont, *A Letter to Rt. Hon Lord Sidmouth*, Cadell & Davies, 1817, p. 13.
24. 1818 *Third Report from the Committee on the State of the Police of the Metropolis*, p. 104.
25. 'Have you any doubt that, from those shops not having tap-rooms, persons reputably dressed, women particularly, are induced to go there to drink spirits, who would be ashamed to pass through a room which was crowded with men?' (*The Times*, 30 August 1816, from 1817 *First Report from the Committee on the State of the Police*). See also 1830 *Report from the Select Committee on the Sale of Beer*, p. 109.
26. Pierce Egan, *Life in London*, Appleton, 1904 [reprint of 1821], p. 143 plate.
27. Letter to *Oracle and Daily Advertiser*, 30 September 1799; see also Colquhoun, *Observations and Facts*, p. 17.
28. *A Dissertation on Mr. Hogarth's Six Prints Lately Publish'd, Viz. Gin-lane, Beer-street, and the Four Stages of Cruelty*, B. Dickinson, 1751, p. 9, quoted in Jessica Warner and Frank Ivis, 'Gin and Gender in Early Eighteenth-Century London', *Eighteenth-Century Life*, 24:2 (2000), pp. 85–105.

29. 1833 *Report from the Select Committee on Manufactures, Commerce, and Shipping*, p. 624.

30. *Manchester Guardian*, 26 February 1848.

31. 1817 *First Report from the Committee on the State of the Police of the Metropolis*, p. 190.

32. Brian Harrison, *Drink and the Victorians*, Faber, 1971, p. 65.

33. *Reports from Committees; Police of the Metropolis: Session 28 January – 12 July 1817*, Vol. VII, p. 21.

34. [Anon.], 'A Friend to Justice', *A Letter Addressed to the Right Honourable N. Vansittart, Chancellor of the Exchequer, &c. &c. on the Revenue and Public Morals . . .*, J.M. Richardson, 1817, p. 28. Witnesses to the 1830 Sale of Beer Committee describe publicans as typically 'men who have begun with a few hundred pounds saved in service' . . . 'persons who have risen from very humble life' . . . 'gentlemen's servants, butlers, coachmen and others'.

35. Pierce Egan, *Real Life in London*, Methuen & Co., 1905 [reprint of 1821 edition], p. 130. Available at: www.gutenberg.org/files/20484/20484-h/20484-h.htm

36. For Thompson's involvement, see [Anon.], 'A Friend to Justice', p. 32.

37. *The Times*, 31 January 1828, an advertisement says that Thompson and Fearon's business had been established 'upwards of thirty years'. The first mention I have found in the press of Thompson keeping a 'gin-shop' on Holborn Hill is in *The Times*, 11 October 1816.

38. [Anon.], 'A Friend to Justice', p. 44.

39. See *John Bull*, 29 March 1824, and *Christian Remembrancer*, Vol. 9, 1827, for two separate instances.

40. *The Times*, 11 December 1816; *Morning Post*, 23 September 1819.

41. '[Thompson] contributes by the liquid poison which he circulates to destroy the constitution of the people, as by his seditious harangues, to calumniate the constitution of the country . . .' (*Anti-Jacobin Review*, Vol. 52, 1817, p. 130).

42. 1816 *First Report from the Committee on the State of the Police of the Metropolis*, p. 160; *Second Report*, p. 354.

43. Thomas Hudson, *Comic Songs*, Gold and Walton, 1818, p. 23.

44. *The Times*, 26 September 1821.

45. *The Gin-shop*, No. 1, 12 November 1836, p. 2.

46. *Hansard*, House of Commons Debates, 22 April 1825.

47. 1834 *Report of the Committee on Drunkenness*, p. 438.

48. 1833 *Tables of the revenue, population, commerce of the United Kingdom and its dependencies. Part I. From 1820 to 1831, both inclusive. Compiled from official returns*, p. 20 shows tax revenue actually rising from £4 million to £5 million. See also Peter Mathias, *The Brewing Industry in England: 1720–1830*, Cambridge University Press, 1959, p. 242, who notes a surge in taxed spirits from 3.68 million gallons in 1825 to 7.41 million in 1826.

49. An Act to regulate the granting of Licences to Keepers of Inns, Ale-houses, and Victualling Houses in England (9 Geo 4 c 61).

50. *Hansard*, House of Commons Debates, 28 and 29 February 1828; 14 March 1828; 21 May 1828.

51. *Caledonian Mercury*, 13 October 1834. The act also stated that its definition of 'inn, alehouse or victualling house' explicitly included any premises selling liquor. Gin-shops, therefore, were no longer outside the legal limits of licensing law, as Colquhoun had argued (see s.37 of the act).

52. 1830 *Report from the Select Committee on the Sale of Beer*, p. 37.

53. Wyatt Papworth, *John B. Papworth*, 1879, p. 68; *The Times*, 31 October 1828. The dates of the rebuild given by Papworth are not entirely certain. They are contradicted by an advertisement in *The Times*, 5 January 1831, which describes the work as recently finished, having been under construction 'for the last five years'.

54. 1830 *Report from the Select Committee on the Sale of Beer*, p. 114.

55. The ground floor of the present building on Essex Road is more recent, late 1800s; but the remainder gives an impression of what was then 'unprecedented'. See *The Times*, 15 October 1829.

56. *The Times*, 6 October 1829; 16 December 1829.

57. *Morning Post*, 7 December 1829.
58. *Morning Chronicle*, 2 January 1830.
59. *The Times*, 1 December 1829.
60. *The Times*, 29 December 1829.
61. *The Times*, 7 December 1829.
62. *Bell's Life in London and Sporting Chronicle* [*Bell's Life*], 3 January 1830.
63. *The Times*, 29 December 1829.
64. Wine merchants were legally restricted to wholesale trade and could sell no *less* than two gallons at a time to the public. Hence, middle-classes families would often send to the nearest public house for a single bottle, if required.
65. *Belfast News-Letter*, 16 February 1830. For a more detailed discussion of the politics of the Beer Act, see Harrison, *Drink and the Victorians*, pp. 74ff.
66. For an excellent assessment of the act, see Nicholas Mason, ' "The Sovereign People are in a Beastly State": The Beer Act of 1830 and Victorian Discourse on Working-Class Drunkenness', *Victorian Literature and Culture*, 29:1 (2001), pp. 109–27.
67. *The Times*, 17 March 1830; see also 14 April 1830.
68. 1833 *Report from Select Committee on the Sale of Beer*, p. 226.
69. See J. Russom, *The Evil Effects of Beer Shops*, Houlston and Stoneman, 1849, for the case against the beer-shop.
70. 1830 *Report from Select Committee on the Sale of Beer*, p. 41, evidence of William Baker, publican.
71. *Standard*, 22 August 1833.
72. John Wight and George Cruikshank, *Sunday in London*, Effingham Wilson, 1833, p. 15. Cruikshank's personal copy included a note that 'This work is my own original idea . . . the text from my suggestions', as documented in Richard A. Vogler, *Graphic Works of George Cruikshank*, Dover Publications, 1979, p. 146.
73. *Monthly Magazine*, November 1834, p. 571.
74. *Bell's Life*, 8 June 1834.
75. *Satirist*, 10 July 1835.
76. *Preston Chronicle*, 26 August 1837, reporting an advert supposedly seen in Seven Dials. This may be comic exaggeration but gives a fair idea of the tone of contemporary advertisements.
77. 1834 *Report of the Committee on Drunkenness*, p. 119.
78. *The Times*, 15 August 1834.
79. '[T]he machine called a beer-engine is so well known in this metropolis, and has been for so many years in general use' (Letter in *Mechanics Magazine*, 7 March 1835, p. 418).
80. John Hogg, *London As It Is*, John Macrone, 1837, p. 289.
81. [Anon.], 'Domestic Notices', *Architectural Magazine*, October 1838, pp. 478–80.
82. *Westminster Review*, October 1829, pp. 301–02.
83. *Examiner*, 1 September 1839.

II The Free-and-Easy

1. The only glaring failure is the Strand Musick Hall (1864–67), a dreary gothic stand-alone theatre, which was burdened with debt from a badly managed, overpriced build. The site would be used for the Gaiety Theatre.
2. The phrase 'From pot-house to palace' probably became commonplace among music-hall historians thanks to W.H. Morton and H. Chance Newton, *Sixty Years' Stage Service: Being a Record of the Life of Charles Morton*, Gale & Polden, 1905, p. 201, and the repeated use of 'pot-house' in the book; but it appears earlier in an interview with Frank Egerton, music-hall manager, in the *Era*, 28 March 1896, and so may be been in common parlance in the 1890s.
3. Thomas Rowlandson, 'The Brilliants' (1801), displays club rules posted on the wall. A 'bumper' was simply a full glass. Rowlandson's satirical sketch, admittedly, targets bibulous middle-class gentlemen at a debating society, and the 'heroic' amounts may be somewhat

exaggerated. Nonetheless, the free-and-easy, patrician and plebeian, had similar roots in Georgian 'drinking-club' culture (cf. frontispiece to Jon Bee, *Sportsman's Slang*, 1825; and Pierce Egan, *Finish to the Adventures of Tom, Jerry and Logic*, C. Baynes, 1830, p. 27; both of which similarly show club rules posted on the wall at the free-and-easy).

4. George Brewer, *Bannian Day*, 1796, p. 11.
5. A plentiful list of useful 'Toasts and Sentiments' appears as an appendix to the song-book [Anon.], *The British Minstrel and National Melodist*, Vol.1, Sherwood, Gilbert & Piper, 1827. They also form part of the idle chatter of Dick Swiveller in Charles Dickens' *The Old Curiosity Shop*.
6. *Morning Chronicle*, 22 November 1824.
7. 1816 *First Report from the Committee on the State of the Police*, p. 153; 'Hell!', *Satirist*, 18 December 1831.
8. *The Times*, 27 January 1819.
9. George Speaight, *Bawdy Songs of the Early Music Hall*, Pan, 1975, p. 10.
10. Hudson, *Comic Songs*, pp. 7,14. Note: 'vig' = Cockney pronunciation of 'wig'.
11. *Blackwood's Magazine*, April 1842, p. 428.
12. The men about town at supper-rooms were not always that dashing. A report about a row with a waiter at Offley's supper-rooms in 1825 describes the crowd as 'bank clerks, half-pay officers, crack deputy drapers' – hardly the most rakish sorts. The row, nonetheless, is partly because a group of glaziers who are considered rather common are in the room (*The Spirit of the Public Journals*, 1824, p. 253). See also *Bentley's Miscellany*, 1839, p. 477, which bemoans the aristocracy having deserted the supper-rooms, once 'all the shop-boys in the metropolis' began to copy their late-night life style.
13. *Bell's Life*, 19 December 1841.
14. *Musical World*, 3 October 1857, pp. 637–38; this is corroborated by an 1820s ditty in *Bell's Life*, 7 May 1826, about Offley's song-and-supper room:

> As day-light approaches the humour grows broad,
> And the song of the Bankers, they hear and applaud;
> And Cr— even adds to his melodies verses
> He had better omit, til the crowd all disperses.

15. An Act for the better preventing Thefts and Robberies and for Regulating Places of Public Entertainment, and Punishing Persons keeping disorderly houses (25 Geo 2 c 36). The act was drawn up following a pamphlet by Henry Fielding, which damned the immoral influence of suburban pubs and pleasure grounds.
16. I have found a handful of prior cases recorded in the press: prosecution for allowing an Indian juggler to perform at the Green Dragon, Stepney, *Morning Chronicle*, 27 August 1823 (the landlord professed his astonishment, as 'such practices [were] continued by all houses in that district'); a prosecution for a 'benefit concert' costing 1s 6d admission held in the 'concert-room' of the London Hospital Tavern, *Morning Chronicle*, 20 March 1823. For the legal significance of the Botheroyd case as a precedent, see 1852–53 *Report from the Select Committee on Public Houses*, where Serjeant Adams' 1850 report is enclosed as an appendix (p. 646).
17. *The Times*, 2 November 1838.
18. The barrister John Adolphus blamed himself for revealing the profitability of music and dancing prosecutions to informers. Adolphus, grubbing up work, requested a music licence for the Golden Lion, Smithfield, in October 1828. Such licences had never been demanded by the City of London authorities; and Adolphus's legal justifications, before bemused City aldermen, may well have inspired Green et al. This, again, was a pub where the landlord had built 'a magnificent room, which he meant to appropriate to concerts and other musical purposes' (*Morning Advertiser*, 23 October 1828; *Public Ledger and Daily Advertiser*, 29 October 1829).
19. Witness statements variously described the audience as 'persons of every description, old and young, male and female'; 'Some very respectable persons and others very indifferent . . . women of no character and boys of about 15 and 17 . . .'; 'boys and girls of very indifferent

character'; 'very mixed company'; 'mostly respectable mechanics . . . he saw children there, attended by their parents' (*Morning Chronicle*, 8 December 1828).

20. *The Times*, 8 December 1828; see also *Morning Chronicle* and *Standard* for variations in the reporting. The *Morning Chronicle* has the most interesting detail.

21. *Bell's Life*, 28 December 1828.

22. See oldbaileyonline.org, case of John Thomas Morgan, 5 January 1832, in which the concert-room of the King's Arms, Mile End, is repeatedly mentioned (incidentally, a venue that *was* licensed by the magistrates, according to the court report). A ground-floor 'saloon' and upper-level gallery form the concert-room.

23. For example, 'Peter Crawley's Free and Easy – on Monday evening next, Jem Ward will take the Chair; he will be faced by Tom Hall, so celebrated for his excellent extemporaneous chanting' (*Bell's Life*, 2 December 1827). From 1828, advertisements for harmonic meetings appear in *Bell's Life*, under the banner 'Fancy Meetings for the Week'. 'The Fancy' was a slang description of the enthusiastic followers of sporting events, particularly young men, keen on sport, gambling and drink. They made a point of patronising 'sporting' pubs, i.e. ones owned/managed by retired stars of the race-track or boxing ring.

24. 'I invited some of them to go – I gave cards to Sullivan and I think to Seale . . .': Case of WILLIAM JORDAN, THOMAS SULLIVAN, HENRY MOTT, THOMAS SEALE, 29 February 1836 (oldbaileyonline.org).

25. The club-goer, however, preferred a more relaxed 'Mine Host' figure in the chair, and this humiliating multi-tasking had died out by the end of the 1830s. See 'The Age Before Music Halls', *All the Year Round*, 20 December 1873, p. 176.

26. *Bell's Life*, 17 November 1833.

27. *Bell's Life*, 6 April 1828; 5 October 1828; 25 January 1829.

28. *Morning Chronicle*, 27 August 1823 (juggler); *Standard*, 22 January 1846 (standing on head); Laurence Selenick, *Tavern Singing in Early Victorian London*, Society for Theatre Research, 1997, p. 16 (playing teeth, in diary of Charles Rice, 11 January 1840).

29. *Examiner*, 15 July 1832.

30. *Bell's Life*, 2 November 1828.

31. *Morning Chronicle*, 2 September 1850.

32. *The Times*, 9 December 1834, for the 2s 6d figure. The anonymous author of 'The Age Before Music Halls', *All the Year Round*, 20 December 1873, p. 176, claims that 'The scale of remuneration ranged from 3s to 5s a night, according to ability and popularity'. The diaries of the minor tavern singer Charles Rice certainly show it was possible to earn 4–6 shillings a night (see Selenick, *Tavern Singing*, p. xviii). It is easy, however, to find other references where singers were less successful, e.g. 'sometimes 9d. and 15d. a night . . . and it is not such easy work as some may imagine' (*Morning Post*, 5 May 1841).

33. *The Times*, 9 December 1834.

34. [Anon.], 'The Age Before Music Halls', p. 178; see also Charles Rice's diary, 26 January 1840, in Selenick, *Tavern Singing*.

35. 'The insolvent had said his house, without a music licence, was worth 600*l.* or 700*l.* but with one it would be worth 2000*l.*' (*London Evening Standard*, 24 October 1845); 'the holder of it could go into the market and sell his house for from 1,000*l.* to 2,000*l.* more' (*Morning Post*, 12 October 1849).

36. 'Mr. Halswell said he knew of cases where petitions were got up . . . solely with the view of extorting money' (*Morning Chronicle*, 6 October 1837).

37. *Preston Chronicle*, 15 September 1838 (re Wigan); 3 April 1841; 8, 18, 24 and 27 December 1841; 8 January 1842.

38. Dagmar Kift, *The Victorian Music Hall: Culture, Class and Conflict*, Cambridge University Press, 1996, pp. 80ff.

39. *Staffordshire Advertiser*, 13 September 1851, re 'Sea Lion' Concert Room, Hanley. Magistrates in Liverpool came to the same conclusion, but found 'no positive law to justify them in doing so' (*Liverpool Mercury*, 1 June 1852).

40. Pierce Egan, *The Pilgrims of the Thames*, W. Strange, 1838, p. 130.

41. Peter Burne, *The Teetotaler's Companion*, Arthur Hall, 1847, p. 98. Burne, however, still considered singing-rooms an attraction to lure the youth to the public house, and thence to alcoholism.

42. The Shepherd and Shepherdess seems to have been renamed c.1817, since the earliest mention of the Eagle Tavern in newspapers appears in *The Times* of 20 August 1817 and pre-dates Rouse's tenancy, which commenced c.1821.

43. John Brown, *Sixty Years Gleanings from Life's Harvest*, J. Palmer, 1858, p. 296. Frances Fleetwood, *Conquest: The Story of a Family*, W.H. Allen, 1913, p. 60, contends that the original charge was tuppence, then soon raised to sixpence.

44. The date of the Grecian opening is often mis-cited as 1825, thanks to a misreading of Warwick Wroth's scant information in *The London Pleasure Gardens of the Eighteenth Century*, Macmillan, 1896. Contemporary newspapers clarify the date; see, for example, *Bell's Life*, 15 May 1831.

45. *Bell's Life*, 21 October 1832; complainants also described it as 'fabricated of wood and covered with pitch' and damned it as a fire risk.

46. *The Times*, 18 October 1834.

47. *Morning Advertiser*, 20 October 1832.

48. Rouse's application for converting the Eagle into a theatre under the 1843 Theatres Act contains a list of dozens of such charitable events, and 'the net profits which have been distributed to the necessitous and deserving poor in bread, coals, blankets and money' (National Archives, LC7/5).

49. *The Times*, 5 December 1834.

50. *Hansard*, House of Commons Debates, 2 July 1835.

51. *The Times*, 29 September 1835.

52. *Bell's Life*, 26 October 1834.

53. The Haymarket Theatre also acquired its own patent in 1766, albeit limited to the summer months, when the other patents were closed.

54. Jane Moody, *Illegitimate Theatre in London 1770–1840*, Cambridge University Press, 2000, p. 46: 'Nevertheless, in 1833 theatrical monopoly had been abolished in all but name . . .'.

55. See the account of the pseudonymous 'Peter Paterson', *Glimpses of Real Life as Seen in the Theatrical World and in Bohemia*, William P. Nimmo, 1864, p. 50 ('Ours was a sickly expedition, and never throve, notwithstanding our having a magic-lantern and three performing dogs, which were the property of the scene-painter').

56. John Hollingshead, 'A Grand Old Music-Hall', *Entr'acte*, 6 June 1896.

57. ibid.

58. *Morning Chronicle*, 8 October 1838.

59. http://acms.sl.nsw.gov.au/album/ItemViewer.aspx?itemid=1114938&suppress=N&imgindex=67, File number FL3776884.

60. *Morning Post*, 11 and 20 September 1839.

61. *Era*, 8 December 1839.

62. *London Courier and Evening Gazette*, 17 October 1839; 'Music and Dancing, as recently introduced into Public Houses, cannot fail to create great disorder and ultimate Demoralization among the lower Classes of the Community, and in a Manufacturing Silks District like Bethnal Green . . .' (MJ/SP/1839/10/034).

63. *Hansard*, House of Commons Debates, 30 June 1842, Vol. 64 c793.

64. National Archives, LC7/5.

65. 1866 *Report from the Select Committee on Theatrical Licences and Regulation*, p. 280.

66. Harold Hartley, *Eighty-Eight Not Out*, Frederick Muller, 1939. Hartley was recalling the late 1860s.

67. *Morning Chronicle*, 20 October 1843.

68. 1866 *Report from the Select Committee on Theatrical Licences and Regulation*, p. 280. A press article on the Albert Saloon from September 1845, presumably before the Lord Chamberlain's intervention, describes waiters serving gin, biscuits and cakes (*Satirist*, 14 September 1845).

69. *Morning Post*, 21 January 1851.
70. *Morning Post*, 4 March 1851; 5 February 1853.
71. 'Penny Theatre in Chadwick's Orchard', letter to *Preston Chronicle*, 20 November 1841.
72. *Daily News*, 6 January 1853; *Lloyd's Weekly Newspaper*, 4 January 1857; cf. James Greenwood, *The Seven Curses of London*, Fields, Osgood & Co., 1869: 'They are *all* children who support the gaff. Costermonger boys and girls, from eight or nine to fourteen years old, and errand boys and girls employed at factories.'; Henry Mayhew, *London Labour and the London Poor*, Griffin, Bohn and Company, 1861, Vol. 1, p. 40: 'The audience is usually composed of children so young, that these dens become the school-rooms where the guiding morals of a life are picked up . . .'
73. Penelope Summerfield makes the Chartist argument in 'The Effingham Arms and the Empire' in E. Yeo and S. Yeo (eds), *Popular Culture and Class Conflict*, Harvester Press, 1981, p. 213, but appears unaware of the Home Secretary's intervention. See also Kift, *Victorian Music Hall*, p. 148. Legal hearings regarding the licence of the Cock and Neptune (*Era*, 1 April 1849) mention the Home Secretary receiving an anonymous letter on the subject. Certainly, such random notes from the Home Office, based on a single report, were not uncommon – see, for example, correspondence between the Manchester Watch Committee and James Graham, Manchester Watch Committee Minutes, 21 January 1843, on the subject of Mancunian shooting galleries.
74. Watts Phillips, *The Wild Tribes of London*, 1855, p. 21.
75. See reports in the *Era*, 1, 8 April and 11 April 1849; 20 May 1849. For the initial threat at the Middlesex Sessions, see *London Evening Standard*, 13 October 1848.
76. *Era*, 1 April 1849.
77. See *Morning Post*, 13 October 1849, for the case made by the East End publicans' barrister.
78. *Lloyd's Weekly Newspaper*, 21 October 1849.
79. 1866 *Select Committee on Theatrical Licences and Regulations*, p. 21. Surrey extended to the Thames in 1849, and hence Surrey magistrates were responsible for Lambeth and Southwark.
80. Report of the Committee appointed by Court on 6 June 1850 to consider the present state of the law as regards the granting of licences for music and dancing by the Court and report to the Court (MJ/SP/1851/08/024).
81. Letter from the National Temperance Society (MJ/SP/1853/10/015).
82. *Daily News*, 5 October 1852.
83. Charles Morton received a 'music only' licence for the Canterbury Arms – the forerunner of the famous Canterbury Hall – in October 1851 at the Surrey Quarter Sessions, 'that being the usual course upon a first application' (*Morning Chronicle*, 16 October 1851). The history of 'music only' in Surrey remains a little opaque. Surrey magistrates discussed the idea of a 'music only' licence with their court clerk in 1830. The clerk's advice was that it was legitimate, and this became a feature of the licence then granted annually to the St Helena Tea Gardens, the venue in question (see *Standard*, 21 October 1830). Surviving records, however, are very patchy for the sessions, and so the extent to which 'music only' was applied to other venues between 1830 and 1850 remains unclear.

III The Music Hall

1. *Kentish Mercury*, 13 June 1840.
2. Robert Poole, *Popular Leisure and the Music Hall in Nineteenth Century Bolton*, University of Lancaster, 1982, pp. 51ff.; *Bolton Chronicle*, 29 March 1845.
3. Horace Heartwell, 'Characteristics of Manchester', *North of England Magazine*, July 1842, p. 348.
4. *Hull Packet*, 7 April 1837; *Manchester Times*, 14 May 1842; *Sheffield Independent*, 10 March 1849; *Era*, 29 July 1849.
5. The case itself hinged on Mrs Montgomery refusing to perform in a ballet. She demanded recompense for her unfair dismissal, and won (*Sheffield Independent*, 13 July 1850; *Era*, 14 July 1850).

6. The first press mention I can find of 'Canterbury Music Hall', rather than 'Canterbury Hall', is *Morning Chronicle*, 15 September 1856, a court case in which Morton's builder claims his bankruptcy was due to being inadequately paid for the job.

7. Various dates are given in contemporary accounts. For example, *Era*, 14 December 1856, says that Morton took the Canterbury Arms in February 1852, began holding harmonic meetings in November 1852, opened the first Canterbury Hall in May 1853, costing £3,000, then proceeded to open the larger version the following year. Official records show that Morton obtained his liquor licence on 20 February 1850 (PS/NEW/1/7); and a 'music only' licence at the Surrey Quarter Sessions in October 1851.

8. *Illustrated London News*, 6 December 1856.

9. H.G. Hibbert, *Fifty Years of a Londoner's Life*, Dodd, Mead & Co., 1916, p. 33.

10. *The Times*, 6 April 1858; 6 August 1858.

11. *Morning Chronicle*, 10 December 1857.

12. *Musical World*, 3 October 1857.

13. Heartwell, 'Characteristics of Manchester'.

14. [Anon.], 'London Tavern Theatres', *Chambers's Edinburgh Journal*, 1 June 1839, pp. 151–52.

15. *Paul Pry*, No.12 [n.d.] c.1855 (source: Museum of London library). A 'pickwick' was a cheap cigar.

16. *Sketch*, 23 August 1893.

17. *Punch*, 23 August 1862.

18. *Musical World*, 3 October 1857.

19. Isabel Brooke Alder, 'Charles Morton, "Father of the Halls"', *The Ludgate*, March 1900, pp. 393–96.

20. 'Noctes Downeyanae no. 5', *Satirist*, 13 May 1838.

21. 'John Smith' [pseud.], *Sketches of Cantabs*, 1849, pp. 69ff.

22. *Era*, 29 January 1854.

23. *Theatrical Journal*, August 1870, p. 277; *Once a Week*, 20 August 1870; *Era Almanack*, January 1871.

24. *Reynolds's Newspaper*, 14 June 1868

25. *Daily News*, 20 September 1862; *Era*, 28 December 1862.

26. *Era*, 15 November 1857; *Building News*, 15 April 1859, quoted in D.F. Cheshire, *Music Hall in Britain*, Fairleigh Dickinson University Press, 1974, p. 24.

27. *Belfast News-Letter*, 26 March 1861. Morton's licence application for the Oxford was opposed, albeit ineffectually, by the lessees of the Haymarket, Adelphi, Princess's, Queen's and Soho Theatres. See *Era*, 14 October 1860.

28. Selenick, *Tavern Singing*, passim.

29. Similar tussles took place in Manchester, Sheffield and elsewhere. See Kift, *Victorian Music Hall*, pp. 88ff.

30. The Alhambra's lessee, Edward Tyrrel Smith, was also in charge of the Theatre Royal Drury Lane and Her Majesty's Theatre in the Haymarket (*Morning Post*, 13 October 1860).

31. *Thorne* v. *Colson*, Queen's Bench, reported in *The Times*, 28 January 1861.

32. *Sheffield and Rotherham Independent*, 3 January 1852; but cf. *Era*, 10 December 1854, where Youdan lost; and *Sheffield and Rotherham Independent*, 26 February 1862, where he got off on a technicality.

33. *Era*, 24 March 1861.

34. *Era*, 12 March 1865.

35. *Era*, 14 May 1865.

36. *The Times*, 14 June 1866.

37. For example, against the Alhambra and the Pavilion (1867), reported in *Standard*, 23 January 1867; Pavilion (1870), *Standard*, 19 December 1870; Oxford (1871), *Morning Post*, 14 August 1871.

38. Review of *Lady Audley's Secret* et al. in *Quarterly Review*, April 1863, p. 482.

39. *Standard*, 21 May 1861; *Morning Post*, 20 June 1861; Dickens, letter to Macready, 11 June 1861 (Graham Storey, Kathleen Tillotson and Madeline House (eds), *The Letters of Charles Dickens*, Oxford University Press, 2002, Vol. IX, p. 424).

40. *Standard*, 16 August 1862.
41. 'In most halls, a net is now suspended below . . .' (*Examiner*, 19 September 1874).
42. *Punch*, 23 August 1862.
43. Seven per cent of acts in 1878 were 'negro delineators' (*Era Almanack*, 1878, p. 76).
44. 'Amongst the Music-Hall Luminaries', in James Greenwood, *The Wilds of London*, Chatto and Windus, 1874, p. 93.
45. *Musical World*, 9 August 1862 ('from "The Observer"').
46. *Era*, 17 May 1863.
47. See also Arnold Bennett, *Hilda Lessways*, E.P. Dutton, 1911, p. 91: 'large overcoat (which Dayson called an "immensikoff").'
48. *Pall Mall Gazette*, 9 March 1868; see Richard Anthony Baker, *British Music Hall*, Sutton Publishing, 2005, pp. 83–5, for Nash's account from his autobiography.
49. Henry C. Lunn, 'The London Musical Season', *Musical Times and Singing Class Circular*, 1 September 1869, p. 201.
50. *All the Year Round*, 25 April 1868, pp. 467–71.
51. *Lloyd's Weekly Newspaper*, 26 January 1879.
52. 'The Healtheries' was a phrase for the Health Exhibition of 1884 in Kensington (see Chapter Six). 'Boko' was (fairly unobjectionable) slang for nose.
53. *Western Mail*, 12 September 1888.
54. [Anon.], *Tempted London*, A.C. Armstrong & Son, [c.1889], p. 186.
55. 1888 *Metropolitan Board of Works Commission. Interim report of the Royal Commissioners appointed to inquire into certain matters connected with the working of the Metropolitan Board of Works*, p. 442.
56. See, for example, Speaight, *Bawdy Songs*, which includes much blunt material from the early nineteenth-century song-and-supper room, including fairly graphic descriptions of sexual activity, e.g. *He Did it before my Face* ('A regular rummy Song'): 'And while I looked at him about, And viewed his manly grace, A certain member he pulled out, He did, before my face . . . Then down he pulled his buckskins new, and commenced his amorous race, And dangled two large apples too – He did, before my face.'
57. See, for example, Thomas Fardell, chairman of the LCC Theatres and Music Halls Committee, questioned in 1892 *Report from the Select Committee on Theatres and Places of Entertainment*, s. 286ff.
58. Kift, *Victorian Music Hall*, p. 120.
59. *Illustrated Police News*, 24 July 1897. Cf. *Hart* v. *Braithwaite*, where the proprietor of the Alexandra Music Hall, Ramsgate, successfully sued a curate who described his venue as a 'moral plague spot' (*The Times*, 8 November 1877).
60. See the Pavilion libel case, reported extensively in the press, e.g. *The Times*, 6, 9 and 10 May 1882.
61. *Era*, 23 September 1877.
62. Peter Bailey, *Leisure and Class in Victorian England*, Routledge, 1978, p. 165.
63. *Leeds Intelligencer*, 20 December 1851; *Leeds Times*, 27 December 1852; *Leeds Intelligencer*, 3 January 1852.
64. *London City Mission Magazine*, April 1862, p. 73; Derek Hudson, *Munby: Man of Two Worlds*, Abacus, 1974, p. 119; *Musical World*, 9 August 1862.
65. The Association for the Improvement of Public Morals, for example, founded in 1879, fretted about music hall and theatre, drink and debauchery, from its very beginnings. See the group's magazine *The Sentinel*, passim.
66. The first halfpenny daily evening paper, which claimed a 200,000 circulation in 1870 (source: *Dictionary of Nineteenth Century Journalism*).
67. *Echo*, 13 September 1877.
68. *Era*, 30 September 1877.
69. Lyon was keen to introduce a formal magisterial check on whether districts 'needed' particular places of entertainment, with particular reference to immorality, as early as 1863. He cited 'lewd exhibition of *poses plastiques*' and sensation acts as something that needed to be checked (*Morning Post*, 18 July 1863).

November 1890; *Era*, 8 November 1890. Charrington
    could still have a say in the general council meetings held to consider the committee's find-
    ings; e.g. 'I once asked a fast man this question: "Are music-hall boxes used for immoral
    purposes?" "Well, you don't suppose they would pay for a box for nothing, do you?"'
    (*Reynolds's Newspaper*, 6 November 1892).

83. Tracy C. Davis, 'Sex in Public Places: The Zaeo Aquarium Scandal and the Victorian
    Moral Majority', *Theatre History Studies*, 10 (1990), p. 2.

84. *Sporting Times*, 4 October 1890.

85. *Licensed Victuallers' Mirror*, 22 May 1888; *Morning Post*, 10 October 1894.

86. W.J. MacQueen-Pope, quoted in Baker, *British Music Hall*, p. 44.

87. Visible use of make-up ('paint') was considered a signifier of dubious morals.

88. 'London County Council Election, 1892: The Elector's Guide, a Popular Hand-book for
    the Election', LSE Selected Pamphlets 1892; 'The London County Council: What It Is',
    LSE Selected Pamphlets 1895; 'New London: Her Parliament and Its Work', LSE Selected
    Pamphlets 1895.

89. *Licensed Victuallers' Mirror*, 26 March 1889.

90. *Illustrated Police News*, 24 November 1896.

91. Susan D. Pennyback, *A Vision for London, 1889–1914*, Routledge, 1995, p. 221.

92. Peter Bailey quotes the useful figure that twenty-one out of twenty-nine halls in the Stoll
    chain of theatres were dry by 1909 (Peter Bailey (ed.), *The Business of Pleasure*, Open
    University Press, 1986, p. xii).

93. *Sheffield Daily Telegraph*, 27 September 1895.

94. The lack of proper consultation on the subject is mentioned at the 1898 licensing sessions (see
    The Times, 26 November 1898) vis-à-vis the Empress Theatre of Varieties, Brixton. Because a
    blanket ban was not within their power, temperance-minded councillors simply introduced a
    'no intoxicating drinks' amendment to pretty much every individual decision after this date.

95. The Empire Palace actually gained an alcohol licence six years after it opened. The manage-
    ment pointed out that '75% of the audience left the theatre [during the show] and frequented
    the public houses in the immediate vicinity' (*Sheffield Evening Telegraph*, 31 July 1901).

96. Letter from J.L. Graydon, as secretary of the Proprietors of Entertainment Association, *The
    Times*, 11 October 1889.

97. 'A Chat with Mr. J.L. Graydon', *Era*, 8 July 1893; see also 'Songs and Suppers', *Era*, 29
    October 1887: 'The drinking customs of the last generation have been greatly modified.
    Many who would have been heavy drinkers fifty years ago are "moderates" at present.'

98. '[A]t most modern music halls these tables have been removed and the auditorium gener-
    ally resembles the stalls, pit, balcony and gallery of a theatre . . . people are now obliged to
    sit side by side' (*Era*, 29 October 1887).

99. *Era*, 6 January 1894.

100. *Era*, 10 February 1900.

101. The LCC Theatres and Music Halls Committee Minutes, housed in London Metropolitan
     Archives, dated 29–30 January 1901, provide a wide range of statistics for the period
     1890–1900.

102. Correspondence, 21 July 1853, re Beehive Public House (MBO/322).
103. The Metropolitan Management and Building Act 1878 was the relevant legislation. For discussion of the need for inspections see 1878 *Report from the Select Committee on Metropolis Management and Building Acts Amendment Bill*. This was followed by the Court of Quarter Sessions in Kent adopting similar rules for licensing beyond the Metropolitan Board of Works' jurisdiction. See *Morning Post*, 2 September 1881.

IV The Dancing-Room

1. [Anon.], *New Guide: An Historical and Descriptive Account of Leamington and Warwick*, 1825, p. 111.
2. Barbara Peel, *Dancing and Social Assemblies in York in the Eighteenth and Nineteenth Centuries*, National Resource Centre for Dance, 1986, p. 4. The York Assembly Rooms were opened in 1732. Girouard notes that they united local Whig and Tory families, who had previously established their own assemblies in private houses (Mark Girouard, *The English Town*, Yale University Press, 1990, p. 134).
3. J.K. Griffith, *A General Cheltenham Guide* [c.1830], p. 38; Philip J.S. Richardson, *The Social Dances of the Nineteenth Century in England*, Herbert Jenkins, 1960, p. 29.
4. Charles Dickens, *The Pickwick Papers*, Penguin, 1994, p. 543.
5. *The Times*, 1 January 1834.
6. John William Kaye, *The Life and Correspondence of Major-General Sir John Malcolm*, Smith Elder & Co., 1836, p. 574 (c.1831–33).
7. John Timbs, *Curiosities of London*, 1855, p. 4.
8. *Sheffield Daily Telegraph*, 24 November 1856.
9. *Morning Chronicle*, 22 September 1822, on public houses in Tooley Street, Southwark.
10. *Morning Post*, 10 December 1833.
11. *The Times*, 11 December 1838.
12. *Hull Packet*, 10 August 1849.
13. *Era*, 21 April 1839. The Grapes had a *music and dancing* licence from 1838.
14. *Morning Post*, 18 October 1841.
15. Mayhew, *London Labour and the London Poor*, Vol. I, p. 12; Vol. IV, p. 229; although the latter volume was written ten years later by co-author Bracebridge Hemyng.
16. *Morning Post*, 7 December 1833; *Preston Guardian*, 2 August 1845.
17. *John Bull*, 6 November 1847.
18. *Morning Chronicle*, 17 December 1833.
19. *Morning Post*, 2 June 1841.
20. *Morning Chronicle*, 23 April 1801.
21. Dickens' 'Dancing Academy' first appeared as a piece in *Bell's Life* on 11 October 1835, and was widely reprinted in other newspapers.
22. John Johnson Collection, *Theatre Royal, Drury Lane Grand Masquerade* [n.d.], London Playbills Drury Lane box 1 (28).
23. Charles Dickens, *Sketches by Boz*, Chapman and Hall, 1854, p. 71.
24. Thomas Frost, *The Old Showmen and the Old London Fairs*, Tinsley Brothers, 1875, p. 263.
25. [Robert Cowtan], *Passages from the Auto-Biography of a 'Man of Kent'*, Whittingham and Wilkins, 1866, p. 38.
26. Dickens, *Sketches by Boz*.
27. *Morning Post*, 11 December 1843.
28. 'Ce bal a deux faces comme Janus; l'hiver, il est établi dans la rue Saint-Honoré, et s'appelle Valentino; l'été, il va dresser sa tente aux Champs-Élysées et prend le nom de Mabille . . .' (Robert Hénard, *La Rue Saint-Honoré*, Émile-Paul, 1909, p. 401).
29. 'The Polka', *The Living Age*, 13 July 1844.
30. Sir F.C. Burnand, *Records and Reminiscences, Personal and General*, Methuen, 1905, pp. 44–5.

31. *World of Fashion*, 1 July 1844; *Aberdeen Journal*, 15 May 1844; 'Ringleader', 'The Polka Considered as a Revolutionary Movement', *Hood's Magazine and Comic Miscellany*, August 1844, p. 169.
32. *Morning Post*, 17 October 1846.
33. *Bell's Life*, 3 October 1847.
34. 'We omitted to notice last week a very unseemly derangement of certain songs from *The Messiah*, which essentials assorted most perversely with the steamy vapourings of Strauss and Musard; certainly *cornet-a-pistonisation* is an honour to which the immortal Handel never aspired' (*Musical World*, 5 November 1840, p. 295).
35. Albert Smith, *Sketches of London Life and Character*, Dean and Son, 1849, p. 30.
36. *Era*, 10 December 1848.
37. *Paul Pry*, No. 6, 18 December 1848.
38. Edmund Yates, *His Recollections and Experiences*, Richard Bentley & Son, 1885, p. 92.
39. Contemporary advertisements suggest that the venue was temporarily converted back into a swimming baths during the summers of 1848 and 1852.
40. *London Daily News*, 18 December 1846; *Standard*, 18 December 1846.
41. 'That apology for a man, little Mr. Grindleigh, acts as master of ceremonies, "assisted by an efficient corps of MCs" or in plain language, two more diminutive bodies . . . Woe to polka maniacs, who break bounds, and trespass out of the magic circle, or to the quadrillers who like to wind up with a galloping sweeping finale, Grindleigh and Co. are quickly on their heels and stop them with the ominous words, "You mustn't do that; it's against the regulations . . ."' (*Satirist*, 31 October 1847).
42. *Huddersfield and Holmfirth Examiner*, 21 August 1852.
43. *Bell's Life*, 19 September 1847; *Morning Advertiser*, 20 July 1848.
44. *Satirist*, 30 September 1848.
45. '"Jeames" at the Walhalla', *Satirist*, 16 December 1848.
46. Thomas Youdan's Casino (1849) was the precursor of his Surrey Music Hall (1856). The latter, as mentioned above, included a ballroom in the complex (see e.g. *Sheffield Daily Telegraph*, 22 November 1856). All advertisements and discussion of the venue at licensing sessions prior to this date, however, focus solely on the music-hall element.
47. *Morning Advertiser*, 12 October 1849.
48. Also appearing as Bignold and Bignall in contemporary documents. Bignall, interestingly, appears as a witness in a case involving the Royal Victoria Saloon, the notorious clip-joint (*Morning Post*, 11 December 1843).
49. Hudson, *Munby*, p. 23.
50. *Sporting Times*, 30 September 1871; *Temple Bar*, July 1877.
51. 1854 *Report from the Select Committee on Public Houses*, p. 93.
52. *Freeman's Journal*, 12 October 1858.
53. *Reynolds's Newspaper*, 20 October 1872; *The Times*, 10 October 1873.
54. See, for fuller details, *The Times*, 9 January 1864; *Morning Post*, 24 January 1864; *Morning Post*, 14 November 1867; *Western Mail*, 27 January 1870; *The Times*, 22 June 1870.
55. *Yorkshire Post*, 28 November 1873.
56. G.F. Train, *Train's Union Speeches*, John Adams Knight, 1862, 2nd series, p. 36.
57. 'One of the Old Brigade' [Donald Shaw], *London in the Sixties*, Everett, 1908. I am also very grateful to Christopher Burton for translating some German accounts of the Portland Rooms on my behalf. See Dr d'Henri, *Geheimnisse der Prostitution*, Verlags-Anstalt, 1871, p. 89; [Anon.], *Die interessantesten Ehescheidungs-Processe der älteren und neueren Zeit*, Carl Minde, 1869, p. 20.
58. Mayhew, *London Labour and the London Poor*, Vol. 4, p. 219.
59. Yates, *Recollections and Experiences*, p. 92. See also *Lloyd's Weekly Newspaper*, 12 February 1893: 'The class of persons frequenting the "rooms" in Holborn was very different to those who visited the Argyll. At the latter place bookmakers, officers in the army, swells and fashionable women . . . while tradesmen, City clerks, lawyers' ditto, &c., went to make up Mr. Hedgeman's company. The women frequenting the place belonged to a more *modest*

station in life, so that taken altogether the Holborn Casino acquired the reputation of being a well-conducted establishment.'

60. *Licensed Victuallers' Mirror*, 15 May 1888.
61. *Cheshire Observer*, 24 October 1874.
62. *Pall Mall Gazette*, 16 February 1874.
63. *Ipswich Journal*, 4 November 1882.
64. *Era*, 21 July 1888.
65. *Morning Chronicle*, 30 October 1829. 'Hops', of course, is also a pun (i.e. dances/beer).
66. *Nottingham Guardian*, 23 February 1877.
67. [Anon.], *Tempted London*, Chapter 12.
68. *Dancing: A Journal Devoted to the Terpsichorean Art*, January 1892, p. 92.
69. *Daily Mail*, 13 September 1897.
70. Charles Booth, *Labour and Life of the People*, Vol. 1: *East London*, Macmillan, 1889, pp. 94ff.
71. *Standard*, 6 January 1888.
72. *Dancing: A Journal Devoted to the Terpsichorean Art*, May 1893, p. 284.
73. James M. Glover, *Jimmy Glover: His Book*, Methuen, 1911, p. 76.
74. Hall Caine, *The Manxman*, Appleton and Company, 1894. Available at: www.gutenberg.org/files/25570/25570-0.txt
75. *Isle of Man Times*, 24 August 1889.
76. *Isle of Man Times*, 16 June 1894.
77. See the excellent book by James Nott, *Going to the Palais*, Oxford University Press, 2015.

V The Pleasure Garden

1. John Evelyn, *Memoirs*, Henry Colburn, 1819, p. 338; Warwick Wroth, *The London Pleasure Gardens of the Eighteenth Century*, Macmillan, 1896, p. 295, quoting Smollett's *Humphry Clinker*.
2. Mollie Sands, *The Eighteenth-Century Pleasure Gardens of Marylebone*, Society for Theatre Research, 1987, p. 50.
3. Pomona Gardens closed as the land was required for the Manchester Ship Canal; Belle Vue went through numerous guises, beginning as a zoo and ending as a twentieth-century theme park; and the Aston Hall and Park Company came to an abrupt end following a fatal tightrope-walking accident, although the parkland was purchased by the City of Birmingham.
4. For example, Boston in Lincolnshire; Norwich (originally Spring Garden/Bunn's Gardens); Manchester (originally Tinkers Gardens, Collyhurst); Birmingham (originally Duddleston Hall Gardens). I am grateful to Ray Newman for alerting me to the Vauxhall in New York.
5. Belatedly introduced in 1846 by Robert Wardell (*Sportsman*, 28 December 1869).
6. [Anon.], *A Brief Historical and Descriptive Account of the Royal Gardens, Vauxhall*, Gye and Balne, 1822. This publicity material produced by the proprietors provides a comprehensive description for this period.
7. In the nineteenth century, the word 'orchestra' was used not only for a group of musicians but, as the Oxford English Dictionary notes, 'The part of a theatre, opera house, or other public building where the musicians perform . . . a building or structure for a band of musicians; a bandstand'.
8. [Anon.], *Brief Historical and Descriptive Account of the Royal Gardens, Vauxhall*, p. 15.
9. Playbill, Lambeth Archives.
10. *Manchester Guardian*, 23 May 1855.
11. *Manchester Courier*, 3 July 1847.
12. Lynda Smith, *The Place to Spend a Happy Day: A History of Rosherville Gardens*, Gravesend Historical Society, 2006, p. 19.
13. *The Times*, 26 and 27 May 1824. Miss Stocks went on to make several balloon ascents at other gardens.

14. *Examiner*, 5 June 1852.

15. *Era*, 20 August 1848.

16. *Dublin Mercantile Advertiser*, 1 June 1835.

17. *Morning Chronicle*, 13 September 1852.

18. *Standard*, 18 June 1834; *The Times*, 10 June 1837; 12 June 1839. The act would be reprised in the 1850s at Cremorne by 'Buono Coré, The Italian Salamander'.

19. *Westmorland Gazette*, 16 August 1823, reporting Mallinson's anecdote of the event. The incident actually happened in 1818, according to local press.

20. Jullien would nonetheless become part of the syndicate that rescued the bankrupt gardens in 1856 and built the lavish Surrey Music Hall within the grounds (a venue for choral and orchestral music, rather than a 'music hall').

21. *Manchester Guardian*, 17 July 1850.

22. *Morning Chronicle*, 25 June 1857.

23. *Morning Post*, 14 September 1803.

24. *Manchester Courier and Lancashire General Advertiser*, 18 May 1850.

25. *Manchester Guardian*, 17 May 1854.

26. *Era*, 27 April 1851; see also playbills, Lambeth Archives.

27. *Theatrical Journal*, July 1858, pp. 220–1.

28. 'Late Hour Memoranda: The Saloons of the Drama', *Satirist*, 31 August 1845.

29. *Manchester Guardian*, 22 July 1854.

30. 'Noctes Downeyanae no. 25', *Satirist*, 7 October 1838.

31. Poster, Museum of London Pleasure Gardens collection, June 1877.

32. *Public Ledger and Daily Advertiser*, 21 June 1823. The theatre's proprietor also offered customers individual rides on the rollercoaster, doubtless for a small extra charge.

33. The same sort of gondola can be seen in the background of E.F. Lambert's *The Annual Fete of the Licensed Victuallers' School* (painted 1831), which took place in the gardens of the Eyre Arms, St John's Wood (Museum of London).

34. *Spectator*, 9 September 1865.

35. James Payn, *Lights and Shadows of London Life*, Hurst and Blackett, 1867, p. 127. The 'Woolly Woman' is an elderly black woman with 7-foot-long locks. Such displays of 'freaks' were commonplace at fairs, and elsewhere in London.

36. James Inches Hillocks, *My Life and Labours in London, a Step Nearer the Mark*, W. Freeman, 1865.

37. *Era*, 20 April 1856.

38. The flyer, which also appeared in *Tomahawk* magazine, was misprinted, skewing the nose of Miss Hamilton's caricature. Giovanelli sued the printer (*Lloyd's Weekly Newspaper*, 3 July 1870).

39. Hudson, *Munby*, p. 271 (diary entry, 21 June 1869).

40. *Era*, 5 August 1855; *Era*, 28 August 1864; *Morning Post*, 15 September 1870.

41. 'London Amusements', *Saint Paul's*, Vol. 9, October 1871, p. 50; *Morning Post*, 15 September 1870; *Era*, 16 July 1881; *Era*, 1 August 1885.

42. *John Bull*, in fairness, considered this was going too far and mocked the 'tender apprehensions for public morality' peculiar to the modern age (*John Bull*, 23 October 1826).

43. 'Late Hour Memoranda: Saloons of the Drama', *Satirist*, 31 August 1845. Despite the libel-avoiding use of 'certain gardens', this appears immediately after a lengthy description of crowds at the Eagle.

44. *Paul Pry*, 8 January 1849.

45. See also *Paul Pry*, 30 April 1849, which accuses the Eagle's proprietor, Tom 'Bravo' Rouse, of being a 'blasphemer' and 'drivelling ribald', maintaining a private parlour in his tavern frequented by prostitutes. Rouse was certainly an eccentric figure, obese and increasingly gout-ridden; but by all accounts he was very popular with his customers.

46. W. Talley, *Man Midwifery and the Results*, Taylor and Greening [n.d.], p. 36.

47. 'Down among the Factories', *National Magazine*, 7, 1860, p. 76.

48. *Manchester Guardian*, 25 May 1853.

49. *John Bull*, 1 July 1822.
50. *Satirist*, 17 July 1831.
51. 1852–53 *Report from the Select Committee on Public Houses*, pp. 311–15.
52. 'Evils of Sunday Taverns', *London City Mission Magazine*, September 1841, pp. 137–42, and October 1841, pp. 157–60; 'The Suppression of the Sunday Taverns', *London City Mission Magazine*, November 1841, pp.169–76. The magazine also returns to the topic in October and November 1842.
53. Arthur G. Credland, 'Charles Random, Baron de Berenger, Inventor, Marksman and Proprietor of the Stadium', *Arms & Armour*, 3:2 (2006), pp. 171–91, provides some detail.
54. *La Belle Assemblée*, 1 August 1831.
55. See e.g. *Bell's Life*, 7 March 1839.
56. *Era*, 14 January 1844. Lord Chief Baron was a genuine judicial title, even though Nicholson himself did not possess it.
57. *Liverpool Mail*, 20 October 1849.
58. Simpson's brother John established Simpson's in the Strand – a 'grand restauratum' for 'those who like good living, choice wines, and fine cigars, blended with economy'; the name and (rebuilt) restaurant survive to this day ('Exit Simpson's', *Daily Mail*, 19 March 1902).
59. The Cremorne-branded restaurant/café flourished in the period 1863–78, when, after the demise of the gardens, it was renamed the Leicester.
60. *Spectator*, 9 September 1865.
61. *Reynolds's Newspaper*, 4 July 1858.
62. *Lloyd's Weekly Newspaper*, 4 July 1858.
63. *Sheffield Daily Telegraph*, 22 December 1865.
64. *Telegraph*, 15 June 1861.
65. *The Times*, 9 May 1846.
66. *Era*, 24 March 1850.
67. *Daily News*, 1 December 1869.
68. *Pall Mall Gazette*, 8 July 1870.
69. *Marylebone Mercury*, 30 May 1863.
70. *Daily News*, 24 June 1882.
71. *The Times*, 10 October 1874.
72. *Daily News*, 28 September 1878; *Morning Post*, 21 January 1880.
73. *Illustrated London News*, 20 June 1874.
74. Charles Selby, *Out on the Sly*, Duncombe and Moon, 1847, p. 9.
75. See Smith, *The Place to Spend a Happy Day* for an excellent history of Rosherville.

VI The Exhibition Ground

1. Paul Greenhalgh, *Ephemeral Vistas: The Expositions Universelles, Great Exhibitions and Worlds Fairs, 1851–39*, Manchester University Press, 1988, p. 10, points out that the international idea had been mooted in France as early as 1834 by a member of the Société Royale d'Émulation, and was again rejected in 1849. Henry Cole, after visiting the Paris Exhibition of 1849, put the international proposal to Prince Albert.
2. See Henry Cole's speech to the City of London for a good summary of early intentions (*The Times*, 18 October 1849).
3. *Punch* referred to the building as 'a palace of very crystal' on 13 July 1850; and the term appears in the press from August (e.g. *Bell's Weekly Messenger*, 18 August 1850). Yet the iron-and-glass Winter Garden that opened in the Champs Élysées in 1846–48 was also referred to as 'a vast conservatory or crystal palace' in the *Illustrated London News*, 22 January 1848. Moreover, the magical 'crystal palace' was a much-used location in pantomime throughout the previous decade (see, for example, a review in *The Odd Fellow*, 28 December 1839: 'up goes the curtain, discovering a crystal palace, inhabited by a queen and several ladies of honour'). It is probably fruitless, therefore, to seek out a particular origin for the name.

4. 1852 *First Report of the Commissioners for the Exhibition of 1851*, Appendix 24: Number of Visitors to National and Other Buildings, Museums &c., p. 21.
5. *The Times*, 5 July 1851; 24 May 1851.
6. J.R. Piggott, *Palace of the People: The Crystal Palace at Sydenham 1854–1936*, University of Wisconsin Press, 2004, p. 38.
7. The West End of London and Crystal Palace Railway, although a separate company, would be operated by the Brighton railway, and sold its principal line, from Pimlico to Norwood, to the Brighton company in the late 1850s.
8. *The Times*, 20 January 1854.
9. *The Times*, 30 December 1853.
10. Report of EGM, 17 March 1853, included in Guildhall Library, Annual Reports 1881–85 COL/LIB/PB02 (Crystal Palace Company).
11. Samuel Phillips, *Guide to the Crystal Palace and Park*, Bradbury and Evans, 1854, p. 15.
12. Prospectus, quoted in *The Times*, 19 May 1852.
13. Dickens' letters, to Wills, 7 August 1853 and to Mrs. Watson, 1 November 1854, in Storey et al. (eds), *Letters of Charles Dickens*.
14. Piggott, *Palace of the People*, p. 122.
15. Samuel Phillips, *Guide to the Crystal Palace and Park*, Bradbury and Evans, 1854, p. 17.
16. ibid., p. 120.
17. Initial estimates of raising £100,000 p.a. were wildly off the mark. The first Statement of Receipt and Accounts for the company after it began trading (to 30 December 1854) shows £17,238 received for 'rental of space'. This was still a respectable sum, but it seems to have been the zenith; the figure swiftly dropped, down to £7,177 in 1858 (*Era*, 27 June 1858) and closer to £4,000 by the end of the century.
18. There has always been some doubt whether the group sat in the mould or a half-completed model. The *Leader and Saturday Analyst*, 7 January 1860, refers explicitly to the 'mould' and indeed it seems unlikely that Hawkins would have risked the dinner party damaging the finished product.
19. 'The Crystal Palace', *Westminster Review*, October 1854, pp. 534ff.
20. *The Times*, 6 August 1856. 'Kiss in the ring' or 'kiss in the green' was a form of kiss-chase played by children and young members of the working class, where the object was to catch a partner, bring them back to the circle of people, and kiss them in front of the assembled crowd. For those in their later teens and twenties, it obviously served as a sort of dating game, a rough-and-ready way of meeting/testing potential marriage partners. The game was often played at fairs on public holidays.
21. Hudson, *Munby*, p. 29 (diary for 26 March 1859). Monday was one shilling entrance, like other weekdays; Saturday was five shillings.
22. ibid., p. 32 (diary for 25 April 1859).
23. ibid., p. 36.
24. Cited in Greenhalgh, *Ephemeral Vistas*, p. 19.
25. *Manchester Guardian*, 25 May 1850.
26. *Era*, 12 April 1868.
27. *Era*, 21 December 1862.
28. *Era*, 22 April 1877.
29. Report of the Directors, 9 February 1888, Guildhall Library, Annual Reports COL/LIB/PB02.
30. A.G.E. Heine, *The Past, Present and Future of the Crystal Palace*, 1874, p. 12.
31. Debt was always a problem, but a steady decline in the Palace's net revenue can also be seen in the annual reports of the 1880s and 1890s. From over £30,000 net profit in the early 1880s, profits gradually fell off.
32. See *Daily News*, 20 July 1857, for the opening of the London Restaurant; *The Times*, 3 April 1858, for the refreshments contract. The Crystal Palace contract involved Sawyer and Strange paying the company 2½ pence for every admission to the grounds; but it still made them a healthy profit. This is not to say that Strange could have extracted more profit from

the Crystal Palace as a whole. When he left the Alhambra Music Hall and attempted to revitalise the Surrey Gardens in the early 1870s, he swiftly went bankrupt.

33. *Era*, 27 June 1858; cf. *Morning Post*, 11 December 1862, which shows that £26,500 out of £85,000 was spent on maintenance, repairs, gardens and grounds and waterworks.

34. *Era*, 12 February 1887.

35. Report of the Directors, 10 February 1887, Guildhall Library, Annual Reports COL/LIB/PB02.

36. George Gissing, *The Nether World*, Oxford University Press, 1992, pp. 106ff.

37. '[N]o person shall be admitted to the said Building or Grounds on the Lords Day in consideration of any money payment.' Available at: www.crystalpalacefoundation.org.uk/history/crystal-palace-royal-charters

38. For example, the New York Exhibition of the Industry of All Nations, 1853–54; the Dublin Exhibition of 1853; the Parisian Exposition Universelle of 1855.

39. Babbage, however, complained that his machine was 'placed . . . in a *small hole* in a *dark corner*' as opposed to 'children's toys, whose merits it is true, the Commissioners were somewhat more competent to appreciate' (Peter Hoffenberg, *An Empire on Display*, University of California Press, 2001, p. 93).

40. 'The International Exhibition: Its Purpose and Prospect', *Blackwood's Edinburgh Magazine*, April 1862, p. 472.

41. *Punch*, 3 May 1862.

42. *John Bull*, 16 March 1861, notes that London's daily capacity for rail traffic had increased from 42,000 to 140,000 in the past decade.

43. *Derby Mercury*, 12 February 1862.

44. For a detailed list of the incomings/outgoings in 1862, see the *Morning Post*, 11 December 1862, presumably drawn from the annual report to shareholders. Receipts fell from £146,000 in 1862 to a little above £100,000 the following year (although the company also managed to slash £20,000 in expenditure) (*Morning Post*, 17 December 1863).

45. 'The "Art Union" was a nineteenth-century institution of art patronage organized on the principle of joint association by which the revenue from small individual annual membership fees was spent (after operating costs) on contemporary art, which was then redistributed among the membership by lot' (Joy Sperling, '"Art, Cheap and Good": The Art Union in England and the United States, 1840–60', *Nineteenth-Century Art Worldwide*, 1:1 (2002)).

46. The reopening season made an operating profit of £21,387, but this was nothing compared to the company's debts. See *Working Revenue Account, Six month ending 31st October 1875*, Haringey Museum.

47. Sir Edward Lee, 'Comments on the Recent Management of the Alexandra Palace', November 1876 (pamphlet), held at Haringey Museum.

48. See the extensive coverage in *The Times* of 21–23 November 1883; 16, 18 and 24 January 1884.

49. Haringey Museum AP1/17.

50. *Nelson Evening Mail*, 13 December 1881.

51. *Newcastle Courant*, 5 August 1881.

52. Gross receipts for 1871 were £76,433. By 1874 they had declined to £16,399 (Henry Cole, *A Special Report on the Annual International Exhibitions 1871, 1872, 1873, 1874*, Eyre and Spottiswoode, 1879, p. xl). Overall the four exhibitions made a loss of £13,000, even putting aside money spent on building work (£126,383).

53. *The Times*, 4 June 1883.

54. For a fascinating article about Indian visitors to the Exhibition, see Joseph W. Childers, 'Peering back: Colonials and Exhibitions' in James Buzard, Joseph W. Childers and Eileen Gillooly (eds), *Victorian Prism: Refractions of the Crystal Palace*, University of Virginia Press, 2007, pp. 203–32.

55. The Imperial Institute would go on to stage its own modest exhibitions for visitors. The 1896 'Summer Season' included colonial and Indian products, an exhibition of horseless carriages, sporting trophies and curiosities, and ancient armour (*Standard*, 27 April 1896).

56. 'Life in London', *Licensed Victuallers' Mirror*, 30 June 1891.

57. *Fun* magazine would mock this in 1888, showing the mountain range and chimneys in a cartoon 'Some Mems. of the Italian Exhibition' (*Fun*, 27 June 1888, p. 277).

58. *Era*, 7 May 1887.
59. *Era*, 14 May 1887.
60. Charles Lowe, *Four National Exhibitions in London*, T. Fisher Unwin, 1892, p. 87, suggests that it took Whitley and colleagues some eight months to build up the requisite list of the great and the good.
61. *The British Architect*, 13 April 1888, pp. 259-60.
62. *Birmingham Daily Post*, 26 May 1888.
63. The *Era* reviewer of 7 July 1888 writes with gentle mockery of Whitley's 'touching conscientiousness' in delaying the arena show for the benefit of the remainder of the exhibition.
64. Lowe, *Four National Exhibitions*, p. 354.
65. ibid., p. 395. John Hart, a businessman involved in Olympia and Earl's Court, also noted that all Hartley's exhibitions lost money, providing detailed figures for each year ('The Losses on London Exhibitions', *Daily Telegraph*, 2 April 1896, p. 6).
66. They were regular performers at the Oxford Music Hall in 1865-66, then subsequently the Alhambra, where they premiered their own short ballet, *The Pearl of Tokay*, which they later took on tour with a forty-strong company. The Kiralfy family were known for their skill, rapid movement and colourful costume, although one harsher critic described their trademark folk dance as 'something apparently in imitation of a lively frog' (*Lloyd's Weekly Newspaper*, 22 April 1866).
67. Brendan Edward Gregory, 'The Spectacle Plays and Exhibitions of Imre Kiralfy 1887-1914', Thesis, University of Manchester, 1988, p. 86. This thesis provides a masterly treatment of Kiralfy's career.
68. A plan of *Venice in London* shows thirteen separate bridges and twenty shops and cafés within the 'city'. There was a central 'grand canal' which bisected the bell-shaped site, connecting with a ring of water around the outside (LMA4684/02/04/1891/001).
69. *Morning Post*, 28 December 1891.
70. Hartley, *Eighty-Eight Not Out*, p. 59.
71. *Era*, 19 December 1891.
72. *Birmingham Daily Post*, 1 June 1892; *Era*, 14 January 1893.
73. Spiers and Pond took £15,000 of the £46,000 issue of debentures which supplemented the original £100,000 raised from ordinary shareholders. See *Financial Times*, 22 July 1910; 26 January 1911; 4 March 1911.
74. See *Financial Times*, 22 July 1910; 26 January 1911; 4 March 1911.
75. The International Universal Exhibition was something of a stop-gap, featuring manufactured goods from a dozen countries and rather miscellaneous attractions. Greater Britain focused principally on large imperial possessions like Canada, Australia and South Africa. From around 1903, Kiralfy began to lose interest in London Exhibitions Ltd, working as a consultant on British sections of foreign exhibitions (1904 St Louis Exposition; 1905 Liege Exposition; 1907 Bordeaux Exhibition) and formulating his plans for White City. See Gregory, 'The Spectacle Plays', pp. 372-73.
76. *Daily News*, 9 May 1888.
77. *Cheshire Observer*, 14 April 1900.
78. *International Universal Exhibition, 1898: Guide and Catalogue*, p. 19.
79. *The Phonogram*, June 1901.
80. Greenhalgh, *Ephemeral Vistas*, p. 54.
81. The 1896 contract for foreign performers at the India and Ceylon exhibition promises to 'board and lodge' employees (Museum of London Kiralfy Collection).
82. *Daily Mail*, 20 June 1899.
83. *Woman's Exhibition, 1900: Guide*, p. 20.
84. *Daily Mail*, 17 August 1899.
85. *Daily Mail*, 29 July 1899; 11, 12, 14 and 15 August 1899.
86. Concessions for amusements and refreshments were also a feature of Cremorne Gardens and Crystal Palace. Records in the Museum of London's Kiralfy Collection show that Kiralfy normally took a 25 per cent cut, although there were exceptions (33 per cent in the case of the rifle range; 60 per cent on deck chairs).

87. *Era*, 21 May 1898.
88. Chetham's Library, F.4.2.1.(a) (online).
89. *Manchester Courier*, 2 March 1907.
90. The origins of the White City lay in an approach to Kiralfy by the British Empire League in 1902 for an exhibition to celebrate, yet again, the Empire and the Coronation. The signing of the *Entente Cordiale* persuaded him to change the theme; and, at the request of the British Olympic Committee in 1906, he incorporated the Games into the site (Gregory, 'The Spectacle Plays', p. 374).
91. *Daily Mail*, 1 April 1908. By way of comparison, Earl's Court as a whole encompassed a mere 22 acres.
92. *Wharfedale and Airedale Observer*, 28 August 1908. See also Programme for the Franco-British Exhibition, 1908, p. 5 (Museum of London). The *Licensed Victuallers' Mirror*, seeing the Danish village at the Anglo-Danish Exhibition of 1888, gave vent to its racism, imagining an Irish village as an exhibition attraction: 'with real Irish pigs and real Irish peasants going about half-naked . . . a real Irish manure-heap with a real Irish M.P. buried in it up to the middle' (*Licensed Victuallers' Mirror*, 22 May 1888).
93. John Home and Gary Whannel, *Understanding the Olympics*, Routledge, 2012, p. 94.
94. *Standard*, 8 July 1908.
95. See Gregory, 'The Spectacle Plays', p. 455 (source: Museum of London Kiralfy Collection). The year 1908 was a bumper one, with £776,163 gross receipts; 1910 was still excellent with £396,705; but in the final years, takings were in the region of £75,000.

VII The Seaside

1. Most famously, the physician Richard Russell (1687–1759), who specialised in diseases of the glands, became convinced of the medicinal properties of seawater in the 1720s. In the 1750s he opened his own clinic in Brighton and did much to popularise it as a fashionable resort.
2. George Keate, *Sketches from Nature; Taken, and Coloured, in a Journey to Margate*, T. Hurst, 1802 (first published 1790), p. 47.
3. *The Times*, 30 September 1805.
4. Keate, *Sketches from Nature*, p. 66.
5. *The Times*, 31 August 1793.
6. [William Hutton], *A Description of Blackpool*, Pearson and Rollason, 1809, p. 5.
7. For the corn trade and the economy of the region, see J. Whyman, 'Aspects of Holidaymaking and Resort Development within the Isle of Thanet, with Particular Reference to Margate, circa 1736 to circa 1840', Thesis, University of Kent at Canterbury, 1980, p. 21.
8. A cabin cost seven shillings; a 'state cabin' thirteen. The stagecoach might cost a guinea and a half for an indoor seat, or eighteen shillings inside. For tourist boats, see Whyman, 'Aspects of Holidaymaking', p. 187.
9. John Feltham, *A Guide to All the Watering and Sea-Bathing Places*, Longman et al., 1813, p. 307.
10. ibid., p. 314.
11. These grounds, within the farm of Thomas Staines, flourished c.1780–1816 as a pleasure garden.
12. *The Family Album of Hawkins Francis James . . . Croydon, July 28th 1828*, Kent Archives R/U2446/F1.
13. R.B. Watts, *The Margate Steam Yachts Guide*, Joseph Mallett, 1820, p. 16; G.W. Bonner, *The Picturesque Pocket Companion to Margate, Ramsgate, Broadstairs and Parts Adjacent*, William Kidd, n.d., p. 2.
14. Watts, *Margate Steam Yachts*.
15. *Bell's Life*, 22 August 1824; Whyman, 'Aspects of Holidaymaking', p. 556.
16. Charles Dickens, *Sketches by Boz*, Penguin, 1995, p. 390.
17. Whyman, 'Aspects of Holidaymaking', p. 211.

18. Whyman's thesis (pp. 233 ff.) provides ample details of a house built and let by one William Stone, 1778–96. The property cost £645 to erect, but made £1,124 in rent over this period, let out to various tenants, principally during the summer.

19. [Anon.], 'Amusements at Margate', *Chambers's Edinburgh Journal*, 15 June 1833, pp. 155–56.

20. *Satirist*, 31 August 1834. A 'castor' was a rabbit-fur hat; 'heavy wet' was strong ale; the 'swell mob' were fashionably dressed thieves and pickpockets, posing as gentlemen.

21. *Fun*, 21 October 1865.

22. *Satirist*, 28 September 1832.

23. *Illustrated London News*, 27 September 1857.

24. *Observer*, 8 October 1865.

25. The houses in Ethelbert Crescent, the first major development in Cliftonville, had just been completed. The *Kentish Gazette*, 11 April 1865, mentions the owners petitioning the council to finish their street paving. By 1900, Cliftonville was considered quite distinct from the more vulgar central Margate, having 'scarcely anything in common with the regions sacred to the tripper' ([English Heritage], *Margate's Seaside Heritage*, English Heritage, 2007, p. 43).

26. *Thanet Advertiser*, 9 December 1865.

27. The Railway Regulation Act 1844 (7 & 8 Vict., c. 85) also provided some encouragement. It demanded 'the provision of at least one train a day each way at a speed of not less than 12 miles an hour including stops, which were to be made at all stations, and of carriages protected from the weather and provided with seats; for all which luxuries not more than a penny a mile might be charged' (p. 2).

28. *Bell's New Weekly Messenger*, 13 August 1843.

29. The price had dropped to three shillings and sixpence by the early 1850s ([Anon.], *Knight's Tourist's Companion*, Nattali and Bond, 1853, p. 22).

30. Susan Major, 'The Million Go Forth', Thesis, University of York, 2012, p. 101; *Manchester Courier*, 19 July 1851.

31. *Lancaster Guardian*, 11 August 1860.

32. *Preston Chronicle*, 11 August 1860.

33. Francis Cobb Jr (1759–1831); not Francis Cobb Sr (1727–1802), although both were influential figures in the town.

34. W.C. Oulton, *Picture of Margate*, Baldwin, Craddock and Joy, 1820, p. 45.

35. *Morning Post*, 25 July 1829.

36. This was very much a new technology. Paul Dobraszczyk, *Iron, Ornament and Architecture in Victorian Britain*, Ashgate, 2014, p. 141, notes that James Brunlees' Southport Pier, among the first iron piers, took engineering inspiration from a railway viaduct over Ulverston Sands.

37. Minutes of the Institution of Civil Engineers, 27 November 1849, No. 804. The naval shipworm *teredo navalis* was the culprit.

38. 'In some resorts, especially Southport, working-class people risked their savings in pier company shares. They included fishermen, domestic servants, a waiter and a barmaid' (John K. Walton, *British Piers*, Thames and Hudson, 1987, p. 13).

39. *Liverpool Mercury*, 10 December 1852.

40. *Bolton Chronicle*, 4 August 1860.

41. For example, steamer trips from Blackpool to the Isle of Man (five hours, with 2–6 hours in Douglas) cost 1s; trips to Llandudno, between 2s 6d and 3s 6d; trips to Southport 2s to 2s 6d ([Anon.], *People's Guide to Blackpool*, n.d. [c.1883]). The opening of a new pier in a rival resort could also be perceived as a positive development for local steamship companies.

42. *Southport Independent and Ormskirk Chronicle*, 28 March 1866.

43. *Southport Independent and Ormskirk Chronicle*, 3 August 1870.

44. See [Anon.], *The New Illustrated Guide to Southport*, Southport Daily News, 1875, p. 45; also *The Times*, 7 July 1888, advertisement for the Trouville Pier and Steamboat Co., quoting statistics.

45. Blackpool North Pier, for example, made £2,303 from its toll; £83 from annual tickets; £88 from monthly tickets; £600 from steamships; £185 from shop rents; £77 from advertising space; £46 from hiring bath-chairs (*Blackburn Standard*, 11 December 1875).

46. *Leeds Mercury*, 8 June 1877.

47. *Preston Herald*, 24 March 1883.

48. *Morning Post*, 9 August 1880. Birch was the designer of Margate Pier (1857), North Pier Blackpool (1863), Deal Pier (1864), West Pier Brighton (1866) and ten others.

49. *Western Morning News*, 6 February 1890.

50. *Exeter and Plymouth Gazette*, 3 October 1889.

51. The company prospectus noted, without naming the Great Western Railway as competition, that the Bristol route cost 5s 6d and took well over two hours, whereas they would charge 1s 6d and the channel crossing would only take half an hour (*Daily Telegraph*, 6 July 1903).

52. Chris Mawson and Richard Riding, *British Seaside Piers*, Ian Allan, 2008, p. 112.

53. Prospectus of the Weston-super-Mare Grand Pier Company (*Daily Telegraph*, 6 July 1903).

54. See, for example, *Reading Mercury*, 28 April 1900; *Mid Sussex Times*, 6 March 1900.

55. *National Observer*, 12 December 1896, p. 90.

56. Richard Marsh, 'The Girl on the Sands', *Strand*, October 1904, pp. 423–33.

57. Frances A. Bailey, 'The Origin and Growth of Southport', *Town Planning Review*, 1 January 1951.

58. 'Some Notes at Starmouth', *Punch*, 24 September 1887.

59. *Liverpool Mercury*, 2 June 1897.

60. Minutes of Aberystwyth General Purposes Committee, 7 May 1897.

61. *Montgomery County Times*, 29 July 1899; 19 August 1899.

62. *Manchester Courier*, 10 September 1890 (reprinted from *Daily Telegraph*).

63. For example, a letter to the papers about promoting amusements in Folkestone describes Blackpool crowds as a 'somewhat rough class . . . [but] I never witnessed the slightest act of indecorum' (*Folkestone, Hythe, Sandgate & Cheriton Herald*, 12 December 1903).

64. John K. Walton, 'Municipal Government and the Holiday Industry in Blackpool, 1876–1914', in John K. Walton and James Walvin (eds), *Leisure in Britain: 1780–1939*, Manchester University Press, 1983, p. 180.

65. John Walton, 'The Social Development of Blackpool 1788–1914', University of Lancaster, 1974, pp. 314–15.

66. Fish was manager at the Pomona Gardens, under James Reilly, the proprietor, from 1868 to 1872. He would return to Manchester in 1880, then go on to manage the Alexandra Gardens, Stockport; Winter Gardens at New Brighton; Aston Lower Grounds, Birmingham; and Hollingworth Lake, before returning to Belle Vue Gardens in Blackpool in 1885, where he died suddenly of a stroke (*Preston Herald*, 6 June 1885).

67. *Preston Herald*, 11 May 1872.

68. *Preston Guardian*, 29 November 1873. By contrast, the Crystal Palace in this period was attracting about 2 million visitors per annum, but struggling to pay a dividend.

69. *Preston Herald*, 22 April 1876.

70. *Era*, 31 March 1888.

71. *Leigh Chronicle*, 8 July 1887; *Preston Herald*, 8 June 1889.

72. *Lancaster Gazette*, 23 May 1877; 12 March 1881; 24 September 1884.

73. *Lancashire Evening Post*, 12 August 1898.

74. The Crystal Palace Aquarium Company initially had a three-year lease, and was established by the Crystal Palace Company as a way of getting in new investment and minimising risk. The aim was for the CPC to buy up the new company after three years, once it had proved profitable (*Morning Post*, 3 June 1870). Typically for the Palace, the company was initially prosperous, with a 10 per cent dividend in 1872, but suffered rapidly diminishing returns as the novelty wore off.

75. *The Times*, 12 August 1872.

76. *Illustrated London News*, 10 August 1872.
77. *Preston Chronicle*, 17 January 1874.
78. *Halifax Courier*, 23 June 1877.
79. *Halifax Courier*, 23 June 1877.
80. See John K. Walton, *The English Seaside Resort*, Leicester University Press, 1983, pp. 60ff., for useful statistics. Southport's fixed non-tourist population was 33,763 in 1881 versus Blackpool's 12,989.
81. *Liverpool Mercury*, 27 October 1874.
82. *Rhyl Record and Advertiser*, 27 April 1878.
83. *Birmingham Daily Post*, 24 March 1877.
84. *Whitstable Times*, 21 August 1875; *Kent and Sussex Courier*, 27 October 1876.
85. *Thanet Advertiser*, 10 September 1881.
86. *Illustrated London News*, 20 July 1878.
87. This power, granted in 1879, initially raised about £500, a sum which would rise to £4,000 by 1914 (Claire Simpson, 'The Economics of a Seaside Resort', Thesis, Lancaster University, 2015, p. 7).
88. Manx Board of Advertising Minutes, 1896.
89. Allen Clarke, *The Story of Blackpool*, Palatine Books Co., 1923, p. 219.
90. *Era*, 6 January 1894.
91. *Manchester Courier*, 10 July 1888. For a list of acts before Holland's tenure, one can scan the advertisements and 'Provincial Theatre' columns of the *Era*.
92. Blackpool Central Property Company 1881, which was wound up in 1885, but instantly replaced by the Central Promenade Estate Company.
93. *Dart*, 9 August 1895.
94. *Lancashire Evening Post*, 6 August 1930.
95. *Era*, 2 November 1895.
96. *Sheffield Daily Telegraph*, 28 May 1898.
97. *Liverpool Mercury*, 5 June 1897.
98. See Paul Watt, 'A "Gigantic and Popular Place of Entertainment": Granville Bantock and Music Making at the New Brighton Tower in the Late 1890s', *Royal Musical Association Research Chronicle*, 42:1 (2009), pp. 109–64.
99. *Yorkshire Post*, 2 December 1909.
100. *Era*, 29 April 1899.
101. I am very grateful to Tim Dunn for pointing out this example.
102. *Lancashire Evening Post*, 7 March 1901.
103. *Era*, 22 December 1906.
104. *Preston Herald*, 17 April 1907.
105. [Blackpool Town Council], *The Guide to Blackpool*, 1913, p. 22.
106. *Southend Standard*, 2 August 1894.
107. I am indebted to Josephine Kane's thesis 'A Whirl of Wonders: British Amusement Parks and the Architecture of Pleasure: 1900–1939', UCL, 2009 (published as *The Architecture of Pleasure*, Taylor and Francis, 2013), for its fascinating information about Blackpool and Southend's Edwardian amusement parks.
108. Ieuan Gwynedd Jones, *Aberystwyth 1277–1977*, Gomer Press, 1977, p. 118.
109. George E. Martin, *Breezy Blackpool*, W. Mate & Sons Ltd, 1899, p. 1. The cover notes 'Published under the auspices of the Blackpool Corporation'; 'Blackpool: The Ideal Holiday Resort', *Sheffield Daily Telegraph*, 25 June 1913.

VIII The Football Field

1. The term 'public school' is a rather confusing one. Its origins lie in the charitable schools of the 1500s, but eventually the expression came to mean a rather select set of establishments, where the wealthy despatched their children for a boarding-school education. The Public Schools Act 1868 created the first batch of 'official' public schools responsible for

their own administration: Charterhouse, Eton, Harrow, Rugby, Shrewsbury, Westminster and Winchester; but the term was also applied more loosely to 'lesser' establishments modelled along the lines of Eton and Rugby. It is in the latter broader, modern sense that I use the term in this chapter.

2. *The Times*, 23 October 1839.

3. The first instance of running with the ball at Rugby was later ascribed to one William Webb Ellis. A commemorative plaque was erected in 1900, testifying to his 'fine disregard for the rules of football' in a game in 1823. There is reason to doubt Webb Ellis's unique contribution, but the practice does seem to have gained currency in the 1820s and 1830s. See Graham Curry, 'Football: A Study in Diffusion', DPhil Thesis, University of Leicester, 2001, pp. 17ff.

4. 'A History of Rugby Football', Rugby School. Available at: www.rugbyschool.co.uk/about/history/a-history-of-rugby-football/

5. *Derby Mercury*, 28 February 1827.

6. *Derby Mercury*, 29 February 1832; *Morning Post*, 6 February 1845.

7. See Adrian Harvey, *Football: The First Hundred Years: The Untold Story*, Routledge, 2005, Chapter 1, for a discussion of Shrove Tuesday matches and their diverse character.

8. *Carlisle Patriot*, 13 April 1839.

9. For example, Londonthorpe v. Welby, *Stamford Mercury*, 2 March 1810; Great Wigston v. Blaby, *Leicester Chronicle*, 14 February 1829; Horbling v. Swaton, *Stamford Mercury*, 5 March 1830; East Kirkby v. Hagnaby, *Stamford Mercury*, 21 April 1837.

10. *Leeds Intelligencer*, 26 February 1848; *Bell's Life*, 28 March 1852. I am grateful to Terry Morris, *Vain Games of No Value?*, Authorhouse, 2016, for pointing me to Holmfirth matches.

11. For recent discussion, see Peter Swain, 'The Origins of Football Debate: The "Grander Design and the Involvement of the Lower Classes", 1818–1840', *Sport in History*, 34:4 (2014), pp. 519–43; John Goulstone, '*Football's Secret History* – chapters 2 and 3', *Soccer and Society*, 19:1 (2018), pp. 35–49.

12. *The Times*, 23 March 1826.

13. *The Times*, 11 March 1830.

14. *Northern Star and Leeds General Advertiser*, 9 November 1863.

15. *Morning Advertiser*, 27 December 1823.

16. *Illustrated London News*, 14 September 1844; *Birmingham Journal*, 27 July 1850; *Derby Mercury*, 15 August 1855.

17. *Illustrated London News*, 8 November 1851.

18. *The Times*, 21 December 1929. Thring remarked on this in his letter to the *Field*, 28 December 1861. Thring had graduated in 1847, taking the curacy of Alford. *Bath Chronicle*, 23 December 1847; *Chelmsford Chronicle*, 8 October 1909.

19. *Sportsman*, 8 January 1898.

20. See Curry, 'Football', pp. 37ff., where he notes Eton's close relationship with King's College Cambridge, which may have contributed to the preference. Secondary sources often confuse Thring's and Malden's efforts at Cambridge, but their careers there did not overlap: Malden began soon after Thring graduated.

21. John Venn and J.A. Venn (eds), *Alumni Cantabrigienses*, Vol. 2, Part 4, Cambridge University Press, 2011. Thanks to Fabian Macpherson for pointing this out to me.

22. *Oxford University and City Herald*, 20 October 1855.

23. *Oxford University and City Herald*, 15 April 1854.

24. George Sills first took a team 'principally of Cantabs' to Westminster School for a match, reported in *Bell's Life*, 21 February 1858. The name 'Dingley Dell' first appears in print in *Bell's Life*, 12 December 1858, and Sills' team at this match included two members from the February game. Dingley Dell also played some cricket matches, e.g. against Charterhouse (*Bell's Life*, 27 June 1858). Sills may well be the George Sills who died in 1905, holding the post of Recorder of Lincoln, an alumnus of St John's Cambridge (*Stamford Mercury*, 8 September 1905).

25. *Bell's Life*, 31 October 1863.
26. *Bell's Life*, 23 January 1859.
27. *Bell's Life*, 19 and 26 December 1858.
28. *Bell's Life*, 16 January 1859.
29. Thring maintained this stance, even as both rugby and soccer prospered. In 1871, he wrote: 'I fear there must be unpleasant personal conflict [in Rugby], in which it is not safe that men should indulge, though boys may enjoy the fun. It is said to increase the spirit of the game. An Indian war-dance is more spirited than a waltz . . . [but] would hardly be admirable in civilized society' (*Bath Chronicle*, 19 October 1871).
30. *Bell's Life*, 5 October 1862.
31. The original letter from 'J.C.T.' appeared in the *Daily Telegraph*, 24 September 1863. Morley's initial reply was published on 28 September under 'Capt. of Barnes F.C.' and Pember's on 1 October under 'The Captain of the N.N. Football Club'.
32. J.D. Cartwright's articles ran in the *Field* between 24 October 1863 and 26 December 1863; a similar series by 'A Lover of Football' would follow in the *Sporting Gazette* beginning 14 November 1863, as noted by Curry, 'Football', p. 73.
33. *Sportsman*, 8 January 1898.
34. *Bell's Life*, 2 March 1867.
35. In the meantime, in 1872 the FA itself would accept Sheffield's less strict offside rule, which allowed for more of a passing game. Previously players were offside if they were further towards the opponent's goal than three of the opposing team. Now one was only offside if 'between the opponent's goal and the goalkeeper'.
36. See advertisements in the *Era*, 18 July 1858; 15 May 1859.
37. *Bell's Life*, 19 December 1863.
38. *Bell's Life*, 20 October 1866; 14 November 1868.
39. *Glasgow Herald*, 7 January 1871.
40. Harvey, *Football*, p. 215.
41. *Sporting Gazette*, 28 November 1863.
42. *Reading Observer*, 24 May 1879.
43. *Northwich Guardian*, 4 May 1878.
44. 'The professional in any branch of sport is, in the first place, the servant of the amateur who practises it for his own amusement. When there is no room for such service, professionals should be rigidly excluded by amateurs for sharing in their sport' ('Professionals in English Sports', *Saturday Review*, 14 April 1888, p. 437); see also 'Professionalism and Sport', *Fortnightly Review*, January 1900, p. 155.
45. 'The Game of Football', *Once a Week*, 2 September 1878, p. 231.
46. *Bell's Life*, 16 January 1864.
47. Alfred Gibson and William Pickford, *Association Football and the Men Who Made It*, Caxton Publishing Company, 1906, Vol. 2, p. 198.
48. *Athletic News*, 1 December 1880.
49. *Sheffield Independent*, 11 November 1879.
50. *Sheffield Independent*, 29 January 1881.
51. *Blackburn Standard*, 4 October 1879.
52. *Blackburn Standard*, 8 March 1879.
53. *Blackburn Standard*, 8 March 1879; 4 October 1879.
54. Admission to Olympic's ground in 1882, for example, was tuppence or threepence, depending on who was playing, with the grandstand the same amount again (*Blackburn Standard*, 12 August 1882).
55. See *Blackburn Standard*, 25 November 1882, in which a letter-writer 'Justicia' puts criticism of Hunter down to sour grapes in Sheffield.
56. *Athletic News*, 22 November 1882.
57. *Manchester Courier*, 16 October 1882.
58. *Manchester Courier*, 8 December 1882.
59. *Sporting Life*, 5 April 1883.

60. *Sporting Life*, 2 April 1883.
61. 'Professionals in English Sports', *Saturday Review*, 14 April 1888, p. 437.
62. Curry, 'Football', p. 151.
63. *Graphic*, 4 February 1882; Dave Russell, *Football in Society*, Carnegie Publishing, 1997, p. 24.
64. *Athletic News*, 16 March 1886, quoted in Morris, *Vain Games*, p. 216.
65. *Blackburn Standard*, 11 June 1887.
66. *Blackburn Standard*, 18 June 1897.
67. *Northern Daily Telegraph*, 19 October 1889; *Blackburn Times*, 19 October 1889.
68. The original League members were Accrington, Aston Villa, Blackburn Rovers, Bolton Wanderers, Burnley, Derby County, Everton, Notts County, Preston North End, Stoke City, West Bromwich Albion and Wolverhampton Wanderers.
69. Gibson and Pickford, *Association Football and the Men Who Made It*, Vol. 2, p. 152.
70. Keith Dewhurst, *Underdogs: The Unlikely Story of Football's First FA Cup Heroes*, Yellow Jersey Press, 2012, p. 229; *Blackburn Standard*, 28 May 1881.
71. *Hampshire Advertiser*, 30 May 1914.
72. Compare *Athletic News*, 5 June 1888, and *Birmingham Daily Post*, 25 May 1889, for the 1887–88 and 1888–89 accounts. For the discussion on incorporation, see *Birmingham Daily Post*, 1 February 1889. Small Heath FC, another Birmingham club (now Birmingham City), was the first club to have made this transition, in 1888.
73. *Birmingham Daily Post*, 1 February 1889.
74. *Belfast Telegraph*, 29 May 1889.
75. *Birmingham Daily News*, 27 February 1893.
76. 'The Degradation of British Sports', *National Review*, August 1891, p. 786.
77. *Sporting Life*, 11 October 1899.
78. Charles Edwards, 'The New Football Mania', *The Nineteenth Century*, October 1892, p. 623.
79. ibid.
80. H.F. Abell, 'The Football Fever', *Macmillan's Magazine*, February 1904, p. 278.
81. 'Professionals in English Sports', *Saturday Review*, 14 April 1888, p. 438.
82. Abell, 'Football Fever', p. 279.
83. *Football Field and Sports Telegram*, 2 January 1886.
84. The football stadium in question was built by the Crystal Palace Company in 1894, by filling in two of Joseph Paxton's dysfunctional fountains.

Conclusion

1. The 'Dingle-Dongle' was a set of 'racing swings'. For a clearer idea of the sorts of rides at White City, see *Farmer Jenkins' Visit to the White City*, a film from 1910 preserved by the British Film Institute, which shows several of the rides in action. Available at: https://player.bfi.org.uk/free/film/watch-farmer-jenkins-visit-to-the-white-city-1910-online
2. Advertisement from the *Era*, 12 March 1887.
3. 'Whenever there was any application of unusual character there was an enormous amount of canvassing, and the mature judgment of those magistrates who were most cognisant with the question of licensing was overriden by gentlemen who really knew nothing about the matter' (*The Times*, 1 May 1889).
4. *Middlesex Sessions of the Peace: Court in Session* MJ/SB/C/001 ff.
5. *Pall Mall Gazette*, 9 April 1880.
6. Entry for Sir Peter Laurie, on *Oxford Dictionary of National Biography* website. Available at: https://doi.org/10.1093/ref:odnb/16133
7. British History Online, *Survey of London*, Vol. 47, pp. 84–108. Available at: www.british-history.ac.uk/survey-london/vol47/pp84-108
8. Heartwell, 'Characteristics of Manchester', p. 349.
9. 1833 *Report from the Select Committee on Manufactures, Commerce, and Shipping*, p. 624.

10. 1907 *Information obtained from certain police forces as to the frequenting of public-houses by women and children.* The figure is perhaps a little exaggerated, as the police were asked to remark on the numbers of women entering pubs, and perhaps sought out the 'worst' examples. Men may also have lingered longer. Nonetheless, the fact that there were two examples where women substantially outnumbered men should give us pause for thought.
11. James F. Lee, *The Lady Footballers: Struggling to Play in Victorian Britain*, Routledge, 2008, p. 81.
12. *Punch*, July–December 1842, p. 60. The 'Taglioni' was an oversized coat, as worn by the well-known, dandyish ballet-master Paul Taglioni.
13. [Cowtan], *Passages from the Auto-Biography of a 'Man of Kent'*, pp. 38ff.
14. *Bentley's Miscellany*, 1839, p. 477.
15. Hartley, *Eight-Eight Not Out*, pp. 76, 78.
16. *Daily Mail*, 11 August 1899.
17. There are, of course, important exceptions, including Lynda Nead's excellent and balanced look at Cremorne Gardens – *Victorian Babylon*, Yale University Press, 2000; and Jonathan Conlin (ed.), *The Pleasure Garden, from Vauxhall to Coney Island*, University of Pennsylvania, 2014, which brings together diverse scholarship on pleasure gardens and amusement parks.
18. *Morning Chronicle*, 27 March 1850.
19. Nead, *Victorian Babylon*, p. 113.
20. Reginald Blunt, *By Chelsea Reach: Some Riverside Records*, Mills and Boon, 1921, p. 185. Smith was also involved in the creation of the Wellington Dining Rooms (arguably London's first restaurant, opened in St James's, 1849) and other restaurants, pubs and cafés, including the Radnor at the northern end of Chancery Lane and the Coal Hole tavern in Covent Garden (of which Nicholson was a famous habitué).
21. Spurgeon, 'Sown Among Thorns, delivered on Lord's Day Morning, August 19th 1888', *Sermons on our Lord's Parables*, p. 476.
22. Brad Beavan, *Leisure, Citizenship and Working-Class Men in Britain, 1850–1945*, Manchester University Press, 2005, p. 73.

ℬibliography

Books and articles

Abell, H.F. 'The Football Fever', *Macmillan's Magazine*, February 1904.

Alcock, Charles W. *Football: Our Winter Game*, Field Office, 1874.

Alder, Isabel Brooke. 'Charles Morton, "Father of the Halls"', *The Ludgate*, March 1900, pp. 393–96.

Altick, Robert. *The Shows of London*, Harvard University Press, 1978.

[Anon.]. 'A Friend to Justice', *A Letter Addressed to the Right Honourable N. Vansittart, Chancellor of the Exchequer, &c. &c. on the Revenue and Public Morals . . .*, J.M. Richardson, 1817.

[Anon.]. *A Brief Historical and Descriptive Account of the Royal Gardens, Vauxhall*, Gye and Balne, 1822.

[Anon.]. *New Guide: An Historical and Descriptive Account of Leamington and Warwick*, 1825.

[Anon.]. *The British Minstrel and National Melodist*, Sherwood, Gilbert & Piper, 1827.

[Anon.]. 'Amusements at Margate', *Chambers's Edinburgh Journal*, 15 June 1833, pp. 155–56.

[Anon.]. 'Domestic Notices', *Architectural Magazine*, October 1838, p. 478–80.

[Anon.]. 'London Tavern Theatres', *Chambers's Edinburgh Journal*, 1 June 1839, pp. 151–52.

[Anon.]. *Knight's Tourist's Companion*, Nattali and Bond, 1853.

[Anon.]. *Die interessantesten Ehescheidungs-Processe der älteren und neueren Zeit*, Carl Minde, 1869.

[Anon.]. 'The Age Before Music Halls', *All the Year Round*, 20 December 1873, p. 176.

[Anon.]. *The New Illustrated Guide to Southport*, Southport Daily News, 1875.

[Anon.]. *People's Guide to Blackpool*, n.d. [c.1883].

[Anon.]. *Tempted London*, A.C. Armstrong & Son [c.1889].

Anthony, Barry. *Murder, Mayhem and Music Hall*, I.B. Tauris, 2015.

Bailey, Frances A. 'The Origin and Growth of Southport', *Town Planning Review*, 1 January 1951.

Bailey, Peter. *Leisure and Class in Victorian England*, Routledge, 1978.

Bailey, Peter (ed.). *Music Hall: The Business of Pleasure*, Open University Press, 1986.

Bailey, Peter. 'Conspiracies of Meaning: Music-Hall and the Knowingness of Popular Culture', *Past and Present*, 144 (1994), pp. 138–70.

Baker, Richard Anthony. *British Music Hall*, Sutton Publishing, 2005.

Beaumont, J.T.B. *A Letter to Rt. Hon Lord Sidmouth*, Cadell & Davies, 1817.

Beavan, Brad. *Leisure, Citizenship and Working-Class Men in Britain, 1850–1945*, Manchester University Press, 2005.

Bee, Jon. *Sportsman's Slang*, 1825.

Bennett, Arnold. *Hilda Lessways*, E.P. Dutton, 1911.

Birley, Derek. *Sport and the Making of Britain*, Manchester University Press, 1993.

Birley, Derek. *Land of Sport and Glory: Sport and British Society*, Manchester University Press, 1995.

Bland, Lucy. 'Purifying the Public World: Feminist Vigilantes in Late-Victorian England', *Women's History Review*, 1:3 (1992), pp. 397–412.

Blunt, Reginald. *By Chelsea Reach: Some Riverside Records*, Mills and Boon, 1921.

Bonner, G.W. *The Picturesque Pocket Companion to Margate, Ramsgate, Broadstairs and Parts Adjacent*, William Kidd, n.d.

Booth, Charles. *Labour and Life of the People*, Vol. 1: *East London*, Macmillan, 1889.

Bratton, J.S. 'English Ethiopians: British Audiences and Black-Face Acts, 1835–1865', *Yearbook of English Studies*, 11 (1981), pp. 127–42.

Brewer, George. *Bannian Day*, 1796.

Bristow, Eric. *Vice and Vigilance*, Gill and Macmillan, 1977.

Brown, John. *Sixty Years Gleanings from Life's Harvest*, J. Palmer, 1858.

Burnand, F.C. *Records and Reminiscences, Personal and General*, Methuen, 1905.

Burne, Peter. *The Teetotaler's Companion*, Arthur Hall, 1847.

Caine, Hall. *The Manxman*, Appleton and Company, 1894.

Carrington, Ron. *Alexandra Park and Palace: A History*, GLC, 1975.

Cheshire, D.F. *Music Hall in Britain*, Fairleigh Dickinson University Press, 1974.

Childers, Joseph W. 'Peering back: Colonials and Exhibitions', in James Buzard, Joseph W. Childers and Eileen Gillooly (eds), *Victorian Prism: Refractions of the Crystal Palace*, University of Virginia Press, 2007, pp. 203–32.

Clark, Peter. *The English Alehouse: A Social History*, Longman, 1983.

Clarke, Allen. *The Story of Blackpool*, Palatine Books Co., 1923.

Coke, David and Alan Borg. *Vauxhall Gardens: A History*, Yale University Press, 2011.

Cole, Henry. *A Special Report on the Annual International Exhibitions 1871, 1872, 1873, 1874*, Eyre and Spottiswoode, 1879.

Colquhoun, Patrick. *Observations and Facts Relative to Public Houses in the City of London and its Environs*, Henry Fry, 1794.

Colquhoun, Patrick. *A Treatise on Indigence*, J. Hatchard, 1806.

Conlin, Jonathan (ed.). *The Pleasure Garden: From Vauxhall to Coney Island*, University of Pennsylvania, 2013.

Conlin, Jonathan (ed.). *The Pleasure Garden, from Vauxhall to Coney Island*, University of Pennsylvania, 2014.

[Cowtan, Robert]. *Passages from the Auto-Biography of a 'Man of Kent'*, Whittingham and Wilkins, 1866.

Credland, Arthur G. 'Charles Random, Baron de Berenger, Inventor, Marksman and Proprietor of the Stadium', *Arms & Armour*, 3:2 (2006), pp. 171–91.

Cruikshank, George and John Wight. *Sunday in London*, Effingham Wilson, 1833.

Cunningham, Hugh. *Leisure in the Industrial Revolution*, Croom Helm, 1980.

Davis, Tracy C. 'Sex in Public Places: The Zaeo Aquarium Scandal and the Victorian Moral Majority', *Theatre History Studies*, 10 (1990), pp. 1–13.

Davis, Tracy C. *The Economics of the British Stage: 1800–1914*, Cambridge University Press, 2000.

Davis, Tracy C. 'The Moral Sense of the Majorities: Indecency and Vigilance in Late-Victorian Music Hall', *Popular Music*, 10:1 (2008), pp. 39–52.

Devereux, Cecily. '"The Maiden Tribute" and the Rise of the White Slave in the Nineteenth Century: The Making of an Imperial Construct', *Victorian Review*, 26:2 (2000), pp. 1–23.

Dewhurst, Keith. *Underdogs: The Unlikely Story of Football's First FA Cup Heroes*, Yellow Jersey Press, 2012.

d'Henri, Dr. *Geheimnisse der Prostitution*, Verlags-Anstalt, 1871.

Dobraszczyk, Paul. *Iron, Ornament and Architecture in Victorian Britain*, Ashgate, 2014.

Donohue, Joseph. *Fantasies of Empire*, University of Iowa Press, 2005.

Dye, William S., Jr. *A Study of Melodrama in England from 1800 to 1840*, Nittany, 1919.

Edwards, Charles. 'The New Football Mania', *The Nineteenth Century*, October 1892.

Egan, Pierce. *Finish to the Adventures of Tom, Jerry and Logic*, C. Baynes, 1830.

Egan, Pierce. *The Pilgrims of the Thames*, W. Strange, 1838.

Egan, Pierce. *Life in London*, Appleton, 1904.

Egan, Pierce. *Real Life in London*, Methuen & Co., 1905 [reprint of 1821 edition]. Available at: www.gutenberg.org/files/20484/20484-h/20484-h.htm

[English Heritage]. *Margate's Seaside Heritage*, English Heritage, 2007.

Evelyn, John. *Memoirs*, Henry Colburn, 1819.

Feltham, John. *A Guide to All the Watering and Sea-Bathing Places*, Longman et al., 1813.

Fleetwood, Frances. *Conquest: The Story of a Family*, W.H. Allen, 1913.

French, Hilary. 'Glamorous Spaces: Public Ballrooms and Dance Halls, 1890–1950', *Interiors*, 6:1 (2015), pp. 41–57.

Frost, Thomas. *The Old Showmen and the Old London Fairs*, Tinsley Brothers, 1875.

Geddes-Poole, Andrea. *Philanthropy and the Construction of Victorian Women's Citizenship*, University of Toronto Press, 2014.

Gibson, Alfred and William Pickford. *Association Football and the Men Who Made It*, Caxton Publishing Company, 1906.

Girouard, Mark. *Victorian Pubs*, Yale University Press, 1984.

Girouard, Mark. *The English Town*, Yale University Press, 1990.

Gissing, George. *The Nether World*, Oxford University Press, 1992.

Glover, James M. *Jimmy Glover: His Book*, Methuen, 1911.

Gorham, Maurice and H.M. Dunnett. *Inside the Pub*, Architectural Press, 1950.

Goulstone, John. 'Football's Secret History – Chapters 2 and 3', *Soccer and Society*, 19:1 (2018), pp. 35–49.

Greenhalgh, Paul. *Ephemeral Vistas: The Expositions Universelles, Great Exhibitions and Worlds Fairs, 1851–39*, Manchester University Press, 1988.

Greenwood, James. *The Seven Curses of London*, Fields, Osgood & Co., 1869.

Greenwood, James. *The Wilds of London*, Chatto and Windus, 1874.

Griffith, J.K. *A General Cheltenham Guide*, [c.1830].

Harrison, Brian. *Drink and the Victorians*, Faber, 1971.

Hartley, Harold. *Eighty-Eight Not Out*, Frederick Muller, 1939.

Harvey, Adrian. *Football: The First Hundred Years: The Untold Story*, Routledge, 2005.

Heartwell, Horace. 'Characteristics of Manchester', *North of England Magazine*, July 1842, pp. 345–58.

Heine, A.G.E. *The Past, Present and Future of the Crystal Palace*, 1874.

Hénard, Robert. *La Rue Saint-Honoré*, Émile-Paul, 1909.

Hibbert, H.G. *Fifty Years of a Londoner's Life*, Dodd, Mead & Co., 1916.

Hicks, Gary. *The First Adman: Thomas Bish and the Birth of Modern Advertising*, Victorian Secrets, 2012.

Hillocks, James Inches. *My Life and Labours in London, a Step Nearer the Mark*, W. Freeman, 1865.

Hindle, David John. *Life in Victorian Preston*, Amberley, 2014.

Hoffenberg, Peter. *An Empire on Display*, University of California Press, 2001.

Hogg, John. *London As It Is*, John Macrone, 1837.

Hollingshead, John. 'A Grand Old Music-Hall', *Entr'acte*, 6 June 1896.

Home, John and Gary Whannel. *Understanding the Olympics*, Routledge, 2012.

Horn, Pamela. *Amusing the Victorians*, Sutton, 1999.

Hudson, Derek. *Munby: Man of Two Worlds*, Abacus, 1974.

Hudson, Thomas. *Comic Songs*, Gold and Walton, 1818.

[Hutton, William]. *A Description of Blackpool*, Pearson and Rollason, 1809.

Inglis, Simon. *League Football*, Collins, 1988.

Jones, Ieuan Gwynedd. *Aberystwyth 1277–1977*, Gomer Press, 1977.

Kaye, John William. *The Life and Correspondence of Major-General Sir John Malcolm*, Smith Elder & Co., 1836.

Keate, George. *Sketches from Nature; Taken, and Coloured, in a Journey to Margate*, T. Hurst, 1802.

Kift, Dagmar. *The Victorian Music Hall: Culture, Class and Conflict*, Cambridge University Press, 1996.

Langford, John Alfred. *A Century of Birmingham Life*, W.G. Moore, 1870.

Lee, Anthony. *Margate in the Georgian Era*, Droit House Press, 2012.

Lee, James F. *The Lady Footballers: Struggling to Play in Victorian Britain*, Routledge, 2008.

Lewis, Robert W. 'The Genesis of Professional Football: Bolton-Blackburn-Darwen, the Centre of Innovation 1878–85', *International Journal of the History of Sport*, 14:1 (1997), pp. 21–54.

Lowe, Charles. *Four National Exhibitions in London*, T. Fisher Unwin, 1892.

Lunn, Henry C. 'The London Musical Season', *Musical Times and Singing Class Circular*, 1 September 1869.

Marsh, Richard. 'The Girl on the Sands', *Strand*, October 1904, pp. 423–33.

Martin, George E. *Breezy Blackpool*, W. Mate & Sons Ltd, 1899.

Mason, Nicholas. ' "The Sovereign People are in a Beastly State": The Beer Act of 1830 and Victorian Discourse on Working-Class Drunkenness', *Victorian Literature and Culture* 29:1 (2001), pp. 109–27.

Mathias, Peter. *The Brewing Industry in England: 1720–1830*, Cambridge University Press, 1959.

Mawson, Chris and Richard Riding. *British Seaside Piers*, Ian Allan, 2008.

Maxwell, John Irving. *The Victuallers Advocate*, 1804.

Mayhew, Henry. *London Labour and the London Poor*, Griffin, Bohn and Company, 1861.

Moody, Jane. *Illegitimate Theatre in London, 1770–1840*, Cambridge University Press, 2000.

Morris, Terry. *Vain Games of No Value?*, Authorhouse, 2016.

Morton, W.H. and H. Chance Newton. *Sixty Years' Stage Service: Being a Record of the Life of Charles Morton*, Gale & Polden, 1905.

Nead, Lynda. *Victorian Babylon*, Yale University Press, 2000.

Nicholson, Watson. *The Struggle for a Free Stage in London*, Houghton Mifflin & Co., 1906.

Nott, James. *Going to the Palais*, Oxford University Press, 2015.

'One of the Old Brigade' [Donald Shaw]. *London in the Sixties*, Everett, 1908.

Oulton, W.C. *Picture of Margate*, Baldwin, Craddock and Joy, 1820.

Papworth, Wyatt. *John B. Papworth*, 1879.

'Paterson, Peter' [pseud.]. *Glimpses of Real Life as Seen in the Theatrical World and in Bohemia*, William P. Nimmo, 1864.

Payn, James. *Lights and Shadows of London Life*, Hurst and Blackett, 1867.

Payn, James. *The Talk of the Town*, Chatto & Windus, 1885.

Pearson, Lynn. *The People's Palaces*, Barracuda Books, 1991.

Peel, Barbara. *Dancing and Social Assemblies in York in the Eighteenth and Nineteenth Centuries*, National Resource Centre for Dance, 1986.

Pennyback, Susan D. *A Vision for London, 1889–1914*, Routledge, 1995.

Phillips, Samuel. *Guide to the Crystal Palace and Park*, Bradbury and Evans, 1854.

Phillips, Watts. *The Wild Tribes of London*, 1855.

Piggott, J.R. *Palace of the People: The Crystal Palace at Sydenham 1854–1936*, University of Wisconsin Press, 2004.

BIBLIOGRAPHY

Playfair, Giles. *Six Studies in Hypocrisy*, Secker and Warburg, 1969.

Poole, Robert. *Popular Leisure and the Music Hall in Nineteenth Century Bolton*, University of Lancaster, 1982.

Raymond, George. *Memoirs of Robert William Elliston*, John Mortimer, 1845.

Richards, Denis. *Offspring of the Vic*, Routledge, 1958.

Richardson, Philip J.S. *The Social Dances of the Nineteenth Century in England*, Herbert Jenkins, 1960.

Roberts, M.J.D. 'The Society for the Suppression of Vice and its Early Critics, 1802–1812', *Historical Journal*, 26:1 (1983), pp. 159–76.

Russell, Dave. *Football in Society*, Carnegie Publishing, 1997.

Russom, J. *The Evil Effects of Beer Shops*, Houlston and Stoneman, 1849.

Rust, Frances. *Dance in Society*, Routledge & Kegan Paul, 1969.

Sands, Mollie. *The Eighteenth-Century Pleasure Gardens of Marylebone*, Society for Theatre Research, 1987.

Sedgwick, Theodore. *Public and Private Economy*, Harper, 1836.

Selby, Charles. *Out on the Sly*, Duncombe and Moon, 1847.

Selenick, Laurence. *Tavern Singing in Early Victorian London*, Society for Theatre Research, 1997.

Slattery-Christy, David. *Royal Palace Gardens: Blackpool's Lost Victorian Pleasure Gardens*, Christyplays, 2016.

Slidell Mackenzie, Alexander. *The American in England*, Richard Bentley, 1836.

Smith, Albert. *Sketches of London Life and Character*, Dean and Son, 1849.

'Smith, John' [pseud.]. *Sketches of Cantabs*, 1849.

Smith, Lynda. *The Place to Spend a Happy Day: A History of Rosherville Gardens*, Gravesend Historical Society, 2006.

Society for Bettering the Condition and Increasing the Comforts of the Poor, *Report of the Society*, 1805.

Speaight, George. *Bawdy Songs of the Early Music Hall*, Pan, 1975.

Sperling, Joy. '"Art, Cheap and Good": The Art Union in England and the United States, 1840–60', *Nineteenth-Century Art Worldwide*, 1:1 (2002).

Spurgeon, C.H. *Sermons on Our Lord's Parables*, Passmore & Alabaster, 1904.

Storey, Graham, Kathleen Tillotson and Madeline House (eds). *The Letters of Charles Dickens*, Oxford University Press, 2002.

Summerfield, Penelope. 'The Effingham Arms and the Empire', in E. Yeo and S. Yeo (eds), *Popular Culture and Class Conflict*, Harvester Press, 1981, pp. 209–40.

Swain, Peter. 'The Origins of Football Debate: The "Grander Design and the Involvement of the Lower Classes", 1818–1840', *Sport in History*, 34:4 (2014), pp. 519–43.

Talley, W. *Man Midwifery and the Results*, Taylor and Greening [n.d.]

Thompson, F.M.L. *The Rise of Respectable Society*, Fontana, 1988.

Thorne, Guy. *The Great Acceptance*, Hodder and Stoughton, 1913.

Timbs, John. *Curiosities of London*, 1855.

Train, G.F. *Train's Union Speeches*, John Adams Knight, 1862.

Vamplew, Wray. *Pay Up and Play the Game*, Cambridge University Press, 1988.

Walker, Emmanuel. 'At Earl's Court', *The Idler*, January 1900, p. 123.

Walton, John K. *The English Seaside Resort*, Leicester University Press, 1983.

Walton, John K. 'Municipal Government and the Holiday Industry in Blackpool, 1876–1914', in John K. Walton and James Walvin (eds), *Leisure in Britain: 1780–1939*, Manchester University Press, 1983.

Walton, John K. *British Piers*, Thames and Hudson, 1987.

Walton, Peter. *Blackpool Tower: A History*, Amberley, 2016.

Warner, Jessica and Frank Ivis. 'Gin and Gender in Early Eighteenth-Century London', *Eighteenth-Century Life*, 24:2 (2000), pp. 85–105.

Watson, Ernest Bradlee. *Sheridan to Robertson: A Study of the Nineteenth Century London Stage*, Harvard University Press, 1926.

BIBLIOGRAPHY

Watt, Paul. 'A "Gigantic and Popular Place of Entertainment": Granville Bantock and Music Making at the New Brighton Tower in the Late 1890s', *Royal Musical Association Research Chronicle*, 42:1 (2009), pp. 109–64.

Watts, R.B. *The Margate Steam Yachts Guide*, Joseph Mallett, 1820.

Wissett, Robert. *Letters to John Bowles*, Shaw, 1815.

Woodman, Deborah. 'Social Order and Disorder in the Nineteenth Century Drinking Place: An Evaluation of Manchester and Salford', *International Journal of Regional and Local Studies*, 6:1 (2010), pp. 72–97.

Wroth, Warwick. *The London Pleasure Gardens of the Eighteenth Century*, Macmillan, 1896.

Wroth, Warwick. *Cremorne and the Later London Gardens*, Elliot Stock, 1907.

Yates, Edmund. *His Recollections and Experiences*, Richard Bentley & Son, 1885.

Periodicals

All the Year Round
Anti-Jacobin Review
Architectural Magazine
Bentley's Miscellany
Blackwood's Magazine
British Architect
British Mothers' Magazine
Christian Remembrancer
Dancing: A Journal Devoted to the Terpsichorean Art
Era Almanack
Fortnightly Review
Fun
The Gin-shop
Graphic
Hood's Magazine and Comic Miscellany
The Idler
The Living Age
London City Mission Magazine
The Ludgate
Macmillan's Magazine
Mechanics Magazine
Monthly Magazine
Musical World
National Magazine
National Observer
National Review
The Nineteenth Century
Once a Week
Paul Pry
The Phonogram
Punch
Quarterly Review
Saint Paul's
Saturday Review
The Sentinel
The Spirit of the Public Journals
Temple Bar
Theatrical Journal
Tomahawk
Vigilance Record

Westminster Review
World of Fashion

Newspapers

Aberdeen Journal
Athletic News
Bath Chronicle
Belfast News-Letter
Belfast Telegraph
La Belle Assemblée
Bell's Life in London and Sporting Chronicle [Bell's Life]
Bell's New Weekly Messenger
Bell's Weekly Messenger
Birmingham Daily Post
Birmingham Journal
Blackburn Standard
Blackburn Times
Bolton Chronicle
Bristol Mercury and Daily Post
Building News
Bury and Norwich Post
Caledonian Mercury
Carlisle Patriot
Chelmsford Chronicle
Cheshire Observer
Daily Advertiser
Daily Mail
Daily News
Daily Telegraph
Dart
Derby Mercury
Dublin Mercantile Advertiser
East London Observer
Echo
Era
Examiner
Exeter and Plymouth Gazette
Field
Financial Times
Folkestone, Hythe, Sandgate & Cheriton Herald
Football Field and Sports Telegram
Freeman's Journal
Glasgow Herald
Halifax Courier
Hampshire Advertiser
Huddersfield Daily Chronicle
Huddersfield and Holmfirth Examiner
Hull Packet
Illustrated London News
Illustrated Police News
Ipswich Journal
Isle of Man Times
John Bull

Kent and Sussex Courier
Kentish Gazette
Kentish Mercury
Lancashire Evening Post
Lancashire Guardian
Lancaster Gazette
Lancaster Guardian
Leader and Saturday Analyst
Leeds Intelligencer
Leeds Mercury
Leeds Times
Leicester Chronicle
Leigh Chronicle
Licensed Victuallers' Mirror
Liverpool Mail
Liverpool Mercury
Lloyd's Weekly Newspaper
London Courier and Evening Gazette
London Daily News
London Evening Standard
Manchester Courier and Lancashire General Advertiser
Manchester Guardian
Manchester Times
Marylebone Mercury
Mid Sussex Times
Montgomery County Times
Morning Advertiser
Morning Chronicle
Morning Post
Morning Post and Gazetteer
Nelson Evening Mail
Newcastle Courant
Northern Daily Telegraph
Northern Star and Leeds General Advertiser
Northwich Guardian
Nottingham Guardian
Observer
The Odd Fellow
Oracle and Daily Advertiser
Oxford University and City Herald
Pall Mall Gazette
Preston Chronicle
Preston Guardian
Preston Herald
Public Advertiser
Public Ledger and Daily Advertiser
Punch
Reading Mercury
Reading Observer
Reynolds's Newspaper
Rhyl Record and Advertiser
Satirist
Sheffield Daily Telegraph
Sheffield Evening Telegraph

Sheffield Independent
Sheffield and Rotherham Independent
Sketch
Southend Standard
Southport Independent and Ormskirk Chronicle
Spectator
Sporting Gazette
Sporting Times
Sportsman
Staffordshire Advertiser
Stamford Mercury
Standard
Telegraph
Thanet Advertiser
The Times
Western Mail
Westmorland Gazette
Wharfedale and Airedale Observer
Whitstable Times
Yorkshire Post

Theses

Curry, Graham, 'Football: A Study in Diffusion', DPhil Thesis, University of Leicester, 2001.

Gregory, Brendan Edward, 'The Spectacle Plays and Exhibitions of Imre Kiralfy 1887-1914', Thesis, University of Manchester, 1988.

Kane, Josephine, 'A Whirl of Wonders: British Amusement Parks and the Architecture of Pleasure: 1900-1939', Thesis, UCL, 2009.

Major, Susan, 'The Million Go Forth', Thesis, University of York, 2012.

Simpson, Claire, 'The Economics of a Seaside Resort', Thesis, Lancaster University, 2015.

Walton, John, 'The Social Development of Blackpool 1788–1914', Thesis, University of Lancaster, 1974.

Whyman, J., 'Aspects of Holidaymaking and Resort Development within the Isle of Thanet, with Particular Reference to Margate', Thesis, University of Kent at Canterbury, 1980.

Legislation and Government Publications

1751 Disorderly Houses Act (25 Geo 2 c. 36)
1816 *First Report from the Committee on the State of the Police of the Metropolis*
1817 *Second Report from the Committee on the State of the Police of the Metropolis*
1818 *Third Report from the Committee on the State of the Police of the Metropolis*
1828 Act to Regulate the Granting of Licences to Keepers of Inns, Ale-houses, and Victualling Houses in England ('Alehouses Act') (9 Geo. 4, c. 61)
1829 Metropolitan Police Act (10 Geo 4., c. 44)
1830 Beerhouse Act ('Beer Act') (11 Geo. 4 & 1 Will. 4, c. 64)
1830 *Report from the Select Committee on the Sale of Beer*
1833 *Report from the Select Committee on Manufactures, Commerce, and Shipping*
1833 *Report from Select Committee on the Sale of Beer*
1833 *Tables of the Revenue, Population, Commerce of the United Kingdom and its Dependencies*
1834 *Report of the Committee on Drunkenness*
1839 Metropolitan Police Act (2 & 3 Vict., c. 47)
1843 Theatres Act (6 & 7 Vict., c. 68)
1844 Railway Regulation Act (7 & 8 Vict., c. 85)

1852 *First Report of the Commissioners for the Exhibition of 1851*
1852–53 *Report from the Select Committee on Public Houses*
1854 *Report from the Select Committee on Public Houses*
1866 *Report from the Select Committee on Theatrical Licences and Regulation*
1878 *Report from the Select Committee on Metropolis Management and Building Acts Amendment Bill.*
1888 *Metropolitan Board of Works Commission. Interim report of the Royal Commissioners appointed to inquire into certain matters connected with the working of the Metropolitan Board of Works*
1892 *Report from the Select Committee on Theatres and Places of Entertainment*
1907 *Information obtained from certain police forces as to the frequenting of public-houses by women and children*

Archives

Aberystwyth
Minutes of Aberystwyth General Purposes Committee
Bodleian Library
Theatre Royal, Drury Lane Grand Masquerade [n.d.]. London Playbills Drury Lane box 1 (28)
Getty Research Institute (via archive.org)
International Universal Exhibition, 1898: Guide and Catalogue
Woman's Exhibition, 1900: Guide
Guildhall Library
Annual Reports 1881–85 COL/LIB/PB02 (Crystal Palace Company)
Haringey Museum
Alexandra Palace Archives
Isle of Man Archives
Manx Board of Advertising Minutes
Kent Archives
The Family Album of Hawkins Francis James . . . Croydon, July 28th 1828 R/U2446/F1
Lambeth Archives
Vauxhall Gardens Collection
London Metropolitan Archives
LCC Theatres and Music Halls Committee Minutes LCC/MIN/
Letter from the National Temperance Society MJ/SP/1853/10/015
Metropolitan Buildings Office correspondence MBO/322
Middlesex Sessions of the Peace MJ/SP/1839/10/34
Middlesex Sessions of the Peace: Court in Session MJ/SB/C
Report of the Committee appointed by Court on 6th June 1850 to consider the present state of the law as regards the granting of licences for music and dancing by the Court and report to the Court, London Metropolitan Archives MJ/SP/1851/08/024
Surrey Magistrates Licensing Minutes 1850 PS/NEW/1/7
Venice in London LMA4684/02/04/1891/001
LSE
'London County Council Election, 1892: The Elector's Guide, a Popular Hand-book for the Election'. LSE Selected Pamphlets 1892
'The London County Council: What It Is'. LSE Selected Pamphlets 1895
'New London: Her Parliament and Its Work'. LSE Selected Pamphlets 1895
Manchester Archives
Manchester Watch Committee Minutes, 21 January 1843
Museum of London
Imre Kiralfy Collection
Pleasure-gardens Collection
National Archives
LC7/5 Lord Chamberlain's Papers

Index

Please note: Music hall artistes and venues are grouped together under the category performers.